PENGUIN BOOKS

MANAGEMENT MATHEMATICS

Peter Sprent was born in Australia in 1923 and is now an adopted Scot who has lived in the ancient Kingdom of Fife since 1967. He is Emeritus Professor of Statistics at the University of Dundee and sees retirement as the time to do the things one really likes. Stimulated by experience as a consultant in fields ranging from agriculture and biology to industry and commerce, his mission is to take the mystery out of mathematics and the stuffiness out of statistics. He is the author of *Statistics in Action*, *Quick Statistics*, *Understanding Data* and *Taking Risks*, all published by Penguin, and has written elementary and advanced texts and numerous papers for professional journals.

Peter Sprent is a Fellow of the Royal Society of Edinburgh and a member of the International Statistical Institute and other professional bodies. His hobbies include hillwalking, flying and golf, but he confesses his scores at that game would bring joy to a first-class cricketer.

MANAGEMENT MATHEMATICS

A User-friendly Approach

PETER SPRENT

PENGUIN BOOKS

PENGUIN BOOKS

Published by the Penguin Group
Penguin Books Ltd, 27 Wrights Lane, London W8 5TZ, England
Penguin Books USA, Inc., 375 Hudson Street, New York, New York 10014, USA
Penguin Books Australia Ltd, Ringwood, Victoria, Australia
Penguin Books Canada Ltd, 10 Alcorn Avenue, Toronto, Ontario, Canada M4V 3B2
Penguin Books (NZ) Ltd, 182–190 Wairau Road, Auckland 10, New Zealand

Penguin Books Ltd, Registered Offices: Harmondsworth, Middlesex, England

First published 1991
10 9 8 7 6 5 4 3 2 1

Filmset in 10/13 Monophoto Times Roman
Printed in England by Clays Ltd, St Ives plc

Contents

Preface

We illustrate the far reaching potential of mathematics in a business or managerial environment largely by annotated worked examples. Basic techniques are explained in an unsophisticated way with mathematical notation and business jargon limited to what is needed for a proper understanding.

In selecting topics we have paid attention to the syllabuses for specific examinations set by professional bodies, but have not slavishly followed these for two reasons. The first is that many of these cover only a restricted range of topics that are important to a particular aspect of management. Secondly, there are many books ranging from little more than recipe books to excellent detailed explanatory texts that cater for candidates for particular examinations. We have included as illustrative exercises a few examination questions set by CIMA (the Chartered Institute of Management Accountants) and ACCA (the Chartered Association of Certified Accountants); also the AEB (Associated Examining Board) and the University of Oxford Delegacy of Local Examinations, since business applications of mathematics appear in some new Advanced Supplementary level syllabuses. The source of each such question is acknowledged and I thank the relevant bodies for permission to reproduce these questions. Many other examples and exercises (marked with an asterisk) are of a style found in a variety of managerial course examinations, although similar questions are likely to be framed in rather different but characteristic ways by each examining authority (often incorporated with questions about the implications for accounting, taxation, etc.). Examination syllabuses for many professional bodies are currently under revision.

Our aim is to supplement the treatment in 'examination targeted' texts with a broad introduction to major topics relevant to all levels of management. To keep it both introductory and user-friendly, the emphasis is on breadth rather than depth.

The book is also designed to help young executives who, for various reasons (e.g. transferring to management after training in a different skill), have had little formal instruction in basic management mathematics and quantitative aspects of decision-making; it may also help those running small business with little or no training in making optimal (or at least good) decisions based on quantitative evidence.

The emphasis is on formulating problems mathematically and developing skills in manipulating data. Working through simple examples helps to build the confidence needed to tackle real-life problems – something that will often involve using a computer. Valuable as computers are, there is a growing history of catastrophes arising from lack of a proper understanding of what one is asking them to do, or a failure to appreciate their many limitations. It is hoped that this book will generate a background awareness that will protect users from such potential disasters.

The final section in each chapter poses two questions: *What?* and *Where?* Brief answers to these are given to help readers decide whether our *user-friendly* introduction suffices for their needs, and, if not, to indicate where they may find further guidance. References given are typical rather than exhaustive; in particular there are many more examination-orientated texts relevant to qualifications for particular professional bodies.

PETER SPRENT
Dundee, September 1990

1 The Quantitative Element in Business

1.1 WHY BOTHER?

The manager who never uses mathematics or statistics is usually a bad manager – one who misses opportunities to improve efficiency or increase profits. What is loosely described as *management* mathematics plays an increasingly prominent role in business-related coursework because it is vital to everyday decision-making from boardroom to shop floor.

We introduce basic principles, using realistic yet straightforward and often simplified examples. Mathematics may help managers and administrators to boost production, reduce costs, increase profits, and streamline processing and marketing. Our broad overview indicates the wide applicability of many techniques and the relationship between them; without this understanding, potential applications to real problems may not be obvious.

Some methods are more important for one type of business; some for another. The detail of how an industrialist allocates resources – men and materials – so that costs are minimized or profits maximized (and minimizing costs does not necessarily maximize profits!) may not be of *direct* interest to a bank manager; he will be more interested in a comparative assessment of several schemes to fund a capital development. A bank manager will, however, expect a manufacturer to have looked at optimum allocation of resources before he pleads for an overdraft.

In this introductory chapter, we look briefly at some mathematical ideas applicable in a business environment, bearing in mind the impact of computers (and the humbler but useful pocket calculator) on the way we do things.

1.2   PERCENTAGES AND INTEREST

The classic application of mathematics to business affairs is *financial arithmetic*; in particular, the calculation of interest, discounts, depreciation, annuities, mortgage repayments, etc.

We learn how to do standard interest calculations at school. Yet, in 1988 the *Sunday Times* reported that a survey of school teachers indicated that many of them could not calculate 15% of £10. The report was critical of their inability to handle such a basic calculation. Do you know the answer? Get your solution before reading on.

How did you go about it? Did you look up some published interest tables and deduce the answer from what you found there? Or did you recall a formula that enables you to do such a calculation, and apply it (perhaps using a pocket calculator)? Have you a desk-top computer that does such calculations almost instantly? Or did you just apply some common-sense rules of logical deduction?

The last approach is straightforward. We argue this way: 15% of £100 is £15; since £10 is $\frac{1}{10}$ of £100, by simple proportions the answer is $\frac{1}{10}$ of £15, i.e. £1.50. The proportionality argument is direct and easy. If you used a computer that only required you to feed in a couple of numbers and wait for the answer, it is likely that the program used this sort of logic.

You may have sympathy for a teacher who had difficulty when faced with this problem with no warning. There can be no sympathy for a manager who cannot (using tables or a calculator if he or she so wishes) come up quickly with the right answer. Business people must be adept at handling percentages, usually in more complicated situations.

1.2.1   Beware of traps

No matter how simple the problem, it is easy to fall into traps. A common one is to solve, unwittingly, a different problem to the one posed.

Example 1.1   The current (1990) standard rate of value added tax (VAT) in the UK is 15%. An item is priced at £10 *inclusive* of VAT. How much is the VAT?

We have just seen that 15% of £10 is £1.50. Is this the amount of VAT? It is not – why? The £10 price is composed of an unspecified amount £x *excluding* VAT *plus* 15% of £x which is £$(x \times 0.15)$.

Solution   To calculate the VAT we note that £$(x + 0.15x) = £10$. This leads to a simple algebraic equation for x:

$$x + 0.15x = 10,$$

that is,

$$(1 + 0.15)x = 10,$$

which gives

$$1.15x = 10, \quad \text{or} \quad x = 10/1.15, \quad \text{or} \quad x = 8.70.$$

Using a pocket calculator for the last step (a sensible thing to do) gives an answer like 8.695 652 174 (the exact answer depends on the particular calculator; yours might give 8.695 652). I have rounded this (as we do in practice) to 8.70, the price to the nearest penny, *excluding* VAT. We get the amount of VAT by subtracting this from £10; it is £$(10 - 8.70) = £1.30$. Alternatively, we could get this by noting again that the VAT is £$(x \times 0.15)$, i.e. £$(8.70 \times 0.15) = £1.30$. When you have done several calculations like this, you would probably simply write your solution as

$$115\% \text{ of } x \text{ is } 10,$$

so

$$\tfrac{115}{100}x = 10, \quad \text{or} \quad x = 8.70.$$

Tables giving the VAT component and the price excluding VAT, corresponding to various total prices T (i.e. price including VAT), are available, but with a pocket calculator, given the total price £T, all we need is a simple formula for calculating the price x excluding VAT at 15%. It is

$$x = T/1.15,\qquad(1.1)$$

where, in Example 1.1, $T = 10$. Algebraic juggling with (1.1) shows that the formula for the amount v of VAT included in a total price T when VAT is charged at 15% is

$$v = 3T/23.\qquad(1.2)$$

[Hint: Multiply both sides of (1.1) by 0.15, then simplify the right-hand side.] The fraction $\frac{3}{23}$ is sometimes called the *VAT fraction* of the total price. If the rate of VAT changes, so does this fraction.

In everyday business, we meet even simpler calculations, ranging from adding sums of money to sharing out money or goods in specified proportions. Such calculations are usually done by clerical and secretarial assistants (with calculator or computer) and are aptly described as *commercial arithmetic*. There is no hard and fast dividing line between *commercial arithmetic* and *financial arithmetic*; simple interest and VAT calculations fall near the divide. Percentages permeate much of financial arithmetic.

1.3   MATHEMATICS AND MANAGEMENT

Juggling with percentages can usually be left to an adequately programmed computer. But computers are dumb. If the percentages you need are a little off-beat, the program you have may not cope. You are back to basics; interest tables (section 2.5) may or may not help. For example, you may have a computer program that can work out the APR (annual, or annualized, percentage rate; see section 2.3.1) given a *monthly* percentage interest rate of 1.5% on a debt initially £90; but could it cope with the problem if the monthly rate jumped from 1.5% to 2% immediately your outstanding debt (including added monthly interest) topped £100? If it can, then fine; but, if not, you will need appropriate tables or some of the formulae in Chapter 2.

Credit card companies have a complicated way of working out interest if you pay *part only* of the money owing by or before the due date each month. Their computers are programmed to cope with this, but few credit card holders have a computer program to check whether the card company computer got it right.

We meet in section 2.2.1 a basic formula (formula (2.4)) used primarily for compound interest problems. Any business-orientated computer program can deal with a whole range of problems using this or a close relative. It is important to know that, with a little adaptation, these formulae can be used for many problems in financial arithmetic; e.g. those concerned with annuities, mortgage repayments, discounting, depreciation, correct instalment payments at given interest rates, etc. We elaborate upon these in Chapters 2 and 3.

In pre-computer/calculator days the heavy-slog arithmetic of compound interest was short-cut by using extensive tables. Interest tables are nearly obsolete, but managers need to use and understand tables and graphs in many other situations.

1.4   TABLES

We distinguish between *mathematical tables* and *data tables*. Typical examples of the former are tables of logarithms and of compound interest, discounting, etc. (all of which, if not yet obsolete, are of decreasing importance thanks to modern calculators). Certain statistical tables (see Chapter 9) also fall into the former category. Tables of the trigonometric functions are another example, but these are of little relevance to business calculations, except in specialized fields like engineering. Data tables are in essence a way of expressing or summarizing acquired information relevant to particular users. Table 1.1 is a simple data table that might be relevant if your business is furniture manufacture.

Clear presentation of data is essential if we are to make the best use of information. This is discussed at some length by Sprent (1988a) and by Ehrenberg (1983).

Table 1.1 Daily output of chairs and tables, week ending 4/11/88.

	Mon	Tue	Wed	Thu	Fri
Chairs	38	61	72	69	83
Tables	17	20	18	22	25

1.5 GRAPHS

We often present information in either tabular or graphical form. The data in Table 1.1 are presented graphically in Fig. 1.1 by what is called a bar chart. These are easy to construct using modern computer graphics. Most real-life data tables, or corresponding graphs, are more complicated; see Tufte (1983) for many inpressive examples of the use of graphs.

Graphs are often an important aid to problem solution. In section 4.1, we explain how to use a graph to solve the following problem.

Example 1.2   A firm makes two kinds of trousers. For type A, material costs £2.50 per pair and it takes one girl 60 minutes to make a pair. Each pair is sold for £9.50. For type B, material costs

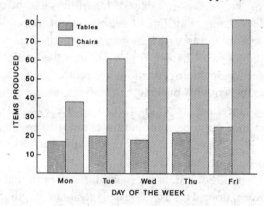

Figure 1.1 Daily output of tables and chairs, week ending 4/11/88.

£2.00 per pair and it takes one girl 20 minutes to make a pair. Each pair is sold for £6.00. The firm employs eight girls who will each work a maximum of eight hours per day and be paid £3.00 per hour worked. Overheads are £240 per day. Market forces limit possible sales of type A to not more than 60 per day and sales of type B to not more than 100 per day. Zip fasteners are in short supply and only 120 are available each day (each pair of trousers must have a zip!). How many of each type should the manufacturer produce to maximize profit?

Have you met a problem like this before? Instinct might suggest solving it by trial and error, calculating the profit for various intuitively appealing solutions satisfying all the stated constraints (e.g. that there are only sufficient zips to make 120 pairs, not more than 60 should be of type A, the limit on the girl-hours available, etc.). With long and tedious trial and error methods, it is easy to miss the best, or optimal, solution. You might like to spend a few moments trying this, but do not waste much time on it.

1.6 CALCULATORS AND COMPUTERS

The pocket calculator has revolutionized financial arithmetic. In some problems in Chapter 2, we have to calculate expressions like $(1.027)^{17}$ or $(1.027)^{-17}$. Before we had modern calculators, this was done using logarithms – a tedious error-prone method. This was why compound interest tables were created. Many calculators now have a y^x key (or it may be labelled x^y) that enables calculations of this type to be done as follows:

1. enter a y value (1.027);
2. strike the y^x key;
3. enter an x value (17);
4. press the $=$ key;
5. read off the answer (1.572 887).

A calculator with a y^x key is a good investment.

Modern computers, from lap-top portable PCs to work-stations or large mainframe units, have added an exciting new dimension to business mathematics. While there is a simple graphical method to solve the trousers problem posed in Example 1.2, it has a serious limitation. It would not work if the firm wanted to maximize profit for three, four, five or twenty different kinds of trousers. Indeed, graphs only work if production is limited to two kinds. A computer-based solution for problems of this type has no such limitation. Many firms have to allocate resources between a large number of options – often 100 or more – with output restricted by availability of raw materials, labour and machines, as well as sales potential or cash flow. A computer can produce in minutes optimum production schedules when fed the relevant data. It can also answer questions about how installing an extra machine, employing one more hand, buying an additional unit of a raw material, and so on, will affect profits.

Problems of this type are called *mathematical programming* problems. In Chapter 4, we consider a sub-species of these called *linear programming* problems. Some managers deplore an emphasis on linear programming in business mathematics courses, saying it is often not what is required in practice. This is partly true. However, it is an important training tool because many of its characteristics extend to more advanced practical techniques. The head of the research and development team of a major UK manufacturer told me, 'In my department we hardly ever use linear programming *per se*, but understanding it helps my team formulate and solve more complex problems.'

1.7   EXAMPLES OF PROBLEM TYPES

We outline some further problems that fall under the broad heading of management mathematics. Simple examples may often be solved with pencil and paper, but most real problems require at least a pocket calculator, and more often a computer.

If a computer can do it, why do we need to understand what goes on behind the scenes or even learn how to solve simple problems manually? The answer comes back to the computer being dumb. Unless we are clear about what we are asking the machine to do, we may ask it to do the wrong thing, or something it is not programmed to do.

Many of the examples below are elaborated upon in later chapters, and we give forward references where appropriate.

1.7.1 Financial arithmetic

Financial arithmetic covers compound interest, annuities, discounting, depreciation, sinking funds, debt repayment, assessment of present values of future payments or receipts, calculating internal rates of return. Many of these topics are relevant to cash flow problems. They may be complicated by allowances for taxation and/or inflation. A good grasp of financial arithmetic is essential for accountants and bankers, desirable for any decision-maker. Basic financial arithmetic is discussed in Chapters 2 and 3.

1.7.2 Optimal allocation of resources

Example 1.2 on trousers was about allocating resources. We often have to allocate limited resources; usually only one (or a few) of all possible allocations will maximize profit while still meeting all relevant *constraints* imposed by the system. For example, an airline may have several different types of aircraft; each type requires different numbers of flight deck and cabin crews; each may carry a different number of passengers; some may be unable to operate a particular route because of constraints imposed by distance or runway limitations; some may be uneconomic if average passenger bookings are below some minima. There are statutory maxima to the number of hours flying *per day* or *per week* or *per month* for crew members. Optimum allocation of an aircraft fleet and crews involves some features of linear programming discussed in Chapter 4, but the allocation is subject to the further restriction that only solutions giving integer (whole) numbers of aircraft and personnel are appropriate, so they are called *integer programming problems*. We meet an example in Chapter 5.

Another problem, called the *transportation problem*, is basically one of linear programming, but its special structure makes it easier to solve by a modified technique. It applies to a distributor who has several different storage depots and wants to supply goods from these to purchasers in a number of different locations. Delivery costs depend on the distances and times taken to effect delivery by appropriate routes, and on the available modes of transport; these costs are supposed known. The problem is to determine how much should be sent from each depot to each purchaser to minimize total transport costs. We consider examples in Chapter 6 and extend the method to problems that have little resemblance to this basic transportation problem, but may be solved in a similar manner.

1.7.3 Network analysis

Network analysis is concerned with finding an optimum path that can be looked upon as a 'trip' through a network. For example, we may wish to travel from city S (for start) to city F (for finish) in Fig. 1.2 at a minimum cost. We may travel by any route through some of the intermediate points A, B, C, D in the directions indicated by the arrows. The figures alongside each sector indicate the cheapest transport cost (in pounds) along that sector by bus, train or taxi (whichever is available). It is obvious by inspection that the cheapest way from S to F is to travel from S to A, then from A to B, from B to C, and from C to F. The cheapest way to travel from S to F in Fig. 1.3 is less obvious. We evolve a systematic way of finding optimal routes in Chapter 8. Note that we have 'simplified' the fare structure by avoiding fares like £1.17 or £2.49. Had we incorporated such fares it might have been a little harder to spot the cheapest route by inspection in Fig. 1.2, but no new principle would be involved. It may seem a little surprising that it is cheaper (Fig. 1.2) to travel from A to C via an intermediate stage B than it is to travel direct. This situation would occur if there were bus services from A

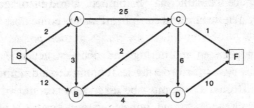

Figure 1.2 Cheapest route from S to F with indicated fares (in pounds) on each sector is S, A, B, C, F.

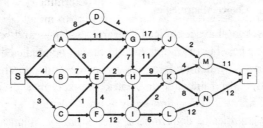

Figure 1.3 Can you spot the cheapest route from S to F with indicated fares for each sector?

to B and B to C, but no direct public transport from A to C, so that one had to resort to a more expensive taxi.

When building a house, we want to complete the job in minimum time or at minimum cost. Some operations must follow certain precedents, while others are interchangeable. One cannot plaster the inside walls before they are built, but one might glaze the windows before, while or after installing the plumbing. Critical path analysis (section 7.3) is one way to find out how jobs must be scheduled to complete a building in minimum time.

1.7.4 Stock policy and inventory control

Customers are frustrated, business is lost, if wanted items are often out of stock. On the other hand, storage of items (especially bulky ones like motorcars, washing machines or electric cookers) is costly and the space available may be limited. During storage, perishable items may deteriorate and equipment may become obsolete before it is sold.

The lag between reordering and delivery, penalties for special quick delivery, or for ordering less than a certain number of units, as well as storage costs, must be taken into account when working out ordering and storage policies. Stock control and inventory methods introduced in Chapter 10 determine policy for reordering that will keep costs to a minimum.

1.7.5 Choice of strategies

A business may have a choice of several strategies and be uncertain which is the best because some factors cannot be predicted accurately in advance. The demand for ice-cream depends on the weather, as does that for raincoats or electric blankets in a different way. Decision theory and decision analysis are tools that take account of such uncertainties to determine a 'best' strategy. What is best may depend upon circumstances. For example, if a firm makes raincoats, it may want to minimize the maximum loss that could occur if the weather is of a kind that does not encourage the sale of raincoats. In the language of decision theory, this would be called a *minimax* decision. A minimax decision strategy is often called a pessimist's solution. Another alternative is to minimize expected loss, or, equivalently, to maximize expected gain. We discuss decision analysis in Chapter 11. If you want an indication of the sort of problem that it may tackle take a quick look at Example 11.5 (p. 281).

1.7.6 Uncertainty

In problems where decision analysis is appropriate, there is usually built-in uncertainty. In predicting ice-cream sales there is uncertainty about the weather. Uncertainty permeates many other business scenarios. Will interest rates go up or down? Will demand for a particular make of washing machine or video recorder increase or decrease? Will the cost of a basic raw material go up? What will be the rate of inflation two years hence? The mathematical tools for dealing with uncertainties are *probability theory* and *statistics*; the science of statistics in this sense should not be confused with the same word used to mean collections of data (as in official Government statistics for production, unemployment, etc.)

Statistical methods (in the scientific sense) are useful when uncertainty can be quantified in probability terms. They are relevant to a number of problems in planning and in studying the reliability of systems. Some applications are considered in Chapters 10 to 14.

1.7.7 Economic indicators

These are important both to governments and to commerce and industry. Indicators are based on statistics in the data sense, and are summaries of large bodies of information. These may be totals (as for imports, exports, number unemployed, etc.) or trend indicators, of which the most important ones with financial implications are *indices* such as the retail price index, or the index of industrial production. Such indices have limitations and to appreciate these limitations it is important to understand how major indices like the retail price index are constructed. We describe this in section 15.3.

1.8 A WARNING

We have indicated some situations facing management where mathematics is relevant; the list is anything but exhaustive. A computer is able to store and process vast amounts of information on costs, outputs, cash flow, etc. Such data can be very useful for determining business strategy; to make the best use of them requires sound (usually mathematical or statistical) analysis. Sadly, some managers hoard data as squirrels do nuts, but they do not always make good use of them when the (financially) rainy day arrives. This book aims to create an awareness of how to use data. The reader will often have to search further to find the detailed technology relevant to specific advanced problems; this may require help from a trained business consultant, a mathematician or a statistician. But *awareness* is the important first step. I hope too that the book will help management teams tackle problems that have relatively simple solutions, but are far from trivial in concept.

1.9 WHAT AND WHERE?

The final section in each chapter has the heading *What and where?* It aims to answer two questions to help the reader assess progress and to give guidance about what to do if something more than a *user-friendly introduction* to a topic is required. The questions are:

> *What skills have we mastered?*
>
> *Where can I read more?*

For this chapter, the answer to the first question is *not many*, for we have simply indicated the scope of *management mathematics*, although in section 1.2.1 we showed how to solve simple problems involving VAT. The answer in later chapters will be more constructive.

Turning to the second question, your further reading may fall in one of two broad categories. The first is that of preparation for specific examinations set by professional bodies; in the UK these include, among others, the Institute of Chartered Accountants, the Chartered Institute of Management Accountants, the Chartered Association of Certified Accountants, the Institute of Data Processing Management, the Rating and Valuation Association. Francis (1988), Lucey (1988), Bancroft and O'Sullivan (1988), and many other course-orientated textbooks cover the syllabuses of these or similar bodies and solve (or give as exercises) many questions set in their examinations. There are texts also that deal specifically with the syllabus of one given body; e.g. Jones and MacKay (1988) deal with the relevant course for the Chartered Association of Certified Accountants. The second broad category of reading consists of course text or background reading for a range of University, Polytechnic or Business School courses. We give references in later chapters to some of these that deal particularly well with specific topics. Two that are useful for parallel reading with this book, each with a somewhat different emphasis, are Waters (1989) and Moore (1986).

EXERCISES

1.1   How much is 20% of £20?

1.2   We showed in section 1.1 that if the VAT rate is 15% the VAT fraction of a total price t is $\frac{3}{23}$. What does this fraction become if the VAT rate is increased to 18%?

1.3   The price of a computer is advertised as £1299 excluding VAT. What is the total price inclusive of VAT at (i) 15% and (ii) 18%?

1.4   A computer is advertised at £1450 inclusive of VAT at 15%. What is the price excluding VAT?

1.5   A computer is advertised at £1500 inclusive of VAT at 18%. How much of the purchase price is VAT?

1.6   If, in Exercise 1.5, the VAT rate were reduced from 18% to 15%, what now is the price of the computer inclusive of VAT if there is no change in its price exclusive of VAT?

1.7   In April 1991 the UK VAT rate was increased to 17.5%. What is the VAT fraction of a total price for this rate?

2 Basic Interest Calculations

2.1 SIMPLE INTEREST

Simple interest calculations are school exercises. Confusion, if any, stems from differing notations arising from the convention of expressing rates as percentages; that convention is not helpful from the mathematical viewpoint! A percentage is a proportion of 100. For calculations, we do better to express rates as a proportion of *one unit*, i.e. divide the percentage rate by 100. Thus 7% expressed as a proportion is $7/100 = 0.07$; similarly 9% as a proportion is 0.09.

We denote by i the *unit proportional rate* equivalent to a *percentage rate R*. In some books and examination questions, our i is replaced by the cumbersome $R/100$, i.e. $i = R/100$. Interest rates are usually expressed on a *per annum* (often abbreviated to p.a.) basis, though a rate per day, per week or per month is sometimes quoted. Credit card companies usually quote a *rate per month*. For simple interest, if the rate per annum (expressed as a proportion) is i, then the rate per month is $i/12$.

Exercise If the annual rate (as a proportion) is i, what is the weekly rate? The usual answer is $i/52$. Pedantically, since there are seven days in a week and 365 days in a year, the correct answer is $7i/365$ providing it is not a leap year! In practice, the slight difference is usually unimportant. Similarly, for one month, $i/12$ is an approximation since months vary in length from 28 to 31 days.

Example 2.1 My building society's Monthly Income Account credits interest monthly as income. I invest £10 000 at 9% p.a. What is my monthly income?

Solution   If $R = 9$, then $i = \frac{9}{100} = 0.09$ is the proportional annual rate. The proportional monthly rate is $i/12 = 0.09/12 = 0.0075$. This is the interest (in pounds) earned on each pound of capital in one month (it equals 0.75 pence). Since my investment is £10 000 the total interest earned is £$(10\,000 \times 0.0075) = £75$ per month.

We may generalize from £10 000 invested at 9% to any amount P (the *principal*) invested at R% p.a. Replacing £10 000 by P and 9% by R in Example 2.1 and following through the argument above, the interest earned each month, denoted by I, is

$$I = (Pi)/12, \qquad (2.1)$$

where $i = R/100$.

If simple interest is paid at a rate R% p.a. on capital P, the interest earned in any one year is Pi, where, as usual, $i = R/100$. Over n years, the total interest earned is n times that earned in one year and is given by

$$I = Pin. \qquad (2.2)$$

You will have met an equivalent formula at school, perhaps written as

$$I = PRn/100 \quad (\text{or } I = PRt/100)$$

These, or (2.2), hold if n (or t) is an integer or a positive fraction. If $n = \frac{1}{12}$ the period is one month and (2.2) reduces to (2.1).

The total *accrued sum* of principal plus interest after n years, denoted by A, is clearly

$$A = P + I = P + Pin = P(1 + in). \qquad (2.3)$$

Example 2.2   I invest £1000 at 10% p.a. simple interest. What is the accrued amount after 18 months?

Solution $P = 1000$, $R = 10$, whence $i = \frac{10}{100} = 0.10$, and $n = 1.5$. Substituting in (2.3) gives

$$A = 1000(1 + 0.1 \times 1.5) = 1150.$$

Thus, in 18 months £1000 grows to £1150 at simple interest.

2.2   COMPOUND INTEREST

Compound interest is usually offered by banks, building societies, etc., if interest is left to accumulate (instead of being withdrawn as income). In the simplest case, a fixed sum (the principal) is invested for several years at a stated interest rate. Interest is 'compounded' or added to the principal at the end of each year, or sometimes more frequently. Unlike simple interest, this added interest is now treated as additional capital which itself earns interest.

Example 2.3   I invest £2400 at a rate of 8% p.a. compounded annually. What will my investment be worth at the end of two years?

Solution   In the first year, as for simple interest, we calculate the interest earned on £2400 using formula (2.2) with $P = 2400$, $i = \frac{8}{100} = 0.08$ and $n = 1$, giving the interest I as

$$I = 2400 \times 0.08 = 192.$$

It is logically correct, but cumbersome, to reapply the simple interest formula in the second year separately to (1) the original £2400 which again earns £192 and (2) the £192 earned in the first year, which is now treated as additional capital. The interest on £192 for one year at 8% is

$$I = 192 \times 0.08 = 15.36.$$

The total interest earned over two years is

$$£192 + £192 + £15.36 = £399.36.$$

Table 2.1 summarizes the interest payments over the two years. The accrued amount A after two years is £2400 + £399.36 = £2799.36. Calculating the second year's interest in two steps wastes effort. We do better to work with the accrued amount at the end of the first year to calculate that at the end of the second year. Formula (2.3) with $n = 1$ gives for the first year $A_1 = 2400(1 + 0.08) = 2400 \times 1.08 = 2592$. Now A_1 is the new 'capital' (or principal) for

Table 2.1 Interest payments on £2400 for two years at 8% p.a.

First year:	Interest on original £2400	192
Second year:	Interest on original £2400	192
	Interest on £192 earned previous year	15.36
	Total interest over two years	£399.36

the second year; to get the accrued amount at the end of the second year we apply (2.3) again with $n = 1$, but with the new capital of £2592, giving (use your calculator) the accrued amount A_2 at the end of the second year as

$$A_2 = 2592 \times 1.08 = 2799.36.$$

Since 2592 is 2400×1.08, it follows that

$$A_2 = 2592 \times 1.08 = (2400 \times 1.08) \times 1.08$$
$$= 2400 \times (1.08)^2 = 2799.36.$$

If this £2799.36 is invested for a third year, it accrues to £$(2799.36 \times 1.08) = £3023.31$ (rounded to the nearest penny). Clearly this can be expressed in terms of the original principal of £2400 and the growth factor 1.08 as

$$A_3 = 2400 \times (1.08)^3.$$

If your calculator has a y^x key (or even a facility to hold a constant multiplier), it is easily verified that this gives $A = 3023.31$ as above.

2.2.1 A generalization

The approach generalizes to any principal P, if we successively apply the simple interest accrual formula (2.3) for one year periods, but replace P each year by the value A generated at the previous step.

This sounds complicated, but it is not. We follow it through for a few steps with slight changes in notation. We (temporarily) denote the initial capital or principal by P_0 and call the accrued amount after one year A_1. If the annual percentage rate is R, then $i = R/100$, and if $n = 1$, (2.3) gives

$$A_1 = P_0(1 + i).$$

For the next year, A_1 becomes the principal, so we rename it P_1; at the end of the second year, the accumulated value A_2 of the investment is

$$A_2 = P_1(1 + i),$$

but $P_1 = A_1 = P_0(1 + i)$, so

$$A_2 = P_0(1 + i)(1 + i) = P_0(1 + i)^2.$$

Proceeding this way, we see that after n years the accrued amount of principal plus compound interest is

$$A_n = P_0(1 + i)^n.$$

It is conventional to drop the subscripts on A and P at this stage because the formula only involves the *initial* principal P, and A is interpreted as the accumulated amount of capital plus interest at the end of n years.

Thus the *fundamental formula for compound interest* is

$$A = P(1 + i)^n. \tag{2.4}$$

Note that (2.3) and (2.4) are identical only if $n = 1$.

The total accumulated interest I after n years is $A - P$, which, using (2.4), is

$$I = P(1 + i)^n - P = P[(1 + i)^n - 1].$$

Example 2.4   I may invest £1000 for three years at 5% p.a. simple interest or at the same rate compounded annually. How much better off am I after three years if I do the latter?

Solution   Using (2.3) with $P = 1000$, $i = 0.05$ and $n = 3$, the accumulated amount at simple interest is

$$A = 1000(1 + 0.05 \times 3) = 1000 \times 1.15 = 1150.$$

Using (2.4), the accumulated amount with interest compounded annually is

$$A = 1000(1 + 0.05)^3 = 1000 \times (1.05)^3 = 1157.625.$$

Thus the second investment produces £7.62 additional interest.

This is hardly a startling difference, but compounding gives a dramatic build up with time.

Example 2.5   I invest £100 at 10% p.a. with interest compounded annually for 50 years. How much better off will I be than if I had withdrawn interest at the end of each year as income (i.e. earned only simple interest)?

Solution   Using (2.3) with $P = 100$, $i = 0.1$ and $n = 50$ gives

$$A = 100(1 + 0.1 \times 50) = 600.$$

In effect I have my original capital intact and have received an income (in the form of interest) over the 50 years of £500 in 50 annual instalments each of £10.

From (2.4), with compound interest my investment grows to

$$A = 100(1 + 0.1)^{50}.$$

If your calculator has a y^x key, you will find this gives

$$A = 11\,739.09.$$

The total interest is this, less £100, i.e. £11 639.09, compared to £500 simple interest. It is to be hoped inflation has not wiped out the benefits!

2.3   MONTHLY, WEEKLY, DAILY OR CONTINUOUS COMPOUNDING

Building societies and banks often credit interest more often than once a year (e.g. at six-monthly, at quarterly or even at monthly intervals). Until recently advertisements used to state something like 'interest at 8% p.a. is credited half yearly'. It is now usual (and sometimes a legal requirement) to qualify such statements by saying that this is equivalent to an APR of 8.16%. What does this mean?

If interest at a nominal rate of 8% p.a. is added half yearly, then interest at *half* the rate is credited every six months; if left in the account, that interest itself earns further interest every six months. We may still use (2.4) to calculate interest when compounding is at *any* given interval if we give new meanings to i and n. If interest is compounded every six months, i now becomes $i = r/100$, where, if R is the annual percentage rate, $r = R/2$ if compounding is done every six months (half yearly). If the compounding period is one month, then $r = R/12$; if it is one week, $r = R/52$; and if it is one day, $r = R/365$. In each case, n, instead of being a number of years, becomes the number of *intervals* over which we compound. Thus, if interest is compounded every six months and we want to know what happens after two years, then $n = 4$. If interest is compounded monthly, then, over nine months, $n = 9$.

Example 2.6   A building society pays interest at a nominal 8% p.a. compounded every six months. How much interest per pound invested do I earn in one year?

Solution   Formula (2.4) gives the accrued sum after one year if we put $P = 1$, $i = 0.04$ (since $i = r/100$, where $r = R/2$ and $R = 8$) and $n = 2$ (one year is two six-monthly intervals). Thus

$$A = 1 \times (1.04)^2 = 1.0816.$$

Thus, in one year, £1 grows to £1.0816. This would also happen if interest was compounded annually (instead of every six months) at a rate of 8.16% (because then the relevant $i = 0.0816$ and $n = 1$).

2.3.1 **APR**

APR stands for *annual* (or *annualized*) *percentage rate*. Given any period of compounding, the APR is the rate that would give the same interest for one year if compounding were done annually.

Financial advertisements, particularly those associated with loans, must, by law, quote the APR. The APR gives a common yardstick for comparing interest rates: this is important because there are so many different ways of quoting rates and of carrying out the compounding. The same building society may compound annually, half yearly, quarterly or monthly on different types of savings account.

2.3.2 **Hybridization**

Since people may deposit or withdraw from accounts, often without giving notice, it is a common and useful practice to calculate interest daily (because the amount of money in the account might alter from day to day) but only to add interest to accounts (so that it starts to 'compound' or earn interest itself) at less frequent intervals (often every six months or annually). This is a hybrid between simple and compound interest.

2.3.3 **Daily interest**

Some sophisticated high interest bank accounts compound interest daily at a rate which is $\frac{1}{365}$ of a quoted annual rate R. We call R the *nominal rate* to distinguish it from the APR.

Example 2.7   A high interest bank account advertises that interest at the (nominal) rate of 8% p.a. compounded daily is paid on credit balances. What is the APR?

Solution   We look at what happens to a principal of £1, since in essence we are interested in proportional increases *per unit*. A nominal 8% p.a. implies that for one day, $i = 0.08/365 = 0.000\,219\,178$. Putting also $P = 1$ and $n = 365$ (the number of days in a year) in (2.4) gives

$$A = 1 \times (1.000\,219\,178)^{365} = 1.083\,278.$$

APRs are usually quoted to one or two decimal places. Since £1 increases by a proportion of 0.083 278 in one year it follows that the APR, to two decimal places, is 8.33%.

We express i to six significant figures (non-zeros after the decimal point) because rounding may affect accuracy when we raise numbers not very different from 1 to a high power. Had we rounded 1.000 219 178 to 1.000 219 we would compute A as 1.083 207, giving an APR of 8.32, so there is an effect on the second decimal place.

> *Exercise*   What would we estimate the APR to be if we rounded to 1.000 22?

The above computations are tedious without a computer or a calculator with a y^x key. For this particular situation, tables are unlikely to be useful unless one had some (easily constructed by computer) giving APRs corresponding to daily compounding at various nominal annual rates. We say more about interest tables in section 2.5.

> *Example* 2.8   What is the APR if interest at the rate of 8% p.a. is credited monthly?

> *Solution*   Arguments similar to those in Example 2.7 give $i = 0.08/12 = 0.006\,666\,7$. Putting $P = 1$ and $n = 12$ in (2.4) gives

$$A = 1 \times (1.006\,666\,67)^{12} = 1.082\,999.$$

Clearly this corresponds to an APR of 8.30%.

The difference in APR between daily and monthly compounding at a nominal 8% p.a. is not dramatic, being only about 3 pence p.a. for each £100 invested; only on large sums is the difference important over one year. It becomes appreciable even for small sums if the amount is left invested for longer periods.

APR tells us what would happen *if* a fixed amount were invested under specified conditions for one year. In practice interest rates or principal often change during the course of a year.

2.3.4 **Continuous compounding**

Occasionally interest is credited even more often than daily. The sums involved are usually large and the period of the loan often short (e.g. overnight loans between merchant banks). Then interest may be credited continuously; at any nominal annual rate this gives the highest possible APR corresponding to that nominal rate.

Mathematically, we consider what happens to (2.4) as i becomes very small and n becomes large, but in such a way that the appropriate i is related to n. We skip the mathematics, called limit theory, needed to get the relevant formula and simply state that, if the nominal annual rate of interest is $R\%$ p.a., then, for continuous compounding, (2.4) is replaced by

$$A = Pe^{im}, \tag{2.5}$$

where A and P are as in (2.4), $i = R/100$, m is the time *in years* (often in practice a small fraction of a year) for which interest is being earned, and e is a constant which is approximately 2.7183. Mathematicians call e the *exponential constant*.

Many calculators have an e^x key which lets us calculate A with a few keystrokes. If there is no e^x key one may use the y^x key, putting $y = 2.718\,281\,828$ (a more precise value of e). The APR for continuous compounding is obtained by putting $P = 1$ and $m = 1$ in (2.5); the resulting A is the increase in unit capital in one year.

Example 2.9   Interest is added continuously at a nominal 8% p.a. What is the APR?

Solution   Putting $i = 0.08$, $P = 1$ and $m = 1$ in (2.5) gives

$$A = e^{0.08}.$$

If your calculator has an e^x key, enter 0.08, press the e^x key and the answer is 1.083 287. Thus the annual increment for one unit invested under these conditions is 0.083 287, so the APR to two decimal places is 8.33. To this accuracy, it is the same as that obtained if interest is credited daily. At commonly occurring rates, there tends to be little difference between continuous and daily crediting so far as APR is concerned. Continuous crediting is largely of interest to somebody who lends several million pounds for a matter of hours.

2.3.5 **Quoted rates**

Nominal interest rates are sometimes quoted *per day* or *per week* or *per month* (rather than *per annum*) if these are the compounding period. Credit card interest is often quoted at a rate currently (January 1990) between 1.5 and 2.4% per month. Following arguments used earlier, we easily verify that a monthly rate of 1.75% implies that each £1 owed would grow in one year to $£(1.017\,5)^{12} = £1.231\,4$, implying an APR of 23.14%.

> *Exercise*   Verify that interest of 2% per month implies an APR of 26.82%.

2.3.6 **Depreciation**

If an item depreciates in value at a rate of 10% p.a., it means that if it is initially worth £100 then it is worth only £90 at the end of one year. In the second year, it decreases in value by 10% of £90; clearly 10% of £90 is £9, so its value at the end of the second year is £81. Depreciation is 'negative' compound interest. To calculate a depreciated value D, we modify (2.4) by replacing i by $-i$, where $i = R/100$ if R is the annual percentage rate of depreciation, i.e.

$$D = P(1 - i)^n.$$

2.4   JUGGLING THE COMPOUND INTEREST FORMULA

We know what happens to fixed amounts invested for various periods under a variety of rules for calculating interest. Three more situations we often meet are illustrated by the following examples:

Case 1   I have £75. I want to invest it to grow to £100 in five years. If compounding is annual, what interest rate must I seek to achieve this?

Case 2   I have to pay a debt of £100 in two years' time. How much should I invest now at a guaranteed 6% p.a. compounded annually to cover that debt?

Case 3   I invest £250 at 7% p.a. compounded annually. How long will it be before I double my money?

Note that formula (2.4) involves P, i, n and A. In the examples in section 2.2, we wanted to find A given P, i, n. In section 2.3, we extended these ideas slightly by looking at equivalences between interest rates with different compounding periods; we effectively looked at equivalent P and A values and how they were maintained by changing the relationship between i and n.

Cases 1 to 3 above involve annual compounding, so the interest rates are essentially APRs. In case 1, we are given P, A and n, and want i (from which we easily deduce R). In case 2, we are given A, n and effectively i (easily obtained from R), and we want to find P. In case 3, we are given P, i (effectively) and A ($=2P$), and want to find n. We express the unknown quantity in each case in terms of the others by juggling formula (2.4) by the rules of algebra (this is sometimes referred to as 'changing the subject' of a formula). If you enjoy algebraic manipulation, you might like to verify that, in this way, we obtain (2.6), (2.7) and (2.8) below. If not, please take these on trust.

$$P = A(1 + i)^{-n} = A/(1 + i)^n, \qquad (2.6)$$

$$i = (A/P)^{1/n} - 1, \qquad (2.7)$$

$$n = \frac{\log(A/P)}{\log(1 + i)}. \qquad (2.8)$$

We use these to solve the problems posed in cases 1, 2 and 3 at the start of this section. Note that an asterisk (*) beside an example or exercise implies that these are of a type often found as questions or part questions in examination papers set by professional bodies or business schools examining in the management or accountancy area.

Example 2.10   Solve the problem in case 1.

Solution   We have $P = 75$, $A = 100$ and $n = 5$, and require i (we easily deduce R since $R = 100i$). Substituting in (2.7) (or starting from $100 = 75(1 + i)^5$), we obtain

$$i = (100/75)^{1/5} - 1 = (4/3)^{1/5} - 1.$$

Using a calculator with a y^x key, (or failing that logarithms), we find $i = 1.059\,223\,8 - 1 = 0.059\,223\,8$. Thus $R = 100i = 5.92$ is the percentage rate correct to two decimal places.

Example 2.11   Solve the problem in case 2.

Solution   We have $A = 100$, $i = 0.06$ and $n = 2$, and we require P. Thus (2.6) is appropriate and

$$P = 100(1.06)^{-2} = 100/(1.06)^2 = 100/1.1236 = 88.999\,6.$$

Thus (to the nearest penny) an investment of £89.00 is needed to produce an accrued amount of £100 in two years if interest is compounded annually at 6%.

In section 3.1.2, we see that the problem typified by Example 2.11 is important in what are called *discounting* and *present value* problems.

Example 2.12   Solve the problem in case 3.

Solution   Here $P = 250$, $A = 2P = 500$ and $i = 0.07$, and we require n. Formula (2.8) is appropriate. Since $\log(500/250) = \log 2$, so

$$n = \frac{\log 2}{\log 1.07}.$$

Using the log key on a calculator (or tables of logarithms), this gives $n = 0.301\,030\,0/0.029\,383\,8 = 10.245$. Thus the money must be left invested for 10.245 years to double. Note that, although we expressly referred to a principal of £250, this is the time taken for *any* sum to double at an interest rate of 7% p.a. If interest is only compounded annually, one would have to wait 11 years before being credited with the accrued double amount (and would then get slightly more).

Bank or building society accounts usually (but not always) allow proportional interest if an account is closed during a compounding period. However, if UK National Savings Certificates are cashed between two interest accrual dates (normally three months apart) no partial interest is allocated.

2.5 INTEREST TABLES

Tables for interest give values of the *accrual factor* $(1 + i)^n$ for selected values of i and n. The availability of y^x key, or a constant multiplier facility, on most calculators makes tables unnecessary. They are still to be found in some offices (and occasionally required in examinations). Table 2.2 is an extract from one.

In tables for *discounting*, the entries are the reciprocals of the corresponding entries in an interest table, i.e. they are tables of $(1 + i)^{-n}$. For depreciation we require tables of $(1 - i)^n$.

Example 2.13   Use Table 2.2 to calculate the accrued value of £150 invested for seven years at 3.5% per annum compounded annually.

Solution   From Table 2.2, we note that the accrual factor for $n = 7$ and $R = 3.5$ is 1.272 3. This is what £1 accrues to under these conditions. The £150 accrues to £(150 × 1.272 3) = £190.85.

Table 2.2 Interest factor $(1 + i)^n$ for selected percentage interest rates $R = 100i$ and stated n

	R								
	1.0	1.5	2.0	2.5	3.0	3.5	4.0	4.5	5.0
n 1	1.0100	1.0150	1.0200	1.0250	1.0300	1.0350	1.0400	1.0450	1.0500
2	1.0201	1.0302	1.0404	1.0506	1.0609	1.0712	1.0816	1.0920	1.1025
3	1.0303	1.0457	1.0612	1.0769	1.0927	1.1087	1.1249	1.1412	1.1576
4	1.0406	1.0614	1.0824	1.1038	1.1255	1.1475	1.1699	1.1925	1.2155
5	1.0510	1.0773	1.1041	1.1314	1.1593	1.1877	1.2167	1.2462	1.2763
6	1.0615	1.0934	1.1262	1.1597	1.1941	1.2293	1.2653	1.3023	1.3401
7	1.0721	1.1098	1.1487	1.1887	1.2299	1.2723	1.3159	1.3609	1.4071
8	1.0829	1.1265	1.1717	1.2184	1.2668	1.3168	1.3686	1.4221	1.4775
9	1.0937	1.1434	1.1951	1.2489	1.3048	1.3629	1.4233	1.4861	1.5513
10	1.1046	1.1605	1.2190	1.2801	1.3439	1.4106	1.4802	1.5530	1.6289

2.6   WHAT AND WHERE?

What skills have we mastered?

Simple interest   The basis formula is (2.2), i.e. $I = Pin$ (or $I = PRn/100$).

Compound interest   The basic formula is (2.4), i.e. $A = P(1 + i)^n$ (or $A = P(1 + R/100)^n$), see also formulae (2.5) for continuous compounding and (2.6) to (2.8) for each of P, i, n in terms of A and the remaining two of P, i, n.

Depreciation   Replace $(1 + i)$ by $(1 - i)$ in (2.4).

Annual percentage rate (APR) provides a comparator between nominal rates with various compounding intervals.

We use these formulae to calculate interest (simple or compound) due at various quoted annual, monthly, weekly or daily rates, and to compare the effect of different compounding periods (weekly, monthly, annual, etc.) at the same nominal annual rate. Continuous compounding for short-term loans and depreciation and discounting can also be dealt with. We may also calculate (1) the interest rate needed to generate in a specific time a stated capital sum with a given initial investment (principal); (2) the principal needed to generate a stated capital sum after a fixed time at a known interest rate; (3) the time taken for a sum of money to double, quadruple, etc., at a given interest rate.

Where can I read more?

Many books that cover specific examination syllabuses have chapters on financial arithmetic. These include Francis (1988: Chaps. 26–28), Lucey (1988: Chap. 28), Bancroft & O'Sullivan (1988: Chap. 3) and Jones and MacKay (1988: Chap. 8).

EXERCISES

2.1   My building society pays simple interest monthly as income; the nominal rate is 7% p.a. If I invest £10 000, what is my monthly income? If the interest rate increases to 7.75%, how much additional income will I receive each month?

2.2   Simple interest is paid quarterly as income by a building society at a nominal 8% p.a. How much must I invest to receive a quarterly income of £500?

2.3   Gilt edge bonds pay simple interest half yearly at a nominal 7% p.a. I invest £100 000. How much interest have I received in total at the end of three years?

2.4   I invest £1000 at 7% p.a. compounded annually. How much interest in total have I received by the end of six years?

2.5   In Exercise 2.4, if, at the end of three years, the rate is increased to 7.5%, how much additional interest would I have at the end of six years?

2.6   In Exercise 2.4, if the interest rate had been 7.5% at first, but was reduced to 7% at the end of year 3, what total interest would I obtain after six years? Explain the difference, if any, between this result and that for Exercise 2.5.

*2.7   I invest a fixed sum at 7% p.a. compounded annually. At the end of three years the accrued value of my investment is £629. How much did I invest initially?

*2.8   If, in Exercise 2.7, the interest had been compounded quarterly at the same nominal annual rate, what would my initial investment have been?

*2.9   Each year a given company's profit is 12% higher than it was the previous year. Will its profit be doubled in size in (a) four years, (b) just over five years, (c) between six and seven years, (d) just under ten years, (e) between 12 and 13 years?

*2.10   A firm calculates depreciation on a machine at a rate of 10% p.a. for the first four years and at 15% p.a. thereafter. What is its value after ten years if it was worth £12 000 when new?

2.11   Complete the following table for interest compounded monthly and verify that the given APRs are correct.

Monthly per cent rate	APR	Monthly per cent rate	APR
1	12.68	3	
1.5		4	
1.75		5	
2		6	101.22

*2.12   At least one APR entry in the following table is incorrect. Identify any that are. Assume interest is compounded weekly.

Weekly per cent rate	APR
0.05	2.63
0.10	5.33
0.50	29.61
1.0	47.77
1.5	96.89
2.0	180.03
5.0	1164.28

Do any of the correct APRs surprise you?

2.13   Interest is compounded daily at a nominal 8% p.a. Does the extra day in a leap year have any practical effect on the APR?

2.14   A merchant bank lends £10 million at a rate of 11% p.a. compounded continuously. How much interest is due after 12 hours?

*2.15   I invest a sum of money at 9% p.a. compounded annually. How long does it take to treble?

2.16   If, in Exercise 2.15, compounding had taken place every six months, how long would my money take to treble?

*2.17   I have £600 to invest and my financial adviser tells me that 'at current interest rates this will grow to £854.75 at the end of four years'. What is the current APR?

*2.18   A piece of machinery depreciates at a rate of 8% p.a. How long elapses before it is worth only half its value when new?

*2.19   When my high interest bank account is in credit, I receive interest at a rate of 9% p.a. net credited daily. When I am in overdraft, I pay interest at a rate of 15% per annum debited monthly. If I have a credit balance of £1000 on 1 January 1990 and leave it and the interest thereon intact for nine months, but then take out an overdraft of £1200 for three months, what is the difference between the interest the bank pays me and that which I pay the bank over the full 12-month period?

*2.20   On deposit accounts, Bank A operates a three-tier interest structure. On any deposit, it calculates interest on the first £10 000 at 7% p.a., on the next £10 000 at 7.75% p.a., and on higher balances at 8.5% p.a., all interest being net and credited annually. Bank B allows interest at the nominal rate of 7.75% p.a. net credited half yearly on all credit balances. Where should I deposit £25 000 if I intend to leave it intact for one year?

*2.21   If the interest rates were the same as in Exercise 2.20, would you give the same advice if I had £50 000 to deposit?

*2.22   Suppose that Banks A and B operate the net of tax interest structures given in Exercise 2.20, but that I also consider a national savings account that pays interest at 10.5% p.a. gross credited annually. If I pay tax on gross income at the rate of 25p in the £, where should I deposit £25 000 if I intend to leave it intact for one year? Would you give the same advice if I had £40 000 to invest?

2.23   The government advertises an issue of National Savings Certificates as '£100 becomes £154 after 5 years'. What is the effective *annual* rate of interest?   [CIMA, part question only. Note that the effective *annual* rate is what we have called the APR.]

2.24   In two years from now some machinery in your company will need replacing. It is estimated that £500 000 will then be required. To provide this £X is to be allocated now, invested at 12% per year, with interest compounded quarterly. What should X be?   [CIMA, part question only.]

2.25   The 31st issue of National Savings Certificates gives £145.92 for every £100 invested if held for the full five years. However, certificates can also be cashed in early. A person cashing in a £100 certificate at the end of year 3 would receive £121.60.

Mrs Smith invested £200 in these certificates.

(a) If she cashes them in at the end of three years, how much does she receive?

(b) Calculate, to two decimal places, the percentage yield of these certificates at the end of year 3.

Half of the certificates purchased are cashed in at the end of year 3 and the remainder are cashed in at the end of year 5.

(c) Calculate the total amount received.

A building society investment account pays interest at $r\%$ per annum compounded annually. Mrs Smith also places £200 in the account and receives the same amount at the end of five years as she did in (c).

(d) Calculate r to two significant figures.   [AEB, AS level.]

3 Regular Payments

These involve extensions of formula (2.4) for compound interest, i.e.

$$A = P(1 + i)^n,$$

and the related (2.6), i.e.

$$P = A/(1 + i)^n,$$

to cover payments at regular intervals, or to compare strategies that involve payments or receipts (i.e. cash flows) in the future.

Simple debt repayment or annuity schemes involve: (1) a fixed initial capital; (2) a fixed number of equal annual payments commencing one year after the capital sum is provided; (3) interest at a specified APR. There are many modifications: e.g. mortgage repayments are often monthly and interest rates may vary; retirement annuity payments are often on a *contingency basis*, i.e. are payable not for a fixed time but until a specified event such as the death of the recipient. Extension from annual to monthly or quarterly payments involves no new principles, but actuarial considerations (not dealt with in this book) are important for contingency annuities.

To calculate loan repayments, or annuities, for the basic fixed interest/fixed period situation, two key ideas are needed: one is the mathematical concept of a *geometric progression*; the other is the financial one of discounting to *present values* of sums payable or receivable in the future.

3.1.1 Geometric progressions

If we take a number, say 6, and repeatedly double it we get a sequence

$$6, 12, 24, 48, 96, \ldots .$$

The 'key' ingredients are *the first term*, 6, and *the ratio of successive terms* or *the multiplier giving the next term*, 2. This is a particular case of a *geometric progression*, which is a sequence of n terms, the *first term* of which is a and the ratio of successive terms, called the *common ratio*, is r. The sequence is $a, ar, ar^2, ar^3, \ldots, ar^{n-1}$. Each subsequent term is obtained from the current term by multiplying the latter by the same constant r. We show in Appendix A.1 that the sum S of all n terms is

$$S = \frac{a(r^n - 1)}{r - 1}, \tag{3.1}$$

so $6 + 12 + 24 + \cdots$ to ten terms equals

$$\frac{6(2^{10} - 1)}{2 - 1} = 6138$$

(check this by writing down all ten terms and adding them).

3.1.2 Discounting and present value (PV)

If I invest money at 10% p.a. compounded annually by using (2.4), I find that after one year this becomes £110, after two years £121, after three years £133.10, and so on.

Ignoring fluctuations in interest rates or effects of inflation, this means that if it can be invested at this rate, £100 now is as good as £110 in one year's time, £121 in two years' time, £133.10 in three years' time. In other words, £100 is today's value of £110 in one years' time, of £121 in two years' time, of £133.10 in three years' time. We call this £100 the *discounted* or *present value* (PV) of these sums.

To get the PV of an amount A in n years' time at a given rate i of discounting, we use

$$P = A/(1 + i)^n.$$

Thus the PV of what becomes £1200 in five years' time if invested at 8% is easily calculated to be $P = 1200/(1.08)^5 = 816.70$. We have here taken i to be a currently available interest rate, but the interpretation may be different; it could, for example, be a projected rate of return on an investment.

3.1.3 Debt repayment

My bank charges interest on a personal loan at an APR of 15%. I arrange a loan of £20 000 to be repaid by ten equal annual repayments, the first due one year after the loan is taken out. The bank informs me that each annual repayment will be £3985.04. They arrive at this figure using formula (3.4) given below. You could, however, check that the bank repayment is correct in a more fundamental way which also gives a hint about how (3.4) is obtained. The key idea is to reduce each repayment to its present value (PV) on the basis of interest being charged at 15%. The sum of these PVs should equal the PV of the total loan, i.e. £20 000. The PV of the first repayment (made one year after the loan is taken out) is

$$\frac{3985.04}{1.15} = 3465.25.$$

Similarly, the PV of that made after two years is

$$\frac{3985.04}{(1.15)^2} = 3013.26,$$

and that after three years is

$$\frac{3985.04}{(1.15)^3} = 2620.23.$$

Proceeding in this way the PV for the final payment after ten years is

$$\frac{3985.04}{(1.15)^{10}} = 985.04.$$

Exercise Compute the present values of all ten payments and verify that these total £20 000.

Your total may differ by a few pence from £20 000. This is due to rounding to the nearest penny both in the original repayment figure of £3985.04 and in the calculated PVs.

We may generalize this to any loan P with equal annual repayments a, for n years at a given interest rate. The above argument then gives

$$P = \frac{a}{1 + i} + \frac{a}{(1 + i)^2} + \frac{a}{(1 + i)^3} + \cdots + \frac{a}{(1 + i)^n}. \quad (3.2)$$

The right-hand side of (3.2) is the sum of n terms of a geometric progression with first term $a/(1 + i)$ and common ratio $1/(1 + i)$. You may like to verify (if not, please take it on trust) that, using (3.1) for the sum of a geometric progression, we get

$$P = \frac{a[(1 + i)^n - 1]}{i(1 + i)^n}, \quad (3.3)$$

which rearranges after some tedious algebra to the useful formula

$$a = \frac{Pi}{1 - (1 + i)^{-n}}. \quad (3.4)$$

The factor by which we multiply P to get a, namely $i/[1 - (1 + i)^{-n}]$ (or equivalently, if you prefer, $i(1 + i)^n/[(1 + i)^n - 1]$), is called the *capital recovery factor*. It is easily computed with a pocket calculator, or may be obtained from published tables for various values of i and n.

Exercise By putting $P = 20\,000$, $i = 0.15$ and $n = 10$, verify that $a = 3985.04$ as stated in the numerical example at the start of this section.

Example 3.1   I borrow £400 at 5% p.a. compounded annually and agree to repay principal plus interest in three equal annual instalments, the first due one year after the loan is made. What should each annual repayment be?

Solution   In (3.4) we put $P = 400$, $i = 0.05$ and $n = 3$, whence

$$a = \frac{400 \times 0.05}{1 - (1.05)^{-3}} = \frac{(400 \times 0.05)(1.05)^3}{(1.05)^3 - 1}$$

$$= (20 \times 1.157\,625)/0.157\,625 = 146.88.$$

Each annual payment should be £146.88. If your calculator has a y^x key, the computation can be telescoped into one operation; intermediate steps are given above only to clarify the calculation.

3.1.4 Obvious checks

In any calculation, it is easy to make a logical error or hit the wrong key on a calculator; whenever possible, check if an answer is at least in the right ballpark. Clearly, if we are repaying capital of £400 in three instalments, each must be more than one-third of the capital to allow for interest, i.e. each must be more than £133.33. Since we have made half the repayments in half the time, the total interest will be of the order of (but not exactly) what would be paid if half the original sum were borrowed for the full term of three years (or the full sum had been borrowed for half the time). It is easily verified (using (2.4)) that the compound interest on £200 borrowed for three years at 5% p.a. is £31.52, suggesting about £10.50 interest per annum. Thus each repayment should be something like £133.33 + £10.50 = £143.83. Each is about £3 more because the 'capital' element of earlier repayments is less than that in later repayments (i.e. earlier repayments have a higher *interest* component; see the comments after Example 3.2 below). However, had we got an answer of £120 or £1468.8, this sort of quick check would immediately indicate that something was seriously wrong. In particular, the latter result suggests a decimal point in the wrong place, one of the commonest errors in arithmetic.

Example 3.2   A company advertises personal loans at a rate of 2% per week compounded weekly. A man borrows £100 repayable by weekly payments starting 13 weeks after the loan is incurred and continuing for two years. How much should each weekly payment be?

      Solution   This is essentially a two-stage problem. First, we consider the capital accumulating at the *weekly* rate of 2% for 12 weeks (we see below why 12 rather than 13). Applying formula (2.4) with $n = 12$, $i = 0.02$ and $P = 100$ gives

$$A = 100 \times (1.02)^{12} = 126.82.$$

Since repayment starts 13 weeks after the original loan, we use a simple adaptation of (3.4) regarding repayments as starting one time unit (a week) after the sum of £126.82 has accumulated, and continuing for 104 time units (weeks) at a rate of 2% per time unit (week). To determine each weekly payment we put $P = 126.82$, $i = 0.02$ and $n = 104$ in (3.4), whence

$$a = (126.82 \times 0.02)/[1 - (1.02)^{-104}] = 2.91.$$

Intermediate steps in the calculation have been omitted; they are analogous to those in Example 3.1.

The total repayment of this loan of £100 in 104 instalments of £2.91 amounts to £302.64. The interest of £202.64 is more than double the amount borrowed! There is a salutory warning here of the danger of being deluded by what seems a low interest rate, 2%, when it is expressed *per week* rather than the more common *per annum*. Note here that early repayments have a large interest component. For example, between week 12 and 13 (when the first payment is made) the loan attracts interest of £2.54 and the offsetting payment of £2.91 gives a net capital reduction of only 47p, from £126.82 to £126.35. The final payment after 104 weeks is, on the contrary, nearly all capital. It is partly to protect people from misapprehensions about interest rates that the law now requires APRs to be stated in loan advertisements. These must also take account of 'hidden' charges such as fees for arranging a loan. Since $(1.02)^{52} = 2.80$, implying that in one year 100 grows to 280, a rate of 2% per week is equivalent to an APR of 180%. You may think that nobody would borrow at a rate of 2% per week, but this rate was commonly charged by unscrupulous money lenders operating in the poorer quarter of one British city until the 1980s.

3.1.5 Annuities

In the simplest annuity problem, an amount P is invested at a fixed rate of interest so that an amount a (the annuity) can be drawn at the end of each year thereafter (often called payment in arrears) for n years until the investment (capital plus interest) is exhausted. Finding the lump sum needed to give a specified annual annuity (e.g. a retirement annuity) of £a payable for n years is essentially the debt repayment problem in reverse, in the sense that we now know a (the required amount of each annual payment), n and also i, the interest rate, but not P.

The solution is given directly by (3.3), which may also be written, after a little algebraic juggling, as

$$P = \frac{a[1 - (1 + i)^{-n}]}{i} \tag{3.5}$$

The coefficient of a is (not surprisingly, but be sure you see why) the reciprocal of the *capital recovery factor* and is often called the *annuity factor*.

Example 3.3   I wish to purchase an annuity to provide annual payments in arrears of £1000 for ten years. If interest on the purchase price is paid at 9% p.a. compounded annually, what is the purchase price? Ignore any administrative charges or provisions for taxation.

Solution   Formula (3.5) is appropriate with $a = 1000$, $i = 0.09$ and $n = 10$, whence

$$P = \frac{1000(1 - 1.09^{-10})}{0.09} = \frac{1000(1.09^{10} - 1)}{1.09^{10} \times 0.09} = 6417.66.$$

Thus the capital required is £6417.66.

This is the reverse of a mortgage repayment situation where the person purchasing the annuity now takes the role of a building society lending £6417.66 to a homebuyer: the provider of the annuity takes the role of a mortgagee repaying that loan in ten annual instalments of £1000 each.

Using an argument like that at the start of section 3.1.3 we may look upon the first payment of £1000 as having earned interest for one year at 9% and thus having a PV at the time the investment is made of $1000/1.09 = 917.43$, that after the second year as having a PV of $1000/(1.09)^2 = 841.68$, and so on.

> *Exercise* By calculating the present value of all ten payments at the time the capital sum was invested, verify that these total £6417.66.

3.2 SINKING FUNDS

A simple sinking fund consists of regular sums set aside to meet a future need such as replacement of equipment or a planned business expansion. If a payment of £a is made annually into a fund now and in each succeeding year until n payments have been made to meet an anticipated expenditure P that is to be incurred n years from now, and interest is compounded annually at a rate R% p.a., we have a situation in which the first payment (made at the current time which we regard as year 0) earns interest for n years, the payment after year 1 earns interest for $n - 1$ years, and so on. The nth payment is made $n - 1$ years from now and earns interest for one year. Using similar arguments to those for mortgage repayments and annuities, we see that, if we write, as usual, $i = R/100$, we have

$$a(1 + i)^n + a(1 + i)^{n-1} + a(1 + i)^{n-2} + \cdots + a(1 + i) = P.$$

Taking out the common factor $a(1 + i)$ on the left, and reversing the order of terms, gives

$$a(1 + i)[1 + (1 + i) + \cdots + (1 + i)^{n-1}] = P.$$

The terms inside the square brackets form a geometric progression of n terms with first term 1 and common ratio $1 + i$. Thus

$$\frac{a(1 + i)[(1 + i)^n - 1]}{i} = P,$$

whence

$$a = \frac{Pi}{(1 + i)[(1 + i)^n - 1]}. \tag{3.6}$$

Example 3.4   A firm plans to replace a piece of machinery in ten years' time. It estimates the cost then will be £10 500. What equal sums must it put aside now and at the beginning of each of the following nine years to meet this commitment if interest is payable at 8% p.a. compounded annually?

Solution   Formula (3.6) is appropriate with $P = 10\,500$, $i = 0.08$ and $n = 10$, giving

$$a = \frac{10\,500 \times 0.08}{1.08(1.08^{10} - 1)} = 671.12.$$

The amount to be put aside each year is £671.12.

We have assumed that interest rates remain constant and that the cost of a project ten years hence has been estimated correctly. In practice, there is unpredictability about effects of inflation and trends in interest rates. These can be taken into account by recalculation of the appropriate future funding level when such changes are detected or predicted. There may also be taxation factors to be considered.

3.3   FUTURE CASH FLOWS

Businesses often have to choose between options that involve different current and future income and expenditure, i.e. cash inflows and outflows. One basis on which to decide on the most favourable option is to reduce all predicted cash flows, both in and out, to their *present value* (PV) (section 3.1.2). The preferred option is the one that produces the greatest *net present value* (NPV) inflow, or, if all produce a net outflow, the one with the smallest NPV outflow. Vital to this approach is a choice of the discounting factors used to calculate the NPV. These may be based on a currently available interest rate, or a rate based on what could be obtained if the money were used for some other feasible activity. A simple example (although it is necessarily rather more complicated than any met previously in this chapter) illustrates the basic idea.

Example 3.5 A firm has a choice of three options regarding policy for photocopying equipment:

(i) invest in new equipment costing £20 000;
(ii) upgrade existing equipment at a cost of £10 000;
(iii) continue using existing equipment without change.

The present resale value of existing equipment is £5000. The firm can obtain maintenance contracts payable annually in advance for six years at rates of £1000 p.a. for option (i), £1200 p.a. for option (ii), and £3000 p.a. for option (iii). Other costs are the same for each option. At the end of six years, resale (or scrap) value of equipment under option (i) is £2000, under (ii) is £1000, and under (iii) is nil.

They decide the appropriate rate for discounting to PV is 14% p.a. Which option is best for the company over a six-year time span?

Solution From a cash flow viewpoint, purchase and maintenance costs are outflows (shown in brackets in Table 3.1). The only inflow is from sale of equipment now or at the end of six years. We use NPVs as an appropriate basis for comparing different outflows at different times. The coefficient of A, i.e. $1/(1 + i)^n$, in (2.6), often called the *present value factor* for discounting (see section 3.1.2), is in this case $1/(1.14)^n$ (where $n = 0, 1, 2, 3, 4, 5$ or 6).

The computations are best set out in a table (although with careful use of a calculator not all this detail need be recorded). In Table 3.1,

Table 3.1 A comparison of three investment strategies using NPVs

| Year | Nominal flows | | | PV factor | Net present values | | |
	(i)	(ii)	(iii)		(i)	(ii)	(iii)
0	(16000)[1]	(11200)[2]	(3000)[3]	1.0000	(16000)	(11200)	(3000)
1	(1000)	(1200)	(3000)	0.8772	(877)	(1053)	(2632)
2	(1000)	(1200)	(3000)	0.7695	(770)	(923)	(2308)
3	(1000)	(1200)	(3000)	0.6750	(675)	(810)	(2025)
4	(1000)	(1200)	(3000)	0.5921	(592)	(711)	(1776)
5	(1000)	(1200)	(3000)	0.5194	(519)	(623)	(1558)
6	2000[4]	1000[4]	0[4]	0.4556	911	456	0
Total six-year flow	(19000)	(16200)	(18000)		(18522)	(14864)	(13299)

Notes:
[1] Consisting of cost £20 000, less resale £5000, plus £1000 maintenance.
[2] Consisting of upgrade £10 000 plus £1200 maintenance.
[3] Maintenance charge. Note that all outflows for years 1 to 5 are also maintenance.
[4] Predicted resale value after six years.

we give on the left annual net cash flows at the end of each year (regarding current time as year 0) in cash values relevant to the stated year for each option. Entries to the right of the *present value* (*PV*) *factor* are for the relevant PVs, all rounded to the nearest £.

The smallest cash outflow expressed on an NPV basis of £13 299 is given by option (iii), so this is the preferred option. In passing, we note that, if we use the left hand data giving actual (i.e. not discounted) cash flows, this would imply a minimum net outflow of £16 200 for option (ii). This option loses out on an NPV basis because it involves a higher initial expenditure than option (iii), and initial expenditure gets no discounting.

The chosen discount rate is crucial. The exercise is only of value if this realistically reflects financial expectations if the money were allocated to other resources and so truly indicates the PV of all cash flows under an alternative allocation.

NPVs are just one way of deciding upon optimum investment strategy and dependence on the choice of discount rate is a disadvantage. Another method commonly used is based on what is called the *internal rate of return*. For any given strategy, this is a discount rate that would give a zero NPV cash flow for that strategy. The optimum strategy is that with the largest internal rate of return as measured by the discount rate for zero NPV. We do not describe the method in detail because it is rather user-unfriendly, largely because a discount rate giving zero NPV can only be determined indirectly for each strategy. This is usually achieved by using a technique called *interpolation*, often in association with another called *iteration*, an approach we describe in broad terms in Appendix A.2. The method involves obtaining the cash flow for two discount rates (preferably chosen so that one gives a negative and the other a positive cash flow); *interpolation* is then used to determine a discount rate that will give a near zero net flow. The process is repeated for improved estimates suggested by this interpolated value; this is the concept of iteration. In practice, NPV or internal rate of return problems are often tackled using computer spreadsheet software.

3.4 OVERSIMPLIFICATION

As this book is about basics, we do not deal with many factors that add complications. Managers and business people must be aware of these; many are dealt with in a routine way by appropriate computer software. Examination questions set by professional bodies also require an understanding of these issues. Here are a few such matters.

3.4.1 Interest rate changes

In recent years, fluctuating interest rates have been the rule rather than the exception. Some of the few guaranteed rates are associated with the nominal value of certain gilt edged stocks (but here the market value of the underlying capital may change); certain UK National Saving Certificates also have guaranteed rates of interest over a five-year period. In general, changes in interest rates keep the financial forecasters busy. The impact of increases in interest rates on mortgage repayments is well known.

3.4.2 Inflation

Rapid inflation in the 1960s and 1970s forced accountants to reconsider the way they valued assets and looked upon depreciation to deal with the (then in many countries) novel situations where equipment could often be sold in three years' time at a higher price in cash terms than it cost, but had in reality depreciated because replacement costs were higher as a result of inflation.

3.4.3 Taxation

Before April 1991, bank and building society interest paid to individuals resident in the UK was paid (by law) effectively *net of basic rate tax*. This made life easy for basic rate tax payers, but difficult for those who paid no tax (because tax deducted at what was called the *composite rate* – a rate determined by the Inland Revenue – could not be reclaimed). It also concerned those who paid higher rate tax. The net interest was 'grossed up' to what one would have got if composite rate tax had not been deducted, and the taxpayer then paid, on this grossed up amount, any difference between the higher rate tax on it and the basic rate tax that had been allowed for in the composite rate. The system has now been changed to be fairer to both taxpayer and non-taxpayer, and in future banks will be allowed to pay gross interest to non-taxpayers but will deduct basic rate tax from taxpayers, and higher rate taxpayers will have to pay additional tax as at present.

Annuities and mortgage repayments are also affected in their *net values* by complex taxation rules. Part of many annuity payments are tax free as they are regarded as a return of capital. The interest component of mortgage repayments on main residences of individuals are also paid net of tax subject to limits on the amount borrowed and dependent also upon the type of mortgage.

3.5 TABLES

In section 2.5, we pointed out that interest and discount tables are now largely irrelevant if one has a computer or even a calculator with a y^x key. This is also true for tables of the *capital recovery factor* giving for selected i and n the values of $i/[1 - (1 + i)^{-n}]$, or for its reciprocal, the *annuity factor*. Few people who do calculations involving these need such tables. The tables are more likely to be of interest to occasional users.

3.6 WHAT AND WHERE?

What skills have we mastered?

Geometric progressions and *present values* (PVs) indicating the present day equivalent of future payments or receipts after discounting to allow for available interest or returns on investment are important ideas for problems involving *mortgage repayments and annuities*. The basic formulae for these are (3.4) and (3.5).
Sinking funds. The basic formula is (3.6).
Net present values provide a useful basis for comparison of cash flows under different strategies, especially when the flows are for different amounts at various times in the future.

With these concepts we may calculate present values, debt repayments or capital required for annuities at fixed interest rates for a fixed period and closely related computations for sinking funds. Exercises 3.5 to 3.7 below extend some of the ideas about sinking funds, but you should be able to cope with these after studying this chapter. Use of NPVs to compare strategies has also been covered.

Where can I read more?

See under this heading in Chapter 2.

EXERCISES

*3.1   I borrow £1000 and interest is charged at a nominal 12% p.a. compounded monthly. I agree to repay the debt in 24 equal monthly instalments, the first due one month after the debt is incurred. How much should each payment be?

*3.2   If I borrow the same amount at the same interest rate as in Exercise 3.1, but the repayment terms are 12 equal monthly instalments, the first being due 13 months after the debt is incurred, how much is each payment? Compare total repayments in Exercises 3.1 and 3.2. Do you think this is a reasonable method of comparing the two schemes? If inflation were increasing rapidly over the two-year period, which method of repayment would you consider to represent the better deal?

3.3   A man wants to receive an annuity of £1000 per annum payable annually for 15 years, the first payment to be made in one year's time. If interest is calculated at 12% p.a., what is the purchase price of the annuity?

3.4   A man purchases an annuity for £12 000 payable annually in arrears for 12 years. If interest is calculated at 10% p.a., how much is each annual payment?

*3.5   A new bridge has just been completed. A replacement will be needed in 20 years' time and this is estimated to cost £200 000. A sinking fund with fixed annual payments is to be started now and followed with a further 19 annual payments. If interest is earned at 9% p.a. compounded annually, how much should each payment be?

*3.6   In the situation in Exercise 3.5, suppose that immediately after ten payments have been made the replacement cost is re-estimated at £250 000. How much should each future payment be if the rate of interest on all invested funds (including capital accrued from the ten earlier payments) is from this date increased to 10%?

*3.7 After setting up a fund as in Exercise 3.6, it is decided at the end of 20 years that replacement of the bridge may be deferred for three years, by which time the cost will have risen to £300 000. Explain why no further contributions to the sinking fund would be needed.

*3.8 A firm has an option of paying for goods with one down payment of £2700 now. Alternatively it may pay £500 now and £500 one year hence, £500 two years hence, £700 three years hence and £700 four years hence. If future payments may be discounted at 12% p.a., use NPVs to determine the more favourable option.

*3.9 A manufacturer of computer accessories wishes to compare three projects, A, B and C which will involve an immediate capital outlay in £ thousand of 1500 for A, 1000 for B and 750 for C. His forecast net cash returns (£ thousand) at the end of each of the next four years are as follows:

Year	1	2	3	4
Project A	850	650	450	250
Project B	600	600	500	500
Project C	400	300	200	100

If the appropriate discounting factor to obtain present values is 10% p.a. which project is to be preferred on the basis of NPVs?

3.10 It has been decided to purchase a new machine by taking out a loan of £40 000 over the 5 years of its life. The loan is being compounded at an interest rate of 17.5% per annum. The loan is to be settled at the end of 5 years by a fund into which equal annual amounts are to be paid at the beginning of each year and on which interest compounds at 15% per annum. Calculate the amount of each of the five equal annual instalments to be paid into the fund. [ACCA]

3.11   In the near future, a company has to make a decision about its computer, C, which has a current market value of £15 000. There are three possibilities:

  (i) sell C and buy a new computer costing £75 000;
 (ii) overhaul and upgrade C;
(iii) continue with C as at present.

Relevant data on these decisions are given below:

Decision	Initial outlay	Economic life	Resale value after five years	Annual service contract plus operating costs (payable in advance)
	£	years	£	£
(i)	75 000	5	10 000	20 000
(ii)	25 000	5	10 000	27 000
(iii)	0	5	0	32 000

Assume the appropriate rate of interest to be 12% and ignore taxation. You are required, using the concept of net present value, to find which decision would be in the best financial interests of the company, stating why, and including any reservations and assumptions. [CIMA]

3.12   (a) One of your clients has a bank credit card and used it to pay £500 for an emergency repair to his car. The client can only repay at most £100 per month to the bank.

   The condition for operating the credit card is that no interest is charged in the month that the repair takes place and thereafter the monthly interest is calculated at 2.5% of the opening balance.
Required:
Draw up a schedule showing the interest charged and the repayments made, if the first repayment is made in the month that the repair is charged.

(b) After his experience with the car your client decides to exchange it and borrow £3 000 from the bank to buy a new one.

The arrangement with the bank is for the client to make five equal annual repayments, being charged interest at 20% per annum on the amount of the loan outstanding. Repayments take place on the anniversary of the original loan.

Required:

Determine the equal annual repayments and draw up a schedule showing the interest charged and repayments made.   [ACCA, part question only]

4 Simple Allocation Problems

4.1 MAKING A CHOICE

Given simple options, it may be easy to see which is best. For example, a smallholder may have room for six rows of potatoes and each row may be either an *early* or a *main* crop variety. He has enough seed to plant four rows of *main* and three rows of *early*. Since he is constrained to six rows in all, a moment's reflection shows he has two options – either four rows of *main* and two rows of *early* or three rows of each. He expects the *main* crop variety to yield 80 kg per row which he can sell at 6p per kg. He expects the *early* variety to yield 50 kg per row which he can sell at 12p per kg. Clearly his expected income per row is £4.80 for *main* and £6.00 for *early*. To maximize his income he should therefore plant as many *early* as possible, i.e. three rows of each.

Allocation problems are usually more complicated. We gave one in Example 1.2 and reproduce it for convenience as Example 4.1.

Example 4.1   A firm makes two kinds of trousers. For type A, material costs £2.50 per pair and it takes one girl 60 minutes to make a pair. Each pair is sold for £9.50. For type B, material costs £2.00 per pair and it takes one girl 20 minutes to make a pair. Each pair is sold for £6.00. The firm employs eight girls, who will each work a maximum of eight hours per day and be paid £3.00 per hour worked. Overheads are £240 per day. Market forces limit possible sales of type A to not more than 60 per day and sales of type B to not more than 100 per day. Zip fasteners are in short supply and only

Table 4.1 Summary of information, Example 4.1

	Material Cost	Time (girl-min)	Sale price
Type A	£2.50	60	£9.50
Type B	£2.00	20	£6.00

Additional information:

Overheads: £240 per day

Wages: £3 per hour

Maximum girl-minutes labour available per day: 3840 (since each girl works a maximum of eight hours (= 8 × 60 = 480 minutes) and eight girls are available, whence 480 × 8 = 3840)

Number of type A that can be sold: Maximum 60

Number of type B that can be sold: Maximum 100

Restriction imposed by zips: Maximum 120

120 are available each day (each pair of trousers must have a zip!). How many of each type should the manufacturer produce daily to maximize profit?

We develop the solution in a stepwise manner. First, we formulate the problem mathematically. Some people find this difficult; it helps to do it in two stages. To start, we summarize our information as in Table 4.1.

4.1.1 **An obvious solution?**

Before we proceed to the next stage, is there a common-sense solution? Because *daily* overheads are fixed, the only scope for adjusting profit per pair made is by maximizing the difference between sale price and cost of material plus labour. First, a pair of type A take 60 girl-minutes to make, the labour cost is £3 per pair; material costs £2.50 per pair. They sell for £9.50 so the profit (ignoring for the moment overheads) is £(9.50 − 3 − 2.50) = £4. Likewise, for type B, the profit is £(6 − 1 − 2) = £3. Trousers of type A produce the higher profit, so it seems we should make as many as possible; however, the market demand is at most 60, so there is no point in making more. Any spare capacity may be used to make type B trousers. Since we only have 120 zips and 60 are needed for type A's, we cannot make more than 120 − 60 = 60 type B's. We can only do this if labour is available. It takes 60 × 60 = 3600 of available girl-minutes to make 60 type A's, so only 3840 − 3600 = 240 remain. At 20 minutes per pair this leaves time to make only 12 type B's. Thus we make 60 type A's at a profit of £4 each and 12 type B's at a profit of £3 each, giving a total profit (excluding overheads) of £(60 × 4 + 12 × 3) = £276. Subtracting overheads of £240 leaves a net profit of £36. A pity about that labour constraint, but we made the most of things by concentrating production on the high profit items – or did we?

Suppose, perversely, we concentrated on the lower profit type B's and made the maximum saleable 100. We still have enough zips left to make 20 type A's (if time is available). Time is available because 100 type B's take 2000 minutes and 20 type A's take 1200 minutes making a total of 3200 minutes – 640 minutes less than our maximum permitted 3840. This is bad luck for the work force, but it does not add to company costs, as girls are paid only for time worked.

The profit on 100 type B's at £3 per pair is £300 and on 20 type A's at £4 per pair is £80, a total of £380 – less £240 overheads – leaving a net profit of £140, compared to £36 by doing the obvious! Or was it the obvious? Things are not as simple as we have tried to make out. We make more profit by concentrating first on lower profit items. Why? Because these take less time per pair to make; in effect they are more profitable per *unit of time*. In our earlier calculation, we concentrated on the highest profit per *item made*.

Are you uneasy? Might some other mix of types A and B make even more profit? It would be tedious to look at all, or even an appreciable number of, possible combinations that satisfied the constraints imposed by daily sales, available labour or supplies of zips. Fortunately we can limit the number of possibilities we have to examine.

4.1.2 A systematic approach

We now put our problem in concise mathematical form. We set up relationships involving two unknowns: the numbers of trousers of types A and B that we make. We use the conventional mathematical symbols for unknowns, x and y. Let x be the number of type A and y the number of type B trousers. We want to find x and y to maximize profit. We know that, apart from overheads, the profit on each pair of type A is £4 and on type B it is £3, whence for sales of x and y we make $4x + 3y$; after allowing for overheads of £240, the total profit £U is clearly

$$U = 4x + 3y - 240.$$

This is called the *objective function* because our aim, or objective, is to maximize U by an appropriate choice of x and y. Both x and y are subject to constraints, which we may write as follows.

1. Sales constraint on type A (60) and type B (100):

$$x \leqslant 60, \qquad y \leqslant 100.$$

   The symbol $\leqslant$ means *is less than or equal to*.
2. Total girl-minutes of labour available (3840):

$$60x + 20y \leqslant 3840.$$

   Dividing each side by 20 (dividing both sides of an inequality by the same *positive* number is allowed), this reduces to

$$3x + y \leqslant 192.$$

3. Availability of zips (maximum 120):

$$x + y \leqslant 120.$$

4. Since x and y are numbers of trousers, they must be non-negative (but one or the other may be zero). We express these constraints as

$$x \geqslant 0, \quad y \geqslant 0.$$

The symbol $\geqslant$ means *is greater than or equal to*.

Mathematicians like problems in a terse form, so they summarize all this without intervening explanations as follows.

Maximize

$$U = 4x + 3y - 240 \tag{4.1}$$

subject to

$$x \leqslant 60, \quad y \leqslant 100, \tag{4.2}$$

$$3x + y \leqslant 192, \tag{4.3}$$

$$x + y \leqslant 120, \tag{4.4}$$

$$x \geqslant 0, \quad y \geqslant 0. \tag{4.5}$$

4.1.3 Using graphs

This problem can be solved graphically because it involves only two variables x and y. The 'equality' parts of (4.2)–(4.4) are represented by straight lines on graphs. Our solution has also to take account of inequalities (sometimes referred to as inequations!).

Since $x \geqslant 0$ and $y \geqslant 0$ (expression (4.5)), we are only interested in the first, or positive, quadrant (sometimes called the north-east quadrant) of the graph as shown in Fig. 4.1; it is the region above the x-axis and to the right of the y-axis. For each remaining inequality, (4.2)–(4.4), we need to know the sub-region in this quadrant where that inequality is true. To find this, we first consider the 'equality' part of each constraint (i.e. that associated with the $=$ part of the $\leqslant$ sign); for example, in (4.4), it is $x + y = 120$, which determines a straight line. We can fix the position of any straight line once we know *any* two points on it. All points on the line (and only

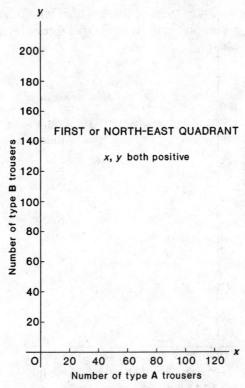

Figure 4.1 The relevant quadrant in Example 4.1; x, y are both positive.

points on the line) satisfy the relationship $x + y = 120$. For instance, when we set $y = 0$ in the equation we see immediately that $x + 0 = 120$ or $x = 120$, thus the point A (Fig. 4.2) with coordinates (x, y) given by (120, 0) lies on the line. Putting $x = 0$ gives $y = 120$, so (0, 120) is also a point, B, on the line. We join A and B by a straight line in Fig. 4.2. All points on one side of the line satisfy the inequality $x + y < 120$; no point on the other side of the line satisfies that inequality. We find on which side points satisfying the inequality lie by testing one point; the easiest to test is the origin

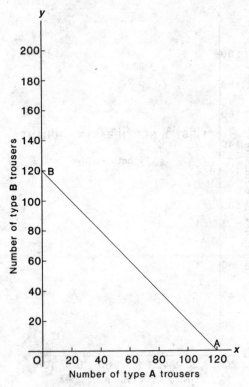

Figure 4.2 AB is the line $x + y = 120$.

(0, 0) (providing, as in this case, it does not lie on the line). If we put $x = y = 0$, then clearly $x + y = 0$; since 0 is less than 120, the inequality is satisfied. It is satisfied by all points in the shaded area in Fig. 4.3. In passing, we note that some authors, and some examiners, shade the area in which an inequality is *not* satisfied.

Similar arguments can be applied to the inequalities (4.2) and (4.3), first putting $y = 0$ and calculating x, then putting $x = 0$ and calculating y, we easily see that the line $3x + y = 192$ passes through the points (64, 0) and (0, 192). Since the inequality $3x + y < 192$ is satisfied for (0, 0), values on the 'origin' side of

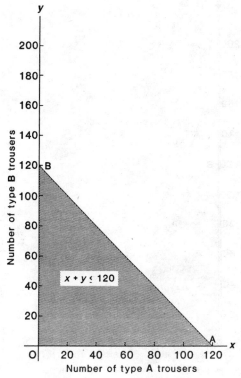

Figure 4.3 The shaded area is that in which $x + y \leqslant 120$, and $x, y \geqslant 0$.

the line satisfy this inequality. By drawing the lines $x + y = 120$ (the line AB) and $x + 3y = 192$ (the line CD) on the same graph (Fig. 4.4), we may shade the area on the 'origin' side of both lines as that in which both inequalities are satisfied.

In like manner, all points for which $x = 60$ lie on a line parallel to the y-axis that passes through the value $x = 60$ on the x-axis, i.e. the point (60, 0). All points to the left of that line satisfy the inequality $x < 60$. This further restricts the values satisfying all

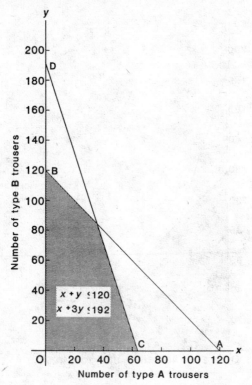

Figure 4.4 The shaded area is that in which x, y are not negative and the inequalities $x + y \leqslant 120$ and $x + 3y \leqslant 192$ are both satisfied.

inequalities, as does the constraint $y \leqslant 100$. The shaded area OPQRST in Fig. 4.5 satisfies all the inequalities. All points in that region, including those on its boundaries, satisfy all constraints and each is a 'feasible' or possible solution to our problem in that all constraints are satisfied. The region as a whole is often referred to as the *feasible region*; any solution corresponding to a point in it is a *feasible solution*. We seek a feasible solution that maximizes profit.

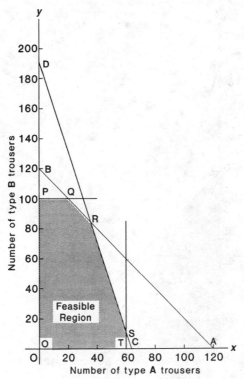

Figure 4.5 The shaded polygon OPQRST is the feasible region for Example 4.1.

4.1.4 **Maximizing the objective function**

We first select any particular value of U: for example, $U = 60$, when the objective function becomes

$$60 = 4x + 3y - 240,$$

which can be rewritten (by adding 240 to each side then reversing sides, operations allowed with equations) as

$$4x + 3y = 300. \tag{4.6}$$

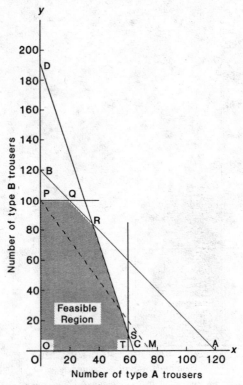

Figure 4.6 The dotted line represents the x, y values for which $U = 60$ in Example 4.1.

Exercise   Check that this line passes through the points (75, 0) and (0, 100), i.e. that the equation is satisfied for these values. The line represented by (4.6) is the broken line in Fig. 4.6. The feasible region is again shaded in that figure. If we now put $U = 120$, we get

$$4x + 3y = 360,$$

a line easily verified to pass through the points (90, 0) and (0, 120). If this is drawn in Fig. 4.6, it is parallel to the line (4.6) corresponding

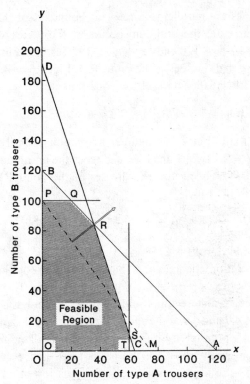

Figure 4.7 As *U* increases the equi-profit line remains parallel to PM and moves upward and to the right in the direction of the arrow. The optimal solution is at R.

to $U = 60$. Indeed, this is general in the sense that if we substitute increasing values of U we get a series of parallel lines that move up and to the right in the direction of the arrow (which is perpendicular to the broken line) in Fig. 4.7. Thus we get a *maximum feasible value* of U when we have a line with (usually just one) point on it that belongs to the feasible region. This point is a vertex of the region. For any greater U, the line lies entirely outside the region. Sometimes any point on a line joining adjacent vertices of the feasible region gives a set of equally favourable optima; this will happen if the equi-profit lines are parallel to a relevant boundary of the feasible region. In our case, the optimum occurs at the vertex where the constraints $x + y \leqslant 120$ and $3x + y \leqslant 192$ 'just' hold in the sense that they are equalities, i.e. at the point R in Fig. 4.6 or 4.7. This is the point which satisfies both of the equations

$$x + y = 120 \quad \text{and} \quad 3x + y = 192.$$

The solution to this pair of simultaneous equations is easily found to be $x = 36$, $y = 84$ (which may be read from the graph directly if it is carefully drawn, being the coordinates of the point R). Putting these values in (4.1) gives

$$U = 4 \times 36 + 3 \times 84 - 240 = 156,$$

i.e. the maximum profit is £156.

The important practical point is that an optimum solution always occurs at a vertex, or on a boundary line joining two adjacent vertices, of the feasible region, if indeed the problem has a solution! (See Exercises 4.7 and 4.9 at the end of this chapter.) This means that in seeking an optimum solution we can ignore all points in the feasible region except those on the boundaries, and even then an optimum can be found by a systematic examination of the vertices.

We have spent a lot of time explaining how to solve this problem. Example 4.2 shows how we streamline a solution in practice.

Example 4.2   A builder's supplier makes both heavy and light prefabricated wall sections. The requirements for a unit of each type are:

	Material (tons)	Machine time (hr)	Finishing (hr)
Heavy	4.5	2	2
Light	2	1.25	2

Available are 180 tons of material, 90 machine hours and 120 hours finishing time. Profit is £5 for a heavy and £4 for a light unit. How many of each should be made to maximize profit?

Solution   All we need do is write down our objective function and constraints, draw a graph indicating the feasible region, determine the direction of equi-probable objective function lines and the vertex at which the maximum occurs, then compute the profit. The objective function is

$$U = 5x + 4y.$$

The constraints are: $x, y \geqslant 0$, together with

material $\qquad$ $4.5x + 2y \leqslant 180,$

machine time $\quad 2x + 1.25y \leqslant 90,$

finishing $\qquad 2x + 2y \leqslant 120, \quad$ i.e. $x + y \leqslant 60.$

The shaded polygon OPQRS in Fig. 4.8 is the feasible region satisfying all constraints and the broken line AS corresponds to $U = 200$. It is clear that the maximum profit is at the vertex Q where the machine time and finishing constraints become equalities. This has coordinates $x = 20$ and $y = 40$, whence $U = 260$ implies a maximum profit of £260 by making 20 heavy and 40 light units.

Examples 4.1 and 4.2 are simple *linear programming problems*, called *linear* because all the constraints and the objective function involve the unknowns x and y in a 'linear' form consisting of sums or differences of each multiplied by constants, plus perhaps an added constant; there are no terms like xy, x^2 or $\log x$.

4.1.5   Effective constraints

All constraints in Example 4.1 are effective in that each is used to define the boundary of the feasible region. However, only two are critical in that they become equalities at the optimum. Constraints

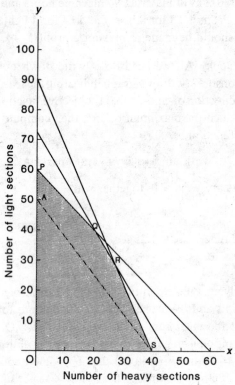

Figure 4.8 The feasible region for solution of Example 4.2.

on total sales of each type are still inequalities at the optimum: i.e. $x = 36$ is less than the maximum permitted $x = 60$; also $y = 84$ is less than the maximum permitted $y = 100$.

A constraint is irrelevant if it holds throughout the feasible region and in an extended region outside its boundaries. If, for example, the firm could obtain a maximum of 170 (rather than 120) zips each day, this would in no way restrict production since the constraints $x \leqslant 60$ and $y \leqslant 100$ already imply jointly that $x + y \leqslant 160$, while the zip constraint is now the less restrictive $x + y \leqslant 170$.

4.2 SENSITIVITY ANALYSIS

Linear programming can be used to answer many relevant questions about the effect on the optimum solution of relaxing constraints in some specified way, or in determining how far constraints may be relaxed without changing those that are critical (i.e. those that are equalities at the optimum). Such investigations are called *sensitivity analyses*.

Example 4.3   If, in Example 4.1, each of the eight workers agree to work an extra 15 minutes per day, increasing the girl-minutes available to $3840 + 8 \times 15 = 3960$ minutes, what effect has this on optimum profits?

Solution   The constraint inequality on time becomes

$$60x + 20y \leqslant 3960,$$

or

$$3x + y \leqslant 198. \tag{4.7}$$

This is satisfied in a region to the left and below the line $3x + y = 198$, a line parallel to the original $3x + y = 192$, but which is moved upward and to the right. The original and new line $(C'D')$ are shown in Fig. 4.9, where the original line is now broken. The new solution is obtained by solving the equations

$$x + y = 120 \quad \text{and} \quad 3x + y = 198,$$

and is $x = 39$, $y = 81$, whence

$$U = 4 \times 39 + 3 \times 81 - 240 = 159.$$

Thus profit may be increased by £3, from £156 to £159, if each girl is prepared to work an additional 15 minutes. In practice, such additional time might involve overtime pay, so that trousers made in overtime will cost more to produce. If the extra time incurred additional payment at a rate of £1.50 per hour, since two hours (120

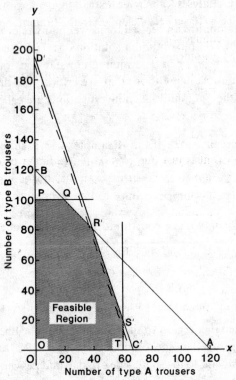

Figure 4.9 The change in the feasible region if the constraint $x + 3y \leqslant$ 192 is replaced by $x + 3y \leqslant 198$. See text.

minutes) of extra time is worked, this payment would wipe out the added profit!

In Example 4.1, constraints on total time and numbers of zips were critical at the optimum. We may ask how much either of these constraints may be relaxed before another constraint becomes critical. For instance, a moment's reflection will show (Fig. 4.7) that if the number of available zips were 140 the constraint $y \leqslant 100$ becomes operative at the optimum in association with the time constraint.

Sensitivity analyses can be extended to deal with a variety of problems such as the effect of changes in the times to make each type of trousers or changes in costs of material. While these analyses may be performed graphically with only two items, we need an appropriate computational method for more than two items and any number of constraints, a point we return to in sections 4.4 and 4.5.

4.3 NOT ALWAYS PROFIT

Maximizing profit is just one context where linear programming is used. We may use it to find, for example, the minimum cost of meeting given specifications, e.g. to find a mixture of ingredients which provides a minimum of some specified component at lowest cost.

Example 4.4   A farmer wishes to apply fertilizer with a phosphate content at least 40%. He can use a basic fertilizer or a mixture of two or more from four basic fertilizers. The phosphate content and the price per bag for each basic fertilizer is as follows.

Brand A	20% phosphate	£8
Brand B	30% phosphate	£6
Brand C	60% phosphate	£10
Brand D	90% phosphate	£11

What is the cheapest way of achieving the required phosphate level?

Rather than plunge into a formal solution, we again proceed by steps. Clearly, if the farmer uses only one basic fertilizer, it must be brand C or D (the ones containing more than 40% phosphate), and use of C is obviously cheaper. He can do better by using some combination of C or D with one of the cheaper brands. For example, it is easy to see that if he uses a mix of equal amounts of A and C the resultant fertilizer contains exactly 40% phosphate – his mini- mum requirement – and the cost per bag will be the average of the cost of each, i.e. £9. This gives a 10% saving on the cost of C alone. Can he do even better? If he used B and D together, it is easy to verify that he would have 40% phosphate if he mixed five bags of the cheaper B with one of the more expensive D. To see this, let us suppose each bag weighs 100 units (e.g. 100 lb). Since each bag of B contains 30 units of phosphate, five bags contain 150 units. One bag of D contains 90 units of phosphate, so six bags of the mixture (weighing 600 units) contains $150 + 90 = 240$ units of phosphate, and 240 is 40% of 600. Now five bags of B and one of D cost £$(5 \times 6 + 1 \times 11) = $ £41. Thus a single bag of the mixture costs £$(41/6) = $ £6.83. Could he further reduce cost by using some other combination of two or more from A, B, C and D? A trial and error approach is time-consuming and we still might miss the optimum if it were an obscure combination of the basic brands.

4.3.1 Graphical aid

A graphical solution simplifies the search. Here is the procedure.

Step 1. Draw axes as in Fig. 4.10 (preferably on graph paper – the grid is omitted on our diagrams to avoid clutter). The x-axis rep- resents phosphate percentage, and the y-axis fertilizer cost (£). We are only interested in positive values of each. The broken vertical line at $x = 40$ corresponds to the minimum phosphate level. Any phosphate content/cost combination to the right of that lines satis- fies the condition *at least 40% phosphate* (the only constraint other than those implicit in the phosphate content of the basic brands). We tie this to prices of possible mixtures to establish a feasible region.

Step 2. Consider first brands B and D or mixtures of these two only. The phosphate content of B is $x = 30$ and the cost is $y = 6$, corresponding to the point B in Fig. 4.11. Similarly for brand D, $x = 90$ and $y = 11$, corresponding to the point D.

The straight line segment BD represents mixtures of B and D. The point B is all brand B, the point D is all brand D, and M is a 5 : 1

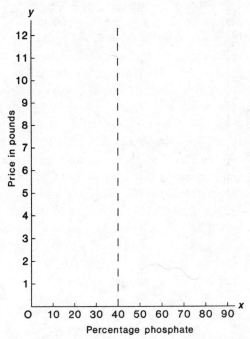

Figure 4.10 The basic graph for constructing a solution to Example 4.3. The dotted line parallel to the y-axis at $x = 40$ represents the minimum phosphate requirement.

mix of B and D. Clearly the point M represents the cheapest mixture of these two containing *at least 40% phosphate*. From an accurate graph, one would find M had y coordinate 6.83; this, as we found arithmetically, was the cost of a mixture of B and D containing 40% phosphate.

From the graph, we may also deduce the proportion of B and D in a mixture corresponding to any point P on BD. If the x coordinates of P, B, D are respectively x_p, x_b and x_d, then the proportion p of brand D is

$$p = \frac{x_p - x_b}{x_d - x_b}. \tag{4.8}$$

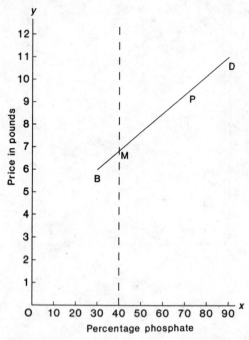

Figure 4.11 The line BD represents mixtures of brands B and D in Example 4.4.

In our example, for the optimum mixture given by M, we have $x_p = 40$, $x_b = 30$ and $x_d = 90$, whence $p = (40 - 30)/(90 - 30) = \frac{1}{6}$, i.e. one bag in six is brand D, as we saw above.

In (4.8), we easily see $p = 0$ when $x_p = x_b$, corresponding to B alone; also that $p = 1$ when $x_p = x_d$, corresponding to D alone. It is good mathematical practice to see if a formula works for simple cases with a known answer. If it does, the formula is still not *proved* correct; but if it gives a wrong answer in a trivial case, it is certainly wrong.

Exercise   If x_p lies midway between x_b and x_d, what are the proportions of B and D?

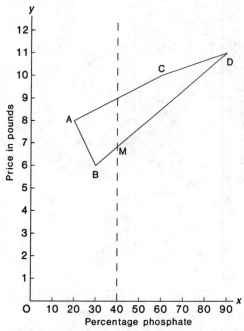

Figure 4.12 Lines representing mixtures of brands (i) B and D, (ii) D and C, (iii) C and A, (iv) A and B in Example 4.4.

Step 3. What about other mixtures? Figure 4.12 shows points A and C, corresponding to brands A and C respectively. We have joined AB, AC and CD to represent phosphate content/cost structures for mixtures of each of these pairs. We could have joined AD and BC also, but it will soon become apparent that there is no need to do this.

Step 4. What about mixtures of three or all four brands? In this example, none of these does better than the optimum mixtures of two brands, but we must establish this. Let us consider all mixtures of A, B and D. Any such mixture can be obtained by first mixing B and D in a certain proportion, then adding a desired amount of A. A mixture of only B and D has phosphate content/cost represented

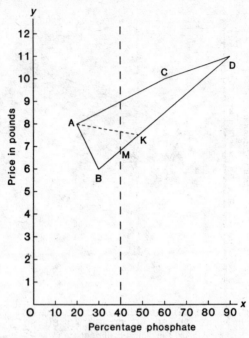

Figure 4.13 The point K represents a fertilizer K which is a mixture of brands B and D. Mixtures of K and A are represented by the line AK.

by some point K in BD (Fig. 4.13). A moment's reflection shows that any mixture of the combination corresponding to K with some brand A added is represented by a point on AK. In effect, this regards the mixture represented by K as a new basic substance (brand K, say) to be mixed with brand A. We may do this for any K in the segment BD. The lines AK corresponding to different choices of K (representing different brand K's) sweep out the triangle ABD, as K moves along BD, so all points in that triangle represent phosphate content/cost for mixtures of A, B, D. The vertices represent one basic fertilizer only, the sides mixtures of two, and the internal points mixtures of all three. Similarly the triangles ABC, BCD, ACD represent possible mixtures of brands designated by their vertices. These triangles overlap to form the quadrilateral

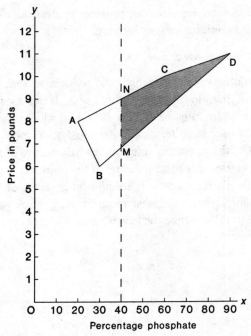

Figure 4.14 The region of feasible solutions for Example 4.4 is the quadrilateral MDCN.

ABDC, which is easily seen also to include all possible mixtures of the four brands. A moment's reflection will show that the internal points of this quadrilateral may be attained in general by more than one possible mix of three or all four fertilizers; and that the quadrilateral ABDC therefore represents all possible mixtures. It is defined once we know A, B, C, D – the four vertices – and, clearly, acceptable mixtures satisfying the condition *at least 40% phosphate* are those corresponding to points in or on the perimeter of the shaded quadrilateral MDCN in Fig. 4.14. We immediately see that the mixture of lowest cost satisfying our phosphate requirement corresponds to M – and we have already found this consists of five parts of B and one part of D and costs £6.83.

In practice, then, we solve our problem by drawing Fig. 4.14 and reading off the minimum cost mixture.

4.3.2 Some points to note

The quadrilateral MDCN defines the feasible region, that is, the region satisfying, in this case, the constraining inequality that phosphate content must be at least 40%, and which covers possible mixes of the four basic fertilizers that satisfy that inequality. As in Example 4.1, the optimum solution lies at a vertex of the feasible region. It corresponds to a minimum of the objective function (here involving the variable cost). A solution at a vertex of the feasible region is characteristic of linear programming problems; our basic tasks are thus (1) to define the feasible region and (2) to examine the

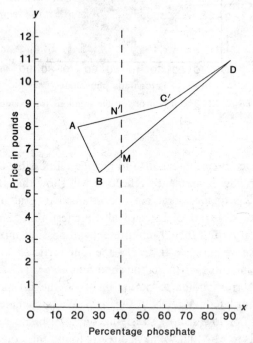

Figure 4.15 A modification of Fig. 4.12 when brand C is replaced by a new brand C'.

vertices to find the optimum solution (or solutions) if indeed a solution exists.

Care is needed to define the correct feasible region. There is no difficulty in Example 4.4 because all the interior angles of the quadrilateral MDCN that defines the feasible region are less than 180°. If brand C in Example 4.4 is replaced by a brand C′ that still contained 60% phospate but costs only £9, then the quadrilateral ABDC in Fig. 4.14 is replaced by ABDC′ (Fig. 4.15). If we replace N in Fig. 4.14 by the corresponding N′ in Fig. 4.15, our feasible region is not MDC′N′ as one might at first suppose. Although, in this particular illustration, it does not alter our optimum solution, the fact that the internal angle at C is greater than 180° is a hint that we have something wrong with our feasible region. The problem is easily tracked down. Applying our earlier arguments for mixtures of brands A, D and C′, we see that mixtures within the triangle AC′D lie outside the quadrilateral ABDC′. Thus our feasible region is given by the shaded area in Fig. 4.16. It is the triangle N″MD, and although the optimum here is still at M, in some problems we may miss an optimum if we examine an incomplete feasible region.

4.3.3 Convexity

If we had had, in Example 4.4, not just four, but any number n of basic fertilizers, where $n > 4$, the quadrilateral with perimeter representing all possible paired mixes would be replaced by a polygon with n sides. If all the internal angles of that polygon are less than or equal to 180°, the feasible region is a sub-polygon with optimal solution (minimum cost satisfying the phosphate requirement) at one of the vertices of this sub-polygon; sometimes there may be an optimum not only at a vertex but at two adjacent vertices and at any point on the perimeter joining those adjacent vertices. These situations are illustrated in Figs. 4.17 and 4.18. In Fig. 4.17, the minimum cost solution corresponds to the point C, implying the corresponding basic fertilizer should be used alone. Note that we would then be applying more than the *minimum* phosphate requirement; this situation may pertain if costs of ingredients other than

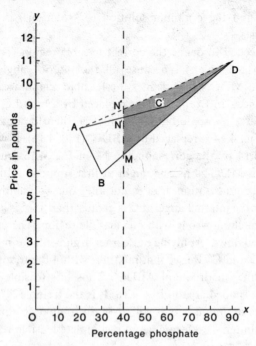

Figure 4.16 The correct feasible region is the triangle N″MD if C is replaced by C′ in Example 4.4.

phosphate are cheaper for one than they are for other basic brands. In Fig. 4.18, either brand C or any mixture of that with brand B containing sufficient brand C to ensure a minimum of 40% phosphate would be optimal.

If any internal angle of the polygon with vertices corresponding to basic fertilizers exceeds 180°, we obtain the feasible region by first forming a reduced polygon by omitting that vertex and joining its neighbours until we obtain a polygon with a lower number of sides that contain no internal angle greater than 180°. The feasible region is a sub-polygon of this. An illustration is given in Fig. 4.19. Mathematicians refer to this final polygon that does not 'turn in' on itself as a *convex hull*. In Fig. 4.19, the convex hull is the polygon AEFGH. The feasible region is now a sub-region of the convex hull

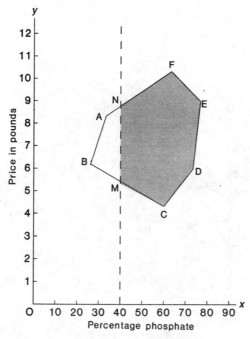

Figure 4.17 A feasible region for determining the minimum cost mixture for six brands A, B, C, D, E, F with given costs and phosphate contents. Minimum cost is achieved by using brand C alone and phosphate content then exceeds minimum stipulated percentage.

and is itself a convex hull. In Fig. 4.19, it is the polygon MEFGN; the optimum corresponds to the point M and could be an appropriate mixture of either brands A and C, or brands A and E (or indeed of A, C and E).

4.4   LINEAR PROGRAMMING AND THE COMPUTER

With only two variables, x and y, graphical solutions are usually straightforward, as in Examples 4.1, 4.2 and 4.4. With more than two variables, graphical solutions are in general no longer feasible. We turn then to computers, after carrying out the basic task of

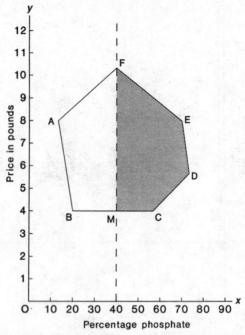

Figure 4.18 Any point on the segment MC represents a minimum cost mixture with at least 40% phosphate.

formulating the problem in mathematical terms. We illustrate the mathematical formulation for such a problem.

Example 4.5   A footwear manufacturer can make boots, shoes, wellies (best green) or carpet slippers. Table 4.2 gives details of cost per unit for materials, labour and for 'finishing' done by outside contractors. Daily total allowable maxima for each category are also given in the final column and the final row gives sale prices per unit for each product.

Formulate mathematically the problem of maximizing profit.

Solution   Given the information in Table 4.2, the formulation is straightforward if one keeps the logic of the problem in

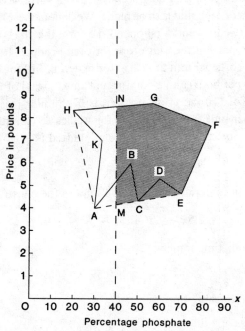

Figure 4.19 Given costs and phosphate contents for brands A, B, C, D, E, F, G, H, K the convex hull giving the cost–content relationship for all mixtures is the polygon AEFGH, and the feasible region is the shaded polygon MEFGN.

Table 4.2 Information on manufacture of footwear

	Boots	Shoes	Wellies	Slippers	Daily maximum
Material (£)	2.5	2	3	1	250
Labour time (hr)	2	1	1	0.5	160
Finishing (£)	0.5	1.0	0	0	100
Sale price (£)	20	15	11	5.5	

Labour costs: £5 per hour

Additional requirement: Number of wellies produced must not exceed 50 mind. There are four products, so we need four variables to represent the numbers of each that is to be made. We denote these by x (boots), y (shoes), z (wellies) and w (slippers). To form the objective function U, we first work out the unit profit for each product. For boots the production costs per unit are £2.50 for material, £10 for labour (two hours at £5 per hour) and £0.50 for finishing, a total of £13, so with a sale price of £20 the profit per unit is £7. Similar reasoning gives the profit per unit for shoes as £7, for wellies £3, for slippers £2.

Thus the objective function to be minimized is

$$U = 7x + 7y + 3z + 2w.$$

Restriction of material costs to £250 implies the constraint

$$2.5x + 2y + 3z + w \leqslant 250,$$

that on labour time implies

$$2x + y + z + 0.5w \leqslant 160,$$

and that on finishing implies

$$0.5x + y \leqslant 100,$$

while finally the restriction on wellies implies

$$z \leqslant 50.$$

With four variables x, y, z, w, graphs will not work. The computer comes to our aid, usually by applying what is called the *simplex method*. This works no matter whether we have two or 102 variables, once we have the problem formulated mathematically. A simplex solution with an appropriately programmed computer then takes only a matter of seconds. With experience, one could get the solution to Example 4.5 using pencil and paper in a few minutes using what is called a *simplex tableau*. We outline the method in section 4.5, but we do not describe the tableau or its use as this would require going into 'user-unfriendly' detail that is best left to a properly pro-grammed computer.

There may be a 100 or more unknowns in real life situations (and a similar number of constraints). The appropriate solutions always occur where certain of the inequality constraints become equalities. The simplex method enables us to form a computer routine that systematically looks at vertices of a region (the feasible region) in multidimensional space (something we cannot represent on graph paper) in such a way that we find at each step a new solution that increases profit as much as possible relative to the previous solution until it eventually converges to the optimum – hopefully after inspecting only a very few of all possible vertices. It provides a definite routine called, in computer jargon, an *algorithm*. Providing the problem is properly posed the method will work in the sense that it will find an optimum if one exists. Proper posing may require some juggling with the form of constraints to ensure that we determine the appropriate feasible region.

We have dodged in our simple examples several practical difficulties that may arise. For example, we sometimes arrive at fractional values of x and y for the optimum when clearly only an integer solution makes sense. We discuss this particular difficulty in section 5.1.

4.5 THE SIMPLEX METHOD

This section is less user-friendly than most in this book, reflecting the nature of the problem. It is important if you want to know the rationale behind the simplex method. If not, you may skip this section as later work does not depend upon it. We indicate the principle behind the simplex method for the two-variables case by applying it to Example 4.1.

Example 4.6   Solve the trousers problem (Example 4.1) by the simplex method.

Solution   Our problem may be summarized as

maximize

$$U = 4x + 3y - 240$$

subject to the constraints

$$x \leqslant 60, \qquad y \leqslant 100,$$

$$3x + y \leqslant 192,$$

$$x + y \leqslant 120,$$

$$x, y \geqslant 0.$$

We introduce new variables called *slack variables* that convert the constraints from inequalities to equalities. We may think of them as representing zero profit items that we never produce. They make the problem more amenable to an analytic solution that can be programmed for a computer. In this example, we require one slack variable for each non-zero inequality constraint. We call these variables s_1, s_2, s_3, s_4, whence

$$x + s_1 = 60, \tag{4.9}$$

$$y + s_2 = 100, \tag{4.10}$$

$$3x + y + s_3 = 192, \tag{4.11}$$

$$x + y + s_4 = 120. \tag{4.12}$$

Clearly all slack variables must be non-negative when they are included in $\leqslant$ inequalities. Thus

$$x, y, s_1, s_2, s_3, s_4 \geqslant 0.$$

The equations (4.9)–(4.12) represent four linear equations in six unknowns x, y, s_1, s_2, s_3, s_4. When the number of equations is less than the number of unknowns, we can find more than one set of values for the unknowns that satisfy all equations. For example, it is easily verified by direct substitution that $x = 0$, $y = 0$, $s_1 = 60$, $s_2 = 100$, $s_3 = 192$, $s_4 = 120$ satisfy equations (4.9)–(4.12). So do the values $x = 36$, $y = 84$, $s_1 = 24$, $s_2 = 16$, $s_3 = 0$, $s_4 = 0$, and also $x = 60$, $y = 0$, $s_1 = 0$, $s_2 = 100$, $s_3 = 12$, $s_4 = 60$. There are two important features common to these three possible solutions.

1. In each, the values of x and y correspond to *one* of the vertices of the feasible region in Fig. 4.6.
2. Two from the six variables take the value zero in each solution.

We do not prove it, but it can be shown that solutions with properties 1 and 2 can be found corresponding to each vertex of the feasible region. These solutions form a set of solutions known as *basic feasible solutions*.

The simplex algorithm explores these systematically until we find the solution for which U is a maximum. Basically, the algorithm works like this

1. Determine any basic feasible solution.
2. Examine U to see if we can increase U by moving along any boundary away from the vertex defined by the current basic feasible solution. If not, we have attained the optimum. If we can increase U, proceed to (3).
3. If we can increase U by moving along one or more boundaries, select one of these and determine the new basic feasible solution corresponding to the next vertex we reach. Taking this as a new current basic feasible solution, return to (2) and repeat this cycle until we have optimal U.

Since each slack variable appears in one constraint equation it is easy to see that, if we set $x, y = 0$, equations (4.9)–(4.12) are satisfied by setting the slack variable in each equal to the numerical value on the right-hand side of that equation. This gives us a basic feasible solution for (1). We now proceed to (2). We express our non-zero variables (usually called the *basic variables*) and also U in terms of the remaining variables (whose values in the basic solution are all zero). These latter variables are sometimes called the *non-basic variables*. Thus, when the slack variables are our basic variables, we write

$$s_1 = 60 - x, \tag{4.13}$$

$$s_2 = 100 - y, \tag{4.14}$$

$$s_3 = 192 - 3x - y, \tag{4.15}$$

$$s_4 = 120 - x - y, \tag{4.16}$$

$$U = 4x + 3y - 240. \tag{4.17}$$

For this basic feasible solution where $x = y = 0$, clearly $U = -240$. Physically, if we regard the slack variables as representing trousers on which there is zero profit, this solution says that if we make nothing profitable we make no profit; indeed we make a £240 loss because our overheads remain!

Because x and y are never negative, clearly we can increase U by increasing either x or y, since each has a positive coefficient in (4.17). Thus we move to (3).

At (3) we have to choose to move to another vertex either by increasing x or by increasing y. Since we increase profit by £4 for each increase of one unit in the x but by only £3 for each such increase in y, a reasonable action is to increase x. But by how much? We see from (4.13)–(4.16) that we may increase x to 60, since this would make $s_1 = 0$, but leave the remaining slack variables positive (all slack variables must be non-negative if the constraints are to hold). This gives a new basic feasible solution with $x = 60$, $y = 0$, and from (4.13)–(4.16) we find $s_1 = 0$, $s_2 = 100$, $s_3 = 12$, $s_4 = 60$.

We now return to step (2) and check whether we can increase U further. To check, we first express the constraints and U in terms of the non-basic variables which are now y and s_1. This requires a little care. Using (4.13)–(4.17), we get

$$x = 60 - s_1, \tag{4.18}$$

$$s_2 = 100 - y, \tag{4.19}$$

$$s_3 = 192 - 3(60 - s_1) - y = 12 + 3s_1 - y, \tag{4.20}$$

$$s_4 = 120 - (60 - s_1) - y = 60 + s_1 - y, \tag{4.21}$$

$$U = 4(60 - s_1) + 3y - 240 = 3y - 4s_1. \tag{4.22}$$

Since the coefficient of y is positive, we can increase U by increasing y. An inspection of (4.18)–(4.21) indicates that the constraints will all still hold if we increase y by a maximum of 12 (if we made a greater increase, (4.20) indicates s_3 would become negative). Our basic variables are now x, y, s_2, s_4.

Exercise Using (4.18)–(4.22), show that expressing the basic variables and U in terms of the non-basic s_1, s_3 gives

$$x = 60 - s_1, \tag{4.23}$$

$$y = 12 + 3s_1 - s_3, \tag{4.24}$$

$$s_2 = 88 - 3s_1 + s_3, \tag{4.25}$$

$$s_4 = 48 - 2s_1 + s_3, \tag{4.26}$$

$$U = 36 + 5s_1 - 3s_3. \tag{4.27}$$

Clearly, since the coefficient of s_1 is positive we can increase the profit by increasing s_1. Further, the constraint equations indicate that we can increase it by a maximum of 24, since for any greater increase s_4 would become negative in (4.26). The basic variables are now x, y, s_1, s_2.

Exercise Using (4.23)–(4.26), show that expressing these basic variables and U in terms of the non-basic s_3, s_4 gives

$$s_1 = 24 - \tfrac{1}{2}s_4 + \tfrac{1}{2}s_3,$$

$$x = 36 + \tfrac{1}{2}s_4 - \tfrac{1}{2}s_3,$$

$$y = 84 - \tfrac{3}{2}s_4 + \tfrac{1}{2}s_3,$$

$$s_2 = 16 + \tfrac{3}{2}s_4 - \tfrac{1}{2}s_3,$$

$$U = 156 - \tfrac{5}{2}s_4 - \tfrac{1}{2}s_3.$$

Remembering that slack variables cannot be negative, it is clear that we cannot increase the profit further by making either s_3 or s_4 non-zero. Thus we have a maximum profit of $U = 156$ when $x = 36$, $y = 84$, in accord with our graphical solution. We in fact started at O and moved to T, then S, then R.

This example makes the simplex method look complicated. Here it is using a sledge-hammer to crack a nut. Its beauty from the computing viewpoint is (1) that it generalizes to the case when we have n unknowns and m constraints and (2) that there are clear and unambiguous instructions for carrying out the process and a defined stopping rule when we attain a maximum. In this brief treatment, we have glossed over additional points that have to be included in a real working algorithm to deal with problems if some constraints are not in the form $\leqslant$ (constraints may be equalities or $\geqslant$), or if some basic variables become zero, etc. There is also a question of determining a stopping rule when no optimum exists, or when there is more than one optimum. The method can also be extended to enable sensitivity analyses to be carried out by considering solution of what are known as *dual* problems.

Even if we use pencil and paper methods, we do not have to write down all the algebra. A *simplex tableau* (which we do not describe) reduces the arithmetic to almost mechanical application of a few simple rules, an important prerequisite for many successful computer programs.

4.6 WHAT AND WHERE?

What skills have we mastered?

We can now solve graphically two-variable linear programming problems for maximization of profit or minimization of costs. If you have read section 4.5, you should have a broad grasp of what a computer program using the simplex method does.

You should be able to solve graphically problems on allocation of resources subject to linear constraints (inequalities) where two processes or products share resources so as to maximize profit, also to determine what mixtures of basic substances produce at minimum cost a product subject to a restriction on some ingredient (e.g. the mixture to contain a minimum percentage of that ingredient). The concept clearly extends to a constraint on the maximum allowable amount of a toxic ingredient (see exercise 4.6 below).

Where can I read more?

Practically any book with the words *operational research* in the title will have a chapter (or chapters) on linear programming. An examination-orientated account that develops both sensitivity analysis and the simplex method beyond our coverage is given by Lucey (1988: Chap. 18–20). Practical examples showing the versatility of linear programming are given by Moore (1986: Chap. 3, 4). A concise treatment of both graphical and simplex methods is given by French *et al.* (1986: Chap. 2). McLewin (1980) is an advanced mathematical text dealing with both the theory and practice of linear programming.

EXERCISES

Unless another method is specified it is intended that these exercises be solved graphically.

*4.1   A pet food manufacturer makes two types of cat food: Megacat and Moggycat. One batch of Megacat requires 50 lb of rabbit and 20 lb of offal. One batch of Moggycat requires 20 lb of rabbit and 40 lb of offal. Profit on each batch of Megacat is £4.50 and on each batch of Moggycat is £2. The manufacturer has 1000 lb of rabbit and 800 lb of offal available. How many batches of each type of food should he make to maximize his profit?

*4.2   A paint manufacturer produces both gloss and matt paints. The times in hours taken for the three processing stages for each batch made are as follows:

	Gloss	Matt
Blending pigments	5	4
Preparation of liquid paint	2	5
Canning, labelling, etc.	2	2.4

Each week the maximum time that can be devoted to blending is 40 hours, to preparation of liquid paint is 31 hours, and to canning, labelling, etc. is 18 hours. If the profit per batch for gloss is £40 and that for matt is £50, how many batches of each would maximize the weekly profit and what would that profit be?

*4.3 Would your conclusion in Exercise 4.2 be altered if a new pigment blending process reduces the time required per batch to 4.8 hours for gloss and 3.6 hours for matt?

*4.4 How would your conclusion in Exercise 4.2 be altered if the profit for matt dropped to £48 per batch?

*4.5 A farmer wants to apply fertilizer with potash content at least 30%. What is the optimum (minimum cost) mixing policy to achieve this using mixtures of any of the following basic fertilizers?

Brand	Percent potash	Cost per bag (£)
A	20	11
B	35	12
C	40	13
D	45	14
E	30	15

*4.6 The maximum permitted level of an impurity in a blended food is 5%. It may be blended from any of the following components, which have the indicated percentage impurity and cost per unit.

Component	Percent impurity	Cost (pence)
A	4	12
B	5	11
C	7	15
D	8	6
E	7	13
F	6	9

What blend or blends are cheapest? If A is in short supply and we want to use the smallest possible amount of it in the blend of minimum cost, what should the mixture be?

4.7 Try solving the following problem graphically. Minimize $5x + y$ subject to $x + y \leqslant 7$, $x > 8$, $y > 0$. What conclusion do you reach?

*4.8 A farmer wishes to apply a minimum of 200 kg potash, 270 kg nitrogen, 180 kg phosphate to a field. He may mix basic fertilizers of two kinds and the number of kilograms of each of these ingredients per 50 kg bag is

	Potash	Nitrogen	Phosphate
Brand A	10	15	15
Brand B	20	15	7.5

However, each bag of brand A contains 40 g of a potentially harmful ingredient and each bag of brand B contains 50 g of that same ingredient. What brand or mixture should he use to meet his fertilizer requirements while minimizing the amount of the potentially harmful ingredient?

4.9   Suppose we have all the conditions in Exercise 4.8 except that the potentially harmful ingredient is replaced by a beneficial ingredient. Explore the problem of nominating a mixture that maximizes the amount of this beneficial ingredient.

*4.10   After an actor has finished recording a television play in which he has a starring role, he always goes on a week-long drinking bout. He will only drink sherry costing £3 a bottle or whisky costing £8 a bottle. His sprees are such that he always imbibes at least 180 units of alcohol. Each bottle of sherry provides 12 units and each bottle of whisky 20 units. He also assigns a personal euphoria rating of 10 units to a bottle of sherry and 25 units to a bottle of whisky and demands a minimum total euphoria rating of 200. How many bottles of sherry and whisky should he buy to satisfy his alcohol and euphoria cravings at minimum cost?

4.11   If, in Exercise 4.10, the price of a bottle of sherry is increased to £4, what now is the optimum solution?

*4.12   Formulate the following mathematically as a linear programming problem. Although it essentially involves three variables, in view of its special nature it is still possible to solve it graphically. See if you can do so. A total of 100 tons of coal is required by an industrial customer who stipulates it must contain not more than 2% sulphur, nor more than 0.05% phosphorus. A merchant has available ample stocks of three kinds of coal with the following specifications.

Type	% Sulphur	% Phosphorus	Profit (£ per ton)
A	1.5	0.06	4.0
B	2.4	0.07	2.5
C	2.1	0.02	3.0

The merchant decides to blend these three types to meet the customer's specifications. How many tons of each should he use to maximize his profit?

4.13 Solve Exercise 4.1 by the simplex method.

4.14 Solve Exercise 4.2 by the simplex method.

4.15 Although it is tedious to solve Example 4.5 fully by the simplex method on the basis of our brief description, you might like to try the first iteration by introducing slack variables in the constraints and getting a first and second basic feasible solution. This will indicate how the method works without involving you in too much tedious arithmetic, which is better left to a computer.

4.16 Your company has to buy immediately two types of tables for its canteens. A maximum sum of £24000 is available for this purpose. A type X table costs £40 and seats four people. A type Y table costs £30 and seats two people. Seating for at least 1800 people is required. There must be at least as many type Y tables as type X tables because the tables are to be used for a variety of functions in the canteens. For reasons of maintenance, storage, etc., the company wishes to buy the smallest number of tables to meet its requirements. You are required to

(a) state the company's objective function;
(b) state all constraints (equations/inequalities);
(c) draw a graph of these constraints, shading any unwanted regions;
(d) recommend the numbers of each type of table the company should buy, justifying your answer.   [CIMA]

5   More about Allocation

5.1   WHEN FRACTIONS ARE A NUISANCE

The optimum numbers of trousers to be made each day turned out to be integers (whole numbers) in Example 4.1. Had they been fractions, it would not have been too disturbing, for an incomplete pair of trousers could be finished the next day, or a nearly optimum solution obtained by rounding first to integer values and checking if all constraints are still satisfied. If they are not, it may be sufficient in a case like this to round down (but see the discussion in Example 5.1 for some warnings). Rounding linear programming solutions to integers will not work in some problems. Airlines want to maximize passenger loadings; they face constraints on fuel availability and crew numbers. It makes little sense if a linear programming solution tells them to use 4.75 aircraft of one type and 8.27 of a second type to carry a maximum of 2761.23 passengers. Rounding numbers of aircraft to the nearest integer values looks to be a way out. Two problems may arise. The first, already mentioned, is that the constraints may no longer be satisfied. That difficulty can be overcome by rounding one or both to the integer below. Even then we face a more serious problem: this solution may not be the optimal integer solution. Example 5.1 shows what may happen.

Example 5.1   To operate a trunk route out of London, an airline has ample flight-deck crews and aircraft of type A and type B, but there are limitations on the available cabin crew and amounts of fuel. Each type A aircraft carries 288 passengers and requires seven cabin crew and 2000 gallons of fuel per flight. Each type B aircraft carries 90 passengers and requires four cabin crew and 600 gallons of fuel. Each aircraft/crew can only make one flight per day. On a day when passenger demand exceeds seating available (ensuring all aircraft take off fully loaded), 56 cabin crew and 11 800 gallons of fuel are available. How many aircraft of each type should be used to maximize the number of passengers carried?

5.1.1 A linear programming approach

If we treat this as a linear programming problem, it is even easier than Example 4.1, for we have only two non-trivial constraints. Let x be the number of type A and y be the number of type B aircraft used. The constraint imposed by cabin crew may be written

$$7x + 4y \leqslant 56, \tag{5.1}$$

and that by fuel

$$2000x + 600y \leqslant 11\,800,$$

which, on dividing both sides by 200, reduces to

$$10x + 3y \leqslant 59. \tag{5.2}$$

The objective function to be maximized (number of passengers) is

$$U = 288x + 90y \tag{5.3}$$

Our linear programming problem then is maximize (5.3) subject to (5.1) and (5.2) and the obvious constraints $x,y \geqslant 0$.

Figure 5.1 is the basis for a graphical solution. The lines AB (cabin crew) and CD (fuel), obtained when we have equality in (5.1) and (5.2), intersect at M and it is easily verified that the feasible region is the quadrilateral OAMD, where the coordinates of A are (0, 14), of D are (5.9, 0) and of M (obtained by solving the equality components of (5.1) and (5.2)) are (3.58, 7.74). If a series of equi-U lines are drawn, the one passing through M turns out to be the broken line lying very close to CD and passing (approximately) through the points (6, 0) and (0, 19.2). All other equi-U lines that pass through the critical region represent lower passenger loads; for example, that

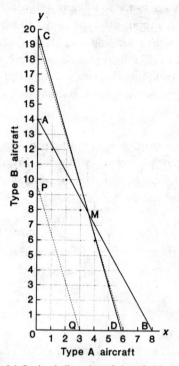

Figure 5.1 Optimal allocation of aircraft. M represents the non-integral optimum. The integer optimum occurs at an integral grid point in the feasible region such that the perpendicular to the equi-profit line through M is a minimum. The relevant point has coordinates (5, 3).

representing a passenger load of $U = 864$ passes through the points (3, 0) and (0, 9.6) and is shown by the broken line PQ in Fig. 5.1. The maximum at M gives a calculated load of 1727.05 passengers, using 3.58 type A aircraft and 7.74 type B aircraft. Rounding these to the nearest integer suggests an optimum with four and eight of each type, but this clearly lies outside the feasible region, for both (5.1) and (5.2) are violated. It is also clear from Fig. 5.1, where we have superimposed an integer grid, that the point (4, 8) is outside the feasible region. If we round down for both types we get three type A and seven type B. Now both constraints are satisfied (verified by substituting these values of x and y in (5.1) and (5.2), or by examining Fig. 5.1 and noting that the point (3, 7) lies in the feasible region. Using (5.3), the passenger load is now $U = 288 \times 3 + 90 \times 7 = 1494$. Do we remain within the feasible region if we round one of the values at M up and one down, i.e. choose four and seven, or three and eight? We easily verify that the former is outside the feasible region, but the latter is within. Obviously we do better using three and eight aircraft of the respective types than if we only use three and seven. With three and eight, we find $U = 1584$. This is the optimum rounding of the linear programming solution, so should we rest on our laurels? Let us try once more – how about four type A aircraft and six type B? Using (5.1) and (5.2) or inspecting Fig. 5.1, it is clear that the point (4, 6) lies in the feasible region OAMD. From (5.3), we now find that $U = 1692$. This is 108 more passengers than we got by the most favourable rounding to integers in our linear programming solution. Can we do even better?

5.2 AN INTEGER FEASIBLE REGION

If realism restricts us to integer values of x and y, this implies that our true feasible region is not *all points in the quadrilateral OAMD* (Fig. 5.1), but a grid of points in and (some perhaps) on the boundary of that quadrilateral with *integer coordinates*. It is further clear that our optimum will be at the grid point within this reduced feasible region that is at the least perpendicular distance from the equi-U line passing through M. This in turn will be a grid point selected from the set of points closest to the bounds AM and MD of the feasible region. We find this set by inspecting the graph at each integer value of x and observing, for that x, the largest integer y which still ensures we are in the feasible region. Inspection shows the paired values of x and y to be those in Table 5.1. All except the last can be read easily from Fig. 5.1.

On the scale used for that figure, it may not be clear whether the point (5, 3) is within the feasible region. It is easily verified that it is, since both constraints, (5.1) and (5.2), are satisfied, (5.2) then being

Table 5.1 Maximum numbers of type B aircraft corresponding to each permissible number of type A aircraft for which both constraints are satisfied

No. of type A	Maximum permissible no. of type B
0	14
1	12
2	10
3	8
4	6
5	3

an equality. For these few solutions, it is easy to calculate U for each, using (5.3). Table 5.2 gives these values, showing that our optimum choice is five type A and three type B aircraft; far from the linear programming solution (after rounding) of three type A and eight type B. We calculated a number of possible optima in Table 5.2, but

Table 5.2 Total number of passenger seats available for potentially optimum allocations of aircraft

No. of type A	No. of type B	Seats available
0	14	1260
1	12	1368
2	10	1476
3	8	1584
4	6	1692
5	3	1710

with experience it becomes clear that the choice of five and three is optimum from our remark that we seek the nearest grid point to the equi-U line through the linear programming optimum point M. This is not necessarily a grid point neighbouring M.

5.2.1 Is this a typical case?

Have I considered a freak case by choosing an example with a rather special property – namely that the equi-U lines are almost parallel to one of the constraint lines? The answer is no. This happens in practical problems, especially when there are many constraints forming part boundaries to the feasible region. In Example 5.1, the data are realistic. The reason the maximum equi-U line through M is close to the line CD representing the fuel constraint is that each type of aircraft is about equally fuel efficient *per passenger carried*.

Exercise Check that fuel requirements per passenger are approximately 6.9 and 6.7 gallons for type A and type B aircraft respectively.

The equi-U lines are far from parallel to the crew constraint boundary because, on a passenger load basis, type A aircraft are more cabin-crew efficient (one per 41.1 passengers) than type B (one per 22.5 passengers).

Because the integer programming solution may be far removed from the linear programming solution, a different approach might be useful. However, in Example 4.1, linear programming worked. Can you see why, in that example, even if we had not had an integer solution, we would almost certainly find a near optimum at an integer point obtained by rounding to a neighbouring integer pair? One approach to integer programming is to use the simplex algorithm as a first step, and if we get a non-integer solution we introduce a second stage algorithm. The procedure is beyond the scope of this book, but the base for one such algorithm is the Gomory method, named after its proposer Ralph E. Gomory (see Gomory, 1958).

5.3 HOW REAL?

Example 5.1 is realistic so far as it goes, but only nibbles at the problems facing airlines. There may be constraints on flight crews as well as cabin crews; it is unlikely there will be an unlimited supply of each type of aircraft, and resources will have to be shared with other routes. It may be relatively easy to work out optimal allocations separately for each of several routes, but impossible to make these optimal allocations to all routes because we would then exceed total resources. More subtle factors then come into play. To give a simple indication, suppose in Example 5.1 where we determined our optimal allocation to be five type A and three type B to carry 1710 passengers we report this to the operations manager. He may have an optimal allocation for a second route that requires seven type A aircraft and those of type B may be unsuitable for that route, so he needs a total of 12 type A aircraft. If he has only 11 of type A available, he cannot meet both demands. He must then look at 'next best' alternatives for each route. From Table 5.2, we see that for the first route the second best solution is four type A and six type B. This enables him to carry 1692 passengers – only 18 less than the optimum. But it releases the extra plane needed for the other route where he can carry an additional 288 passengers. If the latter is a more profitable route per passenger carried, he will want to do this; indeed he would want to do so unless it were very much less profitable.

Profit in cash terms may not be the only factor influencing his decision: he may also consider goodwill. What we have seen is that the basic spade-work for problems of this type can be put on a mathematical footing that leads to better solutions than those based on guesswork or trial and error, the latter being impossible in larger problems.

5.4 ONE-TO-ONE ASSIGNMENTS

Some problems may be posed formally with linear constraints but solutions restricted to integers, but, because the constraints have a special structure, a solution is obtainable by methods specific to the problem, and we arrive directly at a (necessarily integer) solution.

One such is the one-to-one assignment problem. We shall not demonstrate the (not obvious) formal equivalence to a linear programming problem as that is only of academic interest and not user-friendly! We develop a direct solution for a typical problem.

Example 5.2   In an award scheme for physical prowess, each competing club enters a team of four. Each member of a team must tackle one and only one of four challenges designed to test different skills, namely (a) rock climbing, (b) fording a stream, (c) rescuing a swimmer in difficulty, (d) cross-country skiing. At a practice trial, each of the four members of a team attempts each task and the times taken to complete them in minutes are as follows:

| Competitor | Task | | | |
	a	b	c	d
I	12	7	3	18
II	11	10	14	15
III	22	9	8	16
IV	18	22	19	19

If they are expected to record identical times if entered for these events in the final contest, how should the four be assigned to the events so as to minimize the total time the team takes to complete all four challenges?

5.4.1   Trial and error

Professional sport is big business: a lot of money may depend on getting a decision right. In Example 5.2, it is easily seen that if we select competitor I for event a, II for b, III for c, and IV for d that the total time taken will be 12 + 10 + 8 + 19 = 49 minutes. With a trial and error approach we easily pick a better assignment. For

Table 5.3 Number of possible assignments of n individuals to n tasks, with
each individual to perform one and
only one task

n	No. of different assignments possible
2	2
4	24
6	720
8	40320
10	3628800

example, if we select I for c, II for b, III for d, and IV for a, the total
time is $3 + 10 + 16 + 18 = 47$. Is this the best? In this example,
there are 24 possible allocations; it is tedious but not impossible to
write down all of these and compute the total time for each. However, as n, the number of events or number of contestants increases,
the number of possible assignments increases rapidly, as Table 5.3
indicates.

5.4.2 The Hungarian method

To obtain the sums for more than three million assignments of ten
and select the best would be time-consuming for a computer and, for
practical purposes, impossible without. Sometimes there is only one
optimal allocation; in other cases several are equally good. One
routine for getting optima is the *Hungarian method*, or Hungarian
algorithm, so called because it was developed by H.W. Kuhn from
work by a Hungarian, E. Egerváry, in the mid-1950s.

It provides a routine step-wise procedure for making an optimal
allocation corresponding to a minimum. In Example 5.2, we want to
know the minimum total time to complete challenges; in other
examples, it may be a lowest penalty score, or a least cost. For
simplicity, we shall refer to the time, cost, or whatever, whose sum

we wish to minimize as a *penalty*. We outline the algorithm for Example 5.2. The key to the method is as follows. If we add (subtract) a constant c to (from) every entry in a row (or column) of the penalty tableau the total penalty for any assignment will be increased (decreased) by c, but the ranking of the penalties for each assignment is unaltered, because exactly one assignment is made from any given row (or column). This process can be repeated for any desired numbers of rows and columns. In the Hungarian method we proceed as follows.

Step 1. Choose for each row the number c equal to the smallest entry in that row and subtract this from all entries in the row. This ensures we have at least one zero in every row, and all non-zero penalties are positive.

Step 2. Apply an analogous operation to that in Step 1 to columns (if any) that do not yet have a zero element (i.e. in such a column we subtract the smallest entry from each entry in that column, thus ensuring at least one zero entry).

At completion of Steps 1 and 2, there is at least one zero in every row and in every column. We may reverse the order in which we perform Steps 1 and 2. If, at this stage, there are one or more assignments with all zero penalties, these are optimum assignments, for the total penalty is zero, and those for other assignments will be positive. If there are no zero-sum assignments, we proceed to Step 3. However, we first carry out Steps 1 and 2 for Example 5.2. For convenience, we set out the penalties by rows and columns in the order in the tableau given in that example, but omitting labels. Such a display of numbers in ordered rows and columns is called a *matrix*, and, for ease of identification, we shall number this matrix 1.

12	7	3	18
11	10	14	15
22	9	8	16
18	22	19	19

Matrix 1

Step 1. The smallest value in the first row is 3. Subtracting this from each entry in that row gives

$$9 \quad 4 \quad 0 \quad 15$$

Similarly, by subtracting respectively 10, 8 and 18 (the smallest penalties in each) from the second, third and fourth rows, we get matrix 2, which has all elements zero or positive and at least one zero in each row.

9	4	0	15
1	0	4	5
14	1	0	8
0	4	1	1

Matrix 2

Columns 1, 2 and 3 have a zero, so we apply Step 2 to column 4 only, subtracting the smallest entry, 1, from all entries in that column to give matrix 3.

9	4	0	14
1	0	4	4
14	1	0	7
0	4	1	0

Matrix 3

Have we an optimum assignment (i.e. one with zero penalties) in matrix 3? We have this if and only if we can select one or more sets of four zeros such that there is one and only one from each row and column. Inspection shows this is impossible, since for each of the rows 1, 2 and 3 we have only one choice for zero, but two of these are in the same column. As we have no assignment, we proceed to Step 3.

Step 3. We seek the smallest number of horizontal and vertical lines we could draw in matrix 3 that would pass through all zeros. To do this systematically, if there is more than one zero in any row or column, first choose a row or column with as many zeros as possible, next choose a line to go through as many zeros as possible that are not on a line already drawn, proceeding until there are only single zeros remaining and draw appropriate lines through these. We achieve our objective by lines through column 3 and rows 2 and 4 as illustrated in matrix 4.

Matrix 4

We note in passing, but without proof, a useful check. If there has been no assignment possible in Step 2, then we may cover all zeros with less than four lines (in the general *n*-assignment problem with less than *n* lines). Thus, had we found we needed four lines to cover all zeros, it would imply either that we already had an assignment we had not noticed or, alternatively, that we have not selected the minimal set of lines to pass through all the zeros.

In practice, the remainder of Step 3 is carried out as one operation, but to give a better indication of the logic we split it into substeps labelled (a) and (b).

Step 3 (a). We note the smallest penalty not crossed out in matrix 4. Clearly this is 1 in row 3, column 2. We subtract this from all entries in rows 1 and 3 (i.e. the rows that are *not* completely crossed out). This gives matrix 5, where we have suppressed the lines drawn in matrix 4, as they are no longer relevant.

$$
\begin{array}{cccc}
8 & 3 & -1 & 13 \\
1 & 0 & 4 & 4 \\
13 & 0 & -1 & 6 \\
0 & 4 & 1 & 0
\end{array}
$$

Matrix 5

The negative penalties are a problem. Even if we now had an assignment with all zero penalties, it may not be optimum as we might do better by introducing some entries with negative penalties.

Step 3 (b). This step removes the negative penalties. In this case, they are both -1 and occur in column 3. It is easy to see they are removed by adding 1 to all entries in that column of matrix 5, giving matrix 6.

$$
\begin{array}{cccc}
8 & 3 & 0 & 13 \\
1 & 0 & 5 & 4 \\
13 & 0 & 0 & 6 \\
0 & 4 & 2 & 0
\end{array}
$$

Matrix 6

Comparing matrix 4 and matrix 6, we note that the net effect of Steps 3 (a) and (b) is that all elements not struck out in matrix 4 are *decreased* by 1; those struck out by one line only are *unchanged* and those at the intersection of a row and column that are both struck out are *increased* by 1. More generally, the combined effects of the two-stage operation are summed up in the following rule.

> If a is the value of the smallest penalty not struck out, decrease all penalties not struck out by a, leave those struck out by one line only unaltered, and increase those at the intersection of two struck-out lines by a.

This is a telescoping of Steps 3 (a) and (b), and in practice we do both together.

If we have not, at this stage, at least one zero in every row and column we return to Steps 1 and 2 and continue the cycle. If we have zeros in each row and column, we proceed directly to the latter part of Step 2 to check if we have an optimal assignment with total penalty zero. Inspection of matrix 6 shows no such assignment exists so we return to the initial stage of Step 3 and seek a minimal set of struck-out rows and columns. An appropriate set of three lines is given in matrix 7.

$$
\begin{array}{cccc}
8 & 3 & 0 & 13 \\
  & | & | & \\
1 & 0 & 5 & 4 \\
  & | & | & \\
13 & 0 & 0 & 6 \\
  & | & | & \\
0 - & 4 - & 2 - & 0
\end{array}
$$

Matrix 7

We now repeat Steps 3 (a) and (b), telescoping them this time. Again 1 (this time in row 2, column 1) is the smallest penalty not struck out, so we subtract 1 from all elements not struck out, add 1 to those struck out by two lines and leave the rest unaltered. This gives matrix 8.

$$
\begin{array}{cccc}
7 & 3 & 0^* & 12 \\
0^* & 0 & 5 & 3 \\
12 & 0^* & 0 & 5 \\
0 & 5 & 3 & 0^*
\end{array}
$$

Matrix 8

Checking, we find an all-zero penalty assignment for matrix 8. The elements giving it are denoted by an asterisk in that matrix. If there had been no optimal assignment at this stage, the cycle would have been repeated. Returning to our original tableau, as set out in Example 5.2, we see the optimal assignment of competitors is I to c,

II to a, III to b, and IV to d, and the sum of the penalties (here times) is $3 + 11 + 9 + 19 = 42$. There is no other set of zero penalty assignments, so this is a unique optimum. However, had our final matrix for some given set of penalties been

0^{abc}	3	2	5
1	0^a	0^{bc}	5
1	0^b	3	0^{ac}
2	0^c	0^a	0^b

there would have been three minimum penalty assignments illustrated by the sets of zeros with superscripts a, b, c respectively.

The description has made the procedure look long-winded. In practice, one only writes down the matrices 2, 3, 4, 7 and 8 following the rules indicated above.

5.4.3   Unbalanced assignments

Sometimes there are more available people to be assigned to tasks than there are tasks to perform, or more tasks than there are people available. In these situations, there may be penalties for non-assignment. Here is an example.

Example 5.3   In the contest envisaged in Example 5.2, a club can provide only two competitors, and in practice trials the times they take for the four tasks are as follows:

	Task			
Competitor	a	b	c	d
I	6	9	5	17
II	9	7	12	11

As in Example 5.2, each competitor may take part in only one event, but the rules state that if a club cannot provide competitors for each task then they are given a fixed penalty score in any event for which they do not compete (in this example, the penalty might be one and a half times what is considered a reasonable time to complete the task). We suppose these penalties are 14, 9, 8 and 25 respectively for the four tasks. Assuming the competitors will match their practice times in the real competition, for which events should the two be entered to minimize the total time (penalty) score?

Solution We 'convert' this to a problem of assigning four people to four tasks by introducing two fictitious competitors who will score the non-competitor default penalty for the events for which they are 'entered'. Our problem now reduces to the form of Example 5.2, where the default penalties are assigned to the fictitious competitors (labelled IIIf and IVf) in the following penalty tableau.

Competitor	Task			
	a	b	c	d
I	6	9	5	17
II	9	7	12	11
IIIf	14	9	8	25
IVf	14	9	8	25

We leave it as an exercise for the reader to establish that the optimal allocation is to enter competitor I for task a and competitor II for task d. The fictitious competitors may be arbitrarily allocated to tasks b and c. The total penalty for this allocation is 34.

Are you surprised that the optimum strategy assigns competitor II to event d, when his times for events a and b are both superior? Can you see (by inspecting the tableau) why this makes sense?

Sometimes when we make no assignment to certain tasks, we may only in effect wish to minimize penalties for assignments actually made. If so, all fictitious penalties may be given the same arbitrary value, conveniently zero. In this situation, penalties in rows 3 and 4 above corresponding to competitors IIIf and IVf would be set to zero.

Exercise If, in Example 5.3, the penalties are all set to zero for the fictitious competitors, what is the optimum allocation? You should in this case have little difficulty seeing the solution by a careful inspection of the appropriate tableau; if not, it is quickly obtained using the Hungarian algorithm.

5.4.4 How do we deal with a maximum?

If the figures given in Example 5.2 were not the times taken to complete the tasks, but the prize money each competitor could expect to collect, then the winning team is the one that collects the most prize money. We want to assign people to events so as to maximize winnings. Reducing winnings to one zero per row and column, as in the minimization problem, will not help. That would only eliminate the worst allocation. However, we can reformulate the problem to convert it to a minimization problem, the solution of which is a maximum of our original problem. The trick is simple. Assuming the tableau in Example 5.2 is now one of prize money, we select the largest entry in the complete matrix of prize money. If we subtract each entry in the matrix from this, we are left with the 'deficiency' of each competitor's potential winnings compared to the maximum possible win. What we seek is an allocation to minimize these deficiencies. An assignment that does that maximizes the team winnings.

Example 5.4 The tableau in Example 5.2 gives the prize money each competitor could win if he entered that event. What are the maximum possible total winnings?

Here the individual maximum is 22 units (contestant III in event a or contestant IV in event b). Subtracting all entries in the original tableau from 22 gives matrix A:

10	15	19	4
11	12	8	7
0	13	14	6
4	0	3	3

Matrix A

Applying Step 1 of the Hungarian algorithm to obtain row zeros (already present in rows 3 and 4) gives matrix B:

6	11	15	0
4	5	1	0
0	13	14	6
4	0	3	3

Matrix B

Step 2 requires us to reduce column 3 entries by 1 to give a zero, leading to matrix C:

6	11	14	0
4	5	0	0
0	13	13	6
4	0	3	3

Matrix C

Inspection shows an immediate optimal assignment of I to d, II to c, III to a, and IV to b. The total prize for this assignment is obtained from the first tableau in Example 5.2 as $18 + 14 + 22 + 22 = 76$.

5.5   WHAT AND WHERE?

What skills have we mastered?

We have found that linear programming techniques may fail when applied directly to problems that only admit of integer solutions; it does not always suffice to round to the nearest or neighbouring integers. For graphical solutions, examination of a restricted set of points on an integer grid may resolve the problem; more sophisticated methods (not described in this book) are required for more than two variables.

When resources have to be assigned one-to-one to minimize a penalty, the Hungarian algorithm is appropriate in direct application for a balanced assignment of n people to n tasks. Unbalanced problems may often be reformulated as balanced problems by introducing fictitious performers or tasks as appropriate and allocating either pre-assigned penalties or zero penalties to these. We assign the latter if we are indifferent as to how fictitious allocations are made.

A maximization assignment problem may be reformulated as an equivalent minimization problem.

Where can I read more?

French *et al.* (1986: Chap. 4) covers assignment problems in slightly more detail and has some interesting examples. See also Waters (1989: Chap. 7) and Lucey (1988: Chap. 22). A further example of integer programming is given by Hollingdale (1978).

EXERCISES

*5.1   A printer of coloured posters has a choice of purchasing two types of machine. Type A costs £50 000 and can produce 4000 posters per day and running costs are £80 per day. Type B costs £70 000 and can produce 5000 posters per day and running costs are £50 per day. How many of each type of machine should he buy to maximize his daily output of posters if he is prepared to invest up to £500 000 on machines and allocate up to £600 per day for running costs?

*5.2 A local authority wishes to modernize five school buildings during the summer vacation. To expedite the work, it is decided to give one job to each of five different contractors so that all jobs may proceed simultaneously. Each contractor is asked to submit a tender for each of the five schools. The tenders submitted in £ thousand are given below. How should the council award contracts to minimize the total cost. Is more than one optimum allocation possible? What is the total cost under optimum allocation?

Contractor	School				
	1	2	3	4	5
A	7	17	2	12	42
B	9	15	3	9	40
C	8	16	2	10	37
D	12	21	4	11	34
E	11	18	1	8	28

*5.3 Six secretaries are each given a one-week trial work period with each of six executives. Each executive awards each secretary with a mark out of 100 indicating his satisfaction with her work and personality. At the end of the trial period, the secretaries are to be allocated, one to each executive, on a permanent basis. As several executives allocate their top score to the same secretary, clearly not all can have their first choice. Given the satisfaction scores below, how should the secretaries be allocated to maximize the total satisfaction score over all six executives?

Secretary	Executive					
	1	2	3	4	5	6
A	83	75	42	51	62	71
B	92	87	93	84	71	82
C	87	90	73	65	62	72
D	47	62	59	61	64	27
E	94	93	87	77	84	91
F	63	81	74	72	79	61

*5.4   Suppose that in Exercise 5.3 there were only four executives but six potential secretaries. Further, suppose the scores given by the four executives are those given for executives 1, 2, 3, 4 in Exercise 5.3. How do you ensure that the allocation to the four executives will maximize the score? What is this maximum score?

*5.5   Suppose that in Exercise 5.3 executive 1, being the senior person, is allowed to have his favourite secretary – clearly she is E, who scores 94. How should the remaining secretaries now be allocated to maximize the total score over the other five executives?

*5.6   A car rental company has one more car than it needs in each of Newcastle, Carlisle, Edinburgh and Dundee, and one less than it needs in each of Glasgow, Perth, Aberdeen and Inverness. How should it move the surplus cars to meet the deficiencies at minimum total mileage if the mileage between the cities accords with the table below:

	Newcastle (N)	Carlisle (C)	Edinburgh (E)	Dundee (D)
Glasgow (G)	143	94	44	76
Perth (P)	150	137	44	22
Aberdeen (A)	223	210	117	65
Inverness (I)	264	251	158	130

Is there more than one optimal allocation? Are you surprised that any particular routing (i) is, or (ii) is not, used? If so, explain why.

6 The Transportation Problem

6.1 THE TRANSPORTATION PROBLEM

Transportation problems are a generalization of the assignment problem considered in section 5.4; there we assigned n persons (or objects) to m tasks (or destinations) usually on a one-to-one basis where $m = n$. In the transportation problem, we assign groups or sub-groups of objects from m sources to n destinations. The problem has many variants and a number of complications may arise.

Example 6.1 *Whisky galore.*   A whisky distiller has to supply three bottling plants from two distilleries. At distillery I there are 60 barrels of whisky available, and at distillery II there are 120 barrels. Bottling plants A, B and C require respectively 40, 70 and 70 barrels. Entries in the table below gives the cost (£) of transporting one barrel of whisky from the distillery in that row to the bottling plant in that column. For example, the cost of supplying a single barrel from distillery I to bottling plant B is £8. The column on the right gives the numbers of barrels available at each distillery; the final row gives the number of barrels required at each plant. How much whisky should be supplied from each distillery to each bottling plant to minimize transport costs?

| | Plant | | | |
	A	B	C	Available
Distillery I	12	8	5	60
Distillery II	8	10	6	120
Required	40	70	70	

This is called a 'balanced' problem because the amount of whisky available equals the total amount required.

In more general problems, we may have m sources of supply (numbered from 1 to m) and n destinations (numbered from 1 to n) with perhaps a surplus of a commodity available, or else an inability to meet total demand. It is convenient to speak of the route (i, j) between source i and destination j, and to call the cost per unit transported over that route c_{ij}. Thus, in Example 6.1, $c_{11} = 12$, $c_{12} = 8$, $c_{13} = 5$, $c_{21} = 8$, $c_{22} = 10$, $c_{23} = 6$. In an analogous manner, we may write x_{ij} to indicate the number of barrels transported from the distillery in row i to the bottling plant in column j. Formally, then, our problem is to minimize $\Sigma c_{ij} x_{ij}$ subject to constraints on the total available at each source and the total required at each destination. You may not be familiar with the notation Σ. This simply means the costs $c_{ij} x_{ij}$ are to be added over all relevant routes (i, j) *that we actually use*. Like the assignment problem, this is formally one of linear programming, but its special structure leads to easier methods of solution. We do not need to write down the objective function and constraints formally, but an example is given in Exercise 6.15 as a matter of interest.

6.1.1 The basic steps for solution

To solve Example 6.1, we carry out the following procedure.

1. Find any feasible solution (i.e. a solution that meets bottling plant requirements from distillery stocks).
2. Examine this solution to see if we can change some of the x_{ij} and reduce costs. If no reduction is possible, we have an optimal strategy given by the feasible solution in step 1. If we can change some x_{ij} so that costs are reduced, we replace the feasible solution we had at step 1 by this new solution and repeat the process.

In practice, at least three methods are widely used to get a starting feasible solution, and at least two further methods to test whether improved allocation to routes is possible, and, if so, to determine what the improved allocation and the associated costs are. We shall discuss only one procedure for each of these stages.

6.2   GETTING A STARTING SOLUTION – THE BULL AT A GATE APPROACH

This method is formally known as the *north-west corner rule*. It seldom leads to the quickest solution, but it is simple to apply. We demonstrate it for Example 6.1. We first look at route (1, 1) from distillery I to bottling plant A, (the 'north-west corner' route by analogy with a map). The maximum number of barrels we can transfer by this route is 40 (more barrels are available at distillery I, but only 40 are required at plant A). This disposes of all whisky needed by routes in column 1 of the cost table, for no more whisky is required at plant A. We have still, however, 20 barrels for disposal from distillery I. Having started with row 1, column 1, and now finished with column 1, we stay in row 1 but move to column 2; clearly we can assign our remaining 20 barrels from distillery I to this route to meet part of the requirement of plant B. This disposes of all whisky available through routes in row 1. We continue by completing requirements in column 2. Plant B needs a further 50 barrels which must come from distillery II. The remaining 70 barrels from that distillery follow route (2, 3) to meet the requirement of plant C. This feasible solution is summarized in matrix 1 below, where the final column and row give the total 'available' and 'required' numbers of barrels. The feasibility is confirmed by these being equal to the row and column totals for the cell entries.

	A	B	C	Available
I	40	20		60
II		50	70	120
Required	40	70	70	

Matrix 1

The total cost associated with this solution is obtained by multiplying the numbers of barrels in each cell in matrix 1 by the corresponding unit cost given in the original table. The relevant costs are reproduced for convenience in matrix 2.

	A	B	C
I	12	8	
II		10	6

Matrix 2

Thus the total cost is $40 \times 12 + 20 \times 8 + 50 \times 10 + 70 \times 6 = 1560$.

6.2.1 Shadow costs

Is there a feasible solution with a lower cost? The algorithm to test for this uses an ingenious (you may even think it devious) dodge, but it is perfectly legitimate. We introduce what are called *shadow costs*. The concept has a wider applicability to sensitivity analysis in linear programming, although we do not use it in that more general context in this book. Shadow costs are introduced by splitting the total true transportation cost c_{ij} into two additive components.

The first may be looked upon as a charge per barrel released which is levied by a distillery and is the same no matter what the destination; however, these charges will in general not be the same for each distillery. The second is a charge which is incurred by each bottling plant per barrel delivered, irrespective of source distillery, but the amount incurred varies from plant to plant. We denote the distillery charges by u_1 and u_2 respectively, and the bottling plant charges by v_1, v_2, v_3 respectively and equate their sums to the charge c_{ij} *for each route actually used in the feasible solution*. In our example,

$$u_1 + v_1 = c_{11} = 12$$
$$u_1 + v_2 = c_{12} = 8$$
$$u_2 + v_2 = c_{22} = 10$$
$$u_2 + v_3 = c_{23} = 6 \qquad (6.1)$$

We have four equations and five unknowns u_1, u_2, v_1, v_2 and v_3, so, as in the simplex method in section 4.5, there is not a unique solution. If we assume one unknown has a fixed value, we can (not always, but in the situation here) obtain unique solutions for the others. We adopt the convention that $u_1 = 0$. This seems artificial but it suffices for our purposes, for if the true shadow cost for distillery I were some positive quantity £6, say, we would get the same total transport cost structure by reducing this to zero, subtracting £6 from the other distillery charge and adding £6 to each bottling plant charge.

Putting $u_1 = 0$, by solving the equations (6.1) in turn we find $v_1 = 12$, $v_2 = 8$, $u_2 = 2$, $v_3 = 4$. These shadow costs are compatible with the true costs c_{ij} for routes actually used in our feasible solution. Next, we work out what these shadow costs imply for the routes we did not use, i.e. routes (1, 3) and (2, 1). For the former the shadow cost is $u_1 + v_3 = 4$, and for the latter it is $u_2 + v_1 = 14$. These may be compared with the given costs of $c_{13} = 5$ and $c_{21} = 8$.

Since the shadow costs reflect the true costing on the routes we did use, there clearly can be no improvement in switching to a route which has a higher true cost than that given by shadow costing based on the routes actually used. For route (1, 3), this is the position (shadow cost 4, true cost 5, implying it would cost an extra £1 for each barrel transported by this route). For the route (2, 1), the shadow cost is 14, the true cost only 8, so we would save £6 for each unit transported by this route.

So it makes sense to modify our current solution by transferring as many barrels as possible to this route, while maintaining a feasible solution. If we transfer x barrels the saving will be £$6x$.

6.3 IMPROVING OUR SOLUTION

Matrix 3 reproduces the numerical values in matrix 1, but introduces a new number of barrels, x, to route (2, 1). To maintain a feasible solution, we adjust the number of barrels already allocated to maintain all row and column totals with the proviso that there must be no *negative* assignments.

	A	B	C	Total
I	$40 - x$	$20 + x$		60
II	x	$50 - x$	70	120
Total	40	70	70	*Matrix* 3

From matrix 3, we see that, if x does not exceed 40, all cell entries remain positive or zero. Thus we achieve the maximum cost reduction of £(6×40) = £240 by setting $x = 40$, i.e. moving 40 units from route $(1, 1)$ to route $(2, 1)$ with the consequent adjustments. These are reflected in matrix 4.

	A	B	C	Total
I		60		60
II	40	10	70	120
Total	40	70	70	*Matrix* 4

6.3.1 Can we do even better?

In practice, we telescope the above steps into one jumbo tableau. In this, we leave out the distillery labels I and II and the plant labels A, B, C. Also, to avoid confusion because we shall be writing each in the one tableau, we use *small italic* for the costs c_{ij}, larger *italic* for the shadow costs u_i and v_j, and roman (upright) type for the numbers of barrels. Table 6.1 is a completed tableau. Entries were made in the following order.

1. Row and column totals (last column, last row) from data.
2. The true costs in each cell (small italic) from data.

Table 6.1 First working tableau for transportation algorithm, Example
6.1

	12	8	4	
	$40 - x$	$20 + x$		60
0	12	8	5	
	6 $\quad x$	$50 - x$	70	120
2	8	10	6	
	40	70	70	

3. Allocation of 40 to route (1, 1) followed by 20 for route (1, 2), 50 for route (2, 2), 70 for route (2, 3) (north-west corner rule).
4. Arbitrarily set $u_1 = 0$ at left of first row; deduce values *12* and *8* for v_1 and v_2 in top row of tableau by noting that these give correct true costs, i.e. $c_{ij} = u_i + v_j$.
5. Set $u_2 = 2$ at the left of the first column, deducing this from the relation $c_{22} = u_2 + v_2$, where we already know $c_{22} = 10$ and $v_2 = 8$.
6. Clearly now $v_3 = 4$ is the final entry in the top row, as this satisfies the condition that $c_{23} = 6 = u_2 + v_3$.
7. Inspection of the table shows that for the routes not used in the feasible solution, namely routes (2, 1) and (1, 3), $u_2 + v_1 = 14$ and $u_1 + v_3 = 4$. The former shows the greater (in this example the only) excess over the corresponding true cost $c_{21} = 8$. This excess of *6* is indicated in bold italic in that cell above and to the left of the unit cost of *8*. We also enter x for that route and adjust by adding or subtracting x from other allocations as needed to maintain feasibility (we can always find appropriate adjustments by adding or subtracting a suitable x on certain routes).
8. Inspection now shows $x = 40$ gives greatest cost reduction while maintaining feasibility.

Table 6.2 Second tableau for transportation algorithm, Example 6.1

	6	8	4	
0		60		60
	12	8	5	
2	40	10	70	120
	8	10	6	
	40	70	70	

We repeat the cycle using a fresh tableau (Table 6.2) starting with this new feasible solution. The reader should check our computation of the u_i and v_j, remembering that these are determined for *routes with non-zero allocations* after arbitrarily setting $u_1 = 0$. With two rows and three columns, this is always possible providing four cells have non-zero allocations. More generally, if there are m rows and n columns, there must be $m + n - 1$ routes with non-zero allocations to determine all the u_i and v_j. We discuss the situation when this condition breaks down in section 6.5.

6.3.2 Home and dry

In Table 6.2, the shadow costs for the currently unused routes $(1, 1)$ and $(1, 3)$ are respectively 6 and 4, both less than the corresponding true costs of 12 and 5. This means no improvement can be made and we now have an optimum allocation with cost

$$60 \times 8 + 40 \times 8 + 10 \times 10 + 70 \times 6 = 1320.$$

We could also calculate this directly by adjusting the cost of our initial feasible solution which we earlier showed to be 1560, for we pointed out the saving in moving 40 units to route $(2, 1)$ at a reduction of £6 per unit was £240 and $1560 - 240 = 1320$.

In a small problem like Example 6.1, we often find an optimum in one or two iterations, but sometimes many iterations are required.

When there is more than one unallocated route for which a decreased cost would result from a positive allocation, we must choose just one of these for allocation at the next step. It is best to choose the one that will give the greatest cost reduction per unit moved; if more than one will give an equal greatest reduction, an arbitrary choice may be made.

An examination of the tableau of costs and final allocations for Example 6.1 indicates that the lowest cost route of all, (1, 3), is not used. Can you see an explanation for this apparent logical anomaly? The clue lies in relative costs.

In setting out each tableau, we have distinguished numbers allocated from costs by using roman type and italic of two different sizes. In a handwritten tableau, one might use ink and pencil, or pens of different colours. Computer algorithms usually contain some modification to avoid degeneracy problems where we cannot obtain shadow costs, and often use a starting feasible solution that leads more quickly to the optimum than does the north-west corner rule. We illustrate degeneracy in Example 6.3.

6.4   A MORE REALISTIC EXAMPLE

Unless we meet some of the complications to be considered in sections 6.5 and 6.6, there is more arithmetic but nothing new in principle if we have a greater number of supply depots and delivery points. Example 6.2 shows how to obtain a starting feasible solution and calculate shadow costs for three supply depots and four destinations.

Example 6.2   A bus company has seven bus depots; at three of these there are 7, 5 and 12 surplus buses, and the remaining four require respectively 3, 8, 7 and 6 buses. The buses are to be moved as quickly as possible and the times taken in minutes to drive them between depots are given below. Obtain an optimum routing to make the required transfers in minimum total time.

Times to move buses between depots				Buses available
7	2	1	5	7
6	2	4	8	5
5	8	3	1	12
—	—	—	—	
Buses required 3	8	7	6	

Solution We assemble the first iteration tableau by stages. The north-west corner rule assigns buses as follows:

				Total
3	4			7
	4	1		5
		6	6	12
	—	—	—	
Total 3	8	7	6	

The next tableau shows the true route costs (reproduced from the tableau in the example) together with the shadow costs at the top and to the left. Cells corresponding to positive allocations are marked with an asterisk. Remember that the sum of the row and column shadow costs is equal to the route cost for each positive allocation in the current feasible solution. We set arbitrarily $u_1 = 0$; since $u_1 + v_1 = 7$ (the true route cost) it follows that $v_1 = 7$. The remaining shadow costs are now found in the way described in Example 6.1 in the order indicated in parentheses.

u	v			
	7(2)	2(3)	4(5)	2(7)
0(1)	7*	2*	1	5
0(4)	6	2*	4*	8
−1(6)	5	8	3*	1*

The next tableau (it is not necessary to write this in full – it suffices to get the largest values) gives the values of the total shadow cost for each route minus the true cost, e.g. for route (1, 1) it is $4 + 0 - 4 = 0$. (The value is necessarily zero for any cell with a positive allocation.)

$$
\begin{array}{rrrr}
0 & 0 & 3 & -3 \\
1 & 0 & 0 & -6 \\
1 & -7 & 0 & 0
\end{array}
$$

The maximum reduction is 3 for route (1, 3), so we make an allocation to that cell. The effect on the first feasible solution is shown in the following tableau.

					Total
	3	$4 - x$	x		7
		$4 + x$	$1 - x$		5
			6	6	12
Total	3	8	7	6	

Clearly the maximum x for which all allocations remain positive is $x = 1$, giving a new feasible solution

					Total
	3	3	1		7
		5			5
			6	6	12
Total	3	8	7	6	

In practice, these steps are usually telescoped as in Example 6.1. We next work out shadow costs for this new feasible solution. We leave this as an exercise for the reader. The allocation is not optimal and at least one further iteration is needed. The total minimum time turns out to be 50 minutes.

If we calculate shadow costs for a solution and find that shadow costs for some unallocated routes equal the true costs, then clearly any allocation to such routes that maintains a feasible solution may be made without altering the total cost. Thus an allocation need not be (and indeed often is not) unique.

Example 6.2 is essentially a generalization of the allocation problem in Exercise 5.6. In that exercise, there was only one unit to be moved from each source to each destination and the cost or 'penalty' was expressed as distance instead of time.

6.5 DEGENERACY

If we have a route matrix with m rows and n columns, we require a basic feasible solution with $m + n + 1$ positive allocations to determine shadow costs. Either at the start or at a later iteration, we often find we have less than that number of positive allocations. There is a simple dodge to overcome this difficulty. We alter the quantities that are available or to be delivered at certain locations by a small amount – a minute but positive fraction of one unit – which we keep in the system to avoid zero allocations. We ignore these in our final solution, for the cost of transporting a minuscule fraction of a unit is essentially zero.

Example 6.3   A shipping company has nine ships in port A and nine in port B. It requires nine of these to be moved to dock I, six to dock II and three to dock III. The costs in £ thousand for movement between ports and docks are given in the following tableau. Find the optimum movements to minimize costs.

	Dock I	Dock II	Dock III	Ships available
Port A	6	2	5	9
Port B	1	7	1	9
Ships required	9	6	3	

The north-west corner rule gives the allocation

	Dock I	Dock II	Dock III
Port A	9		
Port B		6	3

With two rows and three columns we require at least four positive allocations to determine shadow costs. We only have three, and, if we try to determine shadow cost as we did in Example 6.1, we soon see where we have a problem (try it and see what happens). We overcome the difficulty with a modification. Let e be a very small positive number. We do not need to specify it, but one could, if one wished, give it a specific value such as 0.0001 (or even 0.000 000 1). This is often done in computer programs. We modify our problem but maintain balance by increasing the number at port B to $9 + e$, and the requirement at dock I to $9 + e$. That at the other docks is maintained at 6 and 3 respectively. We apply the transportation algorithm with these new totals.

The north-west corner rule gives the feasible allocation.

	I	II	III	Total
A	9			9
B	e	6	3	$9 + e$
	$9 + e$	6	3	

We now work out shadow costs on the basis of the four positive allocations to the routes (1, 1), (2, 1), (2, 2), (2, 3). Following the telescoped procedure introduced in Example 6.1, we get the shadow costs and potential improvement indicated below

	6	*12*	*6*	
	$9 - x$	x		9
0	*6*	*2*	*5*	
	$e + x$	$6 - x$	3	$9 + e$
-5	*1*	*7*	*1*	
	$9 + e$	6	3	

It is easily verified that the shadow cost for route (1, 2) exceeds the actual cost by 10 and that the greatest reduction is achieved by routing $x = 6$ ships by this route. A further iteration shows that this solution may still be improved and it is left as an exercise to show that the optimal routing and numbers routed by each route are given by

	A	B	C	Total
I		6	3	9
II	$9 + e$			$9 + e$
Total	$9 + e$	6	3	

In this optimal routing, we may now forget about e and set it equal to zero, as this makes a negligible difference to the total cost of £36 000.

6.6   AN UNBALANCED PROBLEM

Sometimes supplies are insufficient to meet all demands, or they may exceed total demand. We restore balance in such problems by adding a dummy row or column to take up any 'slack'. Example 6.4 is a modification of Example 6.1.

Example 6.4 More whisky galore   We amend Example 6.1 by having 80 barrels instead of 60 at distillery I and 130 barrels instead of 120 at distillery II, all other information being unchanged. How much whisky should be supplied from each distillery to each bottling plant to minimize transport costs?

Solution   The data are summarized as

	Plant			
	A	B	C	Available
Distillery I	12	8	5	80
Distillery II	8	10	6	130
Required	40	70	70	

We now have 30 more barrels available from the distilleries than are required by the bottling plants. We restore balance by introducing an imaginary plant requiring 30 barrels. We usually regard the cost of routing to this plant as zero, for in reality any whisky 'routed' to this plant will be left at the distillery. However, there might sometimes be a 'cost' or penalty for supplying this imaginary plant, in the sense that any whisky not supplied may have to be sold off later at a greater loss if it is left at one distillery than if it were left at the other, or storage costs may be higher at one distillery. Therefore we might indicate appropriate penalty cost figures in this dummy column (cf. Example 5.3). For our illustration, we assume costs associated with these routes are zero.

Our cost tableau with the dummy column is then

Plant	A	B	C	Dummy	Total available
Distillery I	12	8	5	0	80
Distillery II	8	10	6	0	130
Total required	40	70	70	30	

Using the north-west corner rule, a feasible allocation is

Plant	A	B	C	Dummy	Total available
Distillery I	40	40			80
Distillery II		30	70	30	130
Total required	40	70	70	30	

The solution proceeds in the usual way for a balanced problem and we leave its completion as an exercise. It is instructive to compare the optimum allocation with that for Example 6.1. You will find the total cost is decreased from £1320 to £1290. Can you see why?

6.7   MODIFICATIONS AND PROBLEMS REDUCIBLE TO TRANSPORTATION PROBLEMS

In transportation-type problems, some routings may be prohibited by an impediment such as an unbridged river or some other factor that makes the route impracticable. We may refrain from using 'forbidden' routes by associating a sufficiently high cost with them – perhaps of the order of 1000 times the cost of any other route. This ensures they will not be included in the optimal routing.

Although not involving physical transport, some problems can be reduced to a transportation problem format. Care is often needed in the formulation to be sure we are minimizing the correct function. A much quoted problem is the so-called *caterer's problem*. A caterer has to provide clean napkins for each guest at dinners held on, say, six consecutive nights. He knows the numbers required for each night and may use either new napkins or laundered ones; there are time lags before used napkins again become available after laundering, so available numbers vary from day to day. He may use several laundry services at different costs (express ones being quicker but more expensive). The problem is to minimize his outlay on napkins. This and other problems of the same ilk are discussed in detail by Wagner (1975) and many other writers.

6.7.1 Formulation as a transportation problem

The following may not look much like a transportation problem, but it can be formulated as one.

Example 6.5 A company undertakes to ship specified numbers of generators at the end of each of January, February and March. The number to be shipped and the numbers the plant can make in normal time and overtime, with costs per unit in £ thousand, in each month are as follows.

Month	Jan	Feb	Mar
Requirement	8	6	12
Max. production in normal time	7	7	7
Max. production in overtime	4	4	5
Cost/unit made in normal time	4	4	5
Cost/unit made in overtime	5	6	8

If any unit has to be stored beyond the end of the month in which it is completed before it is shipped, there is an additional charge of £1000 per unit per month for storage.

Solution The key to formulation as a transportation problem is the recognition of six possible production schedules (January, February, March in normal time, and the same three months in overtime) and three delivery schedules (end January, February, March). There is slack in production since it is possible to produce a total of 34 units (21 in normal time and 13 in overtime) but only 26 are required. To achieve balance we allocate eight production units to a dummy buyer at zero cost (for they will never be made).

We illustrate the determination of typical costs leaving the reader to complete the cost tableau given below. For a normal time unit made and required in January, the cost is clearly 4. For a normal time unit made in January but not delivered until March, there is an additional storage cost of 2 (remembering our cost unit is £ thousand), making the total cost $4 + 2 = 6$. For an overtime unit made in February the cost is 6 if it is delivered in that month, but 7 if it is delivered in March, as one unit is added for storage.

Note that the higher production costs in March may well reflect inflationary trends that could be predicted in advance (e.g. an agreed wages increase or higher costs of raw materials to take effect from that date). We exclude the nonsense of supplying an item to be made in March in, say, January by allocating a high cost (e.g. 1000 units) to the corresponding 'route'. It is left as an exercise to complete the cost tableau:

Production	Sale				
	Jan	Feb	Mar	Not required	*Units*
Jan, normal time	4	5	6	0	7
Jan, overtime	5	6	7	0	4
Feb, normal time	1000	4	5	0	7
Feb, overtime	1000	6	7	0	4
Mar, normal time	1000	1000	5	0	7
Mar, overtime	1000	1000	8	0	5
Units required	8	6	12	8	

Obtaining the optimum is given as Exercise 6.9.

6.8 DEGENERACY OF THE ASSIGNMENT PROBLEM

We have indicated that the assignment problem discussed in the last chapter is a special case of the transportation problem. Since we have one item (person) at each of n supply points, each to be allocated to one of n destinations (tasks) we use a total of n routes only, so in transportation terms the problem is highly degenerate ($2n - 1$ positive allocations are required for a non-degenerate problem) and has to be modified appreciably if we use a shadow cost approach. The methods given in the previous chapter are generally much simpler.

6.9 WHAT AND WHERE?

What skills have we mastered?

A balanced transportation problem where supply equals demand may be solved by first obtaining a feasible solution using the northwest corner rule. Shadow costs are then calculated for this allocation and used as a basis for comparison with true costs on other routes. If the solution is non-optimal, a reduced cost solution may be obtained by shifting units to a route that gives the greatest potential cost reduction; we shift as many units as possible while retaining feasibility. The process is repeated until no further cost reduction is attainable. The solution may not be unique.

Degeneracy will occur in the initial, or sometimes a later, feasible solution if, given m supply points and n demand points, the feasible solution uses less than $m + n - 1$ routes. This difficulty may be overcome by small adjustments to amounts available and required at some of the supply and demand points.

If supply and demand are unequal, dummy routings are used to 'absorb' surpluses or 'supply' deficiencies. Transport over these dummy routes is often (but not necessarily) at zero cost.

Prohibited routes may be effectively excluded by assigning very high costs to them.

Where can I read more?

Nearly all books on operational research have one or more chapters on transportation type problems. See, for example, French *et al.* (1986: Chap. 3) and Wagner (1975: chap. 6). An examination-orientated approach is given by Lucey (1988: Chap 21), and there is a general discussion in Waters (1989: Chap. 7).

EXERCISES

*6.1   A large manufacturer of paint has three factories I, II and III, each producing a full range of products, and four storage depots A, B, C, D. Transport costs per truckload of paint between factories and depots (in units of £10) are given below, together with available supplies and requirements (in truckloads). Determine a distribution schedule to minimize costs.

Factory	Depot				
	A	B	C	D	Available
I	3	6	2	5	50
II	2	5	1	3	80
III	4	8	4	2	40
	70	50	20	30	

*6.2   If, in Exercise 6.1, the route from factory III to depot D becomes unusable because a bridge is destroyed in a flood, what is now the optimal routing and by how much is the cost increased relative to that in Exercise 6.1?   [It may help you to consider Exercise 6.3 at the same time as you are solving this.]

6.3   Application of the north-west corner rule in Exercise 6.2 allots some traffic to the unavailable route. The algorithms given in this chapter can cope with this problem, but many iterations may be needed with such an initial allocation. There are at least two ways of overcoming this difficulty. Can you spot them?

6.4   If, in Exercise 6.1, each depot's requirements remain unaltered but the available supply at factory I is increased to 130, what is now the optimum transport policy? Is the cost reduced compared to the optimum in Exercise 6.1, and if so by how much?

*6.5   If, in Exercise 6.1, the supply at factory I is decreased to 40, all demands cannot be met. If available supplies are to be transported at minimum cost, which depot or depots do not receive their full requirements? [Hint: Introduce a dummy factory that supplies the deficiency at zero cost (because the paint is never actually delivered).]

*6.6   If, in Exercise 6.5, any shortage were more serious at some depots than at others so that penalties per truckload undelivered of 4, 2, 1, 3 are imposed for depots A, B, C, D respectively, what is now the optimum routing and the total associated cost?

*6.7   If, in Exercise 6.4, there is an extra cost of one unit (e.g. for overtime) when more than 50 loads are delivered from factory I in total (i.e. if the demand from factory I exceeds 50, the costs of delivery to A, B, C, D for each additional load are respectively 4, 7, 3, 6), how does this affect the optimum allocation? [Hint: Replace factory I by factories Ia and Ib with 50 and 80 loads available respectively at appropriate costs.]

6.8   Why it is intuitively reasonable that the total cost in Exercise 6.4 is less than that in both Exercise 6.1 and Exercise 6.7?

6.9   Complete the solution of Example 6.5 in section 6.7.1.

6.10   A company has four warehouses from which it supplies a certain item to three customers. The actual transport costs of goods from each warehouse to any customer are the same but there are

differences in loading costs at each warehouse and in unloading costs
at each customer's premises due to differences in access, available
facilities, etc. The loading and unloading charges and numbers of
units available and required are as follows:

Warehouse	Loading charge	Units available	Customer	Unloading charge	Units required
A	2	30	I	1	10
B	3	25	II	2	30
C	4	15	III	5	40
D	1	10			

Determine a minimum cost distribution system.

6.11 In section 6.2, we introduced shadow costs as hypothetical
charges levied by suppliers and incurred by customers. The real costs
indicated in Example 6.10 look much like these shadow costs. In
what essential respect, if any, do they differ?

*6.12 If, in a transportation-type problem, we are given not costs
but bonuses paid to a driver per unit for delivery over each route,
then a driver will wish to maximize his total bonus. Bearing in mind
the way we dealt with maximum assignment problems in section
5.4.4, outline a way we might tackle the problem of maximizing a
driver's bonus payable. [Note that alternative methods are also
possible here.]

  The table below gives such a scheme: entries in the body of the
table are bonuses payable per unit load transported. Find an allocation that maximizes total bonuses. What is this total?

	I	II	III	Units available
A	8	11	19	20
B	11	14	9	10
	15	8	7	

*6.13   A retailer wishes to stock three different kinds of radio: 80 of type A, 60 of type B, 40 of type C. Three wholesalers can supply the following total numbers of radios which may be divided into types A, B, C in numbers to suit the retailer's requirements: wholesaler I, 50; wholesaler II, 70; wholesaler III, 60. The wholesalers charge different prices for each model, but the retailer must sell each particular model at a standard price, so his profit (£) per radio for each model/source combination is that given below. How should he place his order to maximize profit?

Wholesaler	Radio type		
	A	B	C
I	4	3	7
II	6	4	5
III	4	1	2

6.14   If, in Exercise 6.13, the numbers required by the retailer are unaltered and the profits are as given in that exercise, but the wholesalers are willing to supply 60, 80, and 80 radios respectively, how should orders be placed to maximize the retailer's profit? [Hint: Assume zero profit is made on radios not purchased by the retailer and introduce a dummy radio which he sells at zero profit.]

6.15   Writing c_{ij} and x_{ij} for unit transport costs and the numbers transported respectively over route (i, j) in a linear programming formulation of Example 6.4, verify that the objective function may be written

$$U = 12x_{11} + 8x_{12} + 5x_{13} + 8x_{21} + 10x_{22} + 6x_{23},$$

and that two of the constraints are

$$x_{11} + x_{12} + x_{13} \leqslant 80 \quad \text{and} \quad x_{12} + x_{22} = 70.$$

Write down the remaining constraints.

6.16   As a result of expansion in production capacity, the management of Minerva Manufacturing Ltd has decided to take on additional employees at each of their five plants. The numbers required at each are

Plant	I	II	III	IV	V
No. required	45	74	50	82	63

All their employees currently come from three large towns in the area. Upon contacting the main employment agency in each town, Minerva finds that the number of suitable people available for employment are as follows:

Agency in town	A	B	C
People available	120	100	154

Because of the rural situation of the five plants, Minerva has agreed with the trade unions concerned that daily return travelling expenses from each town will be paid by the company to all employees at a rate currently 12p per mile. The distances in miles between each plant and each town are as follows:

	I	II	III	IV	V
A	6	2	2	6	3
B	14	9	4	5	3
C	10	4	11	3	4

Required:

(a) How many men should Minerva aim to employ from each town to minimize the additional travelling expenses incurred? What is the minimum value of these expenses in connection with the additional 314 employees?

(b) In order to appear not to be unfair to potential employees from any one of the three towns, it is decided that the 60 people surplus to requirements should be spread equally between the three towns, i.e. 20 from each. How much more than in (a) would the company have to pay out each day in travelling expenses in order to achieve this at minimum cost?   [ACCA]

6.17   In a certain region of the Republic of Pelion there are five coal mines which have the following outputs and production costs:

Mine	Output (Tons/day)	Production cost ($/Ton)
1	120	25
2	150	29
3	80	34
4	160	26
5	140	28

Before the coal can be sold, it must be 'cleaned' and graded at one of three coal preparation plants. The capacity and operating costs of these three plants are as follows:

Plant	Capacity (Tons/day)	Operating cost ($/Ton)
A	300	2
B	200	3
C	200	3

All coal is transported by rail at a cost of $0.5 per ton kilometre, and the distances (in kilometres) from each mine to the three preparation plants are:

| Preparation plant | Mine | | | | |
	1	2	3	4	5
A	22	44	26	52	24
B	18	16	24	42	48
C	44	32	16	16	22

Required:

(a) Using a transportation model, determine how the output of each mine should be allocated to the three preparation plants.

(b) Following the installation of new equipment at coal mine number 3, the production cost is expected to fall to $30 per ton. What effect, if any, will this have on the allocation of coal to the preparation plants?

(c) It is planned to increase the output of coal mine number 5 to 180 tons per day which can be achieved without any increase in production cost per ton. How will this affect the allocation of coal to the preparation plants?   [ACCA]

7 Scheduling, Sequencing and Critical Paths

7.1 CUTTING THE AVERAGE WAIT

Here is a simple scheduling, or what some writers call a sequencing, problem. The two are interrelated. A schedule includes a sequence; a sequence implies a schedule.

> *Example* 7.1 In less enlightened days (or in less enlightened hospitals), appointments for one doctor at outpatient clinics were often made in blocks, Mrs Alpha, Mr Beta, Miss Gamma and Mrs Delta all being given appointments at 3 p.m. If the doctor knows his patients' conditions, he may estimate consultation time for each to be as follows:
>
> | | |
> |---|---|
> | *Mrs Alpha* | 20 minutes |
> | *Mr Beta* | 15 minutes |
> | *Miss Gamma* | 12 minutes |
> | *Mrs Delta* | 8 minutes |
>
> In what order should he see the patients to minimize the average time they spend at the clinic?

Writers who distinguish between *scheduling* and *sequencing* apply scheduling to the problem of determining the times for each activity (usually including any waiting time before an activity can be started) and sequencing to problems of determining the order in which to perform tasks. We are usually interested in both. In Example 7.1, the doctor might decide to see the patients in the order given above, i.e. in decreasing order of expected consultation time. If these are accurate estimates, the total expected waiting time (time before the patient is seen *plus* expected consultation time) is 20 minutes for Mrs Alpha because she is seen immediately and 35 minutes for Mr Beta (20 minutes' wait while Mrs Alpha receives attention, plus 15 minutes' consultation); similarly Miss Gamma has expected wait $35 + 12 = 47$ minutes and Mrs Delta $47 + 8 = 55$ minutes. The average waiting time is thus the sum of these divided by the number of patients, 4, i.e.

$$(20 + 35 + 47 + 55)/4 = \tfrac{157}{4} = 39.25.$$

What happens if the doctor reverses the consultation order, seeing the patient with shortest expected treatment time first? The expected waits are now as follows:

Mrs Delta		8 minutes
Miss Gamma	$8 + 12 =$	20 minutes
Mr Beta	$8 + 12 + 15 =$	35 minutes
Mrs Alpha	$8 + 12 + 15 + 20 =$	55 minutes

Thus the average expected wait is

$$(8 + 20 + 35 + 55)/4 = \tfrac{118}{4} = 29.5.$$

It is better to see the patients in this order if reducing the queue as quickly as possible is the prime objective. At a hospital, other factors might override this consideration (e.g. a patient with a more serious condition or one requiring special treatment may be seen first).

7.1.2　The best order

Situations like the above are common in social and industrial contexts; in an industrial setting, patients in Example 7.1 are replaced by jobs to be done with known times to do each on a single machine (analogue of the doctor!). For these and for situations like our outpatient example, are there other orderings that give an even shorter expected average wait? Intuitively, you may feel this is unlikely, but can we be sure that the doctor might not do better by seeing first the patient with the shortest expected treatment time, then the one with the longest, then the one with the second shortest, then the one with the second longest, and so on?

Exercise Calculate the expected average wait for the order of treating patients just suggested.

I got 32.75 minutes. Do you agree?

The expected average wait is indeed minimized by seeing patients (or doing jobs on a single machine) in increasing order of time taken. We argue this way. If we have two jobs, the quicker taking time t and the slower the greater time $t + e$ (where e is necessarily positive, i.e. greater than zero), then if we do the quicker job first the total waiting time is

$$t + (t + t + e) = 3t + e. \tag{7.1}$$

If we do the slower job first, the total waiting time is

$$(t + e) + (t + e + t) = 3t + 2e \tag{7.2}$$

Since (7.2) exceeds (7.1) by e, if we do the slower job first, then we increase the total waiting time by e. The same argument applies to the ordering for any pair of jobs, whence it follows that the total (and hence the average) waiting time to completion is minimized by carrying out the jobs in increasing order of times taken. If two jobs take the same time, we may do either first.

7.2 MORE REALISTIC SCHEDULES

Minimizing average times to completion gives what is sometimes called the shortest processing time (abbreviated to SPT) rule for a single machine. This is a confusing terminology, for the same total machine (or processing) time is taken no matter in what order we do the jobs. The adjective 'shortest' applies here to the average *waiting plus processing* time (i.e. it includes queuing time before a job is started).

We do not always want to minimize this average. Some jobs may be wanted by specified times, but it may not matter if others are done later. Sometimes we do not want a job finished too soon, for its early completion may involve storage charges (in hard cash, or as a nuisance factor because the completed product occupies space that could be used more profitably). Penalties for late or early completion may vary from item to item; we would then seek a schedule to minimize total penalties.

These basic ideas generalize to problems where we use several machines for any job, or to scheduling jobs that require the use of two or more machines in a specified order. We shall not deal in detail with problems that require more than one machine, but in section 7.3 we move to complex organizational problems where a number of jobs are carried out, sometimes several proceeding at the same time, but subject to constraints on the ordering. These important scheduling problems are rather different in nature.

7.2.1 Stock-out situations

A *stock-out* situation arises if items are out of stock pending the arrival of fresh supplies. A manufacturer or trader may want to minimize some aspect of the times different items are out of stock. One criterion for comparing scheduling programmes is the average stock-out times for all items. If items are made in sequence on one machine, a common working rule is to produce items in the order in which they are expected to run out of stock. Two examples show ways that this intuitively reasonable rule behaves in practice.

Example 7.2   A bottling machine is used to bottle five different kinds of soft drinks. Batches of 100 dozen bottles of each are made at each processing run on a single machine and the times to complete a run varies between drinks (owing to technicalities such as the time taken to clean and set the machine, mix constituents, etc.)

The table below shows these 'run' times (in days) together with the current stocks (in dozens of bottles) and average daily demands.

Drink	A	B	C	D	E
Current stock (doz)	20	5	30	15	30
Average daily demand (doz)	8	4	15	10	5
Production run time (days)	0.8	0.4	1.0	1.0	0.6

Solution   We first calculate the expected time to stock-out for each drink by dividing current stock by average daily demand, e.g. for drink B it is $\frac{5}{4} = 1.25$ days. For all five drinks, we find

Drink	A	B	C	D	E
Expected time to stock-out	2.4	1.25	2	1.5	6

If we sequence our production in increasing order of expected time to stock-out (i.e. give priority to the shortage areas), the order would be B, D, C, A, E. If we start the first production run now (conveniently designated as time zero), and commence each subsequent run as soon as the previous run is finished, we easily draw up the following time schedule for a complete cycle of all five drinks.

Drink	B	D	C	A	E
Expected time to stock-out	1.25	1.5	2	2.4	6
Production start time	0	0.4	1.4	2.4	3.2
Production run time	0.4	1.0	1.0	0.8	0.6
Production finish time	0.4	1.4	2.4	3.2	3.8

Expected stock-outs occur if production finish time is later than the expected time to stock-out for any drink; otherwise the stock-out time is zero. Inspection of the above tableau shows that in the order given the expected stock-out times are 0, 0, 0.4, 0.8, 0. Adding these and dividing by the number of drinks, 5, gives an average stock-out time of 0.24.

It turns out that this is the lowest average stock-out time of any schedule in this example. However, the rule does not always do this.

Example 7.3   Consider the data in Example 7.2 with the change that the production time for a batch of D is increased to two days. Compare the average stock-out times for the following schedules: (i) B, D, C, A, E; (ii) B, C, A, D, E.

Solution   Analogous tableaux to those in the solution of Example 7.3 for the two cases are as follows:

(i)

Drink	B	D	C	A	E
Expected stock-out	1.25	1.5	2	2.4	6
Production start time	0	0.4	2.4	3.4	4.2
Production run time	0.4	2.0	1.0	0.8	0.6
Production finish time	0.4	2.4	3.4	4.2	4.8

(ii)

Drink	B	C	A	D	E
Expected stock-out	1.25	2	2.4	1.5	6
Production start time	0	0.4	1.4	2.2	4.2
Production run time	0.4	1.0	0.8	2.0	0.6
Production finish time	0.4	1.4	2.2	4.2	4.8

In both cases the total run time, 4.8 is the same. It must be, since the run time for each drink is independent of the order. However, in case (i), which corresponds to scheduling in increasing order of stock-out time, the stock-out periods are respectively 0, 0.9, 1.4, 1.8, 0, giving an average stock-out time of 0.82 days, whereas in the second case the stock-out periods are 0, 0, 0, 2.7, 0, giving an average stock-out time of only 0.54.

Clearly, here, the rule of thumb 'sequence in increasing order of expected stock-out time' does not minimize the average stock-out time. The optimum sequencing to minimize average stock-out time depends not only on the expected stock-out times but also on production times. It does so in a complex manner, and consideration of the optimum procedure to achieve this objective is beyond the scope of this book. In problems of this type, we may seek alternative objectives, e.g. we may wish to minimize the total number of stock-out situations, or minimize the longest stock-out time, rather than the average stock-out time.

7.2.2 Some additional concepts

Even for one machine, one job at a time, situations, additional concepts and more formal definitions are useful. In particular, for any job J, we have the following.

1. The *processing time P* is the machine time required for that job. This is sometimes known precisely, or we may have a reasonable *a priori* estimate.
2. The *due date D* is the time by which the job should be completed.

Both P and D are specified in advance and are outside our control. In Example 7.2, D would be the expected times to stock-out. We may have some control over the following by altering our scheduling.

3. The *completion time C* is the time that processing of the job is completed.
4. The *lateness L* is given by $L = C - D$; L will be negative if the job is completed before the *due date*; if there are penalties in the

form of storage costs for early completion, as well as penalties for late completion, we ideally want $L = 0$. It is usually impossible to achieve this for all jobs.

If there are penalties only for late completion, the quantity of interest is the tardiness, defined as follows.

5. The *tardiness* T is zero if L is negative or zero, but equals L if L is positive.

Some writers use the term lateness for tardiness and do not define the more general concept we have called lateness. If there are different penalties for *tardiness* (or *lateness*) for each job these may be incorporated by assigning a weight W, which indicates the relative penalty per unit time for late completion. It is common, but not universal, practice to set the weight equal to unity for the job or jobs with the smallest penalty weight. Note that, like P and D, the W, if relevant, are pre-specified.

In Example 7.1, we sought a minimum average completion time and showed that this is achieved by sequencing jobs in order of increasing processing time. It is not difficult to show algebraically, though we do not prove it, that this also minimizes the average lateness. In doing so, some of the individual L will almost certainly be positive, and some negative. Depending on the penalties attached to late or early finishes, we may prefer to minimize some weighted mean of lateness or some other function such as the mean tardiness. Both of these problems (as Example 7.3 indicated for mean tardiness) are difficult to tackle and are beyond the scope of an elementary treatment.

7.2.3 Order constraints

Constraints on the order in which jobs are done are common. It may be impossible to perform the mth job J_m before the kth job J_k is completed. Two jobs in preparing a computer program are writing and editing a subroutine, but the subroutine cannot be edited before it is written! In many situations where there are such constraints, we can set up algorithms to minimize the maximum of the latenesses or tardinesses (appropriately weighted) over all jobs. Minimizing a maximum is referred to as a *minimax* problem; such problems are common in operational research. This may only be a 'second best' solution to an overall minimization of average lateness or tardiness, but if a schedule leads to a very small maximum tardiness, or lateness, we may be reasonably happy. An algorithm to determine a schedule that minimizes maximum tardiness was given by Lawler (1973). In the special case of equal weights and no constraints on job order, Lawler's algorithm may be used to show that we minimize the maximum tardiness or lateness by sequencing the jobs in ascending order of due date (i.e. that with the earliest due date is scheduled first). This is what scheduling in increasing order of expected stock-out time does (see section 7.2.1).

We illustrate Lawler's algorithm for a more complicated example.

Example 7.4   An advertising agency has to prepare five publicity pamphlets for a client. Pamphlets 2 or 3 cannot be started before pamphlet 1 is completed because their content will depend upon the selection of material in pamphlet 1. For similar reasons, pamphlet 5 cannot be started before both pamphlets 3 and 4 are completed. Table 7.1 gives, for each pamphlet, the time required

Table 7.1 Scheduling and penalty information for preparation of pamphlets

Pamphlet No.	Time for preparation P_i	Due date D_i	Tardiness penalty weight W_i
1	3	4	2
2	2	8	2
3	4	9	3
4	1	6	1
5	2	10	2

to prepare it (in weeks), the due date (in weeks from commencement of the project) and the tardiness penalty rate (in units of £10) for each week's delay in meeting the due date. Find a schedule that minimizes the maximum tardiness penalty payment associated with the preparation of the pamphlets.

All pamphlets will not be ready on time since the total preparation time (sum of the P_i in Table 7.1) is 12, but the latest due date is 10. Such conflict between what a customer wants and what a supplier can deliver are common. It may seem perverse, too, that the client sets a due date of only six weeks for pamphlet 4 and later dates for pamphlets 2 and 3. However, this sort of situation makes sense if, for example, pamphlet 4 is more technical and the company want it to be available to their marketing department as early as possible so that the sales force have more time to master the detail.

Preparation of pamphlet i may be termed job J_i, with corresponding P_i, D_i and W_i (associated with tardiness) given in the second, third and fourth columns of Table 7.1. The first step using Lawler's algorithm is to decide which job should be done last! This surprises many people, but this 'cart before horse' approach is common in optimization problems. A *backward* stepwise solution is the only feasible way of tackling many problems.

For Lawler's algorithm we first set out the data in Table 7.1 in a horizontal format as follows, using the notation indicated above. We leave a space for another column of figures to left and to right.

	J_1	J_2	J_3	J_4	J_5
P_i	3	2	4	1	2
D_i	4	8	9	6	10
W_i	2	2	3	1	2

The job to be tackled last is the one among all possible last jobs that has the lowest tardiness penalty (obtained by multiplying the tardiness (in weeks) T_i by the appropriate weight W_i). By summing the P_i, we find (as already mentioned) that the last job cannot be completed in less than 12 weeks. Further, the constraints mean that J_1 cannot be the last job because that job must *precede* both J_2 and J_3; it is possible for J_2 to be the last job, but neither J_3 nor J_4 can be the last as they must both *precede J_5*. Thus the last job must be either J_2 or J_5. If we choose J_2, completion at the end of 12 weeks when it is due after eight weeks implies a tardiness $T_2 = 12 - 8 = 4$ weeks; the penalty weight is $W_2 = 2$, so the tardiness penalty is $W_2 T_2 = 2 \times 4 = 8$. Similarly, if we choose J_5, we see that $T_5 = 12 - 10 = 2$ and $W_5 = 2$, whence the tardiness penalty is 4. Clearly we minimize the penalty associated with the final job if we choose J_5 with its associated penalty 4.

We incorporate this decision and the relevant information about the total processing time being 12 weeks in an additional line in the tableau above, so that it now reads as follows:

	J_1	J_2	J_3	J_4	J_5	
P_i	3	2	4	1	2	
D_i	4	8	9	6	10	
W_i	2	2	3	1	2	
12	N	8	N	N	4	J_5

The first entry 12 is the ultimate completion time for the last item processed; the entry N (for not possible) in a column corresponding to any job indicates that it cannot be the last job processed, the numbers 8 and 4 in the columns corresponding to J_2 and J_5 are the weighted tardiness penalties for those jobs. We underline the lowest penalty to highlight it. The J_5 in the final column records that this should be the last job tackled. The process is now repeated after elimination of J_5 to determine which should be the last but one job. We enter relevant information in a further row. Since the processing time P_5 for J_5 is 2, all remaining jobs may be processed in $12 - 2 =$ 10 weeks. Since J_1 must precede J_2 and J_3, it cannot be processed at this stage. We have already excluded J_5 by selecting it as the last to be processed. Thus we have a choice of J_2, J_3 or J_4. Since the chosen job is completed after ten weeks, compared to due completions after 8, 9, 6 (row labelled D_i) with weights 2, 3, 1 (row labelled W_i) respectively, it is easily verified that the corresponding weighted penalties are 4, 3, 4. Thus we choose J_3 at this stage since it involves a minimum penalty of 3. This information is summarized by adding another row:

	J_1	J_2	J_3	J_4	J_5	
P_i	3	2	4	1	2	
D_i	4	8	9	6	10	
W_i	2	2	3	1	2	
12	N	8	N	N	4	J_5
10	N	4	3	4	D	J_3

In this last row, the D (for deleted) indicates that the corresponding job J_5 is already allocated.

Since J_3 takes $P_3 = 4$ weeks, the previous job may be finished after $10 - 4 = 6$ weeks, so this is the first entry in the next row of the algorithm. It is left as an exercise to show that the order of precedence once more means that J_1 cannot be performed at this stage since it has to be done earlier, but both J_2 and J_4 are possibilities. Since the due date for both is six or more weeks, there is no penalty associated with completing either in six weeks. Thus either may be chosen with zero penalty. We arbitrarily choose J_4. Proceeding in this way, we arrive at the conclusion that the job preceding J_4 should be J_2. This leaves no option but to make J_1 the first choice. The steps in the Lawler algorithm corresponding to these choices are

Table 7.2 The Lawler algorithm applied to Example 7.3

	J_1	J_2	J_3	J_4	J_5	
P_i	3	2	4	1	2	
D_i	4	8	9	6	10	
W_i	2	2	3	1	2	
12	N	8	N	N	4	J_5
10	N	4	3	4	D	J_3
6	N	0	D	0	D	J_4
5	N	0	D	D	D	J_2
3	0	D	D	D	D	J_1

given as part of the complete tableau in Table 7.2. In practice, this final table is all that need be written down when using Lawler's algorithm.

From Table 7.2, it is clear that the maximum tardiness penalty is 4 units, associated with J_5, and is achieved if we complete the jobs in the order (reading from the bottom of the final column in Table 7.2) J_1, J_2, J_4, J_3, J_5.

Exercise The ordering is not unique; verify that J_2 and J_4 may be interchanged.

We have considered only jobs scheduled on a single machine. Many interesting problems arise when more than one machine is employed, particularly if items have to be processed in a certain order on several machines M_1, M_2, M_3, ... We may wish to determine schedules that minimize idle machine times, etc. The reader is referred to French *et al.* (1986: Chap. 5) for a general discussion, and to Waters (1989: Chap. 7) for a simple numerical example of one such problem involving two machines using a rule known as Johnson's rule to minimize total time in the system.

7.3   CRITICAL PATH ANALYSIS – SETTING UP A NETWORK

We often want to minimize the total time taken to complete a number (in practice often hundreds or even thousands) of interlocking activities. A computer is essential for dealing with all aspects of large scheduling problems, but the logic can be illustrated by relatively simple examples like building a boat or a house, writing and publishing a book, or even baking a cake. Designing and building a nuclear power station or a space satellite involves major scheduling problems if the end product is to be completed on time and at reasonable cost. Features common to all these situations are as follows:

 (i) there is an order of precedence for certain activities;
 (ii) some activities may be carried out simultaneously;
(iii) the duration of each activity is known precisely, or can be estimated within certain limits, or can be adjusted within a specified range (often at additional cost if the job is speeded up).

For example, in building a house, the foundations must be laid before the walls are erected, the roof must be put on before interior walls are plastered, and for some modes of construction electric wiring and plumbing must be done before plastering the walls. However, electrical work and plumbing may usually proceed simultaneously. A specific time may be laid down for some operations like digging and laying foundations: it may be impossible to reduce this, because it embodies a minimum 'settling period' before further construction can proceed. On the other hand, the time for building walls might be decreased by employing extra bricklayers, perhaps at additional cost. If certain key operations fall behind schedule, completion of the whole project will be delayed (a familiar experience for those waiting to move into a new house).

Critical path analysis (CPA) uses a *network* to represent activities and their interrelationships and determines what are key operations that must not fall behind if a job is to be completed on time. CPA is the first example in this book, apart from a passing mention in section 1.7.3, of widely used techniques grouped under the name of *network analyses*. Further examples of networks are given in Chapter 8. Example 7.5 is a small problem soluble by critical path analysis.

7.3.1 Publishing a book

Example 7.5 A book publisher has to complete the activities listed below between receiving the manuscript for the book *Shady Aspects of Politics* from the author, and publication day. The table indicates the time in days required to complete each. We have labelled the activities *A, B, . . .* and use these labels to indicate in the column headed *Precedents* any that must be completed before that activity can commence.

Activity	Description	Time	Precedents
A	Clear MS with solicitors for libel and copyright queries	10	
B	Copy edit MS and agree any alterations with author	45	
C	Negotiate with author to modify potentially libellous material	40	A
D	Set type	35	B, C
E	Prepare illustrations	22	B, C
F	Assemble page proofs	7	D, E
G	Author corrects proofs	8	F
H	Production editor checks proofs and layout	20	F
I	Author prepares index	8	G

Activity	Description	Time	Precedents
J	Production editor collates author's proof corrections with his own and checks index	9	H, I
K	Printer sets index, corrects proof errors	12	J
L	Design and prepare cover	30	B, C
M	Prepare publicity material	18	J, L
N	Binding and delivery to publisher's warehouse	20	K, L
P	Pre-publication delivery to booksellers and distribution of review copies	30	M, N

What is the minimum time needed to publish the book after receipt of the manuscript?

The times quoted for the various activities reflect the nature of the book. For example, activity C would only take 40 days for a book containing controversial material (the title of this book suggests it might!). For a technical book with mathematical formulae, stages D and G, and perhaps J and K, may take longer. For some books, it may not be practicable to start activity L until after J is completed. For a different breakdown of the publishing procedure, with emphasis on the technicalities of printing and on a costing comparison of different schedules, which introduces ideas beyond the scope of the treatment here, see Moore (1986: Chap. 2).

Publisher's schedules are necessarily based on *estimated* times. All too often there is slippage at a vital stage. Critical path analysis determines the quickest possible time for publication and whether and how much 'slippage' can be allowed in any activity without increasing total time. There are many elaborations such as determining the time-saving by speeding up (usually at extra cost) any part of the process. In essence, all these problems can be solved diagrammatically by a logical representation of the process. Computer programs exploit the logic by using an algebraic and arithmetic translation of the features of these diagrams.

7.3.2 Some conventions

Before using CPA to solve Example 7.5, we need some definitions and conventions and a description of the form of CPA networks. Some conventions are not essential to the logic, but are so widely used that it is wise to adhere to them. For example, we usually represent (as far as is possible) logical sequences diagrammatically progressing from left to right across a page.

An *activity* is a task requiring certain resources (in Example 7.5 the relevant resource is a *time to perform*). An arrow is used to represent an activity in a network, the tail indicating where the activity begins and the head where it ends. The arrows are not drawn to scale. An activity is designated by a letter or number (a letter is to be preferred); we write this designator and associated resource requirement (here time) alongside each arrow in the manner indicated in Fig. 7.1, this being relevant to activity A in Example 7.5.

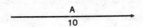

Figure 7.1 Representation of an activity A, and time taken, ten days.

A *dummy activity* is an activity that requires no resources. We introduce these while setting up a network either to meet the logic of a problem, or to help comply with established conventions. Dummy activities are usually denoted by a broken arrow as in Fig. 7.2 and need not be labelled.

$$- - - - - - \rightarrow$$

Figure 7.2 Representation of a dummy activity. No label needed.

Figure 7.3 Circle or node representing an event. Data will later be entered in the three sectors.

An *event* corresponds to the start or finish of one or more activities. It is conventionally denoted by a circle (often referred to as a *node*). It is convenient to divide this circle into three sectors as shown in Fig. 7.3. We put certain information into these sectors as we construct a CPA network.

The CPA *network* is a logical combination of activities, dummy activities and nodes, which must accord with some rules. The first is that there is only one point of entry to a network (the *starting event*) and only one end point (the *finishing event*).

Every activity (including a dummy activity) joins two nodes, one representing the tail or start of the activity and the other the head or finish of that activity. More than one activity may use any tail or head node, but no two activities may jointly use the same tail and head nodes (this restriction is not essential to the logic, but had its origins in an era when its neglect led to difficulties with computer programs). We shall see in section 7.3.3 that such a situation can always be avoided by introducing a dummy activity. The starting event is a tail node only; the finishing event is a head node only. All other nodes are head nodes for some activity or activities and tail nodes for others (dummy activities may be included).

An activity other than the start activity (or activities) uses a tail node that is a head node for some previous activity. The appropriate tail node is chosen to ensure that all activities which must have been completed before the current activity can start have been completed. This implies that, if there are constraints on the order of activities, these are reflected in the choice of tail node. In Example 7.5, since activity C cannot start until A is completed and there is no other

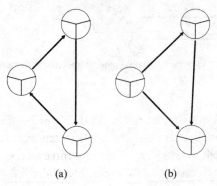

(a)   (b)

Figure 7.4 For CPA, (a) is an impermissible path and (b) is a permissible path.

constraint on C, the head node of A is an appropriate tail node for C.

An *event* or *node* is said to be complete only if all possible activities leading into it (including any logically required dummy activities) have been incorporated.

Loops which lead back (following the direction of arrows) to the same event are not allowed. Thus Fig. 7.4(a) is not an allowable network, but Fig. 7.4(b) is, because the directions of the arrows are contrary.

All activities must contribute to the progression through the network. An activity which does not so contribute is sometimes called a 'dangler' and should be omitted. In a properly formulated problem, danglers are seldom encountered and in essence correspond to irrelevant information (e.g. if, in building a house, it were not necessary for the garden to be landscaped before completion, a statement that landscaping takes ten days would be irrelevant to completion of the house).

Events are numbered progressively in the top sector of the corresponding node, labelling the start node 0 or S (for start) and the first

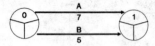

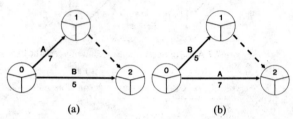

Figure 7.5 Two events should not share both a common tail and head node.

(a)   (b)

Figure 7.6 (a) and (b) indicate two ways of avoiding the difficulty in Fig. 7.5.

head node emanating from it 1, and so on. The final node is labelled either F (for finish) or with the highest node number for the system.

7.3.3 Dummies

We mentioned the convention that two activities must not share the same tail and head nodes. Thus, if I go out and make a cup of tea (activity A taking seven minutes) while my computer prints out the draft of this chapter (activity B taking five minutes), these should not be indicated in a two-node diagram with nodes labelled 0 and 1 as in Fig. 7.5. We overcome this difficulty by introducing a new node 1 and relabelling the old node 1 as 2, then linking 1 and 2 by a dummy activity in either of the ways shown in Fig. 7.6(a) and (b). Another important role of dummy activities is to complete logical paths in a network. Suppose we have the following tasks to perform (for simplicity in this illustration we omit the times required). However, there is an order of precedence given in the last column.

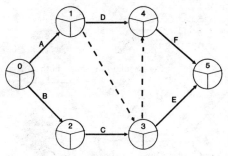

Figure 7.7 A use of dummy activities to preserve the logic of a problem.

Event	Precedents
A	
B	
C	B
D	A
E	A, C
F	C, D

Figure 7.7 is a network representation – our first example of a complete (apart from times) network. Node 0 is the starting node for the network and also the tail node for activities A and B with head nodes 1 and 2 respectively. Since C must follow B (its specified precedent), we may represent C with tail node 2 and head node 3. Since D must follow A, it has tail node 1 and a new head node 4. Now E must follow A and C. This is indicated by joining node 1 to node 3 by a dummy activity. Since F must follow both C and D, we need a dummy activity linking node 3 to node 4. Since E and F must be performed to finish the task, we link these to the final node 5. Although it would be more complicated, and in practice unnecessary,

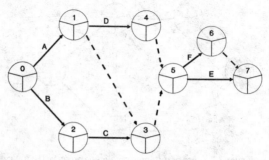

Figure 7.8 A permissible, but not essential, use of dummies connecting nodes 3 and 4 to node 5.

it would still be logical to link nodes 3 and 4 by dummy activities to a new node 5, start activities E and F at the new node 5 and proceed as shown in Fig. 7.8.

Providing the logic is not upset by doing so, it often helps at the initial stages to put in dummy activities fairly freely and some may eventually prove unnecessary. Their effect is to increase the amount of computation needed to establish a critical path, but they can be removed on completing the draft CPA diagram if it is clear that they are not essential. Rules exist (see e.g. French *et al.* 1986: Chap. 6) to determine whether dummy activities may be removed without affecting the logic.

We have explained the rudiments of setting up a network, so try your hand at doing this for Example 7.5. Do so before looking at Fig. 7.9 overleaf. Your version may be correct, yet look very different. If correct, it should be logically (even if not geometrically) equivalent. For example, the following is a potential source of difference that does not affect the logic. In Fig. 7.9, I have connected activity M directly to nodes 10 and 11, and activity N directly from nodes 9 to 11. One could connect M from node 10 to 11 as here, but replace the diagram from nodes 9 and 10 onward by the portion of network shown in Fig. 7.10. If you have had trouble setting up the network, we discuss its construction further in section 7.4.

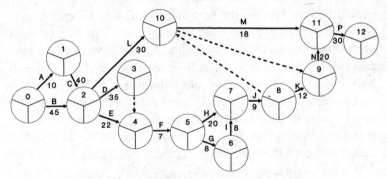

Figure 7.9 A basic CPA diagram for solving a book publishing problem.

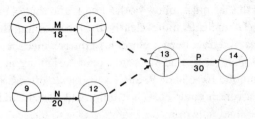

Figure 7.10 A possible modification of the latter part of the network in
Fig. 7.9.

7.4 DETERMINING A CRITICAL PATH

How is our CPA network used to determine what job orderings and
timings are 'critical' for publication in the shortest possible time? To
answer, we must first find the shortest possible time. In Fig. 7.9,
nodes are numbered from 0 to 12. The tail node for any activity
determines the earliest time at which it can start. For example, the
implication of the activity links between nodes 0 (the start) and
nodes 1 and 2 is that A and B may start simultaneously (if we so
wish), so we give each a separate head node (two activities cannot
have the same tail and head nodes). Activity C can only start after
A is complete, so we use the head node for A as C's tail node. We
could, if we like, direct C to a node not so far created, but we choose

node 2 instead, because the next activities D and E depend upon completion of both B and C and can therefore only begin from a node which implies the finish of both of these. Since D and E may proceed simultaneously we direct them to new nodes 3 and 4 respectively, but since F follows completion of both D and E we ensure both are complete by joining node 3 to node 4 with a dummy activity. This join is essential because D takes longer than E; also had we not put it in, D would appear to be a 'dangler' (section 7.3.2), which it certainly is not – the book will not be published if the type is not set! The reader should not find it difficult to follow through the rest of the network, but we draw attention to the dummy activities joining nodes 8 to 10 and 10 to 9. These are needed to comply with the precedents that M must follow both J and L and that N must follow K and L. To indicate more clearly the progression through the network it would have been preferable to interchange the numbering of nodes 9 and 10, so that we could refer to joining node 9 to 10 rather than node 10 to node 9. Such refinements often become clear after the network is completed. It is tidier, but not essential, to make them in the final network.

7.4.1   Minimum publication time

To find the critical path, we need to know, for each activity, its earliest starting time and its latest finishing time if we are to publish the book as quickly as possible. We determine the earliest finishing times by working forward through the network and write these in the lower left sector of each head node. These earliest finishing times become the earliest starting times for subsequent activities with that tail node. These times are included in Fig. 7.11, which represents the same network as Fig. 7.9. The 0 in node 0 is the starting time for the project.

From the data, since A takes ten days we cannot finish A until ten days after the manuscript is received, so we write 10 in the lower left of node 1.

Since B takes 45 days, it is tempting to write 45 in node 2, *but that would not be correct*. We have chosen the event at node 2 to

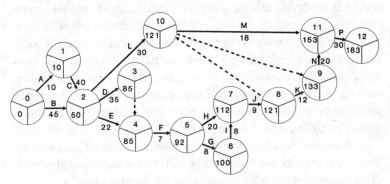

Figure 7.11 Use of a forward pass to determine the minimum publication time.

represent the completion of *both* A and C or the completion of B. Thus the shortest time to reach the event representing completion of both these is the longer of these two times. Now A and C take $10 + 40 = 50$ days, which is more than the 45 days taken for B alone. Thus, the shortest time to do everything needed before we can proceed with the activities D, E, L, which use node 2 as a tail, is 50. Proceeding in this way, it takes another 35 days (the time to complete activity D), to reach node 3, so the minimum total time (from the start) to completion of activity D is $50 + 35 = 85$ days. Event 4 occurs after completion of *both* D and E (plus of course the 'no-time' dummy activity linking 3 and 4). The route $2 \rightarrow 3 \rightarrow 4$ takes the longer time (35 compared to 22 for activity E), so node 4 can only be reached after $50 + 35 = 85$ days. It takes another seven days to reach node 5 by the only route, giving an earliest time of 92. We proceed in this way through the network, remembering that if there are two or more routes into a node we must take the time via the longest route. Checking, you will find the earliest time we can reach node 12 and publish the book is 183 days after delivery of the manuscript. This is useful information, but the publisher will want to know which are the vital activities he must start as soon as each becomes possible if he is to keep to that schedule. Some activities need not be started at the earliest possible dates, or may take extra time without affecting the final completion date. For example, providing the publisher is not slow in starting the job, design of the cover (activity L) will not hold up book production if it takes 40 days rather than 30, but there will be a delay if the author takes 20 days instead of eight over his proof correction (activity G). To decide which activities must be kept to schedule, we determine the latest possible starting date for each activity if we are to finish on time. This is another situation where we work backwards (cf. section 7.2). The book must be finished on day 183. We write this in the lower right sector of the finishing node, node 12. Working back to node 11 we must start activity P at least 30 days before the book is completed (the time taken for that activity), i.e. on day $183 - 30 = 153$. The next backward step to node 10 takes a bit of care. Task M takes 18 days and $153 - 18 = 135$. But there is another path from node 10 to node 11, namely via node 9, and it takes 20 days to work from 9 to 11, therefore, we must be at node 9 after $153 - 20 = 133$ days; this implies we must also be at node 10 by day 133, because of the dummy activity from node 10 to node 9. When there are two (or more) routes leading from a tail node to a head node, the latest date on the tail must allow us to traverse the longest route (in terms of time) and keep on schedule for the start of later activities. For node 8, the latest start time is $133 - 12 = 121$. Proceeding backward in this way, we get the latest start times at all earlier nodes. These are shown in the lower right sector of all nodes in Fig. 7.12.

For many of these nodes, specifically nodes 0, 1, 2, 3, 4, 5, 7, 8, 9, 11, 12, the earliest and latest start times coincide. These determine what is known as a *critical path*. Any delay in the activities A, C, D, F, H, J, K, N, P directly joining these nodes will delay publication of the book. We express this by saying the critical path is ACDFHJKNP. A critical path need not be unique. For example, if activity G had taken 12 days instead of eight, node 6 would also have been critical and the route nodes $5 \rightarrow 6 \rightarrow 7$ and $5 \rightarrow 7$ direct would both require associated activities to start at the earliest possible time.

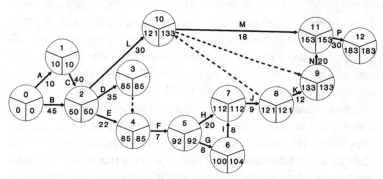

Figure 7.12 Addition of a backward pass to determine critical paths and floats.

On the other hand, since node 10 is not on the critical path, the start of activity L could be delayed appreciably without holding up publication. Inspecting node 10, we see that activities with heads at that node certainly need not be completed until 121 days (the earliest starting time) and indeed completion may be delayed until 133 days (the latest starting time from node 10). If activity L only takes 30 days, there is no slippage in completion time of the whole project providing we start L before day 91. We only need to do this if we want to start activity M after 121 days. Further, unless there are special reasons for starting activity M before day 133, there is no harm in delaying completion of L to day 133, and, if we do this, we may delay the start of L to day 103, providing we keep to the scheduled 30 days for completion. In practice, a publisher resolves a matter like this in the light of available resources and other demands on time.

This flexibility, which applies only to activities not on the critical path, is referred to as *float*. We see that we can start activity L at day 50 (node 2), but to finish it at the earliest finishing time for node 10 we need not start until day 91, leaving a 'float' of $91 - 50 = 41$ days. If we are prepared to finish L only at the latest start time at node 10 of 133 days, we need start only on day 103, giving a float of $103 - 50 = 53$. The first float may be calculated as (earliest head time) $-$ (earliest tail time) $-$ (duration) $= 121 - 50 - 30 = 41$; the second float as (latest head time) $-$ (earliest tail time) $-$ (duration) $= 133 - 50 - 30 = 53$. There is one other type of float, namely (earliest head time) $-$ (latest tail time) $-$ (duration). In our example, this last float is $121 - 50 - 30 = 41$ and is identical in value with the first float we calculated. This is not always so. The three types of float are called respectively the *free float*, the *total float* and the *independent float*. Think carefully what these different floats represent. The total float represents the maximum possible start delay that can occur in a given activity without increasing the critical path length or total duration. The independent float is the maximum delay that can be incurred in an activity without placing any constraints on other activities. The free float is the maximum delay that can be incurred on an activity without placing constraints on *later* activities in the network.

7.4.2 Floats and critical paths

For activities on a critical path all three floats are necessarily zero. However, for an activity such as B, which links two nodes on a critical path, but which is not itself part of the critical path, there is a total float of $50 - 0 - 45 = 5$. This is also in this particular case the value of the free float and the independent float, although in general all three floats will not be equal. Table 7.3 lists each float for Example 7.5.

We have indicated only the simplest form of critical path analyses. The basic principle may be extended to study the effect of altered activity times. If, for instance, in Example 7.5, the time for activity G was increased from eight to 15 days, then this would alter the critical path and the total time to publication. This occurs because the total float associated with G is only 4, and changing the activity time by seven days (from eight to 15) exceeds the total float. Under these new conditions, activity H would no longer be on the critical path. In Exercise 7.7, we explore the implications of this change.

Table 7.3 Floats for Example 7.5.

Activity	ET	LT	EH	LH	D	TF	FF	IF
A*	0	0	10	10	10	0	0	0
B	0	0	50	50	45	5	5	5
C*	10	10	50	50	40	0	0	0
D*	50	50	85	85	35	0	0	0
E	50	50	85	85	22	13	13	13
F*	85	85	92	92	7	0	0	0
G	92	92	100	104	8	4	0	0
H*	92	92	112	112	20	0	0	0
I	100	104	112	112	8	4	4	0
J*	112	112	121	121	9	0	0	0
K*	121	121	133	133	12	0	0	0
L	50	50	121	133	30	53	41	41
M	121	133	153	153	18	14	14	2
N*	133	133	153	153	20	0	0	0
P*	153	153	183	183	30	0	0	0

Earliest tail times (ET), latest tail times (LT), earliest head times (EH) and latest head times (LH), duration (D) of each activity in Example 7.5 and total float (TF) = LH − ET − D, free float (FF) = EH − ET − D and independent float (IF) = EH − LT − D for activities in Example 7.5. ET, LT, EH, LH and D may be read from Fig. 7.12. Activities marked with an asterisk lie on the critical path and all floats for these are zero.

There are many variants of CPA grouped under the title of *programme evaluation and review techniques* – PERT for short. PERT covers problems where activity times may be varied (often at additional cost) and assessment of cost changes if we depart from or modify the critical path.

7.5 (ALMOST) INSOLUBLE SCHEDULING PROBLEMS

We have outlined some important scheduling problems where we arrive at a satisfactory solution without examining every possible schedule. These are usually large in number. For example, if a doctor had to treat ten patients all requiring different treatment times and wanted to minimize the average wait and knew nothing of the results in section 7.1 and tried to find the best solution by writing down all possible treatment orders and calculating the average for each, he would have to make 3 628 800 such calculations (this equals the number of allocations of ten people to ten tasks; see Table 5.3). Even a modern computer would take quite a time to compute these. Many scheduling and sequencing problems cannot be solved by simple procedures like Lawler's algorithm. An apparently simple problem that has intrigued mathematicians and which might well take many years for even a large computer to solve if all of a large number of sequences had to be examined for a network of any size is called the *travelling salesman problem*. The salesman has to start from his base A and visit n cities at least once before returning to base. All are connected to one another by roads and mileages between each are known. The problem is to determine a routing that minimizes his total mileage. If you think it sounds simple try an example with, say, six cities and some known mileages. (Note that the roads need not be straight between the cities, so the triangle property that the distance from A to C direct must be no greater than the sum of the distances from A to B and B to C need not hold.) So far, there is no 'easy to use' algorithm to solve this problem and at least partial enumeration of all possible routings is required.

7.6 WHAT AND WHERE?

What skills have we mastered?

We know that we minimize average processing (including waiting) time for consecutive operations on a single machine by sequencing in increasing order of machine processing time. With penalties for lateness or tardiness, etc., we may prefer (or only be easily able) to minimize maximum lateness or tardiness rather than average lateness or tardiness. Even if minimization of maxima is not our ideal objective, a small maximum may indicate a reasonable *modus operandi* and, in the case of tardiness, is often an easy solution using Lawler's algorithm.

Critical path analysis (CPA) may be used to determine minimum completion time for a complex operation consisting of a number of tasks with constraints upon the order in which they are carried out. *Floats* are important measures of freedom (if any) in start times of activities if completion of the whole process is not to be delayed.

Where can I read more?

Nearly all books on operational research have chapters on CPA (e.g. French *et al.*, 1986: Chap. 6; Moore, 1986: Chap. 2; Waters, 1989: Chap. 5); see also Lucey (1988: Chaps. 23–27) for an extended range of managerial applications. Scheduling problems are discussed in French *et al.* (1986: Chap. 5) and Waters (1989: Chap. 7).

EXERCISES

Exercises 7.1 to 7.6 refer to consecutive processing on a single machine.

7.1   In Example 7.2, determine the average wait + processing time for the sequencing used. Compare this with the average for a sequencing that minimizes this average.

7.2   In Example 7.2, if the sequencing used were that which minimized the average wait + processing time, determine the average stock-out time.

*7.3   If we wish to minimize the number of jobs that exhibit (positive) tardiness when we are given processing time and due dates (e.g.

expected time to stock-out) for each, the following algorithm achieves this.

1. Form the schedule for processing in increasing order of due date. If no job is late, this is a (not necessarily unique) optimal solution. Otherwise, proceed to 2.
2. Identify the first late job in the schedule and the job with longest processing time up to and including that job. Proceed to 3.
3. Remove the longest processing time job identified in 2 to the end of the sequence and update the schedule accordingly. If there are still late jobs other than any already removed to the end of the schedule, return to step 2; otherwise, the solution is optimum.

Apply this algorithm to the following example to determine the minimum number of jobs exhibiting tardiness.

Due date	2	3	5	7	11	13	16
Process time	6	2	3	1	2	1	1

7.4 In section 7.2.3, we mentioned (without proof) that Lawler's algorithm led to scheduling in order of increasing due dates as the solution that minimized maximum tardiness. Set up an appropriate form of Lawler's algorithm to establish that it gives such a solution for the data in Exercise 7.3. What is the least maximum tardiness?

7.5 By how much is the maximum tardiness increased above its minimum for the data in Exercise 7.3 if we take a solution that minimizes the number of jobs with positive tardiness?

*7.6 Use Lawler's algorithm to schedule the six jobs J_1 to J_6 to minimize the maximum weighted tardiness $W_i T_i$ given the due dates, processing times, weights (tardiness penalties) and priority constraints below.

Job	Due date	Processing time	Tardiness penalty	Jobs for prior completion
J_1	5	3	2	J_2
J_2	4	4	1	
J_3	8	5	3	J_1
J_4	10	3	2	J_3
J_5	7	2	1	J_1, J_3
J_6	14	1	5	

*7.7 In section 7.4, we pointed out that, if in Example 7.5 we increased the time of activity G from eight to 15 days, the critical path would be altered. Draw the CPA network for this altered problem; determine the new critical path and draw up a table analogous to Table 7.3 for this amended problem.

*7.8 Pie Piper Fast Foods wish to open a chain of restaurants in ten different cities all on the same day so that they can mount a nationwide publicity campaign to coincide with the opening. The activities involved from the day it is decided to launch the project and the times taken for each activity together with any precedent activities are given below. Perform a CPA to determine the earliest

Designator	Description of activity	Duration (wk)	Precedents
A	Purchase sites and arrange renovation contracts	9	
B	Purchase catering equipment, etc.	3	
C	Obtain liquor licences	7	A
D	Carry out basic site construction	9	C

Designator	Description of activity	Duration (wk)	Precedents
E	Arrange auxiliary contracts	5	C
F	Connect gas, water, electricity, etc.	3	D, E
G	Install catering equipment	2	B, F
H	Hire staff	2	C
I	Train staff	4	H
J	Publicity campaign	3	G, H
K	Open	–	I, J

possible common opening date and draw up a table showing the three float times associated with each activity.

*7.9   By how much, if at all, will the opening time of the Pie Piper chain in Exercise 7.8 be affected if either one or both of the following occur:

  (i) time to obtain liquor licences is increased to nine weeks;
  (ii) time required to train staff is reduced to two weeks?

7.10   An insurance company has decided to modernize and refit one of its branch offices. Some of the existing office equipment will be disposed of but the remainder will be returned to the branch on completion of the alterations. Estimates for the alterations are to be invited from a selection of builders and the builder chosen will be responsible for all aspects of the alterations with the exception of the prior removal of the old equipment and its subsequent replacement.

  The major elements of the project have been identified as follows along with their approximate durations and the immediately preceding elements:

	Element	Duration (wk)	Precedents
A	Obtain estimates from builders	5	E
B	Decide on builder to be used	1	A
C	Arrange details with selected builder	2	B
D	Alterations take place	14	K
E	Design new premises	16	—
F	Decide which equipment is to be retained	1	E
G	Arrange storage of equipment to be retained	2	F
H	Arrange disposal of remaining equipment	3	F
I	Order new equipment	2	F
J	Take delivery of new equipment	3	I, L
K	Remove old equipment to storage or disposal	4	C, G, H
L	Clear up after builder has finished	2	D
M	Return old equipment from storage	2	I, L

Required:

(a) Draw a network to represent the interrelationship between various elements of the project.

(b) What is the minimum time that the alterations can take from commencement of the design stage?

(c) It has been suggested that if the number of builders invited to tender were reduced, the estimates could be obtained in three weeks. What effect would this have on the duration of the project?

(d) What is 'independent' float? Do any of the activities in your network possess it, and, if so, which?   [ACCA]

7.11 On 1 September each year, Salemis Limited begins the task of preparing budgets for the coming year. The various stages in the budgeting process have been identified as follows:

	Stage	Preceding stage(s)	Time (wk)
A	Estimate wage rates	—	2
B	Develop a market forecast	—	4
C	Fix selling prices	—	3
D	Prepare sales quantities budget	B	3
E	Prepare sales revenue budget	C, D	1
F	Prepare selling expenses budget	A, D	3
G	Prepare production quantities budget	D	6
H	Prepare overheads budget	A	4
I	Prepare manpower budget	A, G	2
J	Prepare materials budget	G	3
K	Prepare plant and equipment budget	G	5
L	Produce overall profit forecast	E, F, H, I, J, K, L	1

The whole process must be completed by the end of December which gives a period of 17 working weeks.

Required:

(a) Draw a network to represent the sequence of stages involved in the preparation of budgets. Can the whole process be completed within the required period of 17 weeks?

(b) If it is necessary to reduce the time taken to complete the budgeting process, which stages should be investigated and why?

(c) Explain the difference between total float, free float, and independent float. Show that stage 1 has a free float of 3 weeks, of which 2 weeks is independent float.   [ACCA]

8 Network Analysis in Communication Problems

8.1 A MULTI-PURPOSE TOOL

The CPA diagrams in section 7.3 are only one type of network useful for solving practical problems. Railways often display at stations, or in timetables, schematic diagrams where the nodes are named stations and the joining lines indicate a rail service between pairs of stations.

8.1.1 Rail scheduling

Schematic rail diagrams usually omit features like curves in the track; also, lengths of lines connecting stations are usually arbitrary and do not represent distances or journey times. They simply tell us if a journey is possible between two points, and whether we have a choice of routes. If there is a choice, we need a timetable to find the fastest way of getting from station X to station Y, or a fare schedule to determine the cheapest route. We sometimes include additional information on schematic diagrams to help deduce the fastest, shortest or cheapest routes.

Example 8.1   Figure 8.1(a) is a simple diagram featuring all rail routes between five stations A, B, C, D, E (the nodes). A passenger may travel between two stations by any feasible route for which there is a link represented by a joining line in the diagram, e.g. he may travel from A to E via C and D, via B and D, or via B only; or he may travel from A to C direct, or via B and D, or via B, E and D. In these examples and others in this chapter, we exclude routes that involve back-tracking over the same sector, for clearly if one is

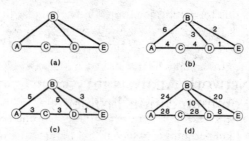

Figure 8.1 (a) Network representation of rail links between five stations A, B, C, D, E; (b) showing distance in kilometres between stations; (c) showing journey times between stations; (d) showing fares between stations.

interested in the shortest, quickest or cheapest route this will not, or need not, involve back-tracking. Londoners familiar with more elaborate 'maps' of this type for the Underground system might sketch a reduced diagram like Fig. 8.1(a) for routes that interest them; e.g. the stations might be Notting Hill Gate (A), Bond St (B), Gloucester Rd (C), Green Park (D) and Oxford Circus (E). The routes between these possible interchange stations are the Central line (AB and BE), the Circle or District lines (AC), Piccadilly line (CD), Jubilee line (BD) and Victoria line (DE).

Whether it is part of the London Underground or any other system, Fig. 8.1(a) is little help to a passenger interested in shortest, quickest or cheapest routes without more information. What is needed depends upon whether one wants to travel as quickly or as cheaply as possible. If trains are frequent on all routes and run at the same speeds on each, knowing the distances between all stations will give the fastest routing between any two. If trains run at different speeds between the various stations, the choice for fastest journey depends on the times taken between each station. If there is a different frequency of service on the routes, one will have to allow for this in selecting the fastest route. Fares for each routing must be known to select the cheapest. The simplest fare structure is one where fares between stations are additive, e.g. if the fare from A to B is 30 pence and that from B to C is 40 pence, then the fare from A to C via B is 70 pence (this simplicity does *not* hold for many rail systems). We now assume there is a frequent service on all routes and ignore delays due to waiting for trains in determining the quickest route. In Fig. 8.1(b), we show alongside each line the distances in kilometres between neighbouring stations. Figure 8.1(c) gives the time in minutes trains take to traverse each sector. It is implicit in Figs. 8.1(b) and (c) that the trains run at different speeds on some sectors than on others: on some they cover more than 1 km per minute, on others less than 1 km per minute. On one sector, they cover exactly 1 km per minute (which is it?). Figure 8.1(d) shows the fare in pence between each pair of stations, these fares being additive in the sense described above. The shortest route (Fig. 8.1(b)) from A to E is A to B to E (6 + 2 = 8 km).

Exercise What are the alternative route mileages from A to E?

The shortest route from A to E is not the quickest. It is evident from Fig. 8.1(c) that the journey would take one minute less using the route A to C to D to E. Inspection of Fig. 8.1(d) shows that neither the shortest nor the quickest route is the cheapest.

Exercise What is the cheapest route?

The above deductions were easy because we only had to examine three routes from A to E: we look at all three and pick the best *for each criterion* shortest, fastest, cheapest. We could have put the separate information in Figs. 8.1(b), (c), (d) on one diagram by writing three numbers alongside each sector representing distance, time and fare in that order. While logical, this would not be aesthetically pleasing and care is needed to pick the right number when making deductions.

8.1.2 Basic properties of networks

Two important properties we explicitly or implicitly assumed in Example 8.1 for distance, time or fares were

(i) each was additive over different sectors of the network;
(ii) none was negative.

Although we represented the links between say B, D, E by a triangle, the Euclidean triangle addition law (the length of any two sides exceeds that of the third) does not necessarily hold for distances, etc.; e.g. the cost from B to D plus D to E is not greater than the cost from B to E direct (Fig. 8.2(d)). This is because we do not relate the physical length of the links to the numbers we associate with that link. This lets us use the same *geometric diagram* when considering distances, time or cost.

Although we found different optimal routes by minimizing distance, time and cost, our method for determining each optimum was essentially the same. For this reason, in many transport or communication problems, we conveniently think of minimizing a 'cost' or 'penalty'. In some problems, we replace 'penalties' by 'rewards' that we wish to maximize.

8.1.3   Complex penalties

Motoring or tourist organizations may recommend best routes between towns by assigning to each some arbitrary measure of 'cost' arrived at by considering a complex of factors depending on the physical nature of alternative routes, traffic densities, safety factors and even aesthetic considerations. Between two points where there are several good roads, choice may be made on minimum mileage. If congestion is likely to be worse on one road than on another, travel time may be the key criterion, while in other sectors safety or meteorological factors (incidence of ice, snow, fog) may be given some weight on alternative routes that require about the same time or are of similar mileage. All other factors being equal, a more scenic route may be preferred. In determining optima for a national road network, one has moved a long way from the simple example of Fig. 8.1.

Example 8.2   Figure 8.2 is a transportation network showing road connections between a potential starting point (labelled S) and two final destinations (labelled F_1 and F_2). The straight lines connecting nodes (towns) represent *all* road connections

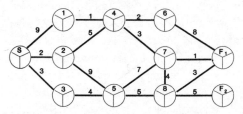

Figure 8.2 A network of routes between S and F_1 and F_2 via intermediate nodes showing penalties associated with traversing each segment.

between intermediate towns. For later convenience, we have divided each node into three sectors with the node number in the top sector. We are interested in the best routes from S to either final destination in the sense that it minimizes the sum of the 'costs' associated with each route sector. Sector costs are indicated by the numbers written beside the line joining each node; they are assumed to be additive. If we sometimes make trips from S only to one of the intermediate towns 1 to 8, we shall be interested also in the shortest route to each of these in terms of our chosen cost measure.

Costs may be mileages, times, bus fares or charges per ton to transport material over each sector, etc., expressed in some appropriate unit.

The network in Example 8.2 is trivial compared to one facing, say, a motoring organization wanting to determine optimum routes from a capital city to the 100 largest towns in a country, or for a manufacturer who wants to determine optimum routings (to minimize costs) from his factory in Birmingham to any city in the European Community that has a population over half a million. Such jobs require a computer for a reasonably quick solution, although the UK Automobile Association produced route advice for its members long before the computer era. Even for the simple network in Fig. 8.2, it is a little harder than it was in Example 8.1 to see the optimum route from S to F_1 or F_2 – perhaps also not quite obvious that, although node 3 is on the optimum route to node 5, it is not on the optimum route to node 7; also, whereas node 4 is on the optimum route both

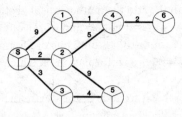

Figure 8.3 Truncated portion of the network in Fig. 8.2.

to node 6 and to F_1, node 6 is not on the optimum route to F_1. Clearly the problem becomes more complicated with additional nodes. Take another look at Fig. 1.3 (p. 11).

When we know our costs for each sector (be it mileage, time, charge or a composite factor) and these are non-negative and additive, there is an algorithm that may be programmed for a computer to determine a best route from any starting node in a network to all other nodes. We say *a* best route, for sometimes more than one routing gives minimum cost. It usually suffices to find one of these, but some computer programs find them all.

Example 8.3   We illustrate the algorithm, known as Dijkstra's algorithm, for an abridged portion of the network in Fig. 8.2, involving only the nodes S, 1, 2, 3, 4, 5, 6 (Fig. 8.3). It is easier to describe it by an example than it is to set it down formally. Failing an available computer program, it can be done with a pencil and eraser. You should work through the procedures given below on a copy (e.g. a photocopy) of Fig. 8.3, although in Fig. 8.4 we illustrate the algorithm step by step.

Solution   We now fill in the remaining lower node sectors, starting by putting zero in the lower left sector of each node. In the lower right sector of S, we also put zero. In the lower right sector of all other nodes, we put L (for *large*) to represent a number much greater than the total cost of travelling from S to that node by any route (many writers use ∞, the mathematical symbol for infinity, in this context). Computers, however, understand a specific large number better than they do the mathematical abstraction of infinity. Our algorithm now starts at node S and works out the cost of getting to other nodes by various routes until one of minimum cost is found. At the same time, it records information on which route is taken for minimum cost.

It costs nothing to get to node S, for we are there at the start. We shall put current calculated minimum costs of reaching any other node from S in the lower right sector of that node. As we already have 0 in the lower right sector of node S, we have finished with this node; to remind us, we put a slash through it. These steps complete the formation of Fig. 8.4(a). Next, we work out the cost of getting to each of the nodes 1, 2 and 3 connected directly to node S. It costs 9 units to get to node 1. When we make a step like this, the rule is to compare this new cost with the entry in the bottom right of the node we are going to: if the new cost is smaller, we replace what is in the bottom right with this new cost. Because L is larger than any cost, we replace L by the smaller 9 at node 1. We also replace the zero in the lower left segment by S to remind us that we calculated the cost 9 by routing *directly* from node S. We refer to the previous node on any route as the preceding node. Similarly L at node 2 is replaced by 2 (the cost of travelling from node S to node 2) and L at node 3 is replaced by 3. In both these cases, we replace 0 in the bottom left sector by S, the preceding node. We now know the cost of travel from node S to each of nodes 1, 2 and 3 by all possible direct routes to them from node S. The one with lowest cost is node 2; we strike this out as we now clearly have the cheapest route to node 2 since any other route to node 2 starting from S (e.g. S to 1 to 4 to 2) must cost more since it would have necessarily to pass through node 1 or node 3 and is therefore inevitably a more expensive route to node 2. The situation now is that in Fig. 8.4(b). Having struck out node 2 with an established lowest cost route to it from S, we examine all routes leading from node 2 to nodes not already struck out; these are nodes 4 and 5. We calculate the cost of reaching these from node S via node 2 by adding the route cost from node 2 to the already established minimum cost (2) given in the lower right segment of node 2. For

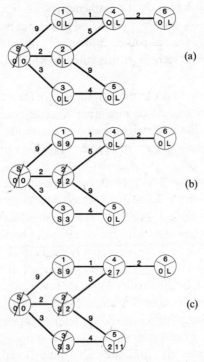

Figure 8.4 Successive stages in applying Dijkstra's algorithm to determining minimum penalty route for traversing the network in Fig. 8.3.

node 4, the cost is 2 + 5 = 7 and for node 5 it is 2 + 9 = 11. These
are both smaller than L, so we replace L in each case by these new
values. Also, to remind us that we reached these totals by travelling
via node 2, we replace the zeros in the bottom left segments of nodes
4 and 5 by 2. We examine all nodes not yet struck out to find the one
with the lowest total cost (bottom right segment). Clearly this is now
node 3 with a total cost of 3. We strike this out and do not need to
consider it further. The situation is now represented by Fig. 8.4(c).
The only relevant route (Fig. 8.4(c)) from node 3 to a node not yet
struck out is that to node 5. Since the minimum cost of getting to
node 3 from S is 3 and it costs 4 units to proceed directly from 3 to

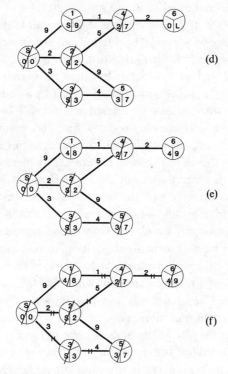

Figure 8.4 Continued.

5, the cost of arriving at 5 by this route is $3 + 4 = 7$. This is less than the cost 11 currently (Fig. 8.4(c)) in the bottom right, so we replace that 11 by 7. We also replace the 2 in the bottom left of node 5 by 3 to indicate we proceed from node 3 for this minimum. This has been done in Fig. 8.4(d). Among nodes not yet struck out, nodes 4 and 5 tie for lowest cost. We may strike out either. As computers like a formal rule, we adopt the convention that in the case of a tie we strike out the node with the lower (or if more than two nodes tie, the lowest) node number. Here it is node 4, so we strike that out; we are now at the stage illustrated in Fig. 8.4(d). We repeat the cycle, calculating the cost of proceeding via node 4 to node 6 and node 1, the only nodes connected to it and not yet struck out. Clearly the cost to node 6 is $7 + 2 = 9$, which is less than our large cost L. We replace L at node 6 by 9 and 0 by 4 to indicate we arrived at the cost 9 by travel from node 4. Similarly, for travelling to node 1 via node 4, the cost is $7 + 1 = 8$, which is less than the current value 9, so we replace the 9 in the bottom right of node 1 by 8 and the S in the bottom left by 4 to indicate we arrived at the cost 8 by proceeding from node 4. At this stage only nodes 1, 5 and 6 are not struck out, and the lowest total, 7, is associated with node 5, so this is struck out. The position is shown in Fig. 8.4(e). Here clearly there are no paths from node 5 to other nodes not already struck out, so we move immediately to the node with the next lowest total which is node 1. Again, when this is struck out, there are no paths from it directly to other nodes not already struck out. Only node 6 remains, and as this is the last node we may formally strike it out as requiring no further attention. The figures in the lower right sector of each node tell us the minimum costs (distance, time or whatever) for travelling from S to that node. The situation is now that shown in Fig. 8.4(f).

To establish routes of minimum cost from S, we work backward starting conventionally at the highest node number, or if we have specifically labelled one with an F (for *finish*), at such a node. We use the 'preceding node numbers' in the lower left segment of each node. From Fig. 8.4(f), the preceding node for node 6 is 4, so we mark the path joining node 4 to 6 by a double slash and now examine node 4, where we find a 2 in the bottom left indicating node 2 is the preceding node, so we double slash the line joining nodes 2 and 4. Node 2 tells us the preceding node is S, so we slash the join of S to node 2. The highest node number not yet dealt with is node 5, so we examine it: we see the minimum cost for node 5 is achieved by proceeding from node 3, so we slash the join of node 3 to node 5. From node 3, we similarly proceed back to S, so we slash the join S to 3. We now have slashed routes from S to all nodes except node 1. Inspecting node 1, we see that the lowest cost route proceeds from node 4, so we slash the join of node 1 to node 4. We need proceed no further, for we already know the optimum route to node 4, as it was determined as part of the route to node 6.

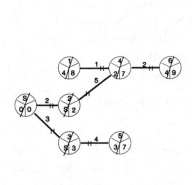

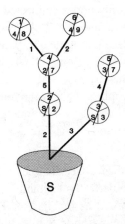

Figure 8.5 Optimum routings from S to other nodes in Fig. 8.3 may be represented as a tree diagram.

Figure 8.6 A more emphatic illustration of the tree structure shown in Fig. 8.5.

You may not be surprised that the routes from node S to node 1 and from node 2 to node 5 are non-optimal, for these are the highest cost segments. However, it must be emphasized that, particularly in larger problems, one may sometimes find that some low cost segments are not used while some high cost ones are included. Indeed, it is easily verified in this example that, if the cost from node 4 to node 1 had been 3 instead of 1, all other costs being as given, the routing from S to node 2 to node 4 to node 1 would not be optimal, while the route S to node 1 would become optimal.

8.1.4 Trees

Figure 8.5 summarizes the optimum routes from S to all other points (obtained by omitting unslashed routes in Fig. 8.4(f)). It has the important characteristic that, starting from node S, once we reach a branching point a route never rejoins the one from which it branched. In operational research jargon, such a network

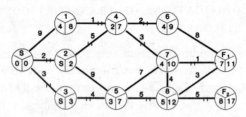

Figure 8.7 Dijkstra's algorithm applied to Example 8.2.

is called a tree. It does not look much like a tree in Fig. 8.5, but it is perfectly legimate (since lines and angles are arbitrary) to redraw it as in Fig. 8.6. This looks more like a conventional tree. Assigning node S to a flower pot is an option omitted by sedate mathematicians.

8.1.5 The main problem

Back now to Example 8.2 and the network in Fig. 8.2; in Example 8.3, we truncated this network by omitting nodes 7, 8, F_1, F_2 and any routes between them, or between them and earlier nodes. A solution for the full network requires a few amendments to, and extensions of, the results for Example 8.3. If we extend a network, we cannot assume the solution obtained for a reduced network will pertain to the corresponding part of the extended network (for there may be cheaper routes to some nodes on the old network that involve the newly introduced sectors and nodes). However, in this example, it turns out that optimum routes from S to nodes 1 to 6 are unaltered. We leave it as an important exercise (Exercise 8.1) to establish the optimal solution indicated by double slashes in Fig. 8.7. Had the cost of travelling from node 5 to node 8 been 7 instead of the given 5, it would have been equally cheap (cost 14) to reach node 8 by the route S, 2, 4, 7, 8, or the route S, 3, 5, 8, or even the route S, 2, 4, 7, F_1, 8, and by implication equally cheap to reach F_2 by any of those routes, demonstrating not surprisingly that a minimum cost route need not be unique.

8.2 MODIFICATIONS OF TRANSPORT COST NETWORKS

To determine optimum minimum cost routes not from a specific starting node S in a network, but from every node to every other node, we could apply Dijkstra's algorithm repeatedly for each different starting node, but a more efficient algorithm exists (see French *et al.* 1986: Chap. 7). However, several modifications of the minimum cost problem can be solved by adapting Dijkstra's algorithm.

8.2.1 Minimum altitudes

Example 8.4 The numbers beside the lines in Fig. 8.8 represent the maximum height (in thousands of feet) of mountain passes on each route sector. Since the likelihood of any pass being blocked by winter snow increases with altitude, a trucking company wishes to determine the route between S and F such that the maximum height of any pass used is as low as possible.

This is another example of a minimax problem (section 7.2.3). In essence, every route from S to F requires the use of several passes, one of which has the maximum height for that complete route. We wish to compare the maxima for all possible routes and select the route with the lowest maximum i.e. the *minimax*.

We modify Dijkstra's algorithm this way. At each step, we seek a route to a given node such that the height of the highest pass on that route is as small as possible. We illustrate this for Example 8.4. Figure 8.9(a) is developed from Fig. 8.8 and closely follows the layout of Fig. 8.4(a). Here L is again a larger number than the height of any pass. We start at node S and compare the pass heights on routes to all nodes connected to S with the current value at that node; e.g. since L is large and the highest pass from S to 1 is of height 5 (5000 ft) we replace L at node 1 by 5, and the 0 in the lower left by S to indicate that we are routing from S. Similarly, for node 2, we replace L by 3, and 0 by S at node 2. At this stage, we formally strike out node 0 in Fig. 8.9(a), and in Fig. 8.9(b) we see that the lowest pass height in the lower right sector of a node not yet struck out is

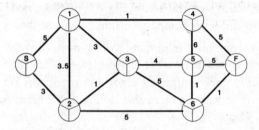

Figure 8.8 The network considered in Examples 8.4 and 8.5.

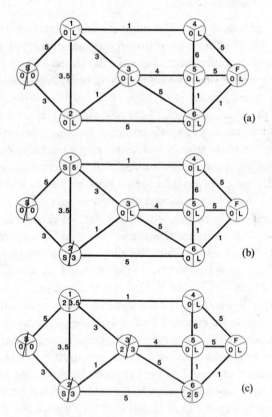

Figure 8.9 First three stages in the solution of Example 8.4.

3 at node 2, which we strike out in Fig. 8.9(b). Since node 2 is joined to nodes 1, 3 and 6, we compare current heights at these nodes with what they would be if we proceed via node 2. If we proceed to node 1 from node 2, the greatest pass height involved is 3.5 (the greater of the current maximum (3) at node 2 and the height of the pass (3.5) connecting node 2 to node 1). Since this is less than the value 5 at node 1 in Fig. 8.9(b), we replace 5 by 3.5 at node 1 (Fig. 8.9(c)). The L at node 3 is replaced by 3 (maximum of the current node 2 value (3) and that of the route connecting node 2 to node 3 (i.e. 1)). Similarly, the L at node 6 is replaced by 5. In Fig. 8.9(c), at each of nodes 1, 3, 6 in the lower left segment, we write 2 to indicate the values were arrived at by travelling via node 2. We now strike out node 3 in Fig. 8.9(c) since this has the lowest pass height among nodes not yet struck out. We leave it as an exercise (Exercise 8.2) to complete the application of the algorithm to this example. However, we point out that at the next step the value of 3.5 at node 1 is further reduced to 3 if we proceed to node 1 from node 3. It is easily verified by reference to Fig. 8.8 or 8.9 that this corresponds to the route S to 2 to 3 to 1. Figure 8.11(a) shows the final result and the optimal routing is indicated by double slashed lines and is determined by a back scan from F. It is from nodes S to 2 to 3 to 5 to 6 to F and the maximum height on this route is 4 (given in the bottom right sector at node F). Inspection of the route shows that this occurs on the sector between nodes 3 and 5.

8.2.2 Maximizing a restriction

Example 8.5 To show the versatility of network analysis, suppose now that the numbers in sectors in Fig. 8.8 represent not heights of passes but the maximum permitted loads on each road in tons (restrictions being determined by the weakest road structure (e.g. a bridge) on each sector. A trucking company will now be interested in determining a route that allows its trucks to proceed from S to F with as large a load as possible. The maximum load on any route will be determined by the sector with the least maximum

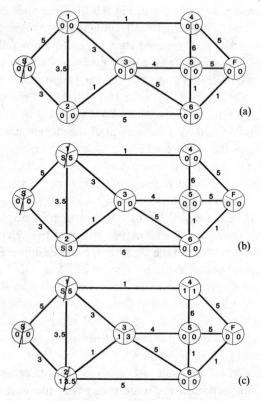

Figure 8.10 First three stages in the solution of Example 8.5.

permitted load. Thus one seeks the route with the greatest 'least maximum permitted' load.

Solution We apply Dijkstra's algorithm in a way not unlike that in our previous example. Figure 8.10(a) indicates our starting point. Since we want to make the load as large as possible, we use as starter values in the lower right of each node, not a load exceeding any real load, but an impossibly small one. The L's in Fig. 8.9(a) are therefore replaced by zeros in Fig. 8.10(a). As usual, the entries in S are formal and we may strike out this node. Node S has

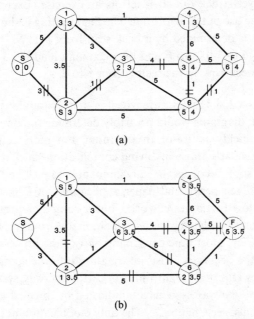

(a)

(b)

Figure 8.11 Final solutions of (a) Example 8.4 and (b) Example 8.5.

links to nodes 1 and 2, and on these routes the respective load maxima are 5 and 3. These are indicated in the usual way in Fig. 8.10(b), and the zeros in the bottom left of these nodes are replaced by S. At this stage, there is another key difference from the last example. We now strike out the node with the *highest* current value in the bottom right sector, since we are seeking a route that will carry as high a load value as possible. Thus we strike out node 1 (Fig. 8.10(b)) and reassess loads via node 1 to all joined nodes not struck out. For example, routing from S to node 1 to node 2 allows a maximum of 3.5 at node 2 (this is the *minimum* of load 5 currently at node 2 and the load of 3.5 on the link from node 1 to node 2). The reader should confirm by a similar argument that the entries at node 3 and node 4 are correctly made in Fig. 8.10(c). The node struck out next is node 2, since it currently has the highest maximum among nodes not yet struck out. It is left as an exercise (Exercise 8.3) to complete the use of the algorithm. The final routing is shown in Fig. 8.11(b) and is determined by a back scan from F to S. It is from S to 1 to 2 to 6 to 3 to 5 to F and the maximum load is 3.5 tons, that restriction occurring in the sector from 1 to 2.

Examples 8.2, 8.4 and 8.5 are trivial in that a careful inspection of the network diagrams would probably determine the optimal route almost as quickly as use of an algorithm. For more complex networks, particularly those involving complications such as one-way routings, it soon becomes virtually impossible to pick best routes by inspection. Even pencil and paper applications of Dijkstra's algorithm are slow for large networks, but a computer program may solve problems involving hundreds of alternative routings in seconds or minutes. The most time-consuming part of the process may well be feeding the necessary 'cost' information into the computer.

How does Dijkstra's algorithm work with one-way systems? Sectors that are one-way systems are indicated by directed joins (as in CPA diagrams; see Chapter 7). The only modification needed to the algorithm is that nodes are assumed to be connected only in the direction of an arrow.

Another modification that may arise, especially if our costs are in the form of time, is that on a two-way route the cost associated with travel from node A to node B may differ from that for travel from node B to node A. We then join the nodes by two directed lines (with arrows) pointing in opposite directions and show the appropriate costs beside each. Different gradients – one uphill, one downhill – or different traffic densities are typical causes of time differences for travel in opposite directions. Figure 8.12 shows a network with a mixture of one-way systems (direction of travel indicated by an arrow), two-way systems with equal costs (joins without arrows), and two-way systems with different costs associated with each direction (indicated by arrows pointing in opposite directions, the different costs being shown beside each arrow). Note that routes from nodes 3 and 4 and between nodes 2 and 6 intersect in Fig. 8.12, but

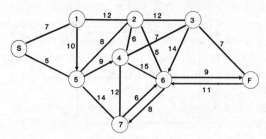

Figure 8.12 A network with some one-way routings and directionally dependent penalties.

that no node is indicated at the intersection. In a road system, this would imply no intersection of these roads (corresponding to a flyover or a junction at which all turns are prohibited).

Dynamic programming, discussed in Chapter 16, provides an alternative approach to the solution of some network problems.

8.3 SOME OTHER NETWORK PROBLEMS

Many other problems are in essence network problems. These include problems of traffic flow, i.e. determining the maximum capacity of a set of roads (or perhaps bridges and tunnels connecting two points) given information about the flow on each sector. The methods employed can be used also to determine maximum flow through complex networks of pipes as in water or gas supply systems. Determination of maximum flow is often based on a principle known as *maximum flow – minimum cut*. The concept of a cut in a network is a division of the nodes into two non-overlapping sets such that one set contains S and the other contains F. The concept is illustrated in Fig. 8.13. Here the lines AB, CD and XY define cuts. However, PQ is not a cut, for S and F are both on the same side of this divide. An important property of a cut is that, if we omit the route segments between all pairs of nodes on opposite sides of the cut, it is no longer possible to travel from A to B (or in the case of a network of pipes or cables there is no possible flow from S to F).

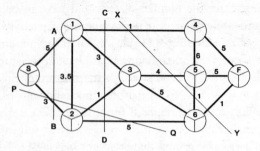

Figure 8.13 AB, CD and XY are cuts. PQ is not a cut.

In Fig. 8.13, the numbers on the edges are the same as those used in Examples 8.4 and 8.5, but here we give them yet another interpretation. We suppose they represent traffic capacity of each road expressed, say, as the number of vehicles (in thousands) per hour which the sector can carry. The minimum cut is a cut that gives the maximum capacity of the road system between S and F. In this example, it is clear that the minimum cut is represented by XY as the flow across the cut, namely $1 + 4 + 1 + 1 = 7$ is less than that across any other cut. This traffic flow (of 7000 vehicles per hour) is the maximum possible between S and F. Whether it would ever be achieved in practice is doubtful, for it depends upon drivers opting for routes that will maximize capacity. However, the concept is important for traffic engineers as it at least indicates where bottlenecks are to be expected in a traffic scheme. It is also of interest, for example, to a police force that wishes to set up road blocks to stop all vehicles that are travelling between S and F. To ensure all vehicles are stopped, a moment's reflection will show that the roads to be blocked must form a cut. For example, if the joins S to 2, 1 to 2, 2 to 3, and 2 to 6 are blocked, then this is not a cut for traffic may route through S to 1 to 4 to F without being stopped. Further, there is no point in setting up blocks on roads additional to those in a cut, for if this is done some traffic will be stopped twice. Also, there is an advantage from the manpower viewpoint of choosing a minimum cut, for the greater the number of cars that have to be stopped if roads are operating at or near their optimum capacity, the greater the number of police required for the job. On the minimum cut, 7000 vehicles an hour is the maximum that will have to be stopped. Had the cut CD (Fig. 8.13) been selected, the maximum possible flow would be $1 + 3 + 1 + 5 = 10$, or ten thousand vehicles per hour, so more police would be required for equally efficient operation of the check. In this latter case, if the roads were at full capacity, the police would stop more cars that were not making the full journey from S to F; in doing so, they may well cause traffic delays that reduce the maximum flow over the minimum cut!

It is easy to spot by 'trial and error' inspection the minimum cut in a simple example like that in Fig. 8.13. However, in more complicated networks, the minimum cut may be far from obvious. Algorithms exist to determine the minimum cut and the flow across it. These are not difficult in principle, but require care and some skill to use. We do not describe them here, but one is described in McLewin (1980: Chap. 11) and there is a more detailed discussion in Appendix 1 of Wagner (1975).

Much of the theory and practice of 'traffic flow' stems from studies of telephone systems and a key element here is the concept of the exchange. In a telephone system with thousands of subscribers, we do not connect every subscriber to every other subscriber by separate lines. It would be inefficient and costly, and many would never be used; Mr Smith of Basingstoke may never want to telephone Mr Brown of Liverpool. Indeed most telephone subscribers wish only to communicate with a very few others. Efficient telephone networking depends upon linking subscribers to local exchanges, which in turn are linked to other exchanges that give access to subscribers in other parts of the system. Each subscriber is connected to one and only one exchange, but exchanges are linked to one another, either directly or through grouping via higher level exchanges. Determination of the number of lines needed to carry traffic between exchanges is a fascinating branch of network analysis, and one we omit reluctantly from this elementary treatment.

8.4   WHAT AND WHERE?

What skills have we mastered?

We have learnt the use of schematic diagrams in the form of networks for optimum routing, using Dijkstra's algorithm to determine routings to minimize cost (in the form of distances, times, fares, etc.). Modifications are available to minimize maxima of some factor such as altitude or to make the best of restrictions imposed by factors such as weight, height or width on vehicles using a route. Networks are easily adapted to allow for one-way flows or direction-dependent costs.

The maximum flow–minimum cut principle is a useful basis for determining network capacity or monitoring flow through a network.

Where can I read more?

French *et al.* (1986: Chap. 7) discuss Dijkstra's algorithm and others in some detail. Potts (1978) gives practical examples of a wide variety of networks. See also the references in section 8.3 for details of maximum flow–minimum cut analysis.

EXERCISES

8.1   Complete the solution of Example 8.2 to determine the minimum cost routing from the stage developed in the text (p. 192).

*8.2   Complete the solution of Example 8.4 to determine the route that involves the lowest maximum altitude.

*8.3   Complete the solution of Example 8.5 to determine the route that maximizes the least maximum permitted load that may be transported subject to the given load restrictions.

*8.4   If the numbers in Fig. 8.12 are sector costs, find the optimum route from S to F. What is the associated total cost? Is your solution unique?

*8.5   Is the optimum route from S to F obtained in Exercise 8.4 the same as that from F to S in Fig. 8.12?

*8.6   Suppose now that in Fig. 8.12 the numbers in the sectors represent the maximum allowable width in metres of vehicles that can use that route (in the directions shown by the arrows for one-way systems, or where different maxima are shown for opposite directions). Determine the optimum route from S to F, so that a contractor can transport loads as wide as possible. What is the widest possible load that can be transported?

8.7   In the situation envisaged in Exercise 8.6, determine the maximum width load that can be transported from F to node 5.

*8.8   If the numbers in Fig. 1.3 (p. 11) represent freight costs (£ per ton) on each sector (all transport is in the direction of the arrows), and costs over sectors are additive, determine a route from S to F that minimizes the total cost. What is the total cost?

8.9   If the data in Fig. 1.3 represent maximum flow through pipes in thousands of gallons per hour of a chemical, what is the maximum hourly flow rate between S and F? [You should be able to find the solution by careful inspection of Fig. 1.3. In more general networks, you will need an algorithm (not given in this book) to determine the minimum cut.]

9 Uncertainty, Probability and Statistics

If a supermarket held all prices steady for the month of August and you bought the same goods each week in that month, you would pay the same each week. This is a deterministic system and in most examples so far in this book we have dealt with deterministic systems – sometimes with tongue (slightly) in cheek by assuming a system is deterministic when strictly it is not, e.g. by assuming that each job will take a pre-specified number of days in CPA (section 7.3).

What if an electrical store sold during each of the last ten weeks respectively 17, 11, 14, 9, 8, 12, 16, 19, 17, 12 washing machines? This does not tell us how many it will sell next week, but we (and the store manager) would be surprised if none were sold, and even more surprised if 100 were sold. Sales forecasts have an element of unpredictability, but past sales give some indication of how things might work out. The unpredictability is often called a *random* element.

What if an opinion poll asserts that, had an election been held last Thursday, 42% of the electorate would have voted Labour. There was no election to test the claim. Do you believe it? If the poll had been conducted by a competent polling organization, it would mean at best we could be reasonably confident that *about* 42% – perhaps something between 40 and 44% – would have voted Labour. Uncertainty arises because the pollsters have interviewed only a sample of voters. Most polls question about 1000 electors chosen to make them more or less typical of all voters. We may also doubt whether all the electors interviewed stated their true voting intention. Taking a sample again introduces a random element.

Most real-world systems have a random element. It may only be incidental: if trains are supposed to depart every hour on the hour, there will be some unpredictable delays, minimal in a well-organized railway system. Many systems, however, are basically random. Checkout times at a supermarket cash desk will vary randomly from customer to customer depending on the size of orders, on whether they pay by cash, cheque or credit card, on the efficiency of the cashier in ringing up items on the till; there may be additional incidental delays due to a missing price sticker or bar code requiring a check with the supervisor, or a customer might dispute the total rung up. There is no preconceived 'correct' or 'ideal' checkout time per customer. Such *essentially* random systems are called stochastic processes. These systems are not without pattern, and because they have a long term stability we get useful information by studying such processes over a reasonable time period. This enables us to make statements along the lines of '95% of all customers take between 25 seconds and 2 minutes 30 seconds to check out and the average checkout time per customer is 57 seconds'. We might make other useful deductions; for example, if the number of customers entering the store between 9 a.m. and 10 a.m. averages about 85 on Mondays and about 147 on Saturdays, we infer that, if there are just enough cashiers on duty on Monday to avoid undue delays, then more will be needed on Saturday.

9.1.1 Probability and statistics

Probability and statistics provide tools to study the consequences of random variability. If you have attended a basic course in probability and statistics, you may find little new in this chapter, whereas, if you have not, the treatment here may seem terse as we concentrate on the minimum needed for applications in the rest of this book. The serious student of mathematics in a business context will have at some stage to delve more deeply into the subject. For other elementary treatments of some of these topics, see e.g. Rowntree (1981) or Sprent (1988b).

9.2   PROBABILITY AND ODDS

There are two kinds of probability: the first is *objective* probability, the other *personal* or *subjective* probability. There is a grey area between the two, but fortunately we may operate on each using the same rules.

Probabilities are associated with *events*, usually possible outcomes of experiments or possible observed states of a system. 'Heads' and 'tails' are events associated with tossing a coin; 'rises' or 'falls' in a stock-market index such as the FTSE 100 (see section 15.3) are events associated with the stock market. A particular event may or may not happen at one particular observation or performance of an experiment. Tossing a coin is a simple experiment. After we toss it, we know whether it fell heads; *a priori* experience tells us it is equally likely to fall heads or tails. We measure probability by a number between 0 and 1 – the nearer that number is to 1, the more likely the event is to happen; the nearer to zero, the less likely. An event certain to happen has probability 1; an event that never happens has probability zero. An event such as 'heads' which is equally likely to happen, or not happen, when a coin is tossed, not unreasonably has probability one-half. Probabilities are closely related to the concept of fair 'odds' in a gambling context; if an event has probability one-half, an even-money bet is fair. If an event has probability $\frac{1}{10}$, odds of 9 to 1 against are fair, in that if one bets repeatedly at these odds one should 'break even' in the long run. In formal mathematics and statistics, probabilities are more widely used than 'odds'; some examination bodies (and many statisticians) frown upon the latter, but in layman terms and in certain modern applications of statistics (e.g. in comparison of the efficacy of drugs) odds is a useful concept.

We write the probability of any event A as Pr(A); here Pr stands for 'probability'. Fair odds against an event with Pr(A) are given by

$$\text{fair odds against A} = [1 - \text{Pr(A)}]/\text{Pr(A)}. \qquad (9.1)$$

Exercises Verify the statements above that fair odds against A corresponding to Pr(A) = 0.5 and Pr(A) = 0.1 are respectively 1 : 1 and 9 : 1. What are fair odds against an event with probability 0.75? If fair odds against an event are 3 : 1, what is the probability the event takes place?

9.2.1 Equally likely outcomes

When we toss a coin, the two possible outcomes heads (H) or tails (T) are equally likely, and Pr(H) = Pr(T) = $\frac{1}{2}$. For a set of n equally likely events, only one of which can occur at a single performance of an experiment, the probability of that one event occurring is $1/n$. For example, if we label each of ten cards with one of the ten digits 0, 1, 2, 3, 4, 5, 6, 7, 8, 9, but they are otherwise identical, then, if one is drawn after shuffling (without the numbers being visible), the probability of drawing any particular number, say 3, is $\frac{1}{10}$, or the odds are 9 to 1 against drawing the card labelled 3. If we have a number of equally likely outcomes, and an event in which we are interested occurs for more than one of these, then the probability of that event is the ratio of the number of favourable outcomes to the total number of outcomes. For example, if we are interested in the probability that the card we draw carries one of the digits 7, 8 or 9, the probability is $\frac{3}{10}$, since three of the ten cards bear one of these digits. More generally, if m out of n equally likely outcomes are favourable to the event A, then the probability that A occurs is m/n. We write

$$Pr(A) = m/n.$$

The *equally* likely proviso is important. Probabilities of the type just described are objective probabilities. The simple experiment of selecting a digit between 0 and 9 such that each has equal probability of selection has many applications in studying industrial and business systems; some of the statistical reasons for this are illustrated in section 9.6 and further applications are given in Chapter 14.

(a)   (b)

Figure 9.1 The two configurations in which a drawing pin may land
when tossed.

9.2.2 More general events

Many events do not involve sets of equally likely outcomes. If a
drawing pin is tossed it may fall in either of the ways indicated in Fig.
9.1; there is no reason to expect each to be equally likely. Indeed
which outcome is the more likely will depend on the shape of the pin.
I tossed a pin 1000 times and found it landed in configuration A of
Fig. 9.1 on 388 occasions and in configuration B on the remaining
$1000 - 388 = 612$ occasions. We call the ratio

$$Fr(A) = \tfrac{388}{1000} = 0.388$$

the *relative frequency* of A. In many situations, the relative frequency
of an event settles down to a fixed value as the number of experiments or observations increases indefinitely. Mathematicians call
this value a *limit*. If this limit exists, it is the probability of A. Had
I tossed the same drawing pin 10 000 times, I might have found
configuration A occurred on 3867 occasions giving $Fr(A) = 0.3867$.
If we are content to express a probability to two decimal places,
clearly in this case it would be reasonable to accept $Pr(A) = 0.39$.
This is an objective probability assessed experimentally.

If we check 1000 invoices from one source and find mistakes in 12
of them, the relative frequency of mistakes is 0.012 and we take this
as an estimate of the probability of mistakes in invoices from that
source. Another way we may look at this is to say that if one invoice
is selected from a very large batch in a way such that any one is
equally likely to be chosen, then the probability that it will have a
mistake is 0.012. The technical jargon for selecting an invoice in this
way is to say it is chosen *at random*.

9.2.3 **Subjective probabilities**

Business decisions are often based on a less precise form of probability called a *subjective* or *personal* probability. We cannot perform an objective experiment to decide today whether a bank's base interest rate will be lower in one month's time, but well-informed bankers and economists may be in broad agreement that this is not likely, a conclusion they reach after considering all the known economic and political indicators and supplementing this information by gut instinct nurtured by experience. It may be that most skilled interpreters of the market would accept that fair odds were 9 to 1 against the rate falling. These odds correspond to a probability of 0.1. Thus if F is the event 'interest rates will fall' we express this as a personal or subjective probability $Pr(F) = \frac{1}{10}$.

Even well-briefed businessmen may not agree that odds of 9 to 1 represent a fair bet. However, there is often widespread agreement that this is not a bad assessment, though some might think $Pr(F) = \frac{1}{12}$ or $Pr(F) = \frac{1}{8}$ to be fairer assessments. Business men often assign such subjective probabilities, at least as a good approximation. A manufacturer may feel strongly that a new model car has an 80% chance of achieving high sales (event H). This can be expressed as $Pr(H) = 0.8$ (expressing 80% as a proportion). How a manufacturer arrives at such an assessment depends upon circumstances. If his company regularly markets new products, long term records may show that about 80% of these have high sales, although it is impossible to be certain how any one new product will sell; an assessment like this is similar to the relative frequency concept of a probability and in that sense is virtually objective. However, in most cases, an assessment of high sales has a greater subjective element; a motor manufacturer, for example, may have the general impression that something like four out of five new models achieve high sales (note that four out of five is 80%), or the conclusion may be based on more specific factors, e.g. a belief that this probability for high sales applies not to all new models, but only to models of the type now being introduced. This could well be the situation for a special type of vehicle such as a four-wheel drive car or a sports model. The probability assessment might also take account of the current or forecast economic outlook, the time of year the model is being launched, how similar it is to other manufacturers' models, what the prospects are in certain export markets. Assessment by such factors is by nature largely subjective. The value of a subjective probability depends largely on how widely it is accepted as reasonable. Even if a precise numerical value is hard to agree, people are often in close agreement about the ordering of probabilities and, in broad terms, whether the probability of a certain event is high, medium or low. For example, if one asks what is the probability that the Prime Minister of the United Kingdom in the year 2000 will be a woman, even astute political observers would disagree on a precise numerical probability, but I suspect most would put this probability at less than one-half. This is because the UK recently had a female Prime Minister; she had already served a near record term and is unlikely to be in office again by the year 2000. It is not obvious who the Prime Minister will be by then, but it is likely to be a person who already has political experience as a member of parliament. Experienced observers might name a dozen potential Prime Ministerial candidates, the majority male. None of these might be the eventual choice, but such considerations suggest odds *greater* than 5 to 1 (probability equivalent $\frac{1}{6}$) against a female Prime Minister might be a reasonable bet. What odds would you accept as fair? The odds against the Archbishop of Canterbury being a woman in the year 2000 would be put by most theologians, indeed by most Christians, as extremely high. Some might put them at 1000 to 1, others at 1 000 000 to 1. Almost certainly, most rational and well-informed people would assign a lower subjective probability to the latter event than they would to Britain having a female Prime Minister in the year 2000.

While people may assign numerically different personal or subjective probabilities for the same event, providing these are assigned on a rational basis, and agreed by those interested to be relevant, each person's subjective probabilities may be manipulated by the mathematical rules used for objective probabilities. The main rules are intuitively reasonable, though care is needed to apply them correctly. We use them to calculate probabilities that cannot be determined by the simple objective or subjective ideas given above.

9.3   MUTUALLY EXCLUSIVE EVENTS AND ADDITIVE PROBABILITIES

There is a simple *addition rule* for *mutually exclusive events*, i.e. only one of which can occur at the one performance of an experiment. If A and B are mutually exclusive with Pr(A) and Pr(B) respectively, the probability that either A or B occurs at one performance is given by

Pr(either A or B occurs) = Pr(A) + Pr(B).

We do not need the more complicated addition rule that holds when events are not mutually exclusive.

Example 9.1   In a check on postal efficiency, it is found that 80% of first class letters are delivered the day after posting and 7% are delivered on the second day after posting. What is the probability a first class letter is delivered within two days of posting?

Solution   Let A be the event 'delivered day after posting' and B be the event 'delivered two days after posting'. 'Delivery within two days of posting' is the event either A or B occurs. By the addition rule

Pr(delivery within 2 days of posting) = 0.80 + 0.07 = 0.87.

Example 9.2   A man has a £500 limit on his store credit card. He is a regular customer and the salesman knows that he never pays cash but charges everything to his card. Assuming he never exceeds his credit limit, if the salesman, when the man walks into the shop, assesses the probability that he will buy a CD stereo unit costing £380 is 0.2 and the probability that he will buy a home computer costing £499 is 0.1, what is the probability he will buy one of these items?

> *Solution*   The rule gives
>
> Pr(buys CD equipment or computer)
>
> = Pr(buys CD equipment) + Pr(buys computer)
>
> = 0.2 + 0.1 = 0.3.

The probabilities are subjective and we would only want to do this calculation if we accept the saleman's assessment. The conditions of the problem make the events mutually exclusive because the man would exceed his credit limit if he bought both.

To save writing, we often abbreviate the event 'either A or B occurs' to 'A or B', whence the addition rule for *mutually exclusive events* may be written

$$Pr(A \text{ or } B) = Pr(A) + Pr(B). \qquad (9.2)$$

A useful special case of the addition rule occurs for an event A and its opposite event, i.e. the event A does not happen, which we denote by A^* (many writers use $\bar{A}$). At any experiment, either A happens with $Pr(A)$ or it does not happen with $Pr(A^*)$. These are mutually exclusive (something cannot happen and not happen at the same time). Also one of the events A or A^* must occur. Thus

$$Pr(A \text{ or } A^*) = Pr(A) + Pr(A^*) = 1,$$

whence $Pr(A^*) = 1 - Pr(A)$, i.e. the probability of any event is (1 − the probability of the opposite event). This apparently trivial result is useful because the probability of A is sometimes easier to calculate directly than that of A^*, or vice versa. From (9.1), it follows that odds against an event A are $Pr(A^*)/Pr(A)$.

9.4 CONDITIONAL PROBABILITIES, MULTIPLICATION AND INDEPENDENCE

We are often interested in the probability that some event occurs when we know another event has already occurred or is occurring simultaneously.

Example 9.3   A machine has two components A and B that are vital in the sense that it stops operating if both fail. It is known from long experience that Pr(A fails on any given day) = $\frac{1}{100}$. Once A fails, there is an extra strain on B, so that the probability the latter fails is now $\frac{1}{40}$. What is the probability the machine breaks down?

Since the above probability that B fails is only relevant after A fails, we say it is a *conditional probability*, i.e. conditional upon A having failed. If we abbreviate the event 'A fails on any given day' simply to A, with a similar notation for B, we refer to 'the event B conditional upon A', which we abbreviate further to B|A. The associated probability is written Pr(B|A). In our example Pr(B|A) = $\frac{1}{40}$.

The probability that A and B both occur is given by the *multiplication rule*:

$$\text{Pr(A and B both occur)} = \text{Pr(A)} \cdot \text{Pr(B|A)}$$
$$= \text{Pr(B)} \cdot \text{Pr(A|B)}. \qquad (9.3)$$

Sometimes one of the above forms is more useful than the other. In Example 9.3, the probabilities for component failure were Pr(A) = $\frac{1}{100}$ and Pr(B|A) = $\frac{1}{40}$, so the probability that both fail and the machine breaks down is

$$\text{Pr(A and B)} = \text{Pr(A)} \cdot \text{Pr(B|A)}$$
$$= \tfrac{1}{100} \times \tfrac{1}{40} = \tfrac{1}{4000} = 0.000\,25.$$

9.4.1 Fail-safe devices

Example 9.3 demonstrates the principle of a 'fail-safe device'. Had there been no back-up component, the probability of a breakdown on any day would be 0.01; with the second or back-up component it reduces to 0.000 25.

If the failure of component B had also had probability $\frac{1}{100}$ irrespective of whether A had failed, we would say the events 'failure of A' and 'failure of B' were independent, and then $\Pr(B \mid A) = \Pr(B)$, so the multiplication rule can be written

$$\Pr(A \text{ and } B) = \Pr(A) \cdot \Pr(B),$$

where we have abbreviated 'A and B both occur' to 'A and B'. So the probability both fail is $0.01 \times 0.01 = 0.000 1$.

The second form of the rule (9.3) implies that, if B is independent of A, then A is also independent of B, i.e. $\Pr(B \mid A) = \Pr(B)$ implies $\Pr(A \mid B) = \Pr(A)$.

9.4.2 Bayes' rule

Sometimes the addition and multiplication rules are both needed. One important case is Bayes' rule given by (9.5) below. The derivation is subtle and not very user-friendly, so if you are prepared to take it on trust go straight to (9.5). Suppose an event B may occur either in association with an event A or in situations where A does not occur. Now 'A does not occur' is the event A* (the opposite event to A). This means that 'B and A' and 'B and A*' are mutually exclusive. Further, if B occurs, then either 'B and A' occurs or 'B and A*' occurs, whence, using (9.2) followed by (9.3), we get

$$\Pr(B) = \Pr[(B \text{ and } A) \text{ or } (B \text{ and } A^*)]$$

$$= \Pr(B \text{ and } A) + \Pr(B \text{ and } A^*)$$

$$= \Pr(A) \cdot \Pr(B \mid A) + \Pr(A^*) \cdot \Pr(B \mid A^*). \qquad (9.4)$$

Turning again to the multiplication rule, we have

$$\Pr(A \text{ and } B) = \Pr(A) \cdot \Pr(B \mid A) = \Pr(B) \cdot \Pr(A \mid B),$$

whence

$$Pr(A\,|\,B) \;=\; \frac{Pr(A)\cdot Pr(B\,|\,A)}{Pr(B)},$$

and, from (9.4), we finally have

$$Pr(A\,|\,B) \;=\; \frac{Pr(A)\cdot Pr(B\,|\,A)}{Pr(A)\cdot Pr(B\,|\,A)\,+\,Pr(A^*)\cdot Pr(B\,|\,A^*)}. \qquad (9.5)$$

Bayes' rule tells us that, if an event B is associated with either an event A or its opposite A*, then if B has occurred, and we know all the probabilities on the right, we can calculate the probability that A (rather than A*) is the associated event. The implications are best seen by an example.

   Example 9.4   In section 9.2.3 (p. 209), we noted that an 80% chance of high sales (H) implied $Pr(H) = 0.8$. The opposite event, low sales, may be denoted by H. We are now told that a market research team may report sales prospects as good (G) or bad (B), and further that they will report prospects good with probability 0.9 if sales are going to be high, i.e. $Pr(G\,|\,H) = 0.9$, or that they will report prospects good with probability 0.25 if sales are going to be low, i.e. $Pr(G\,|\,H^*) = 0.25$. Determine the probability that the market researchers will report good prospects and the probability that sales will be high if they do report good prospects.

   Solution   In our notation, we may rewrite (9.4) as

$$Pr(G) \;=\; Pr(H)\cdot Pr(G\,|\,H)\,+\,Pr(H^*)\cdot Pr(G\,|\,H^*)$$

$$=\; 0.8\,\times\,0.9\,+\,0.2\,\times\,0.25 \;=\; 0.77.$$

Whence, writing (9.5) in the above notation, we have

$$Pr(H\,|\,G) \;=\; \frac{Pr(H)\cdot Pr(G\,|\,H)}{Pr(H)\cdot Pr(G\,|\,H)\,+\,Pr(H^*)\cdot Pr(G\,|\,H^*)}$$

$$=\; 0.8\,\times\,0.9/(0.8\,\times\,0.9\,+\,0.2\,\times\,0.25) \;=\; \tfrac{72}{77} \;=\; 0.935.$$

This implies that, if market research indicates sales prospects are good, then the probability of high sales is 0.935. This means that the odds against high sales are reduced (or the odds in favour increased) over those based on information without market research, since then we had Pr(H) = 0.8, giving odds of $(1 - 0.8)/0.8 = 1:4$ against (or 4 to 1 on). If market research forecasts good prospects, the odds for high sales are reduced to $(1 - 0.935)/0.935 = 1:14.4$ against (or 14.4 to 1 on). The market research has produced useful information. Validity of these calculations depends upon our assertions Pr(G|H) = 0.9 and Pr(G|H*) = 0.25 being reasonable. These will be subjective, but probably based on long term performance of the market research organization. While we hope market researchers will only predict good sales when market prospects really are good, they do sometimes get it wrong! The probability Pr(H) that we attached to high sales before we did the market research is often referred to as a *prior probability*. The probability Pr(H|G) that we attach to high sales after a favourable market research report is called a *posterior probability*.

9.5   RANDOM VARIABLES AND DISTRIBUTIONS

A commuter airline can carry up to 20 passengers on each flight; the numbers carried on any flight will be an integer between 0 and 20. If we observe over a long period the relative frequency with which each number of passengers travel, we may estimate the corresponding *probabilities* that each of these numbers will travel, providing we assume there is no change in the pattern with time (often a rash assumption in view of seasonal fluctuations, economic changes, etc.). When we know these probabilities, we say we know the (*probability*) *distribution* of the numbers of passengers; these probabilities reflect the nature of the 'randomness' in the number of passengers X, which is often called a *random variable*. When we estimate probabilities as long term relative frequencies, we often speak of the distribution more specifically as an *empirical* distribution, empirical meaning determined by observation or experiment. Empirical distributions are common in an industrial context.

Example 9.5 A manufacturer operates six identical machines, each having one component which is subject to heavy wear. In each machine, this component is inspected at the end of each day to see if it needs replacement. For 1000 days, they keep records of the numbers of machines (0, 1, 2, 3, 4, 5, 6) in which the component needs replacement on that day. The records are summarized as

Number replaced	0	1	2	3	4	5	6
No. of days	127	152	175	298	157	43	48

The numbers of times each number of replacements occur are the *absolute* frequencies over 1000 days (note they sum to 1000). We divide them by 1000 to give the relative frequencies, which we take as estimates of probabilities, as follows:

Number replaced	0	1	2	3	4	5	6
Probability	0.127	0.152	0.175	0.298	0.157	0.043	0.048

Note that the sum of these probabilities is 1; it must be since they correspond to mutually exclusive events and one of them must happen. Because they are mutually exclusive, we can use the addition rule to answer questions like the following.

Example 9.6 What is the probability that three or fewer components will need replacement on one day?

Solution The required probability is

Pr(0 or 1 or 2 or 3 replacements)

$= 0.127 + 0.152 + 0.175 + 0.298 = 0.752,$

i.e. there is a probability of approximately 0.75 that three or fewer replacements will be needed on any day.

9.5.1 Expectation and standard deviation

Two important questions about a random variable can be put in non-technical terms:

1. Where is the variable centred?
2. What is the spread of values?

Statisticians use several measures to quantify these ideas. We confine attention almost exclusively to one for each.

The idea of centrality is sometimes associated, not always realistically, with the concept of a 'typical value'. One measure of centrality is the *expected value* or *expectation* (sometimes called also the mean); the *expectation* is the sum of each possible value multiplied by its probability. If we use the symbol X to denote the (random) variable of interest, we denote the expectation by $E(X)$. For Example 9.5,

$$E(X) = 0 \times 0.127 + 1 \times 0.152 + 2 \times 0.175 + 3$$

$$\times 0.298 + 4 \times 0.157 + 5 \times 0.043 + 6 \times 0.048 = 2.527.$$

The expectation is often (but not invariably) somewhere near the middle of the range of values taken by X. This is why it is sometimes called a measure of *centrality*, or a 'typical value'. Of course, it is not typical in the sense that we observe 0, 1, 2, 3, 4, 5, 6 components needing replacement and never 2.527! Another measure of centrality you may meet is the *median* of a distribution, but we do not use it in this book.

The measure of spread we consider is the *standard deviation*. The rules for calculating it are as follows.

1. Multiply each probability by the square of the corresponding X value and add the sum of these products. (This is sometimes called the expectation of X^2, or $E(X^2)$, since it is what the expectation of X becomes if we replace each X value by its square – in this sense it is sometimes regarded as a 'typical value' of X^2).

2. From the sum of products calculated in (1) subtract the square of $E(X)$.
3. Take the positive square-root of the result in (2). This is the standard deviation.

We do not prove it, but in general terms the greater the spread of the X values the higher is the value of the standard deviation.

For Example 9.5, the steps in the calculation are as follows

1. $E(X^2) = 0^2 \times 0.127 + 1^2 \times 0.152 + 2^2 \times 0.175 + 3^2 \times 0.298 + 4^2 \times 0.157 + 5^2 \times 0.043 + 6^2 \times 0.048 = 8.849.$
2. We found above that $E(X) = 2.527$; the square of this is $(2.527)^2 = 6.386$, whence $8.849 - 6.386 = 2.463$.
3. The standard deviation is the square-root of 2.463, i.e. 1.569.

More generally, if a random variable X may take n values (often these will be integers, but this is not essential) $x_1, x_2, \ldots, x_n$, with associated probabilities $p_1, p_2, \ldots, p_n$, then

1. the expectation is given by

$$E(X) = p_1 x_1 + p_2 x_2 + \cdots + p_n x_n; \qquad (9.6)$$

2. the standard deviation is $\sqrt{\{E(X^2) - [E(X)]^2\}}$, where

$$E(X^2) = p_1 x_1^2 + p_2 x_2^2 + \cdots + p_n x_n^2.$$

9.5.2 Theoretical distributions

Another type of distribution that takes a set of n fixed values is a theoretical distribution; these differ from empirical distributions in that the p_i have values assigned by some theory. A very simple distribution of this type is that in which X takes n values $x_1, x_2, \ldots, x_n$ each with an associated probability $p_i = 1/n$. It follows immediately that

$$E(X) = (x_1 + x_2 + \cdots + x_n)/n = \left(\sum x_i \right) \Big/ n.$$

We met Σ in section 6.1, (p. 119). This is simply the average, or arithmetic mean, of the n values of X. Expectation here can be looked upon as a generalization of the idea of arithmetic mean. The standard deviation s in this case reduces to $s = \sqrt{[(\Sigma\,x_i^2)/n - (\Sigma\,x_i)^2/n^2]}$, which, with a little algebraic rearrangement, becomes

$$ s = \sqrt{\left\{\left[\sum x_i^2 - \left(\sum x_i\right)^2 \Big/ n\right]\Big/ n\right\}}, \tag{9.7} $$

a result best thought of in the following words.

1. Square all the x_i and add them; call the sum S_1.
2. Add all the x_i, square their sum and divide by n; call the result S_2.
3. Form the difference $D = S_1 - S_2$, and write $s^2 = D/n$; take the square root to obtain the standard deviation s.

A special case of the above distribution (which in its general form is often referred to as the *uniform distribution*) is where the x_i take the values 0, 1, 2, 3, 4, 5, 6, 7, 8, 9, each with probability $\frac{1}{10}$.

> *Exercise* Verify that in this case $E(X) = 4.5$, $S_1 = 285$, $S_2 = 202.5$ and $s = 2.87$.

In section 9.6, we discuss the role of this distribution in sampling.

9.5.3 The binomial distribution

Another important theoretical distribution where the variable X may take any of the values 0, 1, 2, . . . , n is the *binomial distribution*. It arises when we make n observations (or perform n experiments) at each of which we note whether a certain event, which has a constant probability p of happening, does or does not occur. Its occurrence at one observation does not alter the probability of it occurring at another, i.e. occurrences are independent events. In the n experiments the event will occur r times, r being a number between 0 and n.

For example, if a machine has n similar components and each has a probability p of needing adjustment on a given day, irrespective of whether any other needs adjustment and we examine all n daily, then we might find any number between 0 and n need adjustment. Intuitively we see that the higher the value of p, the more likely we are to observe a high number needing adjustment. If p is known, the probability that we observe a given number needing adjustment on any day is given by the *binomial distribution*. We state the formula for these probabilities without derivation. We denote by X the random variable 'number needing adjustment'; then the probability X takes the value r (where r is one of the numbers 0, 1, 2, . . . , n) is given by

$$\Pr(X = r) = {}^nC_r\, p^r(1 - p)^{n-r}, \qquad (9.8)$$

where ${}^nC_r$ is a shorthand for $[n(n - 1)(n - 2) \cdots (n - r + 1)]/$ $(1 \times 2 \times 3 \times \cdots \times r)$, unless $r = 0$, when ${}^nC_0 = {}^nC_n = 1$.

Some of the terms in numerator and denominator of ${}^nC_r$ may cancel; e.g. ${}^5C_4 = (5 \times 4 \times 3 \times 2)/(1 \times 2 \times 3 \times 4) = 5$. More generally, computation can be saved by noting that ${}^nC_r = {}^nC_{n-r}$.

Example 9.7   A machine has five identical components; the probability that any one of these will need adjusting on a given day is 0.2. What is the probability that 4 or 5 will need adjusting on a particular day?

Solution   Since the outcomes are mutually exclusive, we get the required probability using the addition rule for binomial distribution probabilities with $n = 5$ and $p = 0.2$ (implying $1 - p = 0.8$), i.e.

$$\begin{aligned}
\Pr(X = 4 \text{ or } 5) &= \Pr(X = 4) + \Pr(X = 5) \\
&= {}^5C_4(0.2)^4(0.8) + {}^5C_5(0.2)^5 \\
&= 5 \times 0.0016 \times 0.8 + 0.00032 \\
&= 0.0064 + 0.00032 = 0.00672.
\end{aligned}$$

This implies that on only about 672 days in every 100 000 would we expect to find as many as four or five components need adjusting. Calculation of probabilities for each r gives (rounding probabilities to three decimal places)

Numbers requiring adjustment	0	1	2	3	4	5
Probability	0.328	0.410	0.205	0.051	0.006	0.000

These probabilities sum to unity, as they must (apart from a possible rounding error) for the distribution of any random variable. We could calculate expectation and standard deviation as we did for an empirical distribution, but that is unnecessary, for there are theoretical results for a binomial distribution with specified n and p that give

$$E(X) = np \quad \text{and} \quad s = \sqrt{[np(1 - p)]}.$$

Thus, in Example 9.7, where $n = 5$ and $p = 0.2$, we find $E(X) = 1$ component per day and $s = \sqrt{(5 \times 0.2 \times 0.8)} = \sqrt{0.80} = 0.894$ components per day.

9.5.4 **Poisson processes**

Faults in items often occur at random in the sense that we cannot forecast precisely where they will occur, but they occur independently of one another at a constant average rate. This leads to a long term regularity. For instance, in making glass, a bubble of entrapped air is a common fault that often has these characteristics; in threads, weaknesses that result in breaks may show similar random behaviour. The 'regularity' is that the average or expected number of bubbles per unit area of glass, or the average number of breaks per unit length of thread, remains constant over long production runs. The choice of the unit of area or of length is arbitrary, but for quality glass, unless we choose a very large unit the number of faults per unit area is usually small. Unless the glass were a very cheap kind, where bubbles are of little consequence (e.g. horticultural glass) a manufacturer would not be happy with an average of one or two bubbles per square metre; a figure of between one and three bubbles per 100 square metres would be more acceptable for quality glass. A manufacturer of thread would not be happy with an average of five breaks per 10 metre length; one, two or three breaks per 100 metres might be acceptable, but this would depend on the intended use, and upon what tension had to be applied to cause a break.

When faults occur *at random* (i.e. with a constant long term average rate), the *Poisson distribution* gives the probability for each number of faults per some appropriate unit of area or length. It differs from distributions we have met so far in that there is no theoretically greatest value corresponding to, say, the n in a binomial distribution. In practice, however, we usually deal with situations where the probabilities of faults in excess of a certain number are so small they can be ignored. The mean number of faults per unit area or length is usually denoted by the Greek letter λ (lambda). For any r (where r is zero or a positive integer), if X is the number of observed breaks per unit area, unit length, or whatever, then

$$\Pr(X = r) = e^{-\lambda} \lambda^r / r!$$

where $r!$ (called factorial r) is the product of all the integers between 1 and r, e.g. $4! = 1 \times 2 \times 3 \times 4 = 24$, providing $r \geqslant 1$. If you have a calculator that has a 'factorial' key (usually labelled $n!$), enter 0 and press this key to see what value it gives for 0! It should give the answer 1, for we define $0! = 1$. We met e (the exponential constant) in section 2.3.3.

Example 9.8   Knots in a thread are randomly distributed at an expected rate of 1.5 per 100 metres. If X represents the distribution of knots in 100 metre lengths, find $\Pr(X = r)$ for $r = 0$, 1, 2, 3, 4, 5, 6, 7.

Solution $\Pr(X = 0) = e^{-1.5} = 0.2231$ (since $\lambda = 1.5$, $r = 0$). Have you got an e^x key on your calculator? If not, remember $e = 2.7183$ approximately. Similarly, we find $\Pr(X = 1) = e^{-1.5} \times 1.5/1 = 0.3347$. Again we may work out $\Pr(X = 2) = e^{-1.5} \times (1.5)^2/(1 \times 2) = 0.2510$. There is an easily established recursive relationship that speeds the work with probabilities for higher values of r (see Exercise 9.9), and there are published tables of these probabilities for many values of λ. Continuing calculations, we find $\Pr(X = 3) = 0.125\,5$, $\Pr(X = 4) = 0.047\,1$, $\Pr(X = 5) = 0.014\,1$, $\Pr(X = 6) = 0.003\,5$, $\Pr(X = 7) = 0.000\,7$. These probabilities fall off as r increases. By adding those above, we get $\Pr(X \leqslant 7) = 0.999\,7$, so there is an almost negligible probability for the opposite event, $X > 7$, given by $\Pr(X > 7) = 1 - 0.999\,7 = 0.000\,3$. (This is a good example of using the formula for opposite events A and A*, i.e. $\Pr(A^*) = 1 - \Pr(A)$, given in section 9.3).

Formulae for the expectation $E(X)$ and the standard deviation s are $E(X) = \lambda$ and $s = \sqrt{\lambda}$. In the above example, $E(X) = 1.5$ faults and $s = \sqrt{1.5} = 1.22$. The *Poisson distribution* has many applications. It sometimes provides realistic approximations even when the average rate of occurrence does not quite stay constant.

9.5.5 Random events in time

The Poisson distribution may be applied to events in time. For example, at certain times of day, it is reasonable to assume calls through a telephone exchange are initiated at random at a constant rate per unit time. This may also apply to people, ships, trucks, arriving at some point. For instance, if people arrive singly at a bank or post office, they often do so approximately at random. Although the rate will vary with the time of day, it may well stay fairly constant over limited periods, e.g. from 9 to 10 a.m. If we know that the average rate of arrival is 2.4 customers per minute, we may work out the probability that 0, 1, 2, 3, . . . people arrive in any one-minute interval as it has a Poisson distribution with $\lambda = 2.4$. A process with these random characteristics is called a *Poisson process* and we shall see in Chapter 14 that it is important in studying the behaviour of queues.

So far, we have considered only variables that may take certain discrete values, usually zero or positive integers. If we consider not the number of people arriving per unit time in a Poisson process but the time that elapses between each arrival – often called the inter-arrival time – then, if we can measure it sufficiently precisely, this interval may be anything between a millionth of a second to minutes or hours. Such a variable is said to be continuous.

We do not consider any detailed theory of the distribution of continuous variables here. It suffices for our immediate purposes to say that, if we are studying a Poisson process where arrivals per unit of time have a Poisson distribution with parameter λ, then the inter-arrival times have what is called an *exponential distribution*, which has an expectation $E(X) = 1/\lambda$ (e.g. if there is an average of 2.4 arrivals per minute, the average interval between each arrival is $1/2.4 = 0.417$ minutes (this is 25 seconds). It can be shown that for any positive t_1 and t_2, with $t_2 > t_1$, the probability of an inter-arrival time being between t_1 and t_2 minutes is given by the expression

$$\text{Pr(next arrival in interval } (t_1, t_2)) = \exp(-\lambda t_1) - \exp(-\lambda t_2),$$

(9.9)

where we adopt a commonly used notation of writing $\exp(x)$ instead of e^x to avoid complicated superscripts and subscripts.

Table 9.1 has been prepared using (9.9) for the case $\lambda = 2.4$, i.e. an average arrival rate of 2.4 per minute, or a mean inter-arrival time of $1/\lambda = 1/2.4 = 0.417$. This rate is typical of customer arrivals at a moderately busy bank or post office. We have taken the minute as our time unit and express times in decimal fractions of one minute.

9.5.6 Graphical representation

Figure 9.2(a) represents the probabilities in Table 9.1 on a diagram known as a histogram. The x-axis is divided into intervals each of width 0.2, and on each interval as base we draw rectangles with length (height) equal to $5 \times$ (corresponding probability given in Table 9.1). This is done so that the *area* of each rectangle (width $\times$ height) corresponds to the probability that an inter-arrival time lies in that interval.

We could repeat this process with different interval widths, e.g. 0.1 or 0.005, etc., by using (9.9) with appropriate values of t to calculate the relevant probabilities. When the intervals become very small, the

Table 9.1 Probabilities for random inter-
arrival times for a Poisson process, with
$\lambda = 2.4$

Interval	Probability
0.0–0.2	0.381
0.2–0.4	0.236
0.4–0.6	0.146
0.6–0.8	0.090
0.8–1.0	0.056
1.0–1.2	0.035
1.2–1.4	0.021
1.4–1.6	0.013
1.6–1.8	0.008
1.8–2.0	0.005
2.0–2.2	0.003
2.2–2.4	0.002
2.4–2.6	0.001
2.6–2.8	0.001
2.8–3.0	0.001
> 3	0.001

rectangles become narrower. Mathematically we can equate the area
of the rectangles to an area under a smooth curve. If we choose the
right curve, this works for intervals of any width, e.g. 0.2. For this
example, it has the form

$$y = 2.4e^{-2.4t}. \tag{9.10}$$

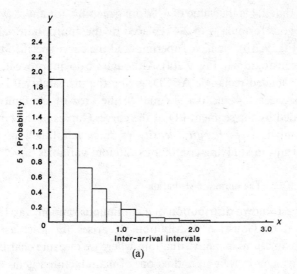

(a)

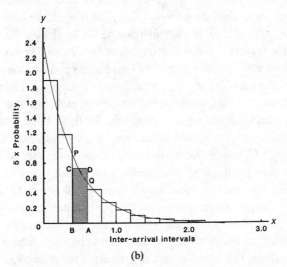

(b)

Figure 9.2 (a) A histogram of probabilities of inter-arrival times in intervals of width 0.2 minutes for random arrivals at an average rate of 2.4 customers per minute. (b) Relationship between the histogram in (a) and a continuous curve (probability density function) for the appropriate exponential distribution.

Note that 2.4 is the value of λ. More generally, for any λ, we use an analogous formula with 2.4 replaced by the appropriate value of λ.

In Fig. 9.2(b), we have superimposed the curve specified by (9.10) on the histogram in Fig. 9.2(a). Although we do not prove it, the area of the shaded rectangle ABCD, giving the probability 0.146 that t lies between 0.4 and 0.6 is equal to the area of the figure ABPQ bounded by the segment PQ of the curve. Curves of the type (9.10) are known as *probability density* or *frequency* functions and are important in studying continuous random variables.

9.5.7 The normal distribution

The best-known distribution of a continuous random variable is the normal or Gaussian distribution. It arises (at least as a good approximation) in many situations where we measure characteristics such as length, weight, and so on, of manufactured items. Production processes often have target values for certain characteristics, but there is inevitable variation about that target. For example, a machine filling bags of cement may be set to deliver 50.5 kg (this being the target). Experience may show that exact deliveries vary in a random way between about 50.1 and 50.9 kg, deviations as far as these extremes being less common than ones close to the target, but deviations of a like amount, either above or below the target of 50.5 kg, being about equally common. In these circumstances the probabilities of getting weights between any two values, say 50.5 and 50.7 or 50.42 and 50.73, accord very closely with that of a normal distribution having a specific mean (expectation) of 50.5. To pinpoint the distribution, we must also specify the standard deviation. In the example above, this would be approximately 0.15 (we do not prove this). If bags were required to have a minimum weight of at least 50 kg the above setting would ensure virtually all bags met that specification. The fact that we do not pursue the normal distribution and its ramifications is not to belittle its importance. To deal with it seriously would add several chapters to this book, but it is a key topic in a more advanced treatment of management mathematics.

9.6 SAMPLES AND POPULATIONS

We pointed out in section 9.1 that political opinion polls are based on interviews with samples of voters; market research is often directed at gauging public reaction to new products or marketing ploys, by testing the reaction of a 'sample' of potential customers. If a sample of consumers do not like a product, it is unlikely to go into mass production. Fundamental to the idea of a sample is some real – or perhaps hypothetical – population from which the sample is taken. In a political opinion poll, the population is all voters; in market research on a new product, it is the less clearly defined 'all potential customers'. Populations need not be people: all items of a certain kind manufactured or marketed by a company form a population. We even extend the concept to embrace all such items that might or will be made. In Chapter 13, where we discuss quality control, we shall be concerned with taking samples from a production run at regular intervals.

If a post office or bank or building society is having problems with long customer queues, a useful approach is to study the behaviour of the queuing and serving system over a period, i.e. consider all customers arriving in a given time interval as our sample, and determine the time each spends in the queue, how the queue length varies and how the times taken to serve each customer differ. This topic is pursued in Chapter 14. Statistical inference – another subject we do not deal with in this book – is largely concerned with using sample information to determine (or infer things about) the distribution of random variables like service time, etc. Once we have established these distributions, we can use that information to study theoretically the effect of increasing, say, the number of tellers in a bank or clerks behind a post-office counter.

Much is often known from past studies about the distribution of service times. These might follow the exponential distribution (section 9.5.5) associated with a Poisson process. Given certain reasonable assumptions, computers make it relatively easy to look at the effects of factors like changing service times on queue behaviour. We take up this topic in Chapter 14. There, we shall need samples from specified distributions which we associate with populations. We need samples that reflect the nature of such a distribution in the sense that the sample values reflect probabilities associated with that distribution, e.g. if there is a probability of 0.3 that a random variable takes a value between 0 and 2, then in the sample this should be the probability that a sample value lies in this range.

9.6.1 Simple samples

In section 9.5.2, we introduced the uniform distribution associated with a random variable X that takes a value 0, 1, 2, 3, 4, 5, 6, 7, 8, 9, each with probability 0.1. We can get a sample of values from this distribution by one of several physical mechanisms. We might write each digit on one of ten identical marbles and put them in a bag. A person is then asked to draw a marble, note the number on it, replace it, draw another marble, note the number on that, repeating the process a fixed number of times. In the long run, each digit should be drawn approximately the same number of times; e.g. if we repeat the experiment, say, 90 times, we *expect* each digit to appear approximately nine times. Some will do so; some will appear rather more, and some rather less. This reflects, basically, the relative frequency concept of probability. The larger our sample, the more faithfully it reflects the characteristics of a population. Table 9.2 is a sample of 200 values generated by computer in a way that mimics mathematically the experiment of drawing marbles labelled 0 to 9 from a bag (with replacement after each is drawn) a total of 200 times. Such tables are called tables of random numbers or random digits. They are important because they can be used to generate samples from virtually any distribution. The general theory is difficult, but we give one example where we quote the appropriate formulae.

Example 9.9   In section 9.5.5, we pointed out that random arrivals at a post office at a rate of 2.4 per minute would given an exponential distribution of inter-arrival times with $\lambda = 2.4$.

Table 9.2 Random digits

8	1	2	8	1	2	7	6	8	9	5	9	5	1	3	3	9	0	8	8
7	7	2	8	3	2	1	4	1	7	4	7	7	6	3	5	5	6	1	9
0	2	3	4	7	7	5	2	9	5	9	6	9	5	7	2	6	9	0	3
4	1	4	8	6	2	2	1	8	8	1	9	3	1	6	7	8	9	7	2
7	0	6	0	3	6	0	4	2	9	1	1	3	6	4	7	2	4	5	6
8	4	8	3	7	8	6	7	8	7	9	0	3	9	3	6	3	0	4	6
1	4	7	0	7	4	8	6	3	6	7	0	1	9	9	8	5	5	2	0
2	4	2	5	1	0	4	5	9	0	9	9	6	9	9	6	9	4	3	8
7	5	6	3	3	9	5	7	2	8	0	0	0	4	9	5	8	9	9	7
8	5	6	8	1	1	0	2	9	5	4	5	1	8	0	0	9	7	6	5

Use random digits to get two samples of 100 from this exponential distribution. This procedure is often referred to as 'simulating' the pattern of arrivals, a topic we develop in Chapter 14.

Solution Without proof, the procedure is as follows.

1. Take random digits in pairs from Table 9.2 or a more extensive table, or random digits obtained by using a computer (most computers have a facility that will do this).
2. Divide the number formed from each pair by 100; call this U.
3. Calculate $(-\ln U)/2.4$, where ln means logarithm to the base e.

Many calculators have a key labelled ln x. For example, the first two digits in Table 9.2 are 81, whence $t = (-\ln 0.81)/2.4 = 0.088$. This would imply that, in a queuing situation with exponential service times averaging $1/2.4$ minutes, the first arrival in our sample took 0.088 minutes to serve. We may repeat the process taking the next pair of random digits working down columns in Table 9.2, then passing to the next column, until we have 100 samples. I used this

Table 9.3 Probabilities for random inter-arrival times for a Poisson process, with $\lambda = 2.4$ and for corresponding samples of 100.

Interval	Probability	Sample 1	Sample 2
0.0–0.2	0.381	0.36	0.42
0.2–0.4	0.236	0.29	0.22
0.4–0.6	0.146	0.14	0.12
0.6–0.8	0.090	0.08	0.10
0.8–1.0	0.056	0.04	0.04
1.0–1.2	0.035	0.03	0.02
1.2–1.4	0.021	0.03	0.02
1.4–1.6	0.013	0.02	0.01
1.6–1.8	0.008		0.02
1.8–2.0	0.005	0.01	0.02
2.0–2.2	0.003		
2.2–2.4	0.002		
2.4–2.6	0.001		
2.6–2.8	0.001		0.01
2.8–3.0	0.001		
> 3	0.001		

procedure for two samples of 100 using computer-generated pairs of random digits. Table 9.3 shows the numbers I found (each divided by 100) in each 0.2 minute interval for these samples of 100, together with the 'population' probabilities for these intervals copied from Table 9.1. For example, the entry 0.29 for sample 1 corresponding to the interval 0.2 to 0.4 means that 29 out of my 100 sample values gave inter-arrival times between 0.2 and 0.4 minutes. We shall see how these ideas are used in Chapter 14. The above method of sampling applies specifically to the exponential distribution with parameter $\lambda = 2.4$. For other values of λ, we generate our sample by using pairs of random digits divided by 100 to form U in $(-\ln U)/\lambda$. Note that, if a table of random digits is used to obtain random pairs the table should be entered at a different point each time it is used, for we would always get the same sample if we all started at the same place each time we used the table. A complication arises if the pair of digits is 00: division by 100 gives 0.00 and the logarithm of 0 to any base is minus infinity. If we get 0.00, we should look at the next digit in the row of the table we are currently using; if this is not zero, but any other digit, say 3 or 5, we replace 0.00 by 0.003 or 0.005 or whatever. If the next digit is zero, we proceed until we get a non-zero digit and base our U on the amended 'near zero' value. The problem should not arise with computers as they effectively give U directly to a very large number of decimal places.

More extensive use of random numbers in sampling is considered in Chapter 14.

9.6.2 Samples from a normal distribution

In Chapter 13, we shall find that we are often interested in samples from a normal distribution. These have a number of important properties that simplify applied statistical calculations. In particular, even if we do not know the mean and standard deviation associated with the distribution, it is relatively easy to get quite good estimates of these from large samples. The techniques are described in elementary textbooks on statistics. The only place we require these in this book is in Chapter 13 and we deal with them briefly in that chapter.

9.7 WHAT AND WHERE?

What skills have we mastered?

We have given rules for basic operations with objective or subjective (personal) probabilities. Specifically, for two mutually exclusive events A and B the addition rule is $\Pr(A \text{ or } B) = \Pr(A) + \Pr(B)$.

The conditional probability $Pr(B|A)$ is the probability B occurs, given that A also occurs. The multiplication rule is $Pr(A \text{ and } B) = Pr(A) \cdot Pr(B|A) = Pr(B) \cdot Pr(A|B)$. If A and B are independent $Pr(B|A) = Pr(B)$ and the multiplication rule becomes $Pr(A \text{ and } B) = Pr(A) \cdot Pr(B)$.

Bayes' rule enables us to calculate $Pr(A|B)$ given $Pr(A)$, $Pr(B|A)$ and $Pr(B|A^*)$, where A^* is the opposite event to A.

Random variables may have empirical or theoretical distributions. Important theoretical distributions include the uniform, the binomial, the Poisson, the exponential, and the Gaussian or normal distributions. Expected (or mean) value and standard deviation are measures of centrality and spread respectively.

Samples from a distribution broadly reflect distribution characteristics. Samples from many distributions may be obtained using tables of, or computer-generated, random digits.

Where can I read more?

Rowntree (1981) covers basic ideas. A general treatment of business and management applications is given by Waters (1989: Chaps. 8–11) and by Ehrenberg (1983). Examination-orientated texts covering statistics include Lucey (1988: Chaps. 2–9), Francis (1988: Chaps. 2–25), Jones and MacKay (1988: part III), and Bancroft and O'Sullivan (1988: Chaps. 8–18).

EXERCISES

9.1   To urge drivers to cooperate in a traffic survey, each driver interviewed is given a numbered ticket. Later one will be drawn to decide the winner of a prize of £10. If 723 out of 2419 drivers interviewed are women, what is the probability that a woman wins the prize?

*9.2   A company checks all invoices for small items from each of two suppliers A and B and categorizes them as follows:

	Overcharge	Correct	Undercharge	Total
Firm A	54	843	103	1000
Firm B	155	1640	205	2000
Totals	209	2483	308	

(i) If one of these invoices is drawn at random and found to be from firm A, what is the probability that it shows an undercharge?

(ii) If an invoice is drawn at random, what is the probability it shows an undercharge?

(iii) An invoice is drawn; what is the probability that it either (a) is from firm A and shows an overcharge or (b) comes from firm B and shows an undercharge.

(iv) An invoice is selected and found to be correct; what is the probability it comes from A?

9.3 A card is drawn at random from ten cards numbered 0, 1, 2, 3, 4, 5, 6, 7, 8, 9. What is the probability that the number on it is

(i) divisible by 4 (assume 0 is divisible by 4)?

(ii) odd?

(iii) either odd or divisible by 4?

(iv) neither odd nor divisible by 4?

9.4 Fifty marbles each bear one of the numbers 1 to 50. One is drawn from a bag. What are the probabilities that the number on it is

(i) divisible by 5?

(ii) divisible by 11?

(iii) divisible by either 5 or 11?

(iv) divisible by neither 5 nor 11?

*9.5 If $Pr(A) = 0.5$, $Pr(B|A) = 0.2$ and $Pr(B*|A*) = 0.3$, then find $Pr(B)$.

*9.6 A company manufactures an item at each of two factories, A and B. A total of 80% of all items are produced at A. The percentage of faulty items in production from A is one-half that in items from B. An item is picked at random and found to be faulty. What is the probability it came from B? If 2% of all items are defective, what is the percentage defectives from B?

*9.7 A commuter airline operates ten-seater passenger planes. It claims that there is a probability of 0.8 that any person booked for a flight actually turns up independently of who else does or does not turn up. If it has 12 people booked on a flight, what is the probability it will be able to accommodate all who turn up? Do you consider the airline's assumptions about the probabilities of people turning up are reasonable?

*9.8 The numbers of days to stock-out for a popular pet food in a supermarket are given below, together with the probability that stock-out will occur at each. Calculate the mean number of days to stock-out and the standard deviation:

Days to stock-out	9	10	11	12	13
Probability	0.1	0.2	0.3	0.2	0.2

9.9 By considering the formula $\Pr(X = r) = e^{-\lambda}\lambda^r/r!$ for the Poisson distribution with mean λ, and the corresponding formula for $\Pr(X = r + 1)$, show that $\Pr(X = r + 1) = \Pr(X = r)\lambda/(r + 1)$. [Note that this is a recursive formula that enables us to calculate $\Pr(X = r + 1)$ knowing λ and $\Pr(X = r)$. We simply multiply the latter by $\lambda/(r + 1)$ to get the former. Apply this recursive formula to work out the relevant probabilities in Example 9.8.]

9.10 Count the number of times each of the digits 0 to 9 occurs in Table 9.2. How many times would you expect each to occur? Do you consider the actual numbers occurring are reasonably consistent with the expected numbers? [Statistical tests exist to quantify such conclusions, although we do not describe them.]

*9.11 Using Table 9.2, and starting from the third and fourth columns take pairs of random digits working down columns to obtain 100 samples from an exponential distribution with mean arrival or service rates of 2.4 persons per minute.

*9.12 Suppose that arrival times at a service point are exponentially distributed with a mean of 1 per minute. Calculate the probabilities of inter-arrival times in each interval of width 0.4 between time 0 and 5.2. What is the probability that an inter-arrival time will exceed 5.2 minutes?

*9.13 Suppose there is a probability of 0.7 that the wait between consecutive buses is five minutes and a probability of 0.3 that the wait is eight minutes. What is the estimated (mean) waiting time between buses? What is the standard deviation of the wait?

*9.14 If, in the situation in Exercise 9.13, each of the digits 0 to 6 is associated with a five-minute wait and each of the digits 7 to 9 with an eight-minute wait, we have a mechanism for sampling from the relevant distribution. Starting with the digits in column 4 of Table 9.2 and working down consecutive columns, obtain 100 sample arrival intervals. Calculate the mean of these 100 sample intervals and compare it with the theoretical expected inter-arrival time obtained in Exercise 9.13. [Note that the sample mean is an estimate of the population mean; it will not in general equal it exactly, but for large samples is likely to be close to it in many circumstances.]

9.15 (a) A glass bottle manufacturer has three inspection points: one for size, the second for colour and the third for flaws such as cracks and bubbles in the glass. The probability that each inspection point will incorrectly accept or reject a bottle is 0.02. What is the probability that:

 (i) a perfect bottle will be passed through all inspection points;
 (ii) a bottle faulty in colour and with a crack will be passed;
(iii) a bottle faulty in size will be passed.

(b) Two machines produce the same type of product. The older machine produces 35% of the total output but eight in every hundred are defective. The newer machine produces 65% of the total output and two in every 100 are defective. Determine the probability that a defective product picked at random was produced by the older machine.   [CIMA]

9.16   Life insurance policies are bought by six men in similar employment, having the same age and health characteristics. The probability that a man in this category will be alive in 20 years' time, at the end of the policy is, according to actuarial tables, 0.6. Find the probability that, after 20 years,

(a) none will be alive,
(b) at least one will be alive,
(c) only four will be alive,
(d) only one will have died.

[AEB, AS level, part question]

10 Stock and Inventory Control

10.1 THE ECONOMICS OF STOCK CONTROL

During the 1980s, UK manufacturing industry usually held between £30 billion (thousand million) and £50 billion of stock at any one time. Official Government statistics divide these into (i) fuel and raw materials, (ii) goods in various stages of production and (iii) finished products. At the end of 1988, the values (to the nearest £ billion) in each of these categories were (i) £14 billion, (ii) £18 billion and (iii) £15 billion, a total of £47 billion. The totals and relative levels change from month to month and depend on market conditions. When allowance is made for the capital tied up, for the cost of warehousing, distribution, ordering and controlling stocks, a conservative estimate of the total holding cost for this stock is between £4 and £5 billion per annum (almost certainly more when interest rates are high). In addition to that held by manufacturers, at the end of 1988 the wholesale trade held stocks valued at £16 billion, and retail trade stocks stood at £13 billion. Classification of stock into the categories (i), (ii) and (iii) above for manufacturing, together with wholesale and retail holdings, as is done in official statistics, is somewhat loose and arbitrary. The finished article for one manufacturer may be the raw material for another. Further, official levels for wholesale and retail stocks do not include motor cars and accessories!

10.1.1 Why hold stock?

Reasonable levels of stock ensure that likely demands can be met, and usually this means allowing some buffer for fluctuations both in demand and deliveries. The fluctuations may be more or less random, or they may have clear seasonal patterns (e.g. demand for ice cream, raincoats, hot-water bottles). In the UK, sales of motor vehicles rise sharply in August for vanity reasons – the prestige of a new registration letter.

Discounts for large orders are an incentive to place these, but if orders grossly exceed current needs the value of any discount must be offset against increased storage costs and lost profits if the items are perishable or likely to become obsolete before they can be used or sold. Stocks may be built up to avoid anticipated price rises. On the negative side, stocks may accumulate simply because demand for an item drops, but nobody does anything about it, thus adding to storage costs of a physical nature (space) and direct financial costs (capital tied up, loss of otherwise recoverable capital due to obsolescence, etc.).

10.1.2 Cost structure

There are three broad types of cost to be considered in assessing any stock control procedure, namely:

1. ordering costs,
2. holding costs,
3. stock-out costs.

Categories 1 and 2 are reasonably clear-cut concepts, although quantification of what is involved in a particular situation may be difficult. Stock-out costs are incurred if an item cannot be supplied on demand.

The objective of inventory, or stock, control – both terms are widely used – is to evolve an ordering and holding policy to minimize total storage costs. Before we see how mathematics might help in simple cases, we list some of the costs that must be taken into account.

Ordering costs include the clerical and administrative costs in placing and receiving an order, as well as transport, packaging and other delivery charges. Also, if a company produces an item 'in house', there may be setting up and tooling up costs for a production run. In practice, it is often reasonable to divide these costs into a fixed component independent of the size of an order, plus an amount 'per item' ordered. The fixed cost per order may include postal and telephone, telex or fax charges in placing an order, a basic charge per delivery, any tooling up costs, etc. The additional costs 'per item' may cover packaging charges, transport, transit insurance, etc., which increase with the size of the order.

Holding costs include interest on capital 'tied up' in the stock, charges for space (rent, rates) and store services such as lighting, heating or refrigeration, staff and maintenance costs, insurance, security, etc. If the goods are perishable, or likely to deteriorate because of vermin attack, or may become obsolete, allowance may be made also for losses in storage from these causes. Even pilfering may have to be taken into account – professional shoplifters are the bane of the retail trade. Petty theft in large offices seldom stops at the odd paper clip!

Holding costs, like reordering costs, can often be reasonably expressed as a fixed cost plus an amount per item in stock for a given unit of time (often per month or per annum). In a well-run organization, the fixed cost per annum is often virtually outside management control (unless they deliberately skimp on insurance, or security, or heating, or something of that sort) and as we shall see in the analysis below, in simple cases the exact level of fixed costs does not affect the policy for reordering stock, whereas costs dependent on stock levels do.

Stock-out costs include additional costs for special deliveries, loss of profit on sales that go to another supplier, or production losses if the item is a raw material. There may be more intangible items like loss of customer goodwill, or industrial unrest if production is held up and this leads to loss of bonuses, overtime payments, etc. Cost of protection against stock-out situations (e.g. for holding buffer stock) is often classed as a stock-out cost.

10.2 INVENTORY POLICY IN AN IDEALIZED SITUATION

The simplest case is one where there is a constant demand for one item like a machine component (e.g. a generator, battery, clutch, gear box, etc.) and supplies can be replenished regularly with a known time for delivery. This situation may pertain, at least as a good approximation, in a factory where there is little change in production levels throughout the year and no difficulties about getting supplies of an item in regular use (e.g. guaranteed next day delivery). Here annual inventory costs are dependent upon ordering costs (governed by the size of each order and the number of orders per annum) and holding costs which will vary with the average number of items in store. Stock-out situations may be avoided with an appropriate ordering policy. We mentioned above that any fixed holding costs not dependent on the number of items in store need not influence ordering policy, but we make provision for them in our analysis as they are relevant to total costs. If we know the delivery time and also know that demand is steady, it is clearly sensible policy to order so that delivery is obtained just before we run out. This avoids stock-out costs and we do not carry items from a previous order in stock longer than necessary. Our problem, given relevant cost information, is to determine the size and frequency of orders to minimize ordering plus holding costs.

Example 10.1   For each order of generators required by a manufacturer of car engines, there is a fixed ordering plus delivery charge of £10 plus an additional charge of 30p ($= £0.3$) per generator ordered. The holding cost per generator per year is £3 in addition to a constant annual storage cost (independent of the number of generators in stock) of £400. Demand is for six generators per day and delivery of orders is guaranteed two days after ordering. What is the optimum ordering policy?

Solution   The ordering cost for one delivery of x generators will be £$(10 + 0.3x)$. It is important to express all costs in the

x	20	30	40	60	80	100	120	140	160
C	2182	1832	1664.5	1512	1450.75	1426	1419.5	1423.43	1433.89

same unit, e.g. pounds, dollars, or whatever, and never in a mixture of pounds and pence or of dollars and cents. If demand is steady and we order so that delivery always occurs just as stock runs out, the average number of generators in hand at any time is $\frac{1}{2}x$, equal to the stock in hand half way between the delivery of each order; this is because the holding decreases uniformly from x to 0. Thus total holding costs are $£(\frac{1}{2}x \times 3 + 400)$ per annum. Since the demand is six generators per day, the annual demand is $6 \times 365 = 2190$ generators (we ignore the minor complications of a leap year). Clearly, then, if we place regular orders for x generators, the number of deliveries per year will be $2190/x$. Since the cost for each delivery is $£(10 + 0.3x)$ this means annual ordering costs will be

$$(10 + 0.3x) \times (2190/x) = (21\,900/x) + 657.$$

The total cost $£C$ per annum for any given order size x is composed of total annual reordering costs + total holding costs and is given by the expression

$$C = (21\,900/x) + 657 + \tfrac{3}{2}x + 400. \tag{10.1}$$

We may plot an approximate graph of cost C against order size x by evaluating C for a set of values of x such as those given in Table 10.1 and drawing a smooth curve through the plotted points. The values are obtained from (10.1); e.g. when $x = 40$, (10.1) gives

$$C = \tfrac{21\,900}{40} + 657 + \tfrac{120}{2} + 400 = 1664.5$$

The values in Table 10.1 suffice for finding an approximately optimal policy to minimize inventory costs, but note that if we put $x = 1$ (i.e. if we reordered items one at a time) then $C = 22\,958.50$, and if we

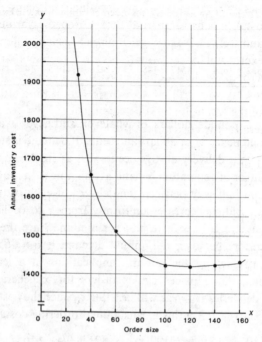

Figure 10.1 Relationship between order size x and total inventory cost C, Example 10.1.

place only one order per annum for all 2190 generators then $C = 4352$. By looking at the general nature of the cost structure, you should see why it is so expensive, relative to the optimum policy, to order the items one at a time or just once a year.

Figure 10.1 is a plot of C against x from the data in Table 10.1 with a freehand smooth curve through the points. The coordinates of the lowest point on the curve give the value of x for minimum inventory cost and the corresponding amount. It occurs for $x = 120$ approximately, and we note from Table 10.1 (or approximately from the graph) that the minimum cost is £1419.50 per annum.

One need not draw a graph to find this minimum. We could obtain it using differential calculus. Calculus has important uses in business mathematics, but we omit it in this introduction because, as here, it is often just a 'means to an end' tool. Given the various costs of ordering and storage, we may generalize (10.1) and differentiate the resulting expression for cost with respect to x, then set that derivative equal to zero, to get the optimum order size. If you are familiar with the calculus, try this with (10.1) or its generalization (10.2); if not, please take the result in (10.3) below on trust.

We generalize by replacing the fixed delivery cost of £10 per order irrespective of size, by a fixed cost £F per order and by writing the additional order cost per item as £c ($c = 0.3$ in Example 10.1). Similarly, we specify a general annual holding cost per item held at £a per item ($a = 3$ in the above example) and annual holding costs that are independent of the number of items held by £P ($P = 400$ in the above example). We write N for the total number of items required per annum. Our total cost C, if we order x items at a time, may then be written

$$C = \frac{(F + cx)N}{x} + \tfrac{1}{2}xa + P,$$

or

$$C = \frac{FN}{x} + cN + \tfrac{1}{2}xa + P. \qquad (10.2)$$

Use of the differential calculus then establishes that the value of x, the reorder quantity giving minimum cost, is

$$x = \sqrt{(2FN/a)}. \qquad (10.3)$$

Returning to our numerical example, we had $F = 10$, $N = 2190$ and $a = 3$. A quick pocket calculator exercise establishes that (10.3) gives

$$x = \sqrt{(2 \times 10 \times 2190/3)} = \sqrt{14\,600} = 120.83,$$

in close agreement with our graphical finding. The calculus result is exact (to two decimal places) and saves the need for a graph. However, the graph is more informative because it shows little difference in costs for reorder sizes between about 80 and 160; costs rise increasingly sharply when order sizes drop below 60 or rise above about 180.

The formula (10.3) does not involve P, the fixed annual storage cost, or c, the order cost per item. This is not unreasonable, since these contribute to the total inventory costs in a way that is unalterable if we change the reorder size. This is clear by the way we define P; as c is a fixed cost per item ordered, and the total number of items ordered equals the annual demand, this also contributes an unalterable amount cN to the annual cost. We cannot adjust either by different choices of x. They do, of course, contribute to the total cost C.

10.2.1 Discounts

Discounts are often allowed for large orders. Their effect can be quite complex, but we can recalculate minimum cost to see if they will make a worthwhile saving. Depending on their nature, discounts may require a reassessment of both reordering and holding costs. We shall consider only a modification where the discount takes the form of reduced reordering costs.

Example 10.2 Suppose that in Example 10.1 a change is made and that for orders of 150 or more generators the fixed delivery charge F is reduced from £10 to £8. What is now the optimum reorder policy?

Solution Equation (10.3) shows the optimum order size for a delivery if the fixed charge is £8 to be $x = 108$. This is not helpful, because we do not get this cheaper rate for deliveries of less than 150! Not surprisingly, the new optimum only tells us that if delivery charges were reduced it may be optimum to place smaller orders, thus reducing average stock holdings. The finding is reasonable, as the whole idea of stock control is to optimize costs by balancing reordering against holding costs; when reordering costs drop, smaller orders become more attractive. Our problem remains, however, that reorder charges only drop if we order 150 or more generators. To see if the reduced reorder cost structure improves things, we must use formula (10.2) to compare the total costs under the original terms with $F = 10$ to those with a new value of $F = 8$, plus the constraint that the minimum value of x must be 150 (to obtain a discount). Putting $F = 8$ and $x = 150$, but leaving all other costs and total requirements the same as before, a simple calculation shows that now $C = 116.8 + 657 + 225 + 400 = 1398.8$. Thus, in placing orders of 150 under these new conditions, there is a slight saving in inventory costs compared to that of £1419.50 under the old regime.

10.2.2 Planning orders

Returning to Example 10.1, we explore further the question of when to place an order. The assumption that the average stock is $\frac{1}{2}x$ depends rather critically on the assumption that new supplies arrive just as stock runs out. If there is a regular guaranteed delivery two days after an order is placed, we should order when there is exactly two days requirements in hand. In our simple example, the daily requirement is 6, so we should reorder when stocks drop to 12. This stock level is often referred to as the *reorder level*.

An important consequence of the 'square-root' aspect of formula (10.3) is that it does not follow that, if the demand for an item doubles, we should double the size of our orders. Indeed only if the demand quadruples should we double our order level. We easily verify this for our numerical example. If demand for the generators doubles, i.e. N increases from 2190 to 4380, it is easily verified that (10.3) gives an optimum order size of 170.88 (which is the original optimum multiplied by the square-root of 2). Only if N increases four times from 2190 to 8760 does the optimum size given by (10.3) double from 120.83 to 241.66. Some firms order all items using a rule of the form 'restock to the amount that customers normally buy in one month' (or it may be one week, or two months, but in essence the same fixed period for all goods). Even if this is a good approximation on average, (10.3) shows it cannot be optimum for all items

if demands (although steady) are not the same for different items
even when the costing structure for ordering and holding is the same
for each. To demonstrate this, suppose that for two items A and B
the monthly demand is 600 for A, and that this happens also to
be the optimum reordering number given by (10.3). Then, if the
demand for B is 1200 per month, the optimum reordering policy
given by (10.3) is 600 multiplied by $\sqrt{2}$ and is easily verified to be 849
(to the nearest integer). This is appreciably less than the 1200 that
would be ordered under the 'order a month's stock' rule. It is easily
shown that under similar circumstances ordering 300, if this were the
anticipated monthly demand for another item, would be ordering
less than the optimum. The general tendency with the 'order a
month's stock' (or a similar policy) is that, if the policy is right for
average turnover items, then fast turnover items will be ordered
in above optimum quantities and slow turnover items in below
optimum quantities. Obviously, the situation may be further complicated by different items having different reordering and holding
costs.

10.2.3 Near optimum solutions

Near optimum solutions may often be obtained even if some costs
are not very accurately determined. This reflects indirectly the
common tendency for the graph relating total cost C and reorder
number x to be rather flat near the optimum. In Example 10.1,
suppose a major mistake had been made in estimating delivery costs
per item and these should have been £0.6 instead of £0.3. This will
alter the total inventory costs per annum, but it has no effect on the
optimum order size, for we saw above that this is uninfluenced by the
delivery cost per item. On the other hand, if the fixed delivery charge
were reduced to £6 per order (the variable charge per item remaining
at £0.3), the total cost for orders of 120 is easily calculated, by
putting the appropriate values in (10.2), to be £1346.50. However,
substituting in (10.3) tells us now that the new optimum order size
is 93.6. In practice, then, we should ideally reorder 94 units, and
(10.2) then gives an optimum cost of £1337.79. Thus the saving in

reducing reorder size to the optimum is less than 1%. In a number of broadly similar numerical cases, savings of less than 5% may be noted for quite drastic changes in fixed reorder component or variable holding component costs. This relative insensitivity to a fairly substantial cost change indicates that unless the sums involved in storage costs are very large, it may suffice to use not very accurate cost approximations. That in many situations the precise reordering size is not too critically dependent upon cost structure should not be taken as an invitation to ignore the whole problem. Remember we indicated that total inventory costs for UK manufacturing industry run to many £ billions per annum. A 1% saving on £1 billion is £10 million. As Example 10.1 shows, a far from optimal reordering scheme (e.g. ordering only annually) can push up costs alarmingly.

10.3 THE REAL WORLD

Inventory problems are seldom as simple as the one considered in the last section: demand may change in a random way from day to day; there may be seasonal changes; deliveries may sometimes take five days, sometimes eight. In such circumstances, stocks may run out and stock-out costs may become important. Suppose we have a reasonably steady demand, but with random fluctuations, and also fluctuations in times to delivery after an order is placed. If stock-out situations lead to lost sales, loss of goodwill, or hold up production, one protection is to keep a 'buffer stock' to meet the possibility of an upward blip in demand or an above average delivery delay leading to a stock-out. A typical situation may be one where demand averages 12 items per day, but varies between 8 and 16 with some fairly clearly defined pattern in that we know the probability that it will take each value between 8 and 16, generally speaking values near the mean of 12 being most common, extremes of 8 or 16 being relatively infrequent, i.e. we know the distribution (section 9.5) of demand. Deliveries may take anything between five and 11 days – it perhaps being more common to be near the latter. How do we use all available information to minimize total costs, which now cover several possibilities and include stock-out costs? The optimum solution involves a blend of deterministic mathematics with ideas from applied probability and statistics. We shall consider only one very simple example in any detail – it is a modification of the problem in Example 10.1. The solution is not very user-friendly, but even if you find the detail hard going it is worth trying to come to terms with the general concepts.

10.3.1 Buffer stocks

Example 10.3   In Example 10.1, we replace a steady demand for six generators per day by a demand that is equally likely to be for five, six or seven per day. The expected demand (section 9.5.1) is clearly still six items per day. We further suppose that delivery is equally likely to take one, two or three days. Again, the expected time is two days. We assume all costs are as in Example 6.1. Explore the pattern of stock-out situations and consider their consequences, if in the event of a stock-out an emergency order must be placed for immediate delivery at an additional cost of £4 per order above normal delivery charges.

Solution   If we considered average demand and average delivery time and ignored all other factors, we would be led to the reordering policy in Example 10.1 with $x = 120$ as the ideal reorder size. This would minimize average annual costs of ordering plus holding if we reordered at the average time of two days before stocks ran out, i.e. adopted a reorder level of 12. However, it takes no account of stock-out costs arising from the random fluctuations in demand or delivery times. Sometimes we may use five, sometimes six and sometimes seven per day and delivery time may be one, two or three days. At the very worst, we might, after ordering, use seven on each of three days – a total of 21 – before receiving a delivery. This is an excess of nine over the average 12. We avoid all stock-outs in this situation by ordering when stocks drop to 21 (i.e. $9 + 12$). If we do so, we will, on average, have $21 - 12 = 9$ surplus items in stock when a new order comes in (it will sometimes be none, but would be 16 if we only used five on the day after the order is placed and the new supplies arrived in one day's time). As it costs £3 per annum to store a generator, the average annual cost of stocking the 'buffer' of nine items is £(9×3) = £27. If we do run out, we have to place an emergency order for immediate delivery at an extra cost of £4 above the usual delivery charges, but it may still pay us to hold a smaller buffer stock and place an emergency order if and only if our buffer stock runs out. If so, what is the best buffer stock? To answer that question, we must know the probability that a stock-out occurs to trigger an emergency order for each buffer stock between zero and nine (it is clearly pointless to hold a larger buffer stock than nine, since nine covers our worst situation of 21 being required in the maximum three days before a normal order arrives). To work out the probabilities, we make further assumptions. We assume that the delivery time and the daily demands are independent, and also that one day's demand is independent of that for another. These assumptions make our mathematics and statistics easier for illustrative purposes; dropping them would not make the problem insoluble, but we would need further information on the nature of any dependence and the calculations would be more difficult. The assumptions are reasonable when the fluctuations in delivery time and in demand are purely chance or random fluctuations and involve a supplier independent of the purchaser. It would be less reasonable if the items for sale were, say ice creams, and sales went up because the weather was hot; delivery times are then likely also to increase because of pressures on the manufacturer with increased demand, i.e. delivery time might be dependent upon demand.

Solution of the problem with independence assumptions can be simplified by using more sophisticated statistical methods, but we break the solution into sets of equi-probable cases using the multiplication rule of probabilities for independent events (section 9.3) and the addition rule of probabilities for mutually exclusive events (section 9.2). If you are not yet happy about calculating probabilities and are prepared to take my calculations on trust, you

Table 10.2 Probabilities for different demands when delivery is made in one day.

Total demand before delivery	Probability
5	$\frac{1}{9}$
6	$\frac{1}{9}$
7	$\frac{1}{9}$

might like to skip directly to Table 10.5, where we summarize the probabilities of having to place an emergency order for each possible buffer size. On the other hand, readers familiar with a concept called the multinomial distribution might like to convince themselves that there are easier ways of obtaining the probabilities given below.

First, suppose that delivery is made one day after we order. The probability of this (since all three delivery days are equally likely) is $\frac{1}{3}$. The demand on that one day is either 5, 6 or 7, each also with probability $\frac{1}{3}$. Since the probability that delivery is made after one day is independent of the demand on that day (our key assumption above), we multiply the probability of each demand by the probability of delivery on day 1 to get the probability that delivery is made after that number of items is demanded. In each case, the probability is $\frac{1}{3} \times \frac{1}{3} = \frac{1}{9}$. We summarize these probabilities in Table 10.2. If delivery takes two days, there are a number of possibilities for total demand each of which, in this particularly simple example, has the same probability. For example, demand on the first day may be 5 (with probability $\frac{1}{3}$) and on the second day 7 (again with probability $\frac{1}{3}$), so the probability of the combined events is given by the multiplication rule as $\frac{1}{9}$. The probability of delivery on day 2 is also $\frac{1}{3}$, thus the overall probability for this situation is $\frac{1}{9} \times \frac{1}{3} = \frac{1}{27}$. There are eight other demand combinations when delivery occurs on day 2 (each with probability $\frac{1}{9}$) and the associated

Table 10.3 Probabilities of different demands when delivery is made after two days.

Demand day 1	Demand day 2	Total demand before delivery	Associated probability
5	5	10	$\frac{1}{27}$
5	6	11	$\frac{2}{27}$
6	5		
6	6	12	$\frac{3}{27}$
5	7		
7	5		
6	7	13	$\frac{2}{27}$
7	6		
7	7	14	$\frac{1}{27}$

probabilities of delivery on day 2 with any of these is again $\frac{1}{27}$. Where two or more of the combinations involve the same total demand, the probability associated with that total combined with delivery at day 2 is $r/27$, where r is the total number of times that combination occurs. These results are summarized in Table 10.3. If delivery occurs after three days, by similar arguments each given set of three demands such as 5 on day 1, 6 on day 2, and 5 on day 3 has probability $\frac{1}{3} \times \frac{1}{3} \times \frac{1}{3} = \frac{1}{27}$. Combining this with the probability of delivery on day 3, again with probability $\frac{1}{3}$, each has probability $\frac{1}{27} \times \frac{1}{3} = \frac{1}{81}$. If the total demand over three days is the same for r of these, the probability of that total demand is $r/81$. All cases are shown in Table 10.4.

As already indicated, with a buffer of 9 all demand can be met from normal orders. With a buffer of 8, a demand of 21 will not be met. The probability of that demand before delivery is $\frac{1}{81}$. If we have

Table 10.4 Probability of different demands when delivery is made after three days.

Demand day 1	Demand day 2	Demand day 3	Total	Probability
5	5	5	15	$\frac{1}{81}$
6	5	5		
5	6	5	16	$\frac{3}{81}$
5	5	6		
5	6	6		
6	5	6		
6	6	5		
7	5	5	17	$\frac{6}{81}$
5	7	5		
5	5	7		
6	6	6		
5	6	7		
5	7	6		
6	5	7	18	$\frac{7}{81}$
6	7	5		
7	5	6		
7	6	5		
5	7	7		
7	5	7		
7	7	5		
7	6	6	19	$\frac{6}{81}$
6	7	6		
6	6	7		
6	7	7		
7	6	7	20	$\frac{3}{81}$
7	7	6		
7	7	7	21	$\frac{1}{81}$

Table 10.5 Probability demand not met before normal delivery with various buffer sizes.

Buffer size, B	Probability demand not met, P
9	0
8	$\frac{1}{81}$
7	$\frac{4}{81}$
6	$\frac{10}{81}$
5	$\frac{17}{81}$
4	$\frac{23}{81}$
3	$\frac{26}{81}$
2	$\frac{27}{81}$
1	$\frac{30}{81}$
0	$\frac{36}{81}$

a buffer of 7, demands of 20 or 21 will not be met. Since these outcomes are mutually exclusive, the associated probability is the sum of the probabilities of each, i.e. $\frac{1}{81} + \frac{3}{81} = \frac{4}{81}$. Similarly, with a buffer of 6, demands of 19, 20 or 21 will not be met, and the sum of the probabilities associated with each is $\frac{1}{81} + \frac{3}{81} + \frac{6}{81} = \frac{10}{81}$. Proceeding in this way, we find the probability that demands in excess of 12 will not be met for each of the buffer sizes 0 (corresponding to reordering when stocks have fallen to 12 and there is no delivery after 12 items have been demanded) to 9 (when all demands including the maximum of 21 ($= 12 + 9$) will be met). These are given in Table 10.5.

If we hold a buffer stock of B, the annual holding cost at £3 per item for this buffer, as we have already seen, is $3B$. If, despite this buffer, stock runs out, there is the additional payment of £4 for

Table 10.6 Expected costs for buffering and stock-out, Example 10.3.

P	$\frac{36}{81}$	$\frac{30}{81}$	$\frac{27}{81}$	$\frac{26}{81}$	$\frac{23}{81}$	$\frac{17}{81}$	$\frac{10}{81}$	$\frac{4}{81}$	$\frac{1}{81}$	0
B	0	1	2	3	4	5	6	7	8	9
S	32.4	30.0	30.3	32.4	32.7	30.3	27.0	24.6	24.9	27

emergency reordering. Our problem is to find the expected, or mean, annual reordering cost for a given buffer stock B. Under the reordering policy of 120 units reordered each time to meet an annual demand of 2190 found as the optimum in Example 10.1, we would place $\frac{2190}{120} = 18.25$ orders per annum on average. If P is now the probability our buffer stock B does not meet demand, the expected number of special orders we have to place annually is thus $18.25P$. If each of these cost £4 the additional cost for special orders has expected value £4 × $18.25P$ = £$73P$ per annum. Thus, if we stock a buffer of B items, the expected total additional costs allowing for stock-out situations is given by

$$S = 73P + 3B. \tag{10.4}$$

where P is the probability of having to place an emergency order for a given buffer B as recorded in Table 10.5. Table 10.6 shows these expected costs calculated from (10.4) for the possible values of B and P (reproduced there from Table 10.5).

Inspecting the row of S values in Table 10.6, it is clear that the expected stock-out protection cost is minimized by holding a buffer of 7 and placing a special order if stock runs out. The normal reorder level would then be when stocks are $12 + 7 = 19$. In this particular example, the additional costs of holding buffer stocks to meet all demands are relatively low, whatever buffer level is used. The situation would be very different if special order costs were high relative to storage costs or if demands and delivery patterns fluctuated more markedly.

The 'statistics' in this particular example needed a bit of explaining, but it is relatively simple even if you did not find it particularly friendly. In practice, it is unlikely that the probability of daily demands for five, six or seven generators would all be equally likely or that delivery would be equally likely to be on any of three days; it might well be between one and five days with different probabilities attached to each. This would increase the number of cases to be enumerated and add to the calculation of appropriate stock-out probabilities with various buffer levels, but the same basic methods would still apply. With larger problems, statistical approximations, such as that based on normal distribution theory (section 9.5.7), may well be appropriate.

10.4 SOME OTHER INVENTORY PROBLEMS

Reordering systems where a fixed size order is placed at intervals determined by a given reorder level is sometimes referred to as a two-bin inventory system – the concept is that of stock held in two bins. The first contains a number of items equal to the reorder level and the other any surplus items in stock; these are to be used first. Reordering is triggered when this second bin is empty; further items are obtained from the first, or reserve, bin until the reordered items are delivered, when the first bin is topped up to the reorder level and additional items are placed in the second bin, which is used until again emptied, which triggers a further reordering.

Another common system is one where orders are placed at regular intervals determined by a time trigger, but instead of a fixed size order being placed items are ordered to bring stocks up to a pre-specified level. The system is appropriate if a number of items have to be ordered from the same source and regular deliveries are made of all these items at specified intervals, say weekly, monthly, etc. The method is widely used by chain stores, which obtain numerous relatively small items from the same source (often a central depot belonging to the company who run the chain). There are also hybrid schemes where certain items may be ordered on a two-bin scheme and others on a fixed time schedule.

Large organizations such as a major chemical plant, or a university, often have central stationery or office or laboratory equipment stores which supply the separate departments. Bulk buying may not only attract discounts, but the total optimum holding stock may well be less than the sum of the optimum holding stocks that would be appropriate to individual departments all purchasing separately without recourse to a central store. Some of these advantages may be offset by additional distribution costs from a central store and higher overheads for security, insurance, etc. The 'central store' concept extends from a single organization to a group of organizations such as all hospitals in a given Health Board area, or a group of production plants belonging to one company but sited in different parts of the country.

We do not describe the appropriate mathematical models to deal with these situations. Some are described in Waters (1989: Chap. 3).

The advantages of a good inventory policy only show when many items are considered or inventory costs are high. The average housewife does not need an inventory scheme for her daily milk purchases, but a supermarket selling 25 000 pints a day in 40 branches might well find a good inventory scheme for distribution of such a perishable commodity makes the difference between profit and loss on its milk sales.

10.5 WHAT AND WHERE?

What skills have we mastered?

We have indicated the costs involved in inventory control and demonstrated how to calculate optimal reorder policies for simple deterministic systems. We have indicated how stochastic elements such as variable demand and uncertainty about delivery can be taken into account, but most practical problems require a deeper understanding of statistics for their solution. We have described several reordering schemes and learnt that some rule of thumb policies are only optimal, or near optimal, in restricted circumstances.

Where can I read more?

If you can get hold of a copy Sasieni *et al.* (1959), Chapter 4 deals very competently with many inventory problems. More accessible sources are French *et al.* (1986: Chaps. 8, 9), Moore (1986: Chap. 7), and Waters (1989: Chap. 3). An examination-orientated treatment is given by Lucey (1988: Chaps. 11–14).

EXERCISES

*10.1   A manufacturer uses 50 control panels each day. Orders may be placed at any time for any number of panels and delivery takes exactly three days after the order is placed. For each order, there is a fixed delivery charge of £20 plus an additional charge of 50 pence per panel. Annual storage costs independent of the number of units held are £1700 and in addition there is a holding cost per unit per annum of £1.50. What is the optimum number to reorder on each occasion, how many orders should be placed annually, and what is the stock reorder level?

*10.2   If, in Exercise 10.1, the supplier offers to reduce the fixed delivery charge to £12 per order if the number of orders per annum is halved but the number of panels per order made double that of the optimum calculated in Exercise 10.1, should the buyer accept this offer and change to a new schedule?

*10.3   If, in Exercise 10.1, any of the following changes is made, how, if at all, will the optimum reorder size be changed in each case?

 (i) the fixed delivery charge per order is increased to £30;
 (ii) the fixed delivery charge per order is decreased to £15;
 (iii) the annual holding costs independent of the numbers of items in stock are increased from £1700 to £2000;

(iv) the change in (iii) is made, and in addition the holding cost per item per annum is reduced by one-third;

(v) the annual holding cost independent of the number of items in stock remains at £1700 but the holding cost per item per annum is doubled.

10.4   Which of the following regimes gives the lowest annual total inventory costs for reordering and storage?

 (i) the optimum associated with Exercise 10.1;
(ii) the optimum associated with Exercise 10.3(iv);
(iii) the optimum associated with Exercise 10.3(v).

What is the total cost for the lowest option?

*10.5   Suppose that in Example 10.3 the only change that is made to conditions specified there is that the cost of a special delivery if a stock-out occurs is reduced from £4 to £3. What is now the optimum buffer stock to carry?

*10.6   Suppose that in Example 10.3 the times to delivery instead of being equally likely to be one, two or three days are such that the probabilities of delivery at days 1, 2 or 3 are as follows:

Days to delivery	1	2	3
Probability	0.2	0.3	0.5

If all other conditions remain as in Example 10.3, what is now the optimum buffer stock?

10.7   [In this examination question EBQ means economic batch quantity and the EBQ model is essentially the one considered in Example 10.1. The formula in part (b) of this question corresponds to our (10.3).]

You are determining the stock policy for Part K and have the following data:

Cost of placing an order and receiving delivery £50
Holding cost per unit of stock for one year £2.40
Annual demand, certain and regular, 48 000 units
Estimated purchase cost per unit £1.00
Delivery time after placing the order 2 weeks

You are required to:

(a) Calculate the total cost of placing orders and holding stocks if
    20, 40, 60, 80 or 100 orders are placed during a year.

(b) Determine the minimum cost using a simple EBQ model of

$$q = \sqrt{(2cd/h)}.$$

(c) Calculate, and comment upon, the effect of a discount of 5% for
    orders in excess of 2000 units.

[CIMA]

11 Making Better Decisions

11.1 FACING UP TO UNCERTAINTY

Major companies once relied upon the shrewd judgement and experience of top managers for major investment and marketing decisions. The successful firms were those who selected, trained and retained such people. Today that is not enough. Shrewdness and experience are still required, but mathematics is now a major tool in decision-making. This stems both from a better understanding of how to quantify uncertainty and from our ability to study the consequences of what might be called 'second-level' uncertainty, i.e. uncertainty about how well we are measuring uncertainty. Here objective and subjective probabilities (section 9.2) play a key role. Whenever there is uncertainty we shall sometimes make wrong decisions, but analysis of the relevant uncertainties will usually disclose how wrong it is possible to be, or reveal the odds against the worst possible consequence materializing if we take a particular decision. Using known facts and rational assessments of uncertainties, the consequences of various possible actions under all conceivable circumstances (the latter often referred to in decision analysis jargon as *states of nature*) may be determined. When the potential consequences of different actions are spelled out, we might make a decision that maximizes our expected profit, or, if we feel it more appropriate, minimizes the maximum possible loss (a minimax decision), or guarantees the best minimum profit (a maximin decision) relative to other possible actions. We may query assessments of uncertainty and explore how critically these influence decision criteria before making our choice. Finally, a manager must take other factors – some psychological, others that may be hard to quantify – into account before making a final decision. The mathematical analysis can only cope with the likely quantitative results of a decision.

11.1.1 Concepts and examples

We illustrate basic concepts by simplified examples; fully realistic examples would involve more computation and consideration of more alternative possibilities, but the basic principles remain unaltered.

Example 11.1   Milk sales at a corner store vary from day to day. The store does not open on Sundays, so more milk is sold on Saturdays (and perhaps Mondays) than on Tuesdays, Wednesdays, Thursdays or Fridays. We concentrate on these last four days when demand varies markedly in a way that the storekeeper cannot predict precisely on a day-to-day basis. However, he observes over a long period how much he sells each day: this varies between 20 and 60 pints. For simplicity, we suppose that customer demand for milk on any day is exactly 20, 30, 40, 50 or 60 pints. This is unrealistic, but it saves a lot of computation, and illustrates the principles involved in the storekeeper's decision on how many pints he should order each day. His problems arise because, in order to keep customer goodwill, he is only prepared to sell milk on the day it is delivered to him (another unrealistic assumption in the case of many shopkeepers!). He pays the wholesaler 20p per pint and sells it for 25p, representing a profit of 5p per pint sold. The wholesaler will not take back unsold milk, so the storekeeper pours this down the drain, losing his 20p purchase price (you might think him very foolish, but more about this below). He cannot predict demand from day to day, but finds on checking his records for a number of weeks that there is a long term stability in the number of days (i.e. the relative frequency, section 9.2.2) on which he sells 20, 30, 40, 50, 60 pints. He uses these relative frequencies as estimates of the *probability* each number is sold in a day. In real life, the probabilities may well turn out to be numbers like 0.287, 0.354, etc., but we simplify arithmetic by taking the following probabilities for 20, 30, 40, 50, 60 sales:

Number of sales	20	30	40	50	60
Probabilities	0.1	0.2	0.1	0.5	0.1

Such long term stability is common in repetitive situations even where we can see no short term pattern. Formula (9.6) for expectation gives expected sales $E(X)$ as

$$E(X) = 20 \times 0.1 + 30 \times 0.2 + 40 \times 0.1 + 50 \times 0.5$$
$$+ 60 \times 0.1 = 43$$

If the wholesaler only supplies milk in multiples of ten pints, how many pints should the storekeeper buy each day to maximize his expected profit?

We intersperse the solution with a number of comments rather than presenting it formally in a compact framework. With an expected demand of 43 pints, it looks reasonable to buy either 40 or 50 pints each day. If the former were chosen, daily demand would not quite be met *on average*, but this does not mean that there would be no milk poured down the drain! The storekeeper's aim is to maximize profit, i.e. his average long run profit. His profit on any one day will depend on how much milk he buys from the wholesaler (an *action* he may control) and on his sales that day (a *state of nature*; he only knows these will lie between 20 and 60 and the associated probabilities given above). Even here there is an act of faith – he cannot be certain that future overall demand patterns will mirror those of the past; he assumes they will. Since he makes 5p profit on each pint sold and loses 20p on any pint not sold, when 40 pints are purchased and 20 sold, the profit on 20 sold is $20 \times 5 = 100$ and the loss on 20 not sold is $20 \times 20 = 400$, so there is a net loss of $100 - 400 = 300$

pence. It is convenient to call a loss of 300p a *profit* of − 300p. Similarly, if he sells 30 pints (leaving 10 unsold) the net profit is $30 \times 5 - 10 \times 20 = -50p$.

If he sells all 40 pints, he makes a profit of $40 \times 5 = 200p$ since no milk is lost. If the demand is for 50 or 60 pints he still makes 200p profit, for he can supply 40 pints and additional demand is recorded as lost sales. If we denote by p_i the probability of a demand for i pints ($i = 20, 30, 40, 50, 60$) and by Q_i the net profit when demand is i (calculated above when he stocks 40 pints), then his expected net profit P is

$$E(P) = \sum Q_i p_i.$$

For a purchase of 40 pints,

$$E(P) = (-300) \times 0.1 + (-50) \times 0.2 + 200 \times 0.1$$
$$+ 200 \times 0.5 + 200 \times 0.1 = 100.$$

To find the order size that maximizes $E(P)$, we perform similar calculations when orders of 20, 30, 50, 60 pints are placed with the wholesaler. Clearly there is no point in ordering more than the maximum demand of 60 pints, nor in ordering less than 20 pints, since there is always a sale for at least that number. The results are summarized in Table 11.1. The reader should verify all expected profits (see Exercise 11.1).

The last line of Table 11.1 shows an order of 30 pints per day maximizes the expected profit; then 125p is the average profit per day that he may expect in the long run. When he sells only 20 pints (on about one day in ten since $p = 0.1$), he loses 100p with this policy. This is compensated for on days when demand is for 30 pints or more (in the long run, this happens on nine days out of ten – do you see why?). Although our description has been long winded, all one need write down is a table like Table 11.1, or even less if you are adept with a pocket calculator!

Table 11.1 Calculation of expected profits for various milk stock levels.

| | | Pints of milk purchased from wholesaler | | | | | | | | |
| | | 20 | | 30 | | 40 | | 50 | | 60 | |
Demand	Prob-ability	Q_i	$Q_i p_i$	Q_i	$Q_i p_i$	Q_i	$Q_i p_i$	Q_i	$Q_i p_i$	Q_i	$Q_i p_i$
20	0.1	100	10	-100	-10	-300	-30	-500	-50	-700	-70
30	0.2	100	20	150	30	-50	-10	-250	-50	-450	-90
40	0.1	100	10	150	15	200	20	0	0	-200	-20
50	0.5	100	50	150	75	200	100	250	125	50	25
60	0.1	100	10	150	15	200	20	250	25	300	30
Expected profit:			100		125		100		50		-125

11.1.2 Expected monetary value

We have used the term 'profit' loosely here, for the storekeeper will have other expenses (e.g. a proportion of overheads) to be deducted before he can call the proceeds 'profit' in a true sense. This type of analysis is also used in contexts where the money is not profit in any accepted sense, so in decision analysis what we have called *expected profit* is often called *expected monetary value* (EMV), a terminology we use henceforth.

11.1.3 Aims

Decision analysis aims to determine a strategy or choice of action(s) that is in some sense optimal when we have information about the states of nature. Usually (but not invariably) that information will be in a quantified form of uncertainty (usually expressed as a probability or as odds). The phrase *in some sense optimal* is deliberately vague. In Example 11.1, we maximized the EMV. This is appropriate for milk sales considered in isolation, for it is a strategy that maximizes the storekeeper's expected earnings from milk sales in the long run (providing his customers' buying habits for milk do not change). EMV is not always an ideal basis for decisions. Suppose, for example, the quantities purchased from the retailer and the demand by customers and the probabilities and cost structure used to construct Table 11.1 did not refer to milk sales and were given not in pence per item, but in £ thousand per machine unit and referred to the profit and losses that may be made if we buy the stated number of machines and can achieve the sales levels indicated by the demand numbers. Further, suppose the person making a deal on this basis (the equivalent of the storekeeper) does not do it every day but only once in a lifetime. Then clearly his EMV strategy is still to purchase 30 items as for the milk example, but in his one-off profit, as the sums involved are now not pence but £ thousand, he might not be happy with the thought that there is one chance in ten that he could lose £100 000. If he were a cautious man, he might well prefer to purchase only 20 items, for then, whatever the demand, he is assured of a gain of £100 000. If potential loss of £100 000 were a disaster, the decision to purchase 20 items only would surely be preferred. Looking at the possible actions, buy 20, buy 30, buy 40, buy 50, buy 60, we see (Table 11.1) that buying 20 minimizes the greatest possible loss (indeed ensures a gain), so in choosing that number he minimizes his maximum loss (or what is equivalent, maximizes his minimum gain), so we have a minimax or maximin decision rule. There are other decision criteria appropriate in some circumstances, but we do not discuss them. The minimax procedure is a pessimist's decision rule – it protects against the consequences of nature doing her worst.

If one makes a large number of decisions about different projects or is evolving purchasing schemes for many commodities, maximizing EMVs for each is usually sensible, because averaged over a number of projects, although some may give less than the EMV and others more, an overall balance close to the EMV is likely. Moore (1986: Chap. 10) cites a situation where EMVs were calculated for 100 capital investment projects, with average costs of over £2 million. Although EMVs were grossly exceeded for a few projects and returns from others fell far short of the EMVs, the total monetary return was close to the sum of the forecast EMVs.

11.1.4 **Other factors – modifying the optimum**

Businessmen and planners often modify an optimum decision based on, say, EMV to take psychological and other not easily quantified factors into account. This does not negate the value of the formal analysis, for the calculations, as well as giving an optimum, will often show the effect of moving away from the optimum, or how alternative optima (e.g. minimax or that based on EMVs) compare.

In Example 11.1, the EMV maximization decision to purchase 30 pints from the wholesaler means the storekeeper never meets demands of 40, 50 or 60 pints. These demands have a total associated probability of $0.1 + 0.5 + 0.1 = 0.7$. So, if each customer purchased exactly one pint, the storekeeper would have between 10 and 30 dissatisfied customers on seven days out of ten. This could be bad for trade, because customers finding milk is frequently unavailable may not only transfer their custom for milk, but in doing so may also take their trade for other goods elsewhere. By buying 40 pints of milk, the storekeeper would be more often able to meet demand, but will cut his EMV from 125 to 100 (Table 11.1). He must now decide whether a drop of 25p a day in net income from milk sales will be compensated for by retaining customers who might otherwise move all their trade elsewhere. If he thinks their custom will bring him a higher net inflow than his lost 25p from milk, clearly he should order the extra milk. Indeed, he might even buy 50 pints a day and reduce his expected net income from this source to 50p if he thinks the drop of 75p from the optimum will be offset by retaining customers with other spending requirements. He might even order 60 pints a day even if, as Table 11.1 shows, it does ensure an expected loss, if he believed certain availability of milk would induce customers to stay with him and purchase more profitable items as well. The 'loss-leader' is a familiar ploy used by supermarkets to attract customers.

11.1.5 **Updates**

One must update decision analyses if possible actions, or the states of nature, or their uncertainty patterns change.

Example 11.2   We return to the situation in Example 11.1, but now a local caterer learns that the storekeeper pours his surplus milk down the drain. The caterer is well aware that properly stored milk is perfectly good for most purposes on the day after purchase (indeed the storekeeper who does not sell milk more than one day old is somewhat altruistic). The caterer has a big turnover, so he will use any day-old milk within hours of getting it. As the caterer's usual source of milk is the same wholesaler that supplies the storekeeper and to whom he also pays 20p per pint, he realizes he will benefit if he takes any day-old surplus at 16p. The storekeeper is delighted – he cuts his losses on unsold milk from 20p to 4p a pint! Let us perform an analysis to check his intuitive belief that he might increase his maximum EMV and also be able to meet higher customer demands. After all, the trouble with large orders before was the possibility of a big loss on unsold pints, and these losses increased with order size.

Solution   He must now recalculate his EMVs for each possible action (purchase 20, 30, 40, 50, 60 pints) for each state of nature (demand 20, 30, 40, 50, 60 pints). Demand here means normal shop sales. Any surplus is now sold to the caterer at a loss of 4p per pint. Thus, if he buys 40 pints and sells 30, he makes a profit of 150p on those sold, but loses 40p on the 10 that are not sold. This gives a net profit of $150 - 40 = 110$p. Table 11.2 shows the complete calculation of EMVs in this case. You should check these calculations (Exercise 11.2). It is clear from Table 11.2 that his EMV is maximized at 178p by purchasing 50 pints per day. Indeed, even if he purchased 60 pints, the EMV would be better than the optimum was in the days when any surplus went down the drain.

Clearly if surplus milk could be sold at a profit, or no net loss, an optimum might be always to buy 60 pints a day, covering all possible demands.

Table 11.2 Calculation of expected profits for various milk stock levels.

Demand	Probability	Pints of milk purchased from wholesaler									
		20		30		40		50		60	
		Q_i	$Q_i p_i$	Q_i	$Q_i p_i$	Q_i	$Q_i p_i$	Q_i	$Q_i p_i$	Q_i	$Q_i p_i$
20	0.1	100	10	60	6	20	2	-20	-2	-60	-6
30	0.2	100	20	150	30	110	22	70	14	30	6
40	0.1	100	10	150	15	200	20	160	16	120	12
50	0.5	100	50	150	75	200	100	250	125	210	105
60	0.1	100	10	150	15	200	20	250	25	300	30
Expected profit:			100		141		164		178		147

11.1.6 Optima that fail to meet other criteria

Bookshops in the UK and many other countries normally obtain books from publishers on a sale or return basis, i.e. they pay the publisher his trade price only for books actually sold. Using the EMV criteria, it is then clear that an optimum procedure would be to stock every book that might conceivably be sold. Why is it then that my local bookshop seldom has the book I want? No, it is not (well, not always) the perversity of the book trade, but the fact that the difference between what the bookseller pays the publisher and what he charges the customer is not all profit – one good reason for talking about EMV rather than profit. Remember those stock holding costs in the last chapter? Booksellers have to face these (as well as reordering costs). If all booksellers were to stock even one copy of every book in print, they would require acres of floorspace in each shop and holding costs would be astronomical, especially for books that are stuck on the shelves for many years with little prospect of a sale.

11.1.7 **Information for decision analyses**

Estimates of EMVs should be based on the best available information. Of course, if the storekeeper knew in advance in Example 11.1 what the exact demand was going to be each day for milk, he would buy that amount daily and could work out his maximum expected profit. In the situation in Tables 11.1 or 11.2, it is obvious that, if he knows he is going to sell, say, 30 pints and buys 30 pints, his profit is 150; similarly if he buys and sells each of 20, 40, 50, 60 pints his profits are respectively 100, 200, 250, 300. Since we know the long run probability for each sale figure, his expected EMV, EMV(max) if he had precise information in advance on each day's demand, would be given by

$$EMV(max) = 100 \times 0.1 + 150 \times 0.2 + 200 \times 0.1$$
$$+ 250 \times 0.5 + 300 \times 0.1 = 215.$$

Thus, if sales could be predicted exactly each day, he could increase his EMV from a maximum of 125 to 215, i.e. by 90p per day in the situation envisaged in Example 11.1. In the situation considered in Example 11.2, he could only increase it from 178 to 215, i.e. by 37p. If custom varies in an erratic manner depending on customers' whims, it is hard to visualize a practical way of getting better indications of demand on a particular day. However, for more costly projects, it may be important to know by how much the EMV could be increased if we had perfect information, i.e. what is the maximum possible EMV? It indicates whether it is worth spending money (and if so how much) on market research, say, to get better information.

The other extreme to complete information is complete ignorance. We assumed above that our storekeeper had records to estimate the probabilities of various demands. If he had only opened his store a few days earlier, he may simply have noted that demand for milk varied between 20 and 60 pints per day. Unless he had some very clear indication that some quantities were more in demand than others, he may reflect his ignorance by assuming each of the sales 20,

30, 40, 50 or 60 had equal probability 0.2. This may lead to a not very reliable estimate of EMVs, but even it might be of some use in that it would warn him against buying too much milk in the situation envisaged in Example 11.1.

11.2   DECISION TREES

A network in the form of a tree (section 8.1.4) – known as a decision tree – may help when making decisions under uncertainty. These are widely used in industrial project planning. We use simple examples only, but these indicate principles and hint at the potential.

11.2.1 Formulating a problem

Example 11.3   A company making video equipment introduces a new line which market research indicates may increase sales by 15% over those for their current model. New products do not always live up to their predicted success, but the management are reasonably confident that if the product meets with a good customer response the forecast percentage increase in sales will materialize, but if it does not then sales will be maintained at something like the level for the product it is replacing. They envisage three possible courses of action:

A1. invest capital in new plant that will enable them to meet the additional demand if it materializes;

A2. cope with any increased demand by working additional shifts for several months of the year or overtime throughout the year (options that they regard as economically equivalent);

A3. use the present plant and work schedules, but meet the additional demand, if it materializes, by sub-contracting the extra work.

What other information is needed to decide on the best course of action, and if you were given it, what action is best?

Again, rather than presenting the solution formally, we intermix it with a discussion of several aspects of the problem. The firm might

Table 11.3 Returns (£ thousand at NPV) for various actions and outcomes, Example 11.3.

	Outcomes	
	R (Rising sales)	S (Steady sales)
Action A1	540	300
Action A2	510	350
Action A3	380	360

consider other possibilities than A1 to A3, but for various reasons reject them. For example, they may reject the possibility of allowing another firm to manufacture the equipment under licence for the export market only, while they concentrate their own production on the home market. Decision analysis can only indicate which, of any nominated actions, are the more desirable: it does not decide which actions should be nominated.

Information is needed about the states of nature. In this example, as already suggested, they decide that either there will be a 15% increase if market research predictions are borne out, or, if they are not, that sales will continue at the present level. On the basis of past experience of new models and their assessment of the retail market for videos in the next 12 months, they entertain no other possibilities. After some discussion, they decide the probability of increased sales is 0.7, and of sales staying at the present level is 0.3. Next, accountants are brought in and asked to estimate the net cash flow (reduced to NPVs; see sections 3.1.2 and 3.3) after one year for each of the three options A1, A2, A3 under conditions of rising sales (R) and under steady sales (S). The company chooses EMV as the appropriate criterion to determine policy. The cash flows estimated by the accountants for the various actions (A1, A2, A3) under each state (R, S) of nature are given in Table 11.3. This information, together with the probabilities 0.7 and 0.3 for R and S, is incorporated in a

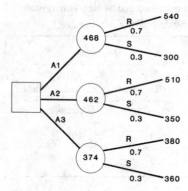

Figure 11.1 A simple decision tree relevant to Example 11.3.

simple decision tree in Figure 11.1. The square on the left represents a decision point (squares are conventionally used to represent decision points). From it, three stems radiate to represent the possible actions (labelled A1, A2, A3). At the end of each such stem is a circle (ignore for the moment the numbers in these circles) from which further stems emanate to represent the possible outcomes or states of nature. These are labelled R and S. We also show on these branches the associated probabilities. At the end of each of these stems, we write the net cash flows for the corresponding action and state of nature; these are obtained from Table 11.3. In this simple example, the decision tree is almost a needless luxury, but we see in Example 11.4 how it may be extended. To determine the optimum action to give maximum EMV, we must calculate the EMV associated with each action. These (in £ thousand) are the numbers given in the circles at the ends of the action lines. That for action A1 is

$$EMV(A1) = 540 \times 0.7 + 300 \times 0.3 = 468.$$

Similarly, EMV(A2) = 462 and EMV(A3) = 374.

Clearly the maximum EMV is obtained by taking action A1; however, returns would only drop by £6000 (about 1.3%) by taking action A2. Action A3 gives a relatively poor EMV. In passing, we note that the maximin criterion of selecting the action that maximizes our minimum return would selection action A3, since this guarantees a minimum return of 360 (compared to 300 for A1 and 350 for A2).

The company might decide that there is little to choose between A1 and A2, and, if they prefer the EMV criterion to maximin, to forget about A3. An astute director might point out that the probabilities 0.7 and 0.3 are based on an experienced assessment of market potential, but they are not sacrosanct. He might consider the probability of 0.7 for a rise in sales is somewhat pessimistic and ask what happens if we calculate the EMVs with this probability increased to 0.75. At this stage, the decision analysis expert points out (somewhat smugly) that he can do even better and determine the range of p values for which A1 dominates A2. He does this by replacing the 0.7 and 0.3 by general probabilities p and $1 - p$ (since the sum of the probabilities for the two states must add to 1). With these, he calculates

$$EMV(A1) = 540p + 300(1 - p) = 240p + 300.$$

Similarly,

$$EMV(A2) = 160p + 350 \quad \text{and} \quad EMV(A3) = 20p + 360.$$

Now, by standard results on inequalities given in Appendix A.3, $EMV(A1) > EMV(A2)$ providing

$$240p + 300 > 160p + 350,$$

$$80p > 50,$$

$$p > 0.625.$$

Although of less interest, a similar analysis shows that A3 would only have a higher EMV than A2 if p were less than 0.071 (see Exercise 11.6). On this basis, the director who felt 0.7 was an underestimate would probably feel reassured that action A1 was best. The analysis implies, however, that for at least some p values there may be little to choose between A1 and A2 so far as EMV is concerned. Looking at estimated net cash flows for A1 and A2, we see that A1 does better than A2 if sales rise, but not so well as A2 if they remain steady. This probably reflects the fact that the extra capital expenditure gives a good return if sales go up and in that sense is less expensive than the labour costs of extra shifts or overtime to meet high demand. On the other hand, if sales remain steady, there is little need for overtime, but the capital expenditure is largely wasted as there is no demand for the extra capacity.

11.2.2 Other factors

With very similar estimates of EMVs for A1 and A2, a final decision might be made on other considerations. The capital for new equipment may not be readily available, and the industrial relations expert might point out that the workforce like overtime and additional shifts. These factors together with some doubt about the true p value might swing the decision towards A2. There is also room for doubts about whether the forecast net cash flows will be exactly matched (accountants are not God).

Is one year too short a time range to consider? Even in the fast changing world of video equipment, many models stay in vogue for a couple of years, so the directors ask for forecasts of returns over two years. As A3 performed so poorly over one year, it is decided to omit it. It is also agreed that different scenarios should be considered in the second year: these are set out in Example 11.4.

Example 11.4   The second-year choice of actions will still be further capital investment (A1) or to meet increased demand by overtime or extra shifts as needed (A2), but we now consider three possible states of nature:

T: second-year demand will be 15% above first-year demand;
U: second-year demand will be the same as the first-year demand;
V: second-year demand will be down 5% on first-year demand.

After considering likely market factors, the directors now believe the probabilities they should associate with T, U, V will depend on whether sales in the first year rose (R) or were steady (S), i.e. the second-year probabilities are conditional on first-year outcomes. They decide that if R is the first year outcome then relevant probabilities for the states of nature T, U, V in the second year are

$$Pr(T \mid R) = 0.6 \qquad Pr(U \mid R) = 0.3 \qquad Pr(V \mid R) = 0.1,$$

and if the first-year outcome is S relevant probabilities are

$$Pr(T \mid S) = 0.2, \qquad Pr(U \mid S) = 0.7, \qquad Pr(V \mid S) = 0.1.$$

These probabilities reflect a not unreasonable expectation that if sales rise in the first year they are more likely to rise in the second year, and if steady in the first year they are more likely to remain steady in the second year. Some allowance is also made for a possible fall in demand that might be caused by market saturation or competition from new rival products. A shrewd manager can often make reasonable subjective assessments of such probabilities.

The accountants also work out the expected cash flow over two years (discounted to NPVs) for all possible combinations of actions and states of nature over the two years. It may not be immediately obvious, but they now have 24 situations to consider. A decision tree makes this clear. The appropriate tree is shown in Fig. 11.2. The tree is formed from left to right. Stems branch initially from the square decision node 1 on the left, where we proceed as in Fig. 11.1 to represent the first-year possible actions (we omit A3 as we do not wish to consider it further). However, at the end of the stems representing first-year states of nature in Fig. 11.2, we now put another series of square boxes to represent decision points where we choose the second-year actions, which we again denote by A1 and A2, analogous to the corresponding first-year actions. At the end of each stem representing these second-year actions, we require three new stems emanating from a circle to indicate possible states of nature T, U, V. Besides the stems representing R, S in the first year and T, U, V in the second year, we show the probabilities of each state of nature (these being conditional in the second year) and, at the end of each second-year 'state of nature' stem, we indicate the accountants' estimates of net cash flow over a two-year period for

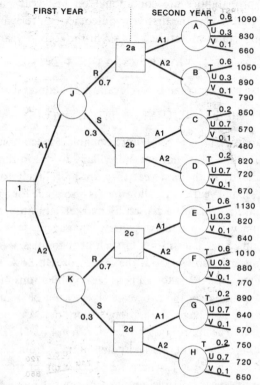

Figure 11.2 The basic decision tree relevant to Example 11.4.

the action/state of nature outcomes associated with that route through stems from the first decision point.

As in many multistage problems, once the tree is constructed, the easiest way is to work backward and find the best second-year decisions irrespective of what happened in the first year. Working backward in decision analysis jargon is often referred to as 'roll-back'. Once we have the optimal second-year decisions, we can work back to see what is appropriate in the first year. We again take EMV as the appropriate criterion. The relevant calculations are shown in Fig. 11.3. In each 'second-year' circle (to which for convenience we

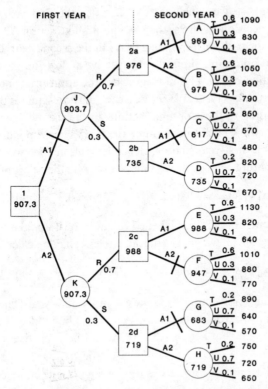

Figure 11.3 Use of roll-back to calculate EMVs in Example 11.4.

have assigned the letters A to H), we give the EMV for the action leading to that circle determined by the cash flows and relevant probabilities for each possible state of nature. For the top circle labelled A in Figs. 11.2 and 11.3, the data in Fig. 11.2 enable us to calculate the EMV as

$$\text{EMV(A)} = 1090 \times 0.6 + 830 \times 0.3 + 660 \times 0.1 = 969.$$

Continuing in this manner, the EMVs at B, C, D, E, F, G, H are as given in Fig. 11.3 (see Exercise 11.8). We now work back to each second-year decision box. For box 2a, the maximum EMV is 976 by taking action A2 in the second year (compared to 969 if action A1 were taken), so we conclude that, if, after the first year, we had arrived at decision point 2a, then we should take action A2. We may now slash the path corresponding to A1 in the second year, to remind us it is non-optimum. Similarly, if we arrive at decision boxes 2b, 2c, 2d, inspection of Fig. 11.3 now indicates the appropriate actions are respectively A2, A1, A2. We show in each of those squares the EMVs corresponding to these optimal actions in the second year.

We now work back to determine the EMVs corresponding to the two possible first-year actions dependent upon the two first-year states of nature R or S. If we take action A1, the relevant EMV is

$$\text{EMV(A1)} = 976 \times 0.7 + 735 \times 0.3 = 903.7,$$

which we enter in the circle labelled J. Similarly, if we take action A2, the EMV is 907.3, which we enter in circle K, having calculated it as

$$\text{EMV(A2)} = 988 \times 0.7 + 719 \times 0.3 = 907.3.$$

The optimum procedure is to take A2 in the first year. Then, in the second year, we would take action A1 if there had indeed been a rise in the first year, but action A2 if there had been no rise in the first year.

Note that once again there is only a small percentage difference (less than 1% between EMVs for A1 and A2 in the first year, although looking at a two-year time span the optimum first-year action is reversed from that if we take a one-year span (Fig. 11.1)). This is a common phenomenon in decision analysis, particularly where one is considering consumer goods that may quickly fall out of fashion. Capital expenditure to meet short term demands might well be a poor long term investment if demand rapidly falls off; it might be better to work overtime or additional shifts. On the other hand, if increased demand is likely to be sustained or even accelerate, capital investment in more equipment may be the more attractive option.

An example very similar in concept to that considered here is given by Moore and Thomas (1988), who expand it to cover facets of decision analysis that are beyond the scope of this elementary account.

11.2.3 A further example

Example 11.5   Sales of the existing model of a car are declining. The manufacturer considers three options.

(1) Continue with the present model in which case current sales of £50 million per annum are expected to decrease by 12% each year.

(2) Without additional investment in capital equipment, replace it by a new model for which, if sales are high, they will amount annually to £70 million, but if sales are low they will amount to only £20 million annually. Previous experience indicates that there is an 80% chance of high sales and a 20% chance of low sales for a new model introduced this way.

(3) Conduct prior market research costing £100 000. It is known that if good prospects are predicted by market research there is a 90% chance sales will be high (and a 10% chance they will be low); also, if bad prospects are predicted by market research, there is a 75% chance sales will be low (and a 25% chance they will be high). If the research predicts sales will be good, then the company will spend a further £20 million on capital equipment and introduce a new model. This will increase annual sales to £120 million if sales turn out to be high; if, despite good predictions, they turn out to be low, sales will slump to £15 million per annum. If the research indicates sales will be bad then the management will proceed with a new model but will make no further capital investment, and if sales indeed turn out to be low they will only amount to £20 million per annum, but if they turn out to be high then capacity limitations mean sales will be restricted to £70 million per annum. (Note here the similarity to sales under option (2).)

If sales predictions under options (2) and (3) are relevant for the next three years, which option should the manufacturer adopt to maximize expected sales return after making deductions for any capital expenditure and cost of market research?

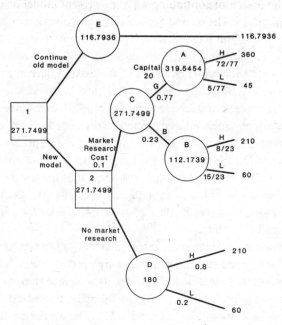

Figure 11.4 A decision tree for Example 11.5.

Solution We have already obtained, using some of the above information in Example 9.4, some further probabilities we need to set up a decision tree. There we deduced the probabilities of good and bad predictions to be 0.77 and (by implication) 0.23 respectively, explaining what these meant in terms of prior beliefs about high or low sales. We also showed in that example that, if we denote high and low sales by H and H* respectively and good and bad predictions by G and G*, then $\Pr(H|G) = \frac{72}{77}$ and (by implication) $P(H^*|G) = \frac{5}{77}$, while similar arguments give $P(H|G^*) = \frac{8}{23}$ and $P(H^*|G^*) = \frac{15}{23}$. You should verify these results by calculations similar to those used in Example 9.4.

An appropriate decision tree is shown in Fig. 11.4. We show two decision points (although the way we draw the tree is not unique); there are other possible logical structures. The first decision point leaves the option of continuing with the present model or introducing a new model. The second decision point involves a sub-branching if the latter decision is taken, i.e. to conduct or not to conduct market research. The relevant probabilities on the different state of nature branches are shown in Fig. 11.4 for this second decision situation. We also show at the end of each branch the expected three-year cash sales. For no new model (option (1)), this is computed from the information that sales will fall by 12% in each of the three years from the current level of £50 million. Thus, in the first year they will be £(50 × 0.88) = £44 million, and in the second year £(50 × 0.88^2) = £38.72 million. In Exercise 11.7, we verify that the third-year sales will be £34.0736 million.

Thus, over three years, sales will be £116.7936 million. It is easily verified from the data that if market research indicated good prospects and sales are high over three years the return is £360 million, and that other returns over three years are those given at the end of each stem of the tree in Fig. 11.4. You should verify these. We have made no attempt to reduce these to NPV. In practice, this would usually be done, but to do so does not alter the principle of the decision analysis, although it will alter the cash values and may well alter the conclusions in many cases.

We now calculate the EMVs shown in each circle emanating from the second decision in Fig. 11.4. For the circle labelled A, we calculate first 360 × (72/77) + 45 × (5/77) = 339.5454. However, since, if we have a good prospect forecast from market research, an extra £20 million is spent on plant, this must be deducted, giving a true EMV at this circle of 319.5454. Similarly, the true EMV at circle B is 210 × 8/23 + 60 × 15/23 = 112.1739. There is no deduction for capital expenditure if the market research gives a bad indication. We use these EMVs at A and B to obtain the EMV at C. Before deducting cost of market research, this is 319.5454 × 0.77 + 112.1739 × 0.23 = 271.8499, from which we deduct £0.1 million, the cost of market research, giving an EMV of 271.7499. For node D, the EMV is 210 × 0.8 + 60 × 0.2 = 180. Since this is lower than the EMV at node C, it is clear that at decision point 2 the firm should opt for market research, because this sharpens up the assessment of prospects for satisfactory sales compared to those assessed using only the prior probabilities of 0.8 and 0.2 (see Example 9.4). The resulting EMV is 271.749 9. Clearly the alternative at the first decision point of continuing with the old model only has an EMV of 116.793 6 (no alternative states of nature are envisaged here). The optimum choice using EMV as a criterion is to opt for a new model and conduct market research before deciding whether or not to spend capital on new equipment. If the market research indicates good prospects, money should be spent on capital equipment. What do you think they should do if market research indicates bad prospects? Do you think the manufacturer chose his options wisely?

11.3 WHAT AND WHERE?

What skills have we mastered

We have established maximum EMV and minimax as two decision-making criteria. Maximum EMV is widely used, but, where consequences may be serious if certain states of nature hold, a minimax or maximin procedure may be preferred.

Decision analysis problems with a probabilistic element are often soluble by use of decision trees. These are useful tools for displaying the logic of a decision analysis and exploring the consequences of various decisions in terms of appropriate criteria.

Where can I read more?

The basic notions in this chapter are extended and illustrated by numerous examples in Moore and Thomas (1988). Several decision criteria are discussed by Waters (1989: Chap. 10). Other useful reading is in Lucey (1988: Chap. 3) and Moore (1986: Chap. 10).

EXERCISES

11.1   In Example 11.1, we computed the expected profit if 40 pints were purchased daily. Carry out the corresponding calculations if

20, 30, 50 or 60 pints are purchased, to verify the results given in Table 11.1.

11.2   Check the calculation of all Q_i and all EMVs in Table 11.2.

11.3   If the storekeeper wishes to maximize his minimum profit in Example 11.2, how many pints should he order each day?

*11.4   Assuming the complete ignorance situation mentioned in section 11.1.7 where demands for 20, 30, 40, 50, 60 pints are assumed to each have probability 0.2, find the storekeeper's optimum strategies to maximize EMV if other conditions are (a) as in Example 11.1, and (b) as in Example 11.2.

11.5   In Example 11.3, verify the values of EMV(A2) and EMV(A3) given on p. 274.

11.6   In the discussion of Example 11.3, we stated that EMV(A3) would only exceed EMV (A2) if $p < 0.071$. Confirm this result.

11.7   In Example 11.5, verify that the third-year sales, if the old model is continued, amount to £34.0736 million as stated.

11.8   Confirm the EMV values in the circles labelled B to H in Fig. 11.3.

11.9   Use Fig. 11.3 to determine the course of action that would maximize minimum profit on the basis of the information given in Example 11.4.

*11.10   Mr Brown is transferred by his Canadian employers to the UK for one year. He needs a car and is referred by a friend to a reliable garage that is willing to repurchase from him at the end of the year at a guaranteed price any car he purchases from them. Three cars meet his requirements and he accepts that basic running costs for each will be the same. Car A is a new car costing £7500, guaranteed repurchase price £5250; any repairs will be covered by guarantee. Car B is a used car costing £4200 with guaranteed repurchase price £2200. The garage will give only a restricted guarantee that covers all repairs except for a new gear box if required. They say there is a probability of 0.4 this will be needed and, if so, they will supply and fit it for £500. Car C is a used car costing £3000 with guaranteed repurchase price £1500, again with restricted guarantee which this time excludes a combined engine and gear box failure. They assess the probability of this as 0.7 and, if needed, they will supply and fit these components for a total cost of £1200. Which car should Mr Brown purchase to minimize his expected net outlay? Which car would minimize his maximum possible outlay?   [Ignore inflation and potential interest if any of the monies were otherwise invested.]

*11.11   A bank manager has a sum of money to lend. He may lend it all to Bones and Shanks. If the venture they finance with it is highly successful (probability 0.6), they will bring the bank £50 000 in interest payments and other service charges. If it is only moderately successful (probability 0.3) they will bring the bank only £20 000, while if it fails the bank will lose £20 000 in default on interest payment.

As Collar and Tie want to borrow half the total amount the manager has available, an alternative would be to lend that amount to them and the balance to Bones and Shanks. A loan to Collar and Tie would guarantee the bank a certain gain of £16 000. The effect of halving the loan to Bones and Shanks would be to halve the profits/losses to the bank given above for that firm, the probabilities of the various outcomes remaining the same. Which lending strategy maximizes the manager's expected gain? Which strategy minimizes his maximum possible loss?

11.12   A centralized kitchen provides food for various canteens throughout an organization. Any food prepared but not required is used for pig food at a net value of 1p per portion. A particular dish, D, is sold to the canteens for £1.00 and costs 20p to prepare.

Based on past demand, it is expected that during the 250-day working year the canteens will require the following quantities:

On 100 days	40
On 75 days	50
On 50 days	60
On 25 days	70

The kitchen prepares the dish in batches of 10 and has to decide how many it will make during the next year.

You are required to:

(a) calculate the highest expected profit for the year that would be earned if the same quantity of D were made each day;
(b) calculate the maximum amount that could be paid for perfect information of the demand (either 40, 50, 60 or 70) if this meant that the exact quantity could be made each day?

[CIMA, part question only]

12 Replacement and Reliability

12.1 THE ECONOMICS OF REPLACEMENT

The problems in this chapter require common-sense adaptations of ideas already met, rather than fresh mathematics. They are concerned, in a broad sense, with replacement of items that deteriorate or fail. Example 3.5, where we examined alternative policies for renewing photocopying equipment, was in essence a kind of decision analysis problem falling into this category.

We often want to know the best policy for replacing equipment that deteriorates and for which maintenance costs rise steadily. We shall in general ignore problems of inflation and assume that monetary values have, where appropriate, been adjusted to NPV.

12.1.1 When to replace

Example 12.1   For polishing stones, a jeweller uses a grinding machine that costs £3500. Maintenance costs in any given year, together with the resale value at the end of the year, are given in Table 12.1; these are based on experience for a number of similar machines and are assumed to be adjusted to present day costs. If kept more than seven years, annual maintenance stabilizes at £1050 and resale value (which is now effectively scrap value) stabilizes at £250. After how many years should the jeweller sell each machine and replace it by a new one, if he wants to minimize his average annual operating costs consisting of depreciation plus maintenance?

Solution   Annual cost is: 'resale value at the beginning of that year − resale value at end of that year + maintenance'.

Table 12.1 Costings for a polishing machine, Example 12.1.

Age in years	Maintenance cost during year	Resale value at end of year
1	220	2600
2	250	2000
3	275	1500
4	300	1100
5	750	700
6	900	500
7	1000	300

The difference between beginning and end of year resale value is the depreciation. So, in effect, the annual cost is *depreciation + maintenance*. Sometimes only this annual total cost is quoted without a breakdown into maintenance and depreciation. The resale value at the beginning of year 1 is the capital (new) value. Thus, in year 1, the jeweller's costs are £(3500 − 2600 + 220) = £1120, i.e. an annual cost of £1120. In the second year, his costs are £(2600 − 2000 + 250) = £850. Thus, over two years, his total costs are £(1120 + 850) = £1970, giving an average annual cost of £985. Alternatively, we can calculate the depreciation over two years as £(3500 − 2000) = £1500, and maintenance over two years as £(220 + 250) = £470, giving a total two-year cost of £1970 as before.

For the third year, the annual cost is £(2000 − 1500 + 275) = £775, giving a three-year total of £(1120 + 850 + 775) = £2745, or an annual average of £915.

For the fourth year, the annual cost is £(1500 − 1100 + 300) = £700. This brings the four-year total cost to £3445, and the annual average to £861 (to nearest £). Similarly the fifth-year annual cost is

Table 12.2 Average annual costs for machine at end of each year, Example 12.1.

Age (years)	1	2	3	4	5	6	7
Av. annual cost	1120	985	915	861	919	949	985

found to be £1150 and the five-year annual average £919. Continuing in this way, you may check that the sixth- and seventh-year averages are £949 and £985. Clearly, after this, annual costs become no lower, since maintenance costs alone are over £1000. Average annual costs for replacement at the end of each year are summarized in Table 12.2, which shows the average annual cost is a minimum if he replaces after four years.

12.1.2 Some approximations

In Example 12.1, we made a simplification by considering one-year periods. Depreciation, in particular, will not go in annual jumps. A machine sold after three years and nine months will have depreciated by an amount somewhere between that at the end of the third year and that at the end of four years. More sophisticated analyses might take this point, and the precise time particular maintenance costs arise, into account. In Example 12.1, as is common, depreciation is at first rapid and then becomes more gradual as the equipment approaches scrap value (or sometimes zero resale value). Maintenance costs tend to increase, often abruptly at a certain age (here after four years). This is usually because replacement of expensive parts then becomes a recurring problem.

12.2 REPLACEMENT OF COMPONENTS

We often have a large number of units, each of which may fail at an unpredictable time, and we seek an optimal replacement policy.

Table 12.3 Percentage of detectors failing after a given time, Example 12.2.

Time after installation (mth)	1	2	3	4	5	6
Percentage unsatisfactory	10	10	20	25	30	5

Example 12.2 A chemical manufacturer is required under the Health and Safety regulations to monitor throughout its plant the level of toxic fumes and to evacuate staff if these levels exceed a specified value. It installs at strategic points 200 automatic detectors that will sound an alarm if the level surrounding any one of them exceeds this critical value. Unfortunately, the sensitivity of these alarms decreases with exposure to the fumes, so each must be tested at monthly intervals after installation, and any that are insufficiently sensitive at a monthly check must be replaced. The cost of each replacement is £6. Records over a long period indicate that the percentages not up to standard at inspection 1, 2, 3, . . . months after installation are those given in Table 12.3. The data are simplified to make the arithmetic easy, but this does not sacrifice any principles.

An alternative strategy is for the company to replace all 200 detectors in bulk at regular intervals and to continue the monthly checks between these regular replacements. Replacement cost per detector is £3 at the bulk replacement. However, any that fail at monthly inspections between these regular total renewals must be replaced at a cost of £6 per unit. Which strategy should the company adopt, and, if the second, at what intervals should bulk replacements be made?

Solution To work out the average monthly cost for the first strategy, we use Table 12.3 to work out the expected life per item. Since the data are percentages we divide by 100 to obtain probabilities, and the expected life in months is

$$(1 \times 10 + 2 \times 10 + 3 \times 20 + 4 \times 25$$
$$+ 5 \times 30 + 6 \times 5)/100 = 3.7.$$

Since there are 200 of these detectors, the expected cost per month for renewal at £6 each is £$(200 \times 6/3.7)$ = £324.32.

The second strategy involves lower unit costs at the bulk replacement. Such cost differentials between individual and bulk replacements are not unrealistic. Individual replacements may involve costs for testing units; there may be additional inventory costs in maintaining stocks to meet varying levels of replacements and technical problems may arise with an individual replacement that increase labour costs (e.g. if an electrical component is involved it may be necessary to isolate part of the circuit for a one-off replacement, whereas for bulk replacement only one switch need be thrown to isolate all units).

To compare (i) individual replacement upon failure with (ii) regular bulk replacements of all units (irrespective of failure) plus replacement of any individual detector found to have failed at a monthly inspection between bulk replacements, we work out the average monthly cost of bulk replacement at intervals of 1, 2, 3, . . . months together with the expected cost of individual monthly replacements between each bulk renewal. Clearly the number of interim replacements will depend on the interval between bulk replacements. If all detectors are replaced monthly, there will be no interim replacements, for monthly checking becomes unnecessary if all items are going to be replaced in any case. The cost per month is then £600. This exceeds the average cost per month of £324.32 worked out above for replacement after individual failure. If we make a full replacement every two months, this will cost £600. In addition there will be an interim inspection at the month's end between successive batch replacements. We expect a 10% failure rate after detectors have been in use for one month (Table 12.3), i.e. that 20 out of 200 will fail. This expected 20 will cost £(6×20) = £120 to replace. Thus, over two months with this policy, expected replacement costs will be (£600 + 120) = £720, giving a monthly average of £360.

If we move to bulk replacement after three months, the situation becomes slightly more complicated; there is still a bulk cost of £600, but there will be inspection replacements one and two months after a bulk replacement. At the inspection after one month, the expected replacement number is again 20 at a total cost of £120. At the inspection after two months, we expect a further 10% failure (Table 12.1) among those installed at the bulk replacement two months earlier, giving a further 20 failures; in addition there is an expected 10% failure rate after one month among the average of 20 installed as a result of the inspection the previous month (i.e. a further two failures). This gives an expected 20 + 2 = 22 failures at the two-month inspection, costing £132. Thus, over the three-month period, total costs are £(600 + 120 + 132) = £852, giving a monthly average of £284. This is better than the monthly average of £324.32 if we replace only on failure.

What if we extend to four-month intervals? We have our bulk replacement cost of £600 plus cost of any replacements at interim inspections after one, two and three months. Our expected replacements at one or two months after a bulk replacement are 20 and 22 respectively (as above). After the third month, we expect a 20% replacement rate among those in the last bulk replacement of all 200 detectors, giving a total of 40; in addition the 20 that were replaced at the end of one month are now two months old and 10% of them (i.e. 2) can be expected to fail, as can 10% (i.e. 2.2) of the expected 22 that were replaced one month previously. Thus the total number to be replaced after three months is 40 + 2 + 2.2 = 44.2 at an expected cost of £265.20, giving total costs over four months of £(600 + 120 + 132 + 265.2) = £1117.2, or a monthly average of £279.3. In Exercise 12.1, we establish that a five-year replacement interval has a monthly average cost of £296.18.

In practice, we stop at this stage, for the monthly average cost is now rising. We do not prove it, but the average monthly cost will continue to rise with longer bulk replacement intervals and

Table 12.4 Numbers of detectors to be replaced on failure, Example 12.2.

Months after last bulk replacement	Total to be replaced
1	20
2	20 + 2 = 22
3	40 + 2 + 2.2 = 44.2
4	50 + 4 + 2.2 + 4.42 = 60.62
5	60 + 5 + 4.4 + 4.42 + 6.062 = 79.882

gradually it approaches the average cost for single replacements at failure only.

To formalize our solution, the computations can conveniently be set out in two tables. In the first, we calculate the expected numbers of replacements at interim inspections one, two, three, . . . months, etc., after a bulk replacement, inspections being made up to the month preceding the next bulk replacement, remembering to take into account at each succeeding month those replaced due to failure at the ends of previous months since the last bulk replacement. Following the procedures above, we easily deduce the totals in Table 12.4. For example, the last entry comprises 30% of 200 that have been in use for five months (= 60) + 25% of 20 that have been in use for four months (= 5) + 20% of 22 in use for three months (= 4.4) + 10% of 44.2 in use for two months (= 4.42) + 10% of 60.62 in use for one month (= 6.062).

In Table 12.5, we set out total and average monthly costs for strategy (ii) with various intervals between bulk replacement. From it we see that the optimum policy, as already indicated, is to bulk replace every four months, with failed detectors replaced one, two and three months after a bulk replacement. The average monthly cost is then £279.30.

Table 12.5 Average costs of various bulk replacement policies, Example 12.2.

Months between bulk replacements (cost £600)	Additional replacement costs	Total costs	Av. monthly cost
1	0	600	600
2	6 × 20 = 120	720	360
3	6 × (20 + 22) = 252	852	284
4	6 × (20 + 22 + 44.2) = 517.2	1117.2	279.3
5	6 × (20 + 22 + 44.2 + 60.62) = 880.92	1480.92	296.18

In this example, failed items were only detected (and could therefore only be replaced) at the end of a month, so, if the information on percentage failures per month is correct, our solution is optimal for average costs. The situation is more complex if failure could occur and be detected at any time during a month and replacement had to be made immediately upon failure, but the mathematics does exist to deal with such situations.

12.3 REPLACING LOST PERSONNEL

A problem that resembles replacement of faulty detector is that of finding an optimum recruitment policy to maintain staff levels at full strength (equivalent to all detectors working) when there is a steady drain due to resignations or retirements (equivalent to failures of a detector). The sort of questions we ask about the system are slightly different.

Example 12.3   A large company wishes to maintain a staff level of 80 graduate engineers. Table 12.6 shows the average percentage of such graduates who leave their employment before the end of any given number of years. (Note that, unlike Table 12.3, the

Table 12.6 Cumulative percentage of graduates resigned by end of each year.

To end of year	1	2	3	4	5	6	7	8	9	10	11	12	13	14	15
Percentage	4	33	48	59	66	70	73	76	80	84	88	91	95	99	100

percentage frequencies here are cumulative. This is an alternative form in which data of this type is sometimes given.)

The figure of 100 in year 15 implies that no recruits stay with the firm's engineering department for more than 15 years. The table also shows that almost half those recruited leave before completing more than three years' service. This may seem a big loss, but it is common in some industrial sectors, where employees who are disillusioned soon leave, especially if they are trained in a skill for which there is a wide demand elsewhere. In many firms, one would expect some engineers to stay longer than 15 years, but this may not be so if conditions are particularly rigorous (e.g. in mining or oil exploration), where men may move to less arduous jobs in middle age, or transfer to other divisions of the same company (e.g. administration). Thus, in some industries, a maximum of 15 years employment in a sector such as engineering will be realistic.

We want to determine a recruitment level such that after a few years, when the system has stabilized, there will be a steady staff level of approximately 80 engineers. A subsidiary question that may be of interest is this: if the ten engineers with longest service in the company are paid a special long service bonus, how many years might a new graduate recruit expect to have to stay with the company before qualifying for this bonus?

Solution There is a simpler approach (given below) to determine the appropriate recruitment level, but we first develop a method that answers both questions. We examine the profile of length of service of people still in employment if 100 are recruited each year. We find the expected number of graduates in employment once this system has stabilized.

We argue this way using information in Table 12.6. When the system stabilizes there will always be 100 (the new recruits) who are in their first year of service. Table 12.6 tells us that four out of each 100 are expected to leave during the first year. This means that from the 100 in the previous year's intake we expect there to be 96 remaining who are in their second-year of service, i.e. have completed one year of service. Considering the recruits one year earlier still, since 33 are expected to leave in the first two years (Table 12.6), the expected number remaining and therefore having completed two years' service is 67. Continuing in this way (Exercise 12.2), we establish the expected numbers on the staff to have completed various lengths of service up to a total of 15 years. These are listed in Table 12.7.

Table 12.7 tells us that if we recruit 100 engineers each year the equilibrium total would be 534. However, we want an equilibrium total of 80, so if recruiting 100 gives an equilibrium total of 534 simple proportions tell us that to obtain an equilibrium total of 80 we should recruit each year $80 \times 100/534 = 14.98$. In practice, this suggests we might recruit 15. However, we implicitly assumed that those who leave during a year do so at the end of that year, whereas in practice people may leave at any time during the year (subject to requirements about periods of notice). If, at the other extreme, we had assumed anyone who left did so at the beginning of each year (e.g. of each 100 recruited, on average four resign on the day they arrive, 33 resigned at the beginning of the second year, and so on, the effect would be to reduce the equilibrium level by 100, giving a total of 434 (check the reasoning carefully to be sure you understand why – looking carefully at the modification needed for the first few entries ·in Table 12.7 may help). On this basis, the recruitment rate needed to maintain equilibrium at 80 would be $80 \times 100/434 = 18.43$. In practice, this suggests recruiting between 15 and 18 – perhaps 16 or 17.

Table 12.7 Number of employees with
given service times per 100 recruited at
year 0.

Years service completed	No. of employees
0	100
1	96
2	67
3	52
4	41
5	34
6	30
7	27
8	24
9	20
10	16
11	12
12	9
13	5
14	1
15	0
Total:	534

Had this been all we wanted to know, it would have been simpler
to calculate the average time graduates stay with the company
(analogous to the average life of detectors in Example 12.1). This
requires deduction from Table 12.6 of the percentage frequency with

which people leave in each year; e.g. from that table we immediately deduce that in year 4 this is $59 - 48 = 11$. In Exercise 12.3, you are asked to complete the table of percentage frequency with which people leave employment in each year and to use it to calculate the mean time in employment.

Your computation should produce a mean of 5.34 on the assumption that all employees leave at the end of a year. If we assume all leave at the beginning, the mean is reduced to 4.34 (i.e. by one year). A reasonable compromise would be to assume that the mean is about five years. To maintain levels at 80, this implies an annual recruitment rate of about $80/5 = 16$, which we have already concluded is reasonable.

12.3.1 Earning a bonus

Our earlier approach is needed to answer the question about how long employees may expect to remain in the job before receiving the long service bonus. To answer this, we calculate the numbers expected to have completed zero, one, two, three, . . . years of service among a total staff of 80. We may do this using simple proportions, making use of the distribution implied in Table 12.7 for 534 employees. For example, we see that 41 of 534 will have completed four years' service, implying that out of 80, about $80 \times 41/534 = 6.14$ will have completed four years' service. We give the approximate length of service distribution for 80 employees calculated in this way and rounded to whole numbers in Table 12.8. From Table 12.8, we see that approximately (because we have rounded off and these are in any case only expected long run frequencies) one employee will have completed 13 years service, two 12 or more, four 11 or more, six 10 or more, nine 9 or more, and thirteen 8 or more. On this basis, a new recruit may expect to have to work between eight and nine years with the company to qualify for the bonus paid to the ten longest service members.

In practice, a company wishing to introduce a long service bonus scheme would probably put a rather different question, but one

Table 12.8 Numbers of employees completing given years of service.

Year completed	0	1	2	3	4	5	6	7	8	9	10	11	12	13	14	15
No. of employees	15	14	10	8	6	5	5	4	4	3	2	2	1	1	0	0

giving much the same answer. They would be more likely to say: 'We want to encourage graduates to stay with the firm by offering a long service bonus after a specified number of years, but we do not want to pay this bonus to more than about ten staff at any one time. What period before paying the bonus should we specify if we want to keep the number of recipients at about ten?' The answer again would be about nine years completed service or perhaps a little less. A caveat here is that, if the bonus were very attractive, this might change employees' length of service pattern, encouraging more employees to complete nine or more years' service if they knew this would qualify them for a good bonus.

12.4 RELIABILITY

Closely related to replacement problems are those of reliability. In advanced applications, equipment may often break down at any time, but there is some long term pattern of relative frequencies of breakdowns after different times in use. A breakdown of one component may place extra strains on others, increasing the likelihood of their failure. In these circumstances, the mathematics in developing a system to ensure reasonable continuity of production or in evolving a policy for replacement that will minimize production loss becomes quite complicated. We look only at simple examples of two types of reliability problem (although we shall see each is closely related). The first is that of assessing how much equipment that is subject to failure should be on hand to give a 'reasonable' assurance that most, if not all, demands can be met. The second is the organization of systems in a way that the breakdown of one or more components will still allow the system almost certainly to function, or to function in a way that meets practical requirements. The human body has many such built-in safeguards. We can breathe through our mouth if our nose becomes blocked. This is not a foolproof system – it will not keep us alive if somebody holds our head under water for an extended period. Sometimes duplicated systems not only protect against the failure of one component but enhance the whole system by the duplication. Having two eyes gives protection against irreparable (or even temporary) damage to one eye. It serves the enhanced function of giving us effective three-dimensional vision. Duplication, triplication and even higher replication of components of a space shuttle in situations where only one functional unit of each type is essential minimizes the probability of complete failure of a vital system due to the high probability of one or two from many millions of components ceasing to function during a space mission even if each individual component has a low probability of failure. Once the reliability of several competing systems is assessed, management and accountants will often take cost considerations into account in deciding which system to adopt.

12.4.1 Remaining airborne

We look at a simple situation, where for each of a number of similar units the probability of breakdown of each in a given period (say one week) is the same. Further, we suppose that a breakdown in any unit occurs independently of a breakdown in any other unit. This is not always the case in practice: all too often, breakdowns in one unit place additional strain on other units, increasing the possibility of further breakdowns.

Example 12.4   A small commuter airline has ten aircraft. There is ample time to do routine (scheduled) maintenance at the weekend when they operate reduced schedules. The probability of any one aircraft being out of service because of an unscheduled maintenance requirement during a given week is 0.1, independent of the status of other aircraft. The airline's flight schedules require eight aircraft to be in serviceable condition at all times on weekdays. What is the probability they will be able to meet this requirement?

Solution This is a situation where the binomial distribution (section 9.5.4) is applicable. If the probability of failure, q say, is 0.1, then the probability of any aircraft being functional when required is $p = 1 - q = 0.9$. The number of aircraft, $n = 10$. The airline can meet its requirements if eight, nine or ten aircraft remain functional all week. Using the binomial formula (9.8), with $n = 10$ and $p = 0.9$, we calculate

Pr(all 10 functional) $= (0.9)^{10} = 0.349,$

Pr(exactly 9 functional) $= 10 \times (0.9)^9 \times 0.1 = 0.387,$

Pr(exactly 8 functional) $= \frac{1}{2}[10 \times 9 \times (0.9)^8 \times (0.1)^2] = 0.194.$

Adding these three probabilities, we find

Pr(8 or more functional) $= 0.194 + 0.387 + 0.349 = 0.930.$

Thus, in the long run, in 93% of all weeks, the airline may expect to have aircraft available for all scheduled services (some services may not operate for a variety of other reasons ranging from air traffic congestion, to weather, to strikes, but that is another story).

A modification of this problem is discussed in Exercise 12.4, namely determining how many aircraft the company needs in these circumstances to be 95% certain of having aircraft available for all scheduled services. The company operating the service may well ask their operations manager for this information.

12.4.2 **All systems go – fail-safe systems**

A closely related problem is that of system reliability. The reliability of a piece of equipment, usually denoted by R, is the probability that it will continue to operate over a specific time period; for most machine components, R will decrease as t, the time period, increases. The study of the behaviour of R as t changes soon gets one involved in advanced mathematics. However, it is often possible to study the reliability of quite complicated systems if R relevant to a fixed time period is known and can be supposed to remain constant (e.g. if R is the probability of a component not breaking down in a day and we assume this remains constant from day to day). This may be realistic over the short term (e.g. for one month in the life of a component that normally lasts several years).

Another useful concept complementary to reliability is that of failure F, defined as the probability of failure in a given time period for an item with reliability R. By the definition of the probability of opposite events (section 9.3), we immediately have $F = 1 - R$.

If a system continues to operate providing at least one of p components with reliabilities $R_1, R_2, \ldots, R_p$ respectively is functional, this means it will only fail if all p components fail. Now the probability that component i fails is $F_i = 1 - R_i$, for $i = 1, 2, \ldots,$ p, and by the multiplication rule for independent events the probability that all fail is the product $F_1 F_2 \cdots F_p$. The required event, that at least one does not fail, is the opposite event to all failing and thus has probability $1 - F_1 F_2 \cdots F_p$. An important practical case is that in which all F_i have the same value F, say. Then the probability the system continues to function becomes $1 - F^p$.

Example 12.5   In a space shuttle system, a component has probability 0.01 of failing. Three of these components are installed in such a way that the system continues to operate as long as at least one of these is functional. If failures in each are assumed independent, what is the probability the system continues to operate?

Solution   Here $F = 0.01$ for each component, so

Pr(system continues to operate) $= 1 - F^3 = 1 - (0.01)^3$

$= 0.999\,999.$

This 'belt + braces + knotted string' type of operation is the kind that might be employed by a pessimist haunted by a fear of losing his trousers in public; it greatly enhances safety compared to the use of one such device, decreasing the probability of failure from one chance in 100 to one chance in a million. Top managers of major projects often have to make decisions on the amount of safety that should be built in by duplication or triplication of equipment where a failure is potentially disastrous.

12.4.3 An electrical analogy

By analogy with electric circuit theory, we often talk about components being in *parallel* if they are such that the system operates as long as at least one of them remains functional. In industrial plants, if a number of machines are capable of making the same component, and production continues as long as at least one is working, these machines are regarded as being in parallel. For example, if one stage in a manufacturing process could in theory be carried out by a single machine as long as it functions properly (i.e. had reliability 1), it is common to install a back-up machine to cope with the fact that in reality all machines have reliability less than 1. The idea can be extended to situations where there may be p machines in parallel and operations can continue normally providing a lesser number r of these remain operational. Indeed that was exactly the situation we considered in Example 12.4 for aircraft availability!

Systems in parallel give increased reliability as we step up the number of units. We have a contrasting situation in chains of production where failure of one unit – one link in the chain – brings the whole system to a halt. Then, the more units in the chain, the more likely it is that the whole system will come to a halt. Such arrangement of components is referred to – again by analogy with electrical networks – as components in *series*. If individual components have reliability R_i, then for a series of n components, if breakdowns are independent, the reliability is the product $R_1 R_2 \cdots R_n$, which, if all $R_i = R$, reduces to R^n. Since, in practice, all $R_i < 1$, it follows that the reliability decreases as the number of components n increases (the product of n positive numbers, all less than 1, decreases as n increases). Most large scale manufacturing processes consist of a

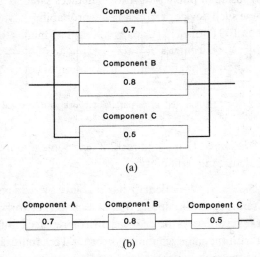

Figure 12.1 (a) Components arranged in parallel and (b) components arranged in series. In each case reliabilities are respectively 0.7, 0.8, 0.5.

mixture of parallel and series components with varying reliabilities. The probability that the whole process remains operational may be obtained by looking upon certain groups of components as equivalent to single components of the same reliability as that of the group, to produce eventually an equivalent system that is essentially either in parallel or in series. Here, network diagrams are extremely useful. Figure 12.1(a) shows the representation of parallel components in a network. The number on each of the parallel components represents the reliability associated with that component. Figure 12.1(b) represents a series network, the numbers on each component again representing the reliability of that component.

Since $F_i = 1 - R_i$, the reliability of the network in Fig. 12.1(a) is $1 - 0.3 \times 0.2 \times 0.5 = 0.97$. The reliability of that in Fig. 12.1(b) is $0.7 \times 0.8 \times 0.5 = 0.28$. Make certain you understand why in each case. Note that in both networks the reliabilities of the three individual components are the same.

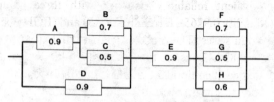

Figure 12.2 A mixed series–parallel network with specified reliabilities. The total reliability of the system is 0.826 (see Example 12.6).

Example 12.6   Figure 12.2 represents a more complex network. Calculate its reliability.

Solution   We calculate its reliability by reducing it to an equivalent series network, noting that in a mixed network a parallel sub-network may always be reduced to (or replaced by) a single component with the same reliability as the total reliability associated with the set of components in parallel. (This is a bit of a mouthful: read it twice, or even three times, to be certain you have grasped this important concept.) Similarly, several components in series can be reduced to a single component with the same total reliability as the series sub-network formed by those components.

We first replace the parallel components B and C by an equivalent single component. By the parallel rule for reliability, this will have reliability $1 - 0.3 \times 0.5 = 0.85$. We refer to this equivalent single component as (BC). We may now work out an equivalent single component A and (BC) which now constitute a series. By the series rule this has reliability $0.9 \times 0.85 = 0.765$. We now regard A, B and C as being replaced by a single component (ABC) with reliability 0.765; this is in parallel with D. We further reduce these two, parallel components to a single equivalent reliability component (ABCD) having reliability, given by the parallel rule, of $1 - 0.235 \times 0.1 = 0.9765$. Thus the components A, B, C, D in Fig. 12.2 are from the reliability viewpoint equivalent to a single component (ABCD) with reliability 0.9765. We next reduce the parallel sub-network F, G, H to a single component. Clearly this has reliability $1 - 0.3 \times 0.5 \times 0.4 = 0.94$. We call this equivalent component (FGH). We now have an equivalent reliability network with three components (ABCD) (reliability 0.9765), E (reliability 0.9) and (FGH) (reliability 0.94) arranged in series. The total associated reliability is 0.9765 × 0.9 × 0.94 = 0.826. Thus, if the reliability data represented the probability that each component would function for one week without a breakdown, the probability that the whole system would function for one week without breakdown would be 0.826. Looked at another way, we might expect it to function satisfactorily in nearly 83 weeks out of every hundred.

Whether or not a manager would be satisfied with that situation would depend very much upon the consequences of a breakdown. If the average breakdown only involved five minutes' lost production this might be tolerable. If each breakdown lost, on average, three days' production, they might be less happy (a euphemism for bloody unhappy) about how their process operated.

Example 12.7 Manufacture of a furniture kit involves the use of two machines, A and B, one after the other (i.e. in series). The reliability of the first machine is 0.9 and that of the second machine is 0.5. What is the reliability of the system? To increase reliability the management consider two options: (i) to duplicate the process by buying an additional pair of machines A and B to run in parallel with the existing machines, or (ii) to buy two additional machines each of type B to be run in parallel with the existing type B machine (i.e. the existing type A machine would run in series with a composite equivalent of three type B machines in parallel). If each type A machine costs £500 and each type B machine costs £250, which option is to be preferred?

Solution The reliability of the existing system is 0.9 × 0.5 = 0.45. Since the capital cost of either option is £500, one should choose the option giving greater reliability. For option (i), the overall reliability is $1 - 0.55^2 = 0.6975$. For option (ii), the three machines in parallel have overall reliability $1 - 0.5^3 = 0.875$, so in combination with machine A in series the overall reliability is 0.7875. Thus option (ii) is preferred.

We have only touched the tip of the iceberg of statistical studies of reliability – whole books at varying theoretical and practical levels have been written on the subject. Experts are needed to assess complex system reliability, but it is important for production managers to understand the rudiments of reliability theory, in particular the very different consequences in series and parallel situations.

12.5 WHAT AND WHERE?

What skills have we mastered?

We have studied replacement policies to minimize cost based on essentially deterministic data (often in the form of estimated costings), taking into account depreciation and maintenance costs.

When many similar units may fail, it is often relevant to compare single replacement on failure with bulk replacement if unit costs for the latter are lower. Optimal recruitment policy to maintain staffing levels has analogies with this problem.

Many reliability problems are closely related to replacement problems. Here the emphasis is on the probability that a system will continue to function. Back-up components are an essential feature of most fail-safe systems.

Overall reliability of production processes is highly dependent upon the layout of machines, in particular whether they are arranged in series or in parallel.

Where can I read more?

Waters (1989: §9.3) provides good supplementary reading and extends some of our notions on reliability. Moore (1986: Chap. 9) deals with a problem similar to that in Example 12.2 in a chapter that links replacement policy with more general financial modelling. A more sophisticated treatment of replacement theory is given by Houlden (1962: Chap. 7).

EXERCISES

12.1 For the data in Example 12.2, verify that the monthly average cost for bulk replacements at five-month intervals with immediate replacement of intermediate failures has a monthly average cost of £296.18.

12.2 In Example 12.3, verify all the entries in Table 12.7 for numbers of employees with given years service per 100 recruited.

12.3 For the data in Example 12.3, complete the table of percentage frequencies with which people leave employment in each year, and use it to verify the given mean time in employment.

*12.4 For the airline data in Example 12.4, determine how many aircraft the airline would need to be 95% certain that it had sufficient aircraft available for all scheduled services. [Hint: You may find a common-sense trial and error method the easiest way to solve this problem.]

*12.5 An illuminated advertising sign has 1000 light bulbs. It is inspected monthly and any bulbs that have failed are replaced at a cost of £1.50 each. The percentage that are expected to burn out during the first, second, third, . . . month of use are as follows:

Month	1	2	3	4	5	6	7
Percentage	5	5	10	10	20	40	10

What is the average monthly cost for replacements?

A maintenance company offers the operators of the sign another arrangement whereby they will replace all bulbs at regular intervals (multiples of one month) at a cost of 50p per unit and replace individual failures at monthly intervals between these total replacements at a cost of £2 per bulb. Should the company operating the sign accept the offer, and, if so, what interval should they specify for complete replacements?

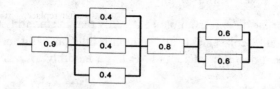

Figure 12.3 Network for Exercise 12.7.

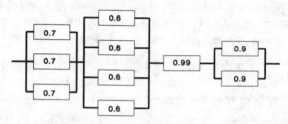

Figure 12.4 Network for Exercise 12.8.

*12.6 A bus company requires 20 drivers for full service on its early morning shift. The probability that any driver who is rostered will turn up is 0.95, independent of whether or not any other driver turns up. If it rosters 22 drivers for this shift, what is the probability it will be able to provide full service on a given morning? During an influenza epidemic, the probability of any driver turning up drops to 0.7. What is now the probability that full service can be operated on a given morning during the epidemic?

*12.7 What is the overall reliability of the network in Fig. 12.3?

*12.8 What is the overall reliability of the network in Fig. 12.4?

12.9 An engineering company is studying a replacement strategy for its metal cutting tools. It has collected the following data on tool life relating to normal load and operating conditions.

	\multicolumn{5}{c}{Months after replacement}
	1	2	3	4	5
Percentage of original tools which have failed by the end of the month (cumulative)	10	25	50	80	100

1000 cutting tools are in use at any given time. They could be replaced by new tools on a mass replacement basis for £1.00 per tool. Alternatively, they may be replaced individually as they fail at a cost of £4.00 per tool. In each case the actual cost of the tool itself is 50 pence, the remainder representing labour and overhead charges.

At present the company replaces tools as they fail.

You are required to:

(a) compare the cost of the current tool replacement system with the alternative of replacing all tools at a certain fixed monthly interval together with individual replacements of those tools which have failed in the preceding interval;

(b) state the best strategy for the company to follow.   [CIMA, part question only.]

[Hint: The situation in this question differs from that envisaged in Example 12.1 in that replacements of individual failures take place immediately they occur.]

13 Process and Product Quality Control

13.1 SOME WAYS OF CHECKING QUALITY

Methods have been developed over the past 50 years to check whether a process is operating satisfactorily – whether goods of marketable standard are being consistently produced. World War II stimulated developments on both sides of the Atlantic. Military equipment, complex both in design and operation, was produced by a variety of suppliers. Raw materials were scarce, and there was a shortage of skilled labour and sometimes, because of the speed at which items were required, a failure to understand fully what was needed or what was technically feasible. Pressures for quick delivery of vital material, and sometimes lust for quick profits, were all factors that resulted in delivery of sub-standard material under defence contracts. Quick and reliable methods were needed to see whether large deliveries were up to specification. Samples were taken; it was assumed that characteristics of the sampled items would be broadly reflected in the batch from which they came. Techniques were developed under the name of acceptance sampling.

13.1.1 Production checks

During production runs, it is clearly useful if checks can be made to detect rapidly anything going wrong. Are some items consistently too heavy or of the wrong dimension? Pistons 10.07 cm in diameter will not fit cylinders of diameter 10 cm! Here a device known as a control chart developed by the American statistician W. A. Shewhart proved useful; these charts may be used on the shop floor by a foreman or skilled operative and quickly indicate when some-thing might be wrong on a production line, e.g. items consistently too heavy or chemically impure. When trouble is indicated, the process may be stopped; hopefully an engineer, chemist or other appropriate expert can suggest what to do – tighten a screw, replace a washer, remove contaminating oil, or whatever. Statistical con-cepts, especially that of a sample (section 9.6), are particularly apposite in both acceptance sampling and in using control charts. On their own, these methods are largely diagnostic; they highlight symptoms and often lead to remedial action that merely relieves the symptoms rather than curing the problem.

In the early days, quality control seldom led to action that brought long term improvement to a process. It even produced hostile responses from some manufacturers because continued failure to supply goods that would pass an acceptance sampling test might cost a firm future contracts, leading eventually to it going out of business. It was left to the manufacturer to find out why his goods were not up to acceptable standard. There was usually little encouragement to explore deep-seated reasons for batches not being up to standard; the testers did not feel it their duty to discuss with manufacturers what problem might be causing batches to be sub-standard, and the manufacturer often received little feedback as to why his goods were being rejected. If, on the shop floor, control charts showed something was going wrong, the immediate aim (particularly if staff were under pressure to meet production targets) was to find a quick way of correcting the difficulty; stopping it happening again by redesigning or modifying a piece of machinery was something for management to worry about – if they even heard of the problem!

World War II quality control methods were carried over to peacetime industrial use with little modification apart from some statistical sophistication to enable quicker detection of problems. New types of control chart were developed and more elaborate sampling techniques were introduced for acceptance sampling to determine whether a batch was of acceptable standard.

The 1970s saw a new ethos developed in quality control. The emphasis shifted from the product to the process. Previously, if the product met specifications, i.e. was within acceptable design limits regarding weight, chemical purity, performance, etc., everybody was happy. It was accepted as a fact of life that some industrial processes produced as many as 8 to 10% defective items, and it was assumed to be prohibitively expensive to reduce these percentages. Acceptance sampling (or sometimes complete inspection of every item) was used to see if 'reasonable' quality levels were being maintained; the defective items were scrapped or sold off cheaply. If acceptance sampling revealed too high a proportion of defective items, you rectified or removed those if possible; if not, you sold the whole batch cheaply. Precisely what one did was a matter of economics.

13.1.2 Total quality control

Control charts, together with certain other well-established statistical ideas, plus some economic principles, together with more sensible management procedures, are now used to improve *process* quality (rather than simply *product* quality), it being argued that if processes are better the finished product will be better. Indeed, given good process control, in many cases, product quality looks after itself, and acceptance sampling or detailed inspection of all finished articles becomes unnecessary.

The new emphasis is epitomized in the phrase *total quality control*. Statistical quality control, the old concept of control charts and other graphical aids, is now allied to specified methods of experimental design (a statistical concept itself dating from the 1930s) to improve processes. This is an important part, but only a part, of total quality control. The old philosophy that come what may a particular process produced $x\%$ faulty goods (where, depending on the product, x tended to be just about any number between 0.5 and 10, sometimes even as high as 20) is dying fast.

The new philosophy had its origins in Japan, born from their post-war industrial conviction that what the consumer wants, above all, is quality and reliability. Japanese manufacturers surmised rightly that the consumer would pay an economic price for this, often a premium that more than covered the cost of building in that higher quality and reliability. While the Japanese adopted, and used, the methods of industrial quality control developed in the West, they applied them differently, making them an integral part of total quality control with its emphasis on controlling the process as the key factor. If a control chart showed a process was getting out of control, they were not content to merely tighten a screw or a nut or a bolt, or to replace a belt drive or some other part of a machine that common experience has shown to be the likely cause of the trouble. They asked instead how that offending part could be redesigned or replaced so that the trouble did not keep resurfacing. In particular, they designed experiments and analysed variability in great detail to determine its sources, to improve processes to reduce the (usually unwanted) variability between products. In some cases, they only reinvented experimental designs and methods of analysis discovered long ago in the West but applied there largely in other fields such as agriculture and biology. Only a handful of enlightened Western industrialists had adapted these methods to their needs; what was important in the Japanese approach was that they applied them in the context of improving a process. Workers on a production line were encouraged to make their own observations of the product they were making and to report and discuss any faults they noted, in contrast with Western counterparts, who so often simply ignored a problem staring them in the face, believing it to be a management worry, not theirs, often oblivious to the fact that management may not even be aware of the difficulty. Sometimes rightly, sometimes wrongly, they assumed management would do nothing about it even if the problem were brought to their attention.

13.1.3 **Back to the West**

The new Japanese philosophy outlined above has been reimported into the West; it would not import lock, stock and barrel, for there are differences in philosophies and educational standards of work-forces in different countries. These differences should not be overemphasized, for Japanese manufacturers setting up production plants in Europe and America have successfully introduced their Western workforce to the philosophy and practice of total quality control. The concept now has many Western evangelists. The idea is spreading, stemming the decline in American and European industrial output as the message is acted upon – the message that people want, and will pay good prices for, quality and reliability. These boost sales and hold them at higher levels than a 'damn the consumer, let's make a fast buck' attitude. As with all rapid changes in outlook, there is a certain amount of ballyhoo. A Japanese engineer, Taguchi, virtually rediscovered many Western ideas on how to experiment and analyse the results to improve processes. 'Taguchi methods' are now OK words with many total quality control experts. It is not decrying Taguchi to say that many of his ideas were known years ago in a different context, for he knew how to sell these ideas, helping to improve the quality of quality control.

Statistical ideas like control charts are fundamental to both process and product quality control; in practice, they are now often automated and computerized. Marquardt (1984) reported that the American chemical giant E.I. du Pont de Nemours & Co. were then using in different parts of their plants, in a variety of control process monitors, over 10 000 computerized CUSUM check systems (a special form of control chart we describe in section 13.2.4). These were involved with the manufacture of products generating billions of dollars' worth of sales annually, and Marquardt indicated that quality control checks of this type were still expanding. The modern shift is from inspection of finished products to control of the process, the ultimate aim being that the finished products will be so good they do not need inspection. The manufacturer who does not heed these trends is in danger of going out of business.

Despite this, the 'all process control, no product inspection' goal is still a long way off. No matter how good the production process, the possibility that goods are damaged in shipment remains: perishable items may deteriorate due to poor storage or adverse weather conditions. Minimizing difficulties arising from these causes might be looked upon as improving the marketing process. So, until we improve marketing control, some acceptance sampling and batch inspection will stay with us, no matter how good the process control.

We describe first one or two elementary control charts, then turn briefly to acceptance sampling in section 13.3. Use of experimental design in controlling and improving processes is a sophisticated technique beyond the scope of this introduction.

13.2 CONTROL CHARTS

Shewhart's original ideas have undergone modifications, some subtle, some important. Three situations where such charts are used include the following.

1. To detect whether a process is on a 'mean' target, i.e. is producing goods with the right mean value (e.g. steel rods of a required length, copper balls of the correct weight, boxes of matches with the appropriate number in each). In mechanized processes, slippage in mean is a common fault. Machines get out of what is called 'statistical control' and suddenly produce items consistently above a required length, below a target weight, etc.
2. To detect increased variability in a characteristic such as a length or weight or number of items per packet.
3. To detect whether the proportion of defective items produced by a process exceeds a permitted or acceptable level.

We give an example of the first of these and comments on the others. An important practical requirement for any control chart in the pre-computer and pre-automatic recording era was that it could be used and interpreted to make *quick* decisions on the shop floor – it was commonly used by a foreman, or by a plant operative himself, without calling on outside expertise. The interpretative issue is to decide whether the chart indicates a need for corrective action because items produced are not meeting standards. Such action can then be taken quickly, before many sub-standard items are produced. With increasing availability of automatic devices for recording characteristics such as weights, lengths or number of defectives, and the ability of computers to do arithmetic on such automatically recorded data, these processes are now often mechanized. We mentioned in section 13.1.3 that one American chemical company used many such control systems with a type of chart known as a CUSUM chart. Whether the whole process is done manually or automatically, the principle of control charts is the same.

13.2.1 Control of the mean

Example 13.1 A manufacturer produces steel rods which ideally should all be 1000 mm long. They are produced by a cutting machine which is fast, producing some 40 such rods per minute. Its sophistication and speed means that there is a slight variability in the lengths of the rods it produces. The buyers of the rods accept this providing rods produced are all between 995 and 1005 mm in length. Set up a control chart to detect slippage in the mean.

We blend the formal solution into a more general discussion. Before he even buys the machine to cut these rods, in the spirit of modern total quality control, the manufacturer will have assured himself that rods it produces fall within these limits when the machine is appropriately adjusted. Any testing he does to confirm this will also give him information he needs for setting up control charts. As we have already indicated in section 9.5.7, measured rod lengths in these circumstances are usually (at least approximately) normally distributed. To estimate accurately the mean and standard deviation of rods produced by this machine, the manufacturer might make 1000 rods and calculate the mean and standard deviation of the lengths. There is a formula for calculating the latter. Indeed it differs only from formula (9.7) in that the final divisor n is replaced by $n - 1$, a difference that has negligible effect when $n = 1000$. Some pocket calculators have a special facility to calculate it. He might find the mean length to be 1000.3 mm and the standard deviation 1.3 mm. It has been established for the normal distribution that there is a probability of only $\frac{1}{20}$ (one chance in 20) of a normally distributed measurement having a value more than 1.96 standard deviations away from the mean and a probability of only about $\frac{1}{500}$ of its having a value more than 3.09 standard deviations away from the mean. Now, if the standard deviation is 1.3 mm, we find $1.3 \times 3.09 = 4.02$, so in the long run we expect only one item in 500 to be either above $1000.3 + 4.02 = 1004.32$ mm or below $1000.3 - 4.02 = 996.2$ mm. This means that we expect virtually all items (i.e. except about one in 500) to have lengths in the range 996.2 to 1004.2 mm, well within the acceptable range 995 to 1005 mm. The machine would be regarded as acceptable from this viewpoint, but of course the manager might take many other considerations (cost, reliability, ease of operation) into account before deciding to buy this particular machine.

The above test results suggest the mean was not spot on the 'target' value of 1000, but very close. This would usually be regarded as acceptably close, bearing in mind (section 9.6) that another sample of 1000 rods could not be expected to have an identical mean, but again one very close to the target value if conditions had not changed. The standard deviation of another sample would also be different, but for a large sample the difference again is unlikely to be of practical importance. For practical purposes, we may regard the machine as capable of making rods of length 1000 with standard deviation 1.3. This is the basis of a control chart to test for slippage in the mean.

To use the control chart described below on the production line, small samples are taken from production at regular intervals and the mean length is measured for each such sample and plotted on the chart. The chart usually has five horizontal lines. The middle of these represents the 'target' value of 1000 for the mean. The position of the other lines depends on the sample size, and the standard deviation (which we take to be 1.3, as estimated from the test run with 1000 rods). One of the convenient properties of this

Table 13.1 Successive mean lengths of samples of four rods; target mean 1000 mm.

999.3	1000.1	1001.1	998.8	999.4	1000.8	1000.1	998.6	999.2
1000.2	998.8	999.1	999.3	998.7	999.4	998.9	998.4	997.8

normal distribution, which we do not prove here, is that for a sample of n observations the sample mean (which of course differs from sample to sample) is normally distributed about the population mean of 1000 with standard deviation $1.3/\sqrt{n}$. Thus, if four samples are taken on each occasion (so that $\sqrt{n} = 2$), there is one chance in 20 that the sample mean will fall outside the range $1000 \pm 1.96 \times (1.3/2) = 1000 \pm 1.27$ and one chance in 500 it will fall outside the range $1000 \pm 3.09 \times (1.3/2) = 1000 \pm 2.01$. This is the information used to position the other four horizontal lines on the control chart. We show how this is done in Fig. 13.1. (The multipliers 1.96 and 3.09 are close to 2 and 3 respectively; British Standard specifications use 1.96 and 3.09, but it is common in many countries to use 2 and 3. There is little difference in practice.) Two lines, usually called (upper and lower) warning lines, are at vertical distances 1.27 above and below the target line and two further lines usually called (upper and lower) action lines at vertical distances 2.01 above and below the target line. The scale on the x-axis represents successive sample numbers. Each time a sample of four is taken, the length of each rod is measured and the mean length for the sample of four is calculated. This mean is plotted on the control chart. Table 13.1 gives a set of successive means of samples of four for the process we have described. These values are plotted in Fig. 13.1.

If the process is working properly (the jargon for this is 'under statistical control'), we would expect only about one sample mean in 20 to lie outside the inner warning lines and only about one in 500 to lie outside the action lines. If the latter occurs, it is an indication the process may be out of control and the rule is to stop and check if the machine is operating properly. Often such a slippage in mean

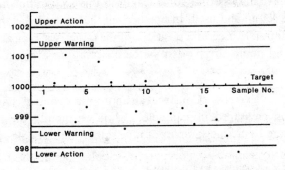

Figure 13.1 A Shewhart control chart for detecting shift in a mean.

is due to wear or loosening of some machine component. Once the slippage is detected, the remedial action (tighten a screw, fit a new belt drive, or whatever) may be obvious. Observations between the inner warning and outer action lines can be expected to occur for about one sample in 20 while the process is in control, so we usually take no action for a single sample value between these limits. However, two successive values between inner and outer lines do give cause for concern and a common rule is to stop the process and check if all is well when this happens. Sometimes more sophisticated rules are used; for example, the rule might be that, if a sample value lies between the warning and action line, do not wait the normal time to take the next sample, but take another immediately. If that too gives a value between warning and action line, then stop the process.

We see in Fig. 13.1 that observations 8 (998.6) and 17 (998.4) fall between lower warning and lower action line. These alone do not warrant a stoppage; the 18th value of 997.8, however, is below the lower action line, so the process would now be stopped and any needed adjustments made.

In our example, we suggested that a simple remedial action like tightening a screw may be appropriate. If the fault recurs regularly, in the spirit of total quality control one would investigate why that screw became loose and perhaps modify the design to eliminate or reduce the problem.

We have discussed at some length in this section how a control chart is set up and used. In practice, all that is needed is the simple computation to ascertain positions of the target, warning and action lines, and points are plotted as the observations are taken on the shop floor.

> *Exercise* Construct an appropriate control chart for the situation envisaged in Example 13.1 if we modify the sampling procedure by taking samples of nine rather than samples of four.

13.2.2 **Changes in variability**

The control chart in section 13.2.1 has the specific aim of detecting slippage in the mean or target value. If this happens, it is intuitively obvious (and not difficult to prove formally) that the probability of getting sample values outside the action lines (above or below depending on whether the slippage is up or down) is increased. However, if the variability of the process increases without any slippage, these probabilities for extremes will also increase. This, together with the fact that increased variability will result in increased production of unacceptable items (with lengths above 1005 mm or below 995 mm) are good reasons why we should also have control charts to test for changes in variability. Although such charts can be based on sample standard deviation, computation of the latter on the shop floor is often regarded as too complicated (modern calculators and computers make this assertion less valid). A more important objection is that, when based on small samples, the values obtained for the sample standard deviation are somewhat unstable. To overcome these problems, control charts to test for changes in variability may be based on the range of sample lengths (the difference between the largest and smallest value in the sample). We shall not discuss such charts in detail. In practice, we are usually interested only in whether variability has increased above that when the machine is under control, so that one need only consider upper warning and action lines. There are recognized methods for obtaining these.

In the spirit of modern total quality control, there is a strong emphasis on reduction of variability, for consistency is a quality attribute that appeals to consumers.

13.2.3 **Other characteristics, including proportion defectives**

Sometimes more than one characteristic may decide whether items are acceptable. Returning to our rods example, an acceptable rod may not only have to have a length between 995 and 1005 mm but may also be required to have a maximum diameter of 4 mm. This can be tested by a 'go – no go' gauge which is passed along the rod, and if the rod slips through it is satisfactory. The specification agreed with the buyer might be that not more than 2% of the rods should exceed this maximum diameter. We shall see in section 13.3 how acceptance sampling provides a means of checking this when batches are delivered, but if production is fast it is better if any departure from standard can be detected on the shop floor. We might then reduce the numbers of rods that would be rejected at the marketing stage if the fault can be easily rectified. To get satisfactory control charts for charges in small proportion defectives, somewhat larger samples are needed than those for checks on length. If the measurement is of the 'go – no go' type the test is often reasonably easy to make on a number of units. Samples of 100 rods might be taken each hour and the number that fail is all that need be recorded. Warning and action lines can be calculated for such sampling plans. We omit details, but for the case of samples of 100 and a 'statistical control target' of 1% defectives, we need only worry about upper warning and action lines (we are usually not worried if the proportion defective drops, although this might have long term interests for total quality control). In practice, we do not even need to draw such a chart. We simply work out the number of defectives that constitute a warning or a need for action. For our example, these turn out to be three or more defectives for a warning, and four or more defectives per 100 for action. Thus, if successive samples had 0, 1, 2, 2, 3, 1, 0, 2, 3, 2, 1, 6, 1, 0 defectives, the process would be stopped after the sample with six defectives. Note that the warning level of three defectives is attained twice in the sequence, but no action is taken as we would only act on warning values (not reaching the action level) if two consecutive values reached that level.

13.2.4 CUSUM charts

We return now to control charts for the mean. Inspection of Fig. 13.1 indicates that, although action was not triggered until sample number 18, all samples after sample 10 had means below the target. This suggests that something might have been starting to go wrong at that earlier stage. It is not uncommon for slight slippage to occur and for this to gradually increase. Until it has become quite marked this slippage may not be detected by the control chart in Fig. 13.1. The essential weakness with this type of chart is that it looks at the evidence from samples one at a time (or at most the evidence of two consecutive samples if we get values between warning and action lines).

Instead of plotting means, we might examine deviations from the target mean for successive samples. If the process is under control, we expect a fair mixture of plus and minus deviations and the sum of these will fluctuate around a mean value of zero. If, on the other hand, there is either a sudden or gradual slippage, we expect a preponderance of deviations of one sign. This idea led to a proposal that we consider a control chart in which we looked at the *cumulative sum of deviations from the targets for successive samples*. This cumulative sum (often abbreviated to CUSUM) would indicate that the process was going out of control if it showed marked departure from the base or zero line. Table 13.2 gives the deviations from the target mean of 1000 for the data in Table 13.1. Table 13.3 gives the

Table 13.2 Deviation from 1000 of sample means in Table 13.1.

-0.7	0.1	1.1	-1.2	-0.6	0.8	0.1	-1.4	-0.8
0.2	-1.2	-0.9	-0.7	-1.3	-0.6	-1.1	-1.6	-2.2

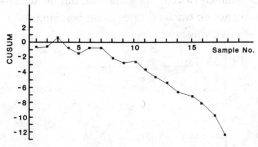

Figure 13.2 A basic CUSUM chart based on the data used in Fig. 13.1.

sums of successive deviations. For example, successive values are -0.7, $-0.7 + 0.1 = -0.6$, $-0.7 + 0.1 + 1.1 = -0.6 + 1.1 = 0.5$, and so on. These CUSUMS are plotted against sample numbers in Fig. 13.2, where we have joined successive points to highlight the downward trend from about sample 7 onward. By what criterion do we decide when a CUSUM chart indicates slippage? We can obtain numerical criteria on which a decision can be based, but perhaps the simplest method on the shop floor is to use a geometric device known as a V-mask. This, in effect, provides a decision rule corresponding to those used with the earlier control charts. The basic concept on which any decision rule is based is that if a slippage of amount m occurs, then on average one step after slippage the CUSUM has average value m; two steps after, it has average value $2m$, and more generally r steps after it has average value rm. Mathematically we say the line has slope m. In essence it is the average additional distance the new trend line moves above (or below, if m is negative) the base line for each additional sample. The slope indicates both the presence of and amount of slippage. Altering the scale of one or both

Table 13.3 Cumulative sums of deviations in Table 13.2.

-0.7	-0.6	0.5	-0.7	-1.3	-0.5	-0.4	-1.8	-2.6
-2.4	-3.6	-4.5	-5.2	-6.5	-7.1	-8.2	-9.8	-12.0

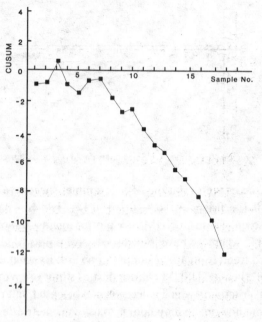

Figure 13.3 The effect of increasing the *y*-scale on a CUSUM chart. Data is the same as in Fig. 13.2.

axes in Fig. 13.2 makes the pattern either more or less clear. If we squeeze up the vertical scale, the trend line is squashed down towards the base line and visual detection of slippage becomes more difficult. If we expand the vertical scale (as we have done in Fig. 13.3), quite small deviations give the appearance of trend, and large deviations may well push the points off the top or bottom of the chart. For sensible visual interpretation, care is needed in the choice of scales; the choice also influences the shape of the V-mask we describe below. The best vertical scale for detecting slippage depends on the standard deviation, but details are too technical for discussion here.

The V-mask was suggested by a British statistician G. A. Barnard, and we illustrate its use in Fig. 13.4. The mask consists of a piece of still paper, card or perspex, with a V cut out of one side of it. It is

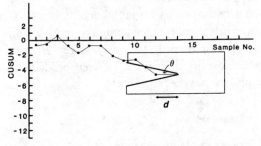

Figure 13.4 Use of a V-mask with a CUSUM chart.

placed on the CUSUM chart in the manner illustrated in Fig. 13.4 with the vertex of the V pointing forward and at a designated horizontal distance d in front of the last observed point.

The angles (both equal in magnitude) between the horizontal base line and a mask boundary (arm of the V) are denoted by θ. The choice of θ depends upon the scales used and the behaviour of the mask depends upon the values of d and θ. Wetherill (1977) describes ways in which d and θ may be chosen. Having chosen an appropriate d and θ, the rule is that we stop the process as soon as either of the mask boundary lines intersects the trend line joining successive sample points. Thus we would stop the process in the situation illustrated in Fig. 13.4, there being an indication of slippage below the target mean. This situation pertains at sample 12, whereas with a Shewhart control chart we would not stop until sample 18.

13.3 ACCEPTANCE SAMPLING

Acceptance sampling is usually associated with inspection of completed products either to estimate the proportion of defectives in large batches or to see whether there is evidence that the proportion of defectives exceeds an agreed pre-specified number. The disadvantage, compared to shop floor quality control for defectives, is that any fault is only detected long after the difficulty leading to it occurred; there may have been many faulty items produced in the meantime and at best corrective action is long delayed. This is a major reason why the emphasis in total quality control is on process control. Nevertheless acceptance sampling may be important for perishable goods, or even at the early stages of purchasing raw materials where quality differences between products from several potential suppliers may be important.

13.3.1 A simple scheme

We give a basic example of acceptance sampling.

Example 13.2   A buyer regards batches of rods as unsatisfactory if they contain more than 2% with maximum diameter exceeding 4 mm. As it would be extremely time-consuming to test every rod in batches of, say, 10 000 rods, the supplier suggests that a fair test would be to take a random sample of 100 from each batch and accept that batch if it contains less than two defectives; if it contains two or more defectives, the whole batch should be checked and all defective rods removed. (The latter is likely to be a costly and time-consuming process unless it could be mechanized. If it could be, there might well be a case for incorporating such a check in the manufacturing process.) Explore the characteristics of the proposed sampling procedure.

A rigorous treatment is complicated, so the statistical aspects are usually modified in a way that makes virtually no difference to the final answers. The key question that concerns us is this: if we have less than two defectives in a sample of 100 from a batch of 10 000, can we reasonably conclude that there are less than 2% defectives in the batch? We suppose temporarily that there are exactly 2% defectives in the batch, i.e. a total of 200 defectives in 10 000. Then, if we select a rod at random the probability it is defective is $p = 0.02$. If we now select a second rod, the probability it is also defective will not quite be 0.02, for we now select a rod from the 9999 remaining; the probability it is defective is a conditional probability, dependent upon whether or not the first rod were defective. If the first were not defective, we have 200 defectives in 9999 giving (by the equally likely events concept) a probability of $\frac{200}{9999}$ that the second rod selected is defective. If the first had been defective, the corresponding probability would be $\frac{199}{9999}$. Neither of these differs from 0.02 until the fifth decimal place. Generally speaking, when we sample from a large batch (without replacing items for reselection) and p is small, the value of p varies little unless we take a very large sample. We therefore feel justified in supposing p is constant and that our sample is analogous to the situation where one has a set of $n = 100$ observations for each of which the probability of the event we are interested in (a defective) is $p = 0.02$. This is a situation where the binomial distribution holds. Thus we can work out the probability of getting zero or one (or any other number of) defectives. It is intuitively obvious and not difficult to prove that if $p < 0.02$ there will be a higher probability of getting zero or one defectives in our sample, because there are fewer defectives in the batch. When $p = 0.02$, the probability of getting zero or one defectives – the criterion that makes the batch acceptable – is (using formula 9.8)

$$\begin{aligned}
\text{Pr(0 or 1 defectives)} &= \text{Pr(0 defective)} + \text{Pr(1 defective)} \\
&= 0.98^{100} + 100 \times 0.98^{99} \times 0.02 \\
&= 0.1326 + 0.2706 = 0.4032.
\end{aligned}$$

This tells us that *if the true percent defectives is* 2%, then in the long run we expect to accept about 40% of all batches with 2% defectives. It also implies that some 60% of all batches that just meet the requirement of not more than 2% defectives would be rejected and thus need full inspection. Whether or not supplier and buyer would be happy with that state of affairs may depend on the cost of full inspections, and how critical it was to reject batches with too many defectives. Clearly it would be useful to know more about how this sampling scheme and the acceptance criteria operate for other values of p.

Indeed, given $n = 100$, we may set up an equation giving the probability of accepting a sample for any given value of p. If we

Table 13.4 Probability of acceptance with given p; sampling scheme in Example 13.2.

p	0	0.005	0.01	0.015	0.02	0.03	0.04	0.05	0.06
Pr(A)	1	0.910	0.736	0.557	0.403	0.195	0.087	0.037	0.015

call the probability of acceptance Pr(A), this equals the probability our sample contains zero or one defectives, i.e.

$$\Pr(A) = (1 - p)^{100} + 100(1 - p)^{99}p$$
$$= (1 - p)^{99}(1 + 99p). \tag{13.1}$$

Substituting appropriate values of p in (13.1) gives the values of Pr(A) for various p shown in Table 13.4. If we draw a smooth curve through the corresponding (p, Pr(A)) values given in Table 13.4 we obtain what is called the operating characteristic curve – commonly abbreviated to OC curve – for the sampling scheme. This is plotted in Fig. 13.5. As we would expect intuitively, the probability of accepting a batch decreases as the number of defectives it contains increases. From Table 13.4 (or from Fig. 13.5), we see that we are certain to accept a batch with no defectives (for obviously there will then be no defectives in a sample), and that we will also accept about 91% of all batches with 0.5% defectives, but as we saw earlier once we get to the critical level of 2% defectives we only accept about 40% of all batches without further inspection. If producer and consumer have a common interest and want to avoid inspection of batches living up to the guarantee, they may be unhappy about the need to inspect many good batches. On the other hand, the consumer does not want to accept too many faulty batches because these pass the test despite the fact that they contain too many defectives, so we are interested in the behaviour of the OC curve when there may be, say, three, four or five defectives in the batch. From Table 13.4, we immediately see that when there are 4% defectives ($p = 0.04$) there is a probability of 0.087 that a batch is accepted, i.e. that in the long

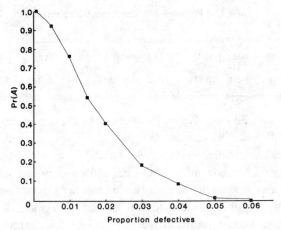

Figure 13.5 Probability of accepting a batch with various proportion defectives using samples of 100 and accepting batches only if there are zero or one defectives.

run we would accept 8.7% of all batches that had 4% defective rods. The buyer may well feel unhappy about this, but it is in the very nature of sampling schemes that some unacceptable batches will slip through, and also that some acceptable ones will be rejected (and either subjected, as here, to complete inspection, or, in some other cases, sold off as second grade if inspection were too expensive or impossible because testing was destructive). Compromise helps us get round some of the difficulties. There is nothing sacred about either (i) a sample size of 100 or (ii) accepting only samples with zero or one defectives. We might decide to take large samples, say 200, and accept if we have less than four defectives. We shall look at this example further in Exercises 13.2–13.4. We simply give at this stage Table 13.5 which is analogous to Table 13.4 for this modified sampling scheme.

Comparing Tables 13.4 and 13.5, it is clear that the change in sample size and acceptance criteria have increased the probabilities of accepting batches with 2% or less defectives and decreased the probabilities of accepting those with 3% or more defectives. This is

Table 13.5 Probability of acceptance; sample of 200, three or less defective, for various *p*.

p	0	0.005	0.01	0.015	0.02	0.03	0.04	0.05	0.06
Pr(*A*)	1	0.981	0.858	0.647	0.431	0.147	0.040	0.009	0.002

what we would wish. We may explore a variety of sampling schemes with different OC curves. We plot those corresponding to the schemes exemplified by Tables 13.4 and 13.5 in Fig. 13.6. On that figure, we also show an ideal OC curve for a sampling scheme that would accept all batches with two or less defectives and reject all those with more than 2% defectives. Sadly, because of sampling variation, we can only achieve this goal by full inspection of all batches. However, there are many more sophisticated techniques giving OC curves that are not too far from this ideal. There are a number of other important concepts associated with acceptance sampling that we do not consider here such as producer's risk and consumer's risk; these are discussed by Wetherill (1977). Tables are

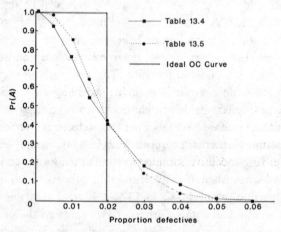

Figure 13.6 A comparison of OC curves for two sampling schemes and the ideal OC curve if we wish to accept all batches with not more than 2% defective.

available that give characteristics of various sampling schemes, but, as with interest tables, these are increasingly giving way to computer programs to compare various schemes.

13.4 WHAT AND WHERE?

What skills have we mastered?

We have learnt how to construct control charts for slippage and how to determine OC curves in acceptance sampling. We have also discussed the rudiments of CUSUM charts, although the construction of appropriate V-masks requires theory not given here. Although not exactly a skill, we have tried to explain the ethos of *total quality control*.

Where can I read more?

Wetherill (1977) provides a compact account of the statistical aspects of quality control. Although quality control is of increasing importance in a managerial context, it does not seem to have penetrated many professional examination syllabuses. The statistical aspects are covered in many standard statistical texts, especially those dealing with engineering or industrial applications.

EXERCISES

*13.1   Mean weights of samples of three bags of cement filled by a machine should be normally distributed with a mean of 51 kg and a standard deviation of 0.3 kg when the machine is operating properly. Construct a Shewhart control chart for shift in the target mean of 51 kg. If consecutive samples have the mean weights in kilograms given below, when, if at all, should the process be stopped to check if it is out of control?

51.5, 51.7, 50.4, 51.2, 50.0, 50.6, 51.2, 51.7,

51.8, 50.4, 50.9, 51.3, 51.0, 49.8, 50.6.

*13.2   Assuming that the proportion p of defectives in samples of size 200 from large batches has a binomial distribution, show that, if the acceptance rule is to accept batches if there are three or less defectives, then the formula for calculating the probabilities in Table 13.5 may be put in the form:

$$Pt(A) = q^{197}(q^3 + 200q^2p + 19\,900qp^2 + 1\,313\,400p^3),$$

where $q = 1 - p$. Use this formula to verify the probabilities given in Table 13.5.

13.3   If p is small and n large, the binomial distribution may be approximated to by a Poisson distribution with parameter $\lambda = np$. If $n = 200$, we have $\lambda = 200p$. Substituting the values of p in Table 13.5, we find the values of λ corresponding to the p values in that table are respectively 0, 1, 2, 3, 4, 6, 8, 10, 12. Show that, using this approximation, for any given value of λ the probability of three or fewer defectives is given by

$$Pr(A) = e^{-\lambda}(1 + \lambda + \lambda^2/2! + \lambda^3/3!) \quad \text{(see section 9.5.4)}.$$

Use this result to evaluate the probabilities corresponding to those in Table 13.5, and compare your results with those given in that table.   [A calculator with an e^x key is useful.]

13.4   Use the Poisson approximation to calculate the probabilities corresponding to those in Table 13.4. Would you regard the approximations as reasonable for these smaller samples?

14 Modelling, Simulation and Queues

14.1 PLANNING AND MODELLING

Here is an organizational type problem that is usually solved by trial and error. A factory's 'in house' component store has a single counter to which employees requiring components bring their orders. Storemen then get goods from storage shelves arranged in parallel behind the counters as in Fig. 14.1. The demand for each of perhaps several hundred components will vary: some will be in almost constant demand; others will be required only infrequently, perhaps about once a month. Related items will often be required at the same time, e.g. nuts and bolts, power sockets and plugs, picks and shovels. Storemen will spend a lot of time walking to and from shelves collecting the items required. To minimize this time, common sense demands that frequently required items should be stored near the service counter. It is clearly sensible to put a commonly required item in position A rather than in position B (Fig. 14.1). It also makes sense to store items, such as nuts and bolts, that may often be required on the same order close to each other, so that they can be collected by the storeman in one trip. It would be silly to have nuts in position C and bolts in position D in Fig. 14.1. Frequency of demand may not be the only factor that determines shelf position. Heavy items might be placed near the front, even if not in great demand, to save having to carry them long distances; items that are too bulky to be handed over the counter may be placed near a service door so that they can be easily taken into or removed from the store using a trolley or a forklift truck. A good layout may well be

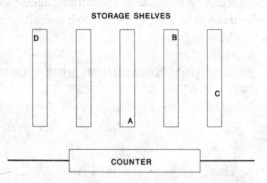

STORAGE SHELVES

Figure 14.1 Layout of a service counter and shelves in a component store. Items in high demand should be stored near to the service counter, and items often required together stored near to each other. It would waste storemen's time if nuts were stored in position C and bolts in position D.

achieved by trial and error, although 'time and motion' experts may recommend a layout on a more sophisticated basis. The store manager has to take factors other than layout into account; the customers (here employees requiring components needed for work of the various departments in the factory) do not want to be kept waiting too long because all the storemen are busy. Serious delays in getting service may even hold up factory production. Also, the store manager does not want to employ so many storemen that some are idle for much of the day. If customer delays or server idleness (when there are no customers) are too common, these are again circumstances where a little trial and error, by, say, reducing or increasing staff by one, may provide a solution that balances the conflicting problems of customer delay and employing too many storemen. Here we face a simple queuing problem; more sophisticated problems of this type are not easy (or cheap) to solve by trial and error.

14.1.1 Queues

We are all familiar with queues: at supermarket checkouts, at the post office or bank (even at hole-in-the-wall ATMs outside banks, regardless of whether the cashiers inside are busy doing nothing), at our local GP surgery. We queue in cars at traffic lights. Ships queue to enter harbours or to be loaded or unloaded; aircraft queue to land or take off at a busy airport. In a manufacturing process, there may be queues of partly made items waiting until there are machines ready to carry out the next stage of the process, and queues of completed items waiting for a buyer.

Even for simple situations like supermarket checkouts, there are a lot of different formats a queue may take, called, in the jargon of queuing theory, *queue discipline*. There may be only one checkout operating – this is a *single-server system*; more likely there are several – a *multiserver system*. Usually in a supermarket, the customers form separate queues for each cashier. Customers choose their queue by a series of, often ill-defined, rules. Most of these are more or less intuitive, but vary from customer to customer: some will join the queue with the fewest people; others will do a quick scan of the contents of the trolleys and baskets of those already in the queues and prefer one with three people each only having one or two items to a queue where one person is waiting with a heavily loaded trolley. An experienced customer may shun the shortest queue if he knows that the cashier on that till is particularly slow.

In banks and post offices, a common queuing system is that of a single customer queue where the person at the front goes to the first of several service points to become free. This system is less common in supermarkets because one long queue may be spatially inconvenient if it stretches back along the aisles between shelves where other customers are still selecting goods.

Queuing patterns are influenced not only by queue discipline but by factors such as irregularity in arrival and in service times. The interval between successive customers joining supermarket checkout queues may be, 25, 7, 3, 15, 9, 42, 3, 1, 7, . . . seconds. The time a particular cashier takes to service successive customers in her queue may be 25, 41, 23, 79, . . . seconds; had the same customers distributed themselves differently among the cashiers, the service times for that cashier would almost certainly have been different.

14.1.2 **The mathematics of queues**

There is a large corpus of mathematical theory about queue behaviour, but complex queuing systems may lead to mathematically intractable problems. Most queues have a strong probabilistic or stochastic element. The mathematical theory of queues is unlikely to help a supermarket manager worried about whether he should employ another cashier and risk her being idle quite a bit of the day, or whether he should tolerate occasional long queues of grumbling customers likely to transfer their custom elsewhere. He does better to experiment for a few weeks with an extra cashier and see what happens.

On the other hand, if an airport suffers congestion problems because it has only one runway, the owners will be less happy about building a second runway costing £10 million just to see if that will cure the problem. They might want at least to compare this with other alternatives: diversion of some traffic to another airport, increased hours of airport operation (and the anti-noise lobby will rightly have something to say about that), or perhaps investment in an improved air traffic control system that will speed up landings and take-offs. This is a situation where we would like some sort of model to tell us what *might* happen under these various alternatives.

The idea of physical models to tell us what may happen in a new development is well established. When designing a new ship, scale models are subjected to testing under storm conditions in tanks; models of new aircraft are tested in a wind-tunnel. The designing and testing takes account of known theories about the behaviour of various materials under stress, of the aerodynamic behaviour of bodies of different shape and weight, and so on.

Queuing problems, and other problems with a stochastic element, lend themselves to one of two kinds of mathematical modelling. The first is a complete mathematical specification of the system which has an analytic solution. For some simple queues (and even for some complicated systems), we have such models and we use them to get probabilistic distributions of the waiting time, to work out expected queue length and other features. In practice, such solutions are only available for a few specific queue disciplines. *Whether or not* analytic solutions are available, providing we have reasonable information about the stochastic behaviour of the individual *components* of the queue – the pattern of arrivals, the distribution of service times – we may *simulate* the behaviour of queues extending over many hours or days in a matter of minutes or, if we use a computer, in microseconds. It is also easy to study the effect of changes in the arrival or service pattern. How well these simulations will reflect reality depends on how well we model reality with our assumptions about arrival and service time patterns.

We confine our examples of simulation to queues but the idea can be applied elsewhere. Sprent (1988b: Chap. 10) illustrated the use of simulation to study the distribution of the breakdown times of a machine which stops when any one of three components fails and the distribution of the lifetimes of each such component is known; he also used simulation to study the effects of replacing some of these with alternative components having a different lifetime distribution.

14.2 SIMULATING A QUEUE

Even when a simple queue with specific patterns of arrival and service times can be studied analytically, we may still learn about its behaviour from appropriate simulations. A system that has been widely used to demonstrate the basics (often using a simplified model of reality) is that of appointments at a hospital outpatients clinic. Sprent (1977) and Hollingdale (1978) independently illustrated this application using very similar models. Moore (1980, 1986) used Sprent's model for illustrative purposes and extended it to include further realistic factors. We use an example inspired by happy hours spent watching ships passing through locks on the Crinan and Caledonian canals.

14.2.1 'Locked' in

Example 14.1   Boats arrive randomly at a canal lock at an average rate of one every half-hour. The lock can only handle one boat at a time, and the time taken to handle each can conveniently be split into two parts. The first is the time required to position the boat in the lock. This depends on the size of the boat and the skill of its crew, and experience has shown that it is equally likely to take 3, 4, 5, 6 or 7 minutes. The second part is that needed to adjust the water level in the lock to the required departure level and for the boat to clear the lock, together with adjusting water levels in the lock to accept the next boat. Experience has shown that is equally likely to take any time between 20 and 29 minutes. Simulate the time for the passage of ten boats through the lock, commencing from an arbitrary zero time at which the lock is not currently in use, but is ready to receive a boat.

Solution   We explained in section 9.5.5 what we mean by events taking place randomly in time; the arrival of boats corresponds to a Poisson process with mean time between events of, in this case, 30 minutes. What we have to do now is to get a random sample of times up to the first arrival and between successive arrivals (usually called the inter-arrival times, using a method like that outlined in Example 9.9). We get an appropriate random sample using random digits (section 9.6.1) in pairs. If U represents a pair of random digits, then the rule we use is similar to that in Example 9.9, i.e. that $V = -30[\ln(U/100)]$ may be taken as the first arrival time in a random arrival process with mean 30 (here ln stands for 'the logarithm to the base e'). If your pocket calculator has a key labelled ln, just enter the number U, divide by 100 and press the ln key (if you have no ln key, first get the common logarithm (i.e. log to the base 10 of U) and multiply by 2.303 to get $\ln U$); finally multiply by 30 and change the sign. We take the next pair of random digits (from a table, or computer-generated) and calculate the V corresponding to this U. This gives the interval between the arrival of the first and second boat. We repeat this process to get the inter-arrival intervals for ten boats.

We illustrate this process using paired random digits from Table 9.2. In accord with good practice when using random numbers, we enter the table at an arbitrary point and select digits either by rows or by columns. For the pairs to determine inter-arrival intervals of boats, we select pairs of digits from columns 13 and 14 starting in the first row for our values of U, namely 51, 76, 95, 31, 36, 39, 19, 69, 04, 18. We calculate the time V after the system opens to arrival of the first boat to be $V = -30(\ln 0.51) = 30 \times 0.6733 = 20.20$. We round this to the nearest minute, i.e. $V = 20$. Continuing in this way for the remaining U, we calculate the successive inter-arrival times as 20, 8, 2, 35, 31, 28, 50, 11, 97, 51. Note that the mean of these is 33.3, which is not far from the population value 30 and well within the expected variation from sample to sample (section 9.6). You may be surprised at the wide spread of inter-arrival times ranging from two to 97 minutes: a spread like this is fairly typical for random arrivals with a mean of one every 30 minutes. For each boat arriving, we now allocate times for it to enter and be secured in the lock (based on the information that this is any number of minutes from three to seven, each with the same probability (i.e. 0.2)). We allocate each time by assigning two of the ten random digits 0 to 9 to each time, e.g. if we select a 0 or 1 we say the ship requires three minutes for positioning in the lock, if 2 or 3 it requires four minutes, if 4 or 5 it requires five minutes, if 6 or 7 it requires six minutes, and if 8 or 9 it requires seven minutes. We use the random digits in column 9 of Table 9.2 to assign the relevant times. These digits are given below and under each we give the time allocated by the above rule.

Digit	8	1	9	8	2	8	3	9	2	9
Time	7	3	7	7	4	7	4	7	4	7

It is reasonable to work to the nearest minute, so it is easy to allocate the times between 20 and 29 minutes for complete passage through the lock and for readjusting water levels. Since there are ten equally likely times, i.e. 20, 21, 22, . . . , 29 minutes, an obvious choice is to allocate digit 0 to 20 minutes, digit 1 to 21 minutes, digit 2 to 22 minutes and so on, up to digit 9 for 29 minutes. Using digits 8, 1, 0, 7, 5, 4, 2, 3, 9, 6 from column 19 of Table 9.2 this gives the times 28, 21, 20, 27, 25, 24, 22, 23, 29, 26. Adding these times to those above for positioning the boats gives a total time for handling each boat in the lock. For boat 1, it is $28 + 7 = 35$, for boat 2 it is $21 + 3 = 24$, and so on, totals for all boats being 35, 24, 27, 34, 29, 31, 26, 30, 33, 33. It is easily verified that the mean of these ten times is 30.2, reasonably close to the theoretical or population mean of $5 + 24.5 = 29.5$. Note that, because these 'service' times are uniformly distributed in certain defined and restricted intervals, they are less variable than the inter-arrival times, and range only from 24 to 35 minutes.

14.2.2 The traffic flow pattern

Practical interest in this simulation lies in how traffic moves through the canal: are there times when there is no activity at the lock and other times when boats are delayed waiting for one or more of those in front to clear? We can answer these questions most easily by drawing up a table; Table 14.1 is such a table based on Example 14.1.

We write the entries in the following order. In the first column, we put the time of arrival of each boat (in minutes) after an arbitrary starting time. These are obtained from the inter-arrival data given in section 14.2.1 above. The first entry is 20. Since the next boat arrives eight minutes later, its arrival time is recorded as $8 + 20 = 28$. The next arrival is at time 30 $(28 + 2)$, and the following one at time 65 $(30 + 35)$. We proceed in this way to complete the column. Column 2 gives the total servicing time each boat takes to enter, pass through the lock and for the lock water level to be adjusted to take the next boat. We obtained these in section 14.2.1. Column 3 gives the entry time to the lock. For the first boat this is 20, since it enters the lock as soon as it arrives. In column 4, we put the time service is

Table 14.1 Simulation of the passage times of ten boats through a canal lock.

Arrival time (1)	Process time (2)	Entry time (3)	Exit time (4) (2) + (3)	Delay in entry (5) (3) − (1)	Time lock traffic free (6)
20	35	20	55	0	20
28	24	55	79	27	0
30	27	79	106	49	0
65	34	106	140	41	0
96	29	140	169	44	0
124	31	169	200	45	0
174	26	200	226	24	0
185	30	226	256	41	0
282	33	282	315	0	26
333	33	333	366	0	18
Averages:				27.1	6.4

completed: this is 55, since it takes 35 minutes to service this boat. Generally, the entry in column 4 is the sum of the entries in column 2 and 3. In column 5, we record any waiting time for the boat before it enters the lock. For the first boat, this is zero. In column 6, we record any time the lock is not in use prior to the entry of the boat we are dealing with in the current row of the table. In this case it is 20, reflecting the 20 minutes from the start time to the arrival of this first boat.

We now move to column 3 for the second boat (columns 1 and 2 having been completed already). Although it arrived 28 minutes after starting time, it cannot be processed through the lock until time

55 (completion of the first boat's passage), so we enter 55 in this column. Since it takes 24 minutes to service, we enter $55 + 24 = 79$ in column 4. Since the boat had to wait $55 - 28 = 27$ minutes before entering the lock, we write 27 in column 5. We enter zero in column 6, since the lock was occupied with the passage of the previous boat until this one entered. Proceeding in this way, we complete the entries for each boat in Table 14.1. At the foot of columns 5 and 6, we give the averages associated with each of those columns. For column 5 it is 27.1, and for column 6 it is 6.4. Clearly the early arrivals in fairly rapid succession cause a bottleneck at the lock which is not cleared until the 97 minute gap between arrival of boats 8 and 9. Even if we assume our information about the nature of arrivals and distribution of service time is realistic, we would need a much longer simulation to see just how bad delays may be in the long run and how the canal is coping with traffic.

14.2.3 How realistic?

Were our assumptions in Example 14.1 realistic? Approximately 'random' arrivals are common and so are assumed in many simulations (and indeed in mathematical analyses) of queuing systems. It would be suspect, however, for traffic through a canal at certain times of the day, or in certain parts of a canal. For example, in many British canals most of the traffic is pleasure craft. These often set out from the same boat hirer's premises about 9 a.m. each Monday morning, so traffic on Monday, and possibly Tuesday, is not likely to have a random pattern. After several days of canal cruising, boats are likely to be well spread out, depending upon the different itineraries, so the approximation to randomness in time may be quite reasonable except that sometimes two or more boats hired by one group, or whose crews are close friends, may tend to stick together (often referred to in statistical jargon as clumping). We shall see in Example 14.2 that an assumption of approximate randomness in time even allows a possibility of busy and slack periods.

The assumptions about times taken to process a boat through the lock are a simplification. We have specified that boats take an exact number of minutes both for entry and for processing through the lock once they have entered and been secured. In reality, a boat might take 3.6 minutes for entry and 25.9 minutes for processing, or other times involving fractions of a minute. However, if the spread is fairly even across the given time span, little useful information is lost by what effectively amounts to rounding these times to the nearest minute. We could elaborate on our model by allowing finer tuning in the distribution of arrival times. We may also allow for minor mishaps. For example, there may be a probability of 0.03 that a boat will get jammed in the lock; experience may show that if this happens the time taken to release the boat is normally distributed with a mean of 17 minutes and a standard deviation of five minutes. Such possibilities can be 'built in' to a simulation model without altering the basic principles; the modelling (and computer programming if the simulation is done on a computer) just becomes more complicated.

14.2.4 Ringing the changes

Simulation is useful for studying how some change, such as one in queue discipline, will affect a system. In Example 14.1, the canal management may expect that, in future, traffic will increase (perhaps because the pleasure boat companies are providing more boats for hire, or an increasing number of private boats are using the canal). They consider plans for speeding up passage through the lock by redesigning it so that it can be filled or emptied of water more rapidly. The cost of such a project will depend on the amount by which the process is speeded up. So, to get an indication of the likely consequences of different schemes, they perform simulations for different amounts of speeding up and for different forecasts of traffic flows. To illustrate, we consider just one possible modification, taking the case where a new filling process lops, on average, ten minutes off the phase of getting boats through the lock after they have entered and been secured, i.e. instead of being uniformly distributed between 20 and 29 minutes, it is now uniformly distributed between ten and 19 minutes. We could do a new simulation (indeed

Table 14.2 Revised simulation of the passage times of ten boats through a canal lock.

Arrival time (1)	Process time (2)	Entry time (3)	Exit time (4) (2) + (3)	Delay in entry (5) (3) − (1)	Time lock traffic free (6)
20	25	20	45	0	20
28	14	45	59	17	0
30	17	59	76	29	0
65	24	76	100	11	0
96	19	100	119	4	0
124	21	124	145	0	5
174	16	174	190	0	29
185	20	190	210	5	0
282	23	282	305	0	72
333	23	333	356	0	28
Averages:				6.6	15.4

several new, or longer, simulations) with these times. However, first let us study the effect on the previous simulation of a reduction of every service time by ten minutes, but with the arrival pattern unchanged. This alters all columns in Table 14.1 except the first. Results for this revised simulation are given in Table 14.2. You should form this table yourself as an exercise to be sure you follow all the steps.

How does the reduction in mean waiting time for boats to enter the lock strike you? Intuitively, you might argue that if the process time is reduced by ten minutes, the average waiting time would be reduced by the same amount. However, the average waiting time reduction is from 27.1 to 6.6 – more than 20 minutes. This would certainly please boat users, but whether it would be economic for a canal operating company to make such changes would depend very much on the capital cost and whether this could be recouped from increased dues or perhaps increased traffic (which might of course mean that delays would once again build up). A decision on whether to reconstruct would be based not on ten simulations but more likely on 1000 (or even 100 000) simulations done on a computer, and simulations would also be carried out for other assumed traffic densities and rates of servicing.

14.2.5 Trying again

Example 14.2   To indicate the scope for variation in even ten simulations, we consider one more simulation for the proposed new lock system (with processing times ten minutes lower than in Example 14.1).

This time, columns 3 and 4 of Table 9.2 were used in pairs to determine the inter-arrival intervals. These turn out to be 38, 38, 32, 22, 15, 6, 11, 42, 14, 12 minutes – an average of 23.0 minutes. Again, this is not too unreasonable for a sample of ten from a random process with mean 30, although it suggests 'above average' traffic density on the canal. This indicates flexibility in the random arrivals model to reflect comparatively 'busy' spells. Conversely, a simulation may sometimes reflect behaviour in a slack spell.

Columns 8 and 11 respectively of Table 9.2 were used to get the times taken to secure boats in the lock and to process them through and refill the lock once they were secured. We record only the total service times obtained in this way in column 2 of Table 14.3. The table is completed in a similar manner to Tables 14.1 and 14.2.

It is interesting to compare the average delays before entering the lock and the average time the lock is not being used with those in Table 14.2. Although the traffic density is higher (on average one boat every 23 minutes, compared with one every 33 minutes in the previous simulation), the average wait is increased by less than one

Table 14.3 A further simulation of the passage times of ten boats through a canal lock.

Arrival time (1)	Process time (2)	Entry time (3)	Exit time (4) (2) + (3)	Delay in entry (5) (3) − (1)	Time lock traffic free (6)
38	21	38	59	0	38
76	19	76	95	0	17
108	23	108	131	0	13
130	14	131	145	1	0
145	16	145	161	0	0
151	25	161	186	10	0
162	23	186	209	24	0
204	24	209	233	5	0
218	16	233	249	15	0
230	18	249	267	19	0
Averages:				7.4	6.8

minute, but there is a substantial reduction in the time the lock is traffic-free. The system is such that it can absorb, at least temporarily, an increased traffic density by using up some slack time.

14.3 Some general comments on queues

Queues that are completely free of stochastic elements are rarely considered in simulations, not because they are non-existent, but because they need virtually no study. On many factory production lines, conditions are often very stable. Processing each item on one machine may take exactly ten seconds; the next stage may take exactly 30 seconds. Thus, if one machine only is used for the first stage, we need three machines for the next stage if there are to be no processing delays (if no time is lost in transfer between stages). However, in transport-type queues (ships entering ports, aircraft landing, cars at traffic lights), marketing queues (banks, supermarkets), or communication queues (telephone, telex, fax systems), there are nearly always stochastic elements. In our canal lock example, we had random arrivals and uniformly distributed service times in a single queue.

It is intuitively obvious, that, if we had a deterministic queue where arrivals are regular at a rate of one every five minutes, say, and if service is also completely deterministic in a constant time which does not exceed five minutes, then nobody would have to wait However, if people arrive steadily at four-minute intervals and it takes five minutes to serve each arrival, then a queue soon builds up; the second arrival will have to wait one minute while service is completed for the first arrival, the next arrival will have to wait two minutes, the next three minutes, and so on. The situation is more complicated with exponentially distributed arrival times and stochastic service times, as we saw in the canal example when we reduced the processing time. The average interval between arrivals (30 minutes in theory, but 33 minutes in one simulation and 23 minutes in the other) exceeded the average service time of 19.5 (closely approximated in both simulations), but still some customers had to wait. Once again, if average service time had exceeded the average inter-arrival time, a queue would soon have built up, and continued to grow. Studies of the equilibrium of queuing systems are extremely important.

14.3.1 A special type of queue

A simple system that has been widely studied analytically is one where customers arrive randomly at a certain rate and are served by a single server at some other random rate. This is the Poisson process for both arrivals and service. We quote some results for this system where arrivals follow a Poisson process with mean inter-arrival time A and service time is also random with mean S. Clearly, if S is greater than A, the server cannot cope and the queue will eventually become infinite in length. The quotient, or ratio, $T = S/A$ is called the traffic intensity. Indeed, this definition is used also for other distributions of inter-arrival and service times; however, in the special case of the Poisson or 'random' processes for arrival and service, the following important results hold when $T < 1$:

1. The average total time spent in the system per customer is $S/(1 - T)$.
2. The average waiting time prior to service is $TS/(1 - T)$.

Note the requirement that $T < 1$ (otherwise the queue becomes infinite). We do not prove the above results.

Example 14.3   In a single-server queue with random inter-arrival times averaging 2.5 minutes and random service times averaging two minutes, determine the average time spent by a customer in the system (waiting plus service times) and the average time in the queue prior to service.

Solution   Here $A = 2.5$ and $S = 2$, so $T = 2/2.5 = 0.8$, and the total time spent in the system is on average $S/(1 - T) = 2/0.2 = 10$ minutes. The average wait prior to service is $TS/(1 - T) = 8$ minutes.

In Exercise 14.5, we find that the average waiting times in the canal lock example calculated by these formulae greatly exceed those noted in the simulations. There are two reasons for this. The first and most important is that the distribution of service times is not completely random; these involve, as we pointed out in Example 14.1, a relatively short range of times, so we never get the odd very long service time that is characteristic of a completely random process. The second point is that these averages reflect long term trends when the system is in so-called equilibrium. Early fluctuations in a short term simulation may well not reflect such long term trends.

14.4   WHAT AND WHERE?

What skills have we learnt?

We have learnt that many queues may be simulated once the queue discipline – pattern of arrivals and departures – is determined.

Queuing systems may be partly deterministic and partly stochastic. The stochastic element is usually strong in any system where there is a human factor, i.e. queues formed by humans or involving services under control of people (ships, aircraft, etc.). In well-controlled industrial processes the deterministic element may often (but by no means always) predominate.

Simulations, usually done in practice on a computer, are particularly useful for studying the effects of potential changes in queue discipline. How well a simulation study will mirror reality depends on how well the specifications on which the simulation is based (nature of arrival and service patterns) accord with reality.

For Poisson processes, where inter-arrival times and server times are exponentially distributed, simple formulae exist for average waiting times and average service times expressible in terms of traffic density defined as the ratio of mean service time to mean inter-arrival time.

Where can I read more?

Moore (1986: Chap. 5) gives a more detailed discussion of queues with several practical examples. Other numerical examples of simulation are given in Sprent (1988b: Chap. 10).

EXERCISES

14.1   In the solution to Example 14.1, an explanation is given of how the total times for passage through the lock for each boat were obtained. Using this explanation, verify that the total times stated in that solution are correct.

14.2   Verify that the inter-arrival times used to form the entries in column 1 of Table 14.3 accord with the use of random digit pairs from columns 3 and 4 of Table 9.2 to calculate those inter-arrival times.

14.3   Perform a similar check to that sought in the previous exercise for the process times given in column 2 of Table 14.3.

*14.4   In a Poisson arrival/service queue, the mean inter-arrival time is ten minutes and the mean service time is seven minutes. What is the traffic density? Determine the average time each arrival spends in the system and the average waiting time per customer prior to service. Study the effects on these quantities of the following changes:

  (i) a reduction to eight minutes in the mean inter-arrival time;
 (ii) an increase in the mean service time to 7.5 minutes;
(iii) both a reduction to eight minutes in mean inter-arrival time and an increase in mean service time to 7.5 minutes.

Do your conclusions accord with your intuition? If not, why not?

*14.5   Apply the formulae for average total time in the system and average service time given in section 14.3 to the relevant theoretical average times in Examples 14.1 and 14.2, and compare them with your observed results for the simulations. How might any discrepancies be explained?

*14.6   People join a queue either alone (with probability 0.8), or in pairs (with probability 0.1), or in triples (with probability 0.1). People in the queue are served individually and each takes three minutes to serve (e.g. if a pair arrive it will take six minutes to serve them). There is only one server. The interval between arrivals (whether alone or in pairs or triples) is equally likely to be any number of minutes between one and nine. Perform a simulation of the system using random digits from Table 9.2 to show arrival times, service start times, service finish times, customer wait and time the server is free for 15 arrivals assuming the system opens at 9 a.m. [Note a simulation of such a system for 30 arrivals is given in Sprent (1988b: Chap. 10).]

15 Index Numbers

15.1 HOW TO BE BORING WITHOUT REALLY TRYING

Index numbers measure changes with time; they are important but boring. They are just summary statistics (as are means and standard deviations), but ones that are often grossly misunderstood and generally of limited value. They cannot be ignored, for a small change in, say, the retail prices index often has important economic or political consequences; if the nature and limitations of indices were more widely understood, irrational reactions to small changes in key indices might be avoided. It is a moot point to what extent the October 1987 stock-market crash was triggered by the automatic programming of dealers' computers to give warnings to sell once the Dow-Jones index fell more than a certain number of points in a given time.

The weakness of most important indices is that they measure only broad *average* changes. Although the retail prices index is constructed in a careful and elaborate way, an increase in its value means only in broad terms that the cost of living has gone up. It does not necessarily mean that my cost of living or your cost of living has gone up; it does, however, mean that for the average family with average spending habits living in a part of the country where costs are in some sense average (and each of these is a vague concept), the cost of living has gone up by an amount indicated by the change in the index. An official justification for its use was given in the *Employment Gazette* in August 1987 as, 'It is less confusing and more useful

Table 15.1 Changes in the retail price of butter.

1 Jan 1984	49p	1 Jan 1987	57p
1 July 1984	50p	1 July 1987	58p
1 Jan 1985	50p	1 Jan 1988	61p
1 July 1985	52p	1 July 1988	61p
1 Jan 1986	53p	1 Jan 1989	61p
1 July 1986	56p	1 July 1989	63p

to have a single measure of inflation which, though not necessarily strictly relevant to any one household, will be close to the experience of the great majority of them'. This naïve assertion begs the question of how close is close. In fairness though, this is a difficult question to answer, and to attempt to do so in any meaningful way would be costly.

Because indices are limited in usefulness, this does not mean we should abandon attempts to measure trend. It is simply pointing out that indices are for some purposes woefully inadequate; their very inadequacy leads to misapprehensions that often unsettle the stock or currency markets. Index changes encourage politicians to make claims they may regret a month later (perhaps that matters little now it is accepted widely that a week is a long time in politics).

Mistakes made by decision-makers who do not understand the limitations of indices are at best frustrating; at worst they may have serious economic consequences.

We discuss several types of indices of increasing complexity; even brief explanations of how the more complex indices are constructed serve to highlight the limitations.

Example 15.1 The retail price of butter per 250 gram pack on certain dates is given in Table 15.1. Construct a butter price index taking 1 January 1984 as base.

Table 15.2 A butter price index; base 100, 1 January 1984.

1 Jan 1984	100	1 Jan 1987	116.32
1 July 1984	102.04	1 July 1987	118.36
1 Jan 1985	102.04	1 Jan 1988	124.49
1 July 1985	106.12	1 July 1988	124.49
1 Jan 1986	108.16	1 Jan 1989	124.49
1 July 1986	114.29	1 July 1989	128.57

Solution The basic idea is to express the price at a given date as a percentage of that at the base date. On 1 July 1984, the price is 50p, which is $100 \times \frac{50}{49}\%$ of the price on 1 January 1984, so the index is 102.04. Similarly, at 1 January 1989, the index was $100 \times \frac{61}{49} = 124.49$. This means that the amount of butter that cost 100 price units (be it £ sterling, US dollars or South African rands) on 1 January 1984 would cost 124.49 price units on 1 January 1989. The indices for each of the dates given above with 1 January 1984 as base is given in Table 15.2. You should check each entry.

To describe the above simply as a butter price index is glib. Most supermarkets stock about a dozen different brands of butter with prices for a 250 gram pack varying by 5p or more between brands. In a small store, a brand currently selling in a supermarket for 55p might cost 59p. In the Western Isles of Scotland, butter tends to cost more than it would in a similar shop in Edinburgh or London. I had tongue in cheek, too, when I said it did not matter if unit prices were in £ sterling, US dollars or South African rands. The price of butter in the UK, USA and South Africa is generally different and changes at a different rate in each; changes in the exchange rate between different currencies is an added complication if we try to compare price trends in different countries and currencies.

Thus we oversimplify if we call our index simply a butter price index without qualification or explanation. If Table 15.1 applied to the same brand in the same supermarket at each date, it would reflect price trends for that brand in that supermarket, but would have little wider relevance unless we knew that price trends in other stores and for other brands of butter followed similar patterns.

A more interesting index would be one that reflected price trends for butter in the whole country. The average price paid per 250 gram pack could be calculated exactly if we knew the total number of packs sold, say, in a given week at each price. We would need price information for the base date and any other date for which we wanted to calculate the index.

It is not practicable to get all this information. We would do better to conduct a sample survey to estimate the average price of butter at any given time. If good survey practice is adopted, information from a small proportion of retail outlets about prices and sales will give a good approximation to the overall situation. This is broadly how prices are determined for a wide variety of goods and services in calculating the retail prices index, an index we describe in detail in section 15.3. If the indices in Table 15.2 were based on results of such a survey, then we would have a reasonable index for the average price of butter on the stated dates. If this, perchance, reflects accurately what happens in Glasgow or London, there is still no guarantee it also does so for Cornwall or the Isle of Skye.

15.1.1 The scope of indices

The general form of a simple price index (sometimes called a price relative) is that it has a value 100 at an arbitrary time (time 0) and a value $I_{n,0}$ at a given later time n, where

$$I_{n,0} = 100 p_n / p_0.$$

Here p_n is the price of a unit quantity at the (current) time n, and p_0 is the price of the same unit at the base time. The subscripts on I indicate it is the value of the index at time n with base time 0. In Example 15.1, taking 1 January 1984 as base, the July 1988 index might be written $I_{\text{Ju88, Ja84}}$ in a fairly obvious notation to show that it is the index value on 1 July 1988 with base 1 January 1984.

Indices are not always for prices. They may refer to quantities manufactured or consumed, to costs, to changes in volumes, to numbers engaged in particular activities, to share values, and so on. If we take 1987 as base year, and a smelter produces 4500 tons of aluminium in that year and 5200 tons in 1989, then we write the production quantity index for 1989 in an obvious notation as $I_{89,87} = 100 \times 5200/4500 = 115.56$. If the context makes it clear (e.g. if it is explained in the text what the base and current times are), the suffixes may be omitted from I. The general formula for a quantity index is analogous to that for a price index, but it is customary to replace p_0 and p_n (for price) by q_0 and q_n (for quantity).

15.2   MORE COMPREHENSIVE INDICES

Before considering the UK retail prices index, which takes into account price movements over a broad field of consumer expenditure, we look at some intermediate steps with indices for several commodities. In practice, these are nearly always what are called 'weighted' indices. The need for weighting becomes clear if we consider, say, a price index for butter and pepper. If we want this index to reflect changes in expenditure per individual (the average cost of, or the price paid by an individual for, these commodities), we must not only consider changes in the price of unit packages of both pepper and butter, but make allowance for the relative quantities of each used by individuals. This will vary from person to person. A survey is a possible way to get an average figure.

Example 15.2   A survey shows the average purchase of butter per person is 220 grams per week and that of pepper 0.5 grams per week. Taking a base date of 1 January 1985, the average retail prices then are 22p for a 20 gram pack of pepper and 50p for a 250 gram pack of butter. How should this information be used to construct a 'butter + pepper' price index?

Solution   To make the units comparable, we express the cost per some standardized amount (the same amount for each commodity). We arbitrarily choose this to be 1 gram. Then for pepper the cost per gram is clearly $\frac{22}{20}$p, while for butter it is $\frac{50}{250}$p. A realistic price or cost index must also take account of average quantities consumed per person; these are what we mean by 'weights'. For butter, since the average consumption is 220 grams and the cost is $\frac{50}{250}$p per gram, the average expenditure is $220 \times \frac{50}{250} = 44$p. For pepper, since each person uses on average 0.5 grams and the cost is $\frac{22}{20}$ per gram the average expenditure is $0.5 \times \frac{22}{20} = 0.55$p. Thus the weekly expenditure on butter and pepper is $44 + 0.55 = 44.55$ pence.

The weekly expenditure of 0.55p on pepper (largely because such a small quantity is consumed) is almost negligible compared to that on butter, so that a quite sharp change in the price of pepper will have less effect on the appropriate 'butter + pepper' price index than a corresponding change in the price of butter.

Example 15.3   Calculate a 'butter + pepper' index for 1 July 1989 using the information in Example 15.2 for the base date, given that the price of pepper has doubled to 44p per 20 gram pack while butter has risen (as it did in Example 15.1) only to 63p.

Solution   We may summarize the price information as follows:

	Butter	Pepper
1 January 1985	50	22
1 July 1989	63	44

The prices per gram on 1 July 1989 are now $\frac{63}{250}$ and $\frac{44}{20}$p and since the average purchase of butter is 220 grams and of pepper 0.5 grams, the average person's expenditure on butter plus pepper is now

$220 \times \frac{63}{250} + 0.5 \times \frac{44}{20} = 56.54$. To calculate the corresponding 'butter + pepper' index for 1 July 1989 relative to the base of 1 January 1985, we use these expenditure figures as 'costs' (or prices in the sense of prices that the consumer pays) at the two dates and find the index is $I = 100 \times 56.54/44.55 = 126.91$.

Note that for the above period the price index for pepper alone (since the price doubled) is 200. That for butter alone would be $100 \times \frac{63}{50} = 126$. Thus, quite sensibly, the combined index is very close to that for butter alone; the steep increase on the pepper alone index is 'downweighted' because we use so little pepper. The index we have just calculated is usually called an aggregate weighted price index.

15.2.1 Weighted relatives indices

Another weighted index commonly used is a weighted relatives price index. This is an index based on the separate price indices and is the mean of these weighted by the quantities used of each commodity. In the above example, the weights are 220 for butter and 0.5 for pepper (average consumptions per person in grams). The respective single commodity indices have the values 126 and 200. Their weighted relatives mean is obtained by multiplying each by its respective weight, adding these products and dividing by the sum of the weights, i.e.

$$I = (220 \times 126 + 0.5 \times 200)/220.5 = 126.17.$$

15.2.2 Comparing and extending indices

There is little difference between the weighted aggregate and relatives indices for butter and pepper, but Example 15.4 will show that there may sometimes be appreciable differences. First, we formalize and extend slightly the ideas just developed. We have restricted ourselves so far to two commodities, but the ideas extend to any number. For each commodity, we must know the prices at the base date and at a later date (or dates) n at which we want to calculate the index. We suppose we have m commodities in all. We denote by p_{i0} and p_{in} the prices of commodity i at times 0 and n respectively, and by q_i the amount of commodity i used. Then the weighted aggregate price index is defined by

$$I_{A,n,0} = \left(\sum q_i p_{in} \bigg/ \sum q_i p_{i0} \right) \times 100,$$

and the weighted relatives price index as

$$I_{R,n,0} = \left(\sum q_i I_{i,n,0} \right) \bigg/ \left(\sum q_i \right),$$

where $I_{i,n,0}$ is the price index for the ith commodity at time n with base 0 and all summations are over the m commodities. The notation looks formidable, and we give these formulae for completeness, but we see in Example 15.4 that the full expression for only two commodities is simple to write down.

   Example 15.4   The prices in pounds per 50 kg bag of waste offal and of rabbit meat blended in a pet food in 1984 (year 0) and 1990 (year 6) are given below, together with the quantities of each used in a batch.

	Price in year 0	Price in year 6	Quantity used
Offal	1.5 (p_{10})	3 (p_{16})	7 (q_{10})
Rabbit	20 (p_{20})	10 (p_{26})	1 (q_{26})

Compare the weighted aggregate and the weighted relatives purchase price indices for the pet food ingredients.

   Solution   Using the above formulae, the weighted aggregate price index is

$$100(7 \times 3 + 1 \times 10)/(7 \times 1.5 + 1 \times 20) = 101.6.$$

For the weighted relatives index, we note that the 'relative' for offal is 200 (a doubling in price from 1.5 to 3) and that for rabbits is 50 (a halving in price from 20 to 10). Thus the weighted relatives price index is

$$(7 \times 200 + 1 \times 50)/(7 + 1) = 181.25.$$

Can you explain the difference? Think carefully before reading on.

The key factor is that the actual prices per unit for offal are low but a large number of units are used (making total or weighted cost relatively high), whereas for rabbit the prices are relatively high but the number of units used are low (somewhat off-setting high costs per unit). The aggregate index tends to compare expenditures at given prices and the two expenditures here are somewhat comparable (the low unit cost being heavily weighted and the high one lightly weighted). Now since unit costs for offal double and those for rabbit are halved, this tends to balance out expenditure, whereas if we take a weighted relative index, this gives extra weight to the relative where more units are used (offal), but ignores the fact that rabbit has the higher unit cost. The effect here is perhaps unusual in that we have one commodity price rising steeply, while the other drops (perhaps because there was a local plague of rabbits in 1990). The effect of inflation in recent years has generally precluded situations like this. However, it occasionally happens that while prices generally are rising, that of a particular commodity may drop because a new source is found, or a cheaper manufacturing process is introduced. Thirty years ago, computers with only 1% of the computing power of that on which I am preparing the manuscript for this book cost about £50 000 at *then* current prices, compared to £3000 at *today's* prices for my equipment. The ravages of inflation make the contrast even more startling in real (present value) money terms.

There is no question of one of the above indices being correct, or the other wrong. Each measure a different aspect of price changes. Generally speaking, the aggregate price index is the preferred indicator of expenditure changes, while the relatives index gives a better reflection of relative increases or decreases for costs in proportion to the number of units used. These differences make for confusion, with people often quoting the index that best suits their case, without stating which has been calculated. The basis of calculation of these, or any other index, should always be clearly indicated.

15.2.3 Choice of weights

Our examples so far have concentrated mainly on price or cost indices and we have described their weighting by quantities. Quantity indices, measuring, say, the output of several different factories, may often appropriately be weighted by prices. The computations proceed in similar manner with quantities and prices interchanged in their role. A difficulty that commonly arises is that relevant prices and quantities are often not independent. A rise in price might alter the demand for a commodity; for instance, returning to Example 15.2, if butter prices rose to 90p per 250 gram pack, people might either cut their butter consumption or switch to another product such as margarine, so that average consumption of butter of 220 grams per week might fall to 170 grams. Of course, consumption may also change for reasons entirely unconnected with price; health scares often lead to dramatic changes in people's eating habits.

If we are calculating a price index $I_{n,0}$, and quantities purchased or produced change between times 0 and n, should we choose the quantities at time 0 or at time n as weights? If we use the quantities at time 0, we are essentially studying an index which reflects changes in costs if demand patterns had stayed as they originally were, whereas if we use quantities at time n we are comparing changes in costs corresponding (i.e. weighted) to accord with our current demands. It may be tempting to use a hybrid index with current q values in the numerator and base time q values in the denominator. This index is not, however, an aggregate price or cost index (weighted by quantity) or an aggregate quantity index (weighted by prices). It is, if anything, a total expenditure index measuring changes in

Table 15.3 Output of vehicles and cost per unit 1986, 1988.

	1986		1988	
	Cost per unit	No. produced	Cost per unit	No. produced
Cars	4800	850	5100	928
Trucks	9850	105	10200	85
Vans	3700	450	4700	220

overall expenditure on goods of a certain type as a result of changes in both costs and quantities involved.

Weighted aggregate indices of prices or quantities using base date weights are called *Laspeyres indices*; those using current time weights are called *Paasche indices*. Calculation of each is straightforward; given base year and current year prices and quantities; it is possible to calculate both Laspeyres and Paasche price and quantity indices as Example 15.5 shows. If such indices (for prices for example) are being calculated for several different years, we need to know the q values (weights) for each of these years to calculate the Paasche indices. Sometimes these are not as readily available as prices.

Example 15.5   A motor manufacturer produces cars, trucks and vans. Cost per vehicle for manufacture and numbers of each made in 1986 and 1988 are given in Table 15.3. Calculate Laspeyres and Paasche cost and quantity indices for the firm's output with 1986 as base.

Solution   The reader should check through the calculations outlined below to be sure the relevant processes are understood.

Laspeyres cost index:

$$100(850 \times 5100 + 105 \times 10\,200 + 450 \times 4700)/$$

$$(850 \times 4800 + 105 \times 9850 + 450 \times 3700) = 110.94.$$

Paasche cost index:

$$100(928 \times 5100 + 85 \times 10\,200 + 220 \times 4700)/$$

$$(928 \times 4800 + 85 \times 9850 + 220 \times 3700) = 108.65.$$

Laspeyres quantity index:

$$100(4800 \times 928 + 9850 \times 85 + 3700 \times 220)/$$

$$(4800 \times 850 + 9850 \times 105 + 3700 \times 450) = 90.06.$$

Paasche quantity index:

$$100(5100 \times 928 + 10\,200 \times 85 + 4700 \times 220)/$$

$$(5100 \times 850 + 10\,220 \times 105 + 4700 \times 450) = 88.18.$$

For both price and quantity, the Paasche index has the slightly lower value, but the difference is only small. An interesting point is that, while the cost indices have risen (they exceed 100), the quantity indices have fallen; this reflects the fact that, while all prices have risen, production of both trucks and vans has fallen and only that of cars has risen.

Sometimes (see Exercises 15.4 and 15.5) the difference between a Paasche and Laspeyres cost or price index (or the corresponding quantity indices) may be more dramatic. Again it is not a question of one being right and the other being wrong. Each measures something different and it is important to quote which is being used, especially when each has a very different value.

15.3 SOME IMPORTANT INDICES

Many major indices, such as the retail prices index (RPI), the taxes and prices index (TPI), the index of industrial production, the trade weighted sterling index, or the FTSE 100 shares index (affectionately, or less affectionately, depending on the state of the stock market, known in financial circles as the *Footsie*), are complex in structure although in principle they are either weighted aggregate or weighted relative indices.

15.3.1 The retail prices index

The retail prices index is calculated monthly using weights that are revised annually on the basis of changing household expenditure patterns revealed in a nationwide survey called the *Family Expenditure Survey*. These weights reflect the relative proportions spent by an *average* household on items under each of (currently) five major headings, which are subdivided into about 80 categories. Prices are checked regularly for about 600 items covering all categories. Prior to 1987, there were 11 major headings. In any given year, the weights for each group are based on information gleaned from the Family Spending Survey for the year ending in the previous June. The units in this survey are households. A household is defined as all who live at the same address and share common catering facilities, but excludes hotels, hostels and boarding houses. There is no implication of a blood or marriage relationship between members; domestic servants are included. While family homes or flats are obviously covered, groups with looser associations such as students or workers sharing a flat also qualify. To conduct the survey some 11 000 addresses are selected annually, although the precise basis of selection is not made clear in the brief description given in the 'Definitions' and 'Explanatory notes' pertaining to the official publication the *Monthly Digest of Statistics*. Effectively the approach leads to selection of some 10 400 families, because selection of addresses on a national scale – no matter what care is taken to pinpoint only residential properties – will inevitably lead to some failures (houses may have been demolished or changed to other uses, or be unoccupied, etc.). Participation in the survey is not compulsory, but it is reported that about 70% of those selected respond and fill in the questionnaire and partake in interviews. This, in practice, is a good response to such a survey, but there is a danger of a bias introduced by non-response. For example, most non-responses may be from poorer families, or families of a particular political or religious persuasion, whose expenditure patterns may be rather different from those among respondents. Year-to-year results from the survey should be compared with caution, for definitions used in the survey may vary slightly between years to reflect social trends. This is desirable in a survey designed to get information useful for calculating the RPI. Care is taken in defining items of income and expenditure so that one gets meaningful and comparable results from all respondents. For example, respondents are asked for *gross* income before deduction of tax and national insurance contributions, but *excluding* proceeds from the sale of cars or other capital assets, legacies, proceeds of maturing insurance policies, windfalls and most in-kind payments (use of company cars, free suits, etc., although luncheon vouchers are included in income!). An imputed cost for owner-occupier or rent-free accommodation is included. Expenditure includes outlay on goods and services, but *not* savings and investment, nor income tax and national insurance payments, mortgages (other than interest payable thereon) and other costs for purchase of or additions and extensions to a house. There are special provisions for hire purchase and credit finance. What housing expenditure is included depends upon the type of accommodation, but rents, rates and insurance are covered. Persons classified as working include temporary absentees from work and the unemployed and the self-employed. Students and housewives are classed as 'unoccupied', which presumably makes more sense to an economist than to a student or housewife. This brief description only touches on main features of the survey. The whole procedure and the derivation of weights from these data is highly technical. However, the weights reflect relative expenditures; for example, the survey showed that in 1986 the average family expenditure on bread was £1.68 per week and on butter 43p, representing respectively proportions of about 0.009 and 0.002 of family expenditure. They are therefore given weightings of 9 and 2 respectively where the total of weights for all expenditure items is 1000.

Table 15.4 Weights (total 1000) used in RPI calculation.

	Year		
	1962	1973	1986
Food	350	248	185
Alcohol	71	73	82
Tobacco	80	49	40
Housing	87	126	153
Fuel and Light	55	58	62
Durable household goods	66	58	63
Clothing and footwear	106	89	75
Transport and vehicles	68	135	157
Miscellaneous goods	59	65	81
Services	58	53	58
Meals outside home	—	46	44

15.3.2 The weights

Table 15.4 gives the weights used for the 11 different expenditure headings used prior to 1987 for each of the years 1962, 1973, 1986. The category *meals outside home* was not included in 1962.

A decrease in weights between any two dates indicates that families were on average spending a lower proportion of their income on items under that heading at the latter date. Some of the changes, such as the decrease in tobacco, will cause little surprise. The decrease for clothing and footwear looks to have a less obvious explanation; it may result from a combination of factors – trends towards wearing less formal attire, perhaps clothes becoming out of fashion less quickly, and improvements in quality resulting in clothes being kept longer, or a combination of these and a less steep rise in clothing prices relative to other goods. There is indeed some evidence of the last: in the 11 years from 1974 to 1984, the price of tobacco goods rose more than twice as fast as that of clothing. This may have helped reduce the demand for tobacco (although health considerations may be a greater contributory cause), but the lower price rise in clothing does not appear to have increased demand substantially; and therefore the proportion of total income spent on clothing has dropped. The sharply increased weighting for transport and vehicles may reflect both more travel and a relatively fast increase in cost, although the index for that category over the period was not much in excess of that for all items (400 compared to the 'all items' 394.6 on 13 January 1987). At the same time, the indices for clothing with the 1974 base of 100 was 266 and that for tobacco was 603.

15.3.3 Revised heads

Prices used in calculating the RPI cover all the heads in Table 15.4, and also the revised combined heads adopted from 1987, namely

1. food and catering,
2. alcohol and tobacco,
3. housing and household expenditure,
4. personal expenditure,
5. travel and leisure.

The list of items included under each head, with weights and separate indices calculated for each, are given every month in the *Monthly Digest of Statistics*.

The single RPI quoted in the press is a weighted relative of the indices for the five categories above. There are some noteworthy exclusions from the index. The chief factors not taken into account are (i) income tax payments; (ii) national insurance contributions; (iii) pension and life insurance premiums; (iv) subscriptions to professional bodies or trade unions; (v) the capital element of mortgage repayments (although interest repayments are included). Other exclusions are contributions to church collections, cash gifts, betting, and doctor's and dentist's fees.

With a base of 100 on 1 January 1974, the index stood at 189.5 on 1 January 1978 and at 358.5 on 1 December 1984 and at 394.5 on 13 January 1987. At this last date, the base was changed to 100 at the same time as the 11 major category base was reduced to the five given above.

Annual revision of weights is a slight compromise over the use of exact current weights: it reflects the fact that the Family Spending Survey is an annual event and provides a sensible basis for recalculation of weights. It would be very costly to carry out this survey monthly and expenditure patterns seldom change dramatically except in crisis situations like the outbreak of war or introduction of rationing, situations where people are likely to have more to occupy their minds than the RPI. Another argument against monthly surveys is that the time taken to process the results would make the information available too late for use in calculating current RPIs for a particular month.

15.3.4 **Commodity prices**

Besides weights, the other essential information needed to calculate the index is a set of average prices for many commodities. For expenditure within each category, a representative list of items is selected and priced at regular intervals in a wide selection of urban and rural retail outlets; some 130 000 separate items throughout the UK are priced each month. A suitably weighted index is worked out for each of the five expenditure groups and, as already explained, the RPI is a weighted relatives index based on these group indices with weights given in Table 15.5 (updated as appropriate). So far as possible, goods of unchanged quality are priced on successive dates. Clearly this aim is sometimes difficult to achieve, particularly for goods like vehicles and durable items, where new models are constantly being introduced and older ones withdrawn, where yesterday's optional extras become today's standard equipment. For example, a car windscreen wash was once an optional extra; it is now a mandatory requirement in new cars. The same applies to seat belts. Seasonal foods also pose problems. For example, over some years, it has been noted that in March the price of new potatoes is approximately 2.2 times that of old potatoes. Thus, at that time of year, it is deemed appropriate in the price survey to regard the price of 5 lb of new potatoes as comparable to the price of 11 lb of old potatoes. By June, there is no price differential (in practice, new potatoes have by then virtually taken over from old).

Much criticism of the RPI arises from misconceptions about how it is constructed, and what it is supposed to measure. It is based on average prices nationwide and the items included are commodities and services used by the great majority of households in the UK (although some may not use any items from particular groupings such as alcohol or tobacco). The households include practically all wage-earners and most small and medium salary earners. It excludes pensioners solely or largely dependent upon State pensions (some 14% of all households) and certain high income families (about 4% of all households). Obviously the expenditure pattern of a single person living alone is likely to be very different from that of a married couple with five young children. Also, a single person on a low income has a different pattern from one on a high income.

15.3.5 The RPI and inflation

Changes in the RPI are often looked upon as measures of inflation, and one hears people say, 'Inflation is only supposed to have gone up 5% last year, but my expenses have gone up 10%'. This could well be true, but has that person based his statement on expenditure and prices covered by the RPI? Are the weightings used in the RPI relevant to that individual's expenditure? Or, for example, does he or she spend considerably more (or less) on alcohol and less (or more) on clothes than the index weightings for those categories imply? Further, price changes in a local area may not be reflected in a national average.

Table 15.5 RPI weights and group indices, 15 August 1989; base 100, 13 January 1987.

Group	Food	Alcohol & tobacco	Housing	Personal	Travel & leisure
Weight	203	119	341	110	227
Index	112.1	111.3	123.2	110.9	113.4

Different people express displeasure at the RPI at different times. Because indices may be sensitive to weightings and sudden changes in one factor, it is inevitable that there will be grumbles about what is included and what is left out. Some UK Government ministers in 1989 – when mortgage interest payments rose sharply as an inevitable but indirect result of Government policy – suggested that including this element in the RPI gave an exaggerated inflation rate and they quoted what the RPI would be if this item were omitted. Had interest rates dropped when other inflationary factors were high, these same ministers could have been expected to remain silent. In fairness to those who complained about their inclusion when rates went up, we point out that part of their argument was that in making comparison between the UK inflation rate, as measured by the RPI, and that of other countries, some of the latter did not include mortgage interest in their equivalent measures of price changes. This is a valid point, but their methods of calculation probably differ in other respects as well; this places serious restrictions on the validity of comparisons, restrictions that apply in many other contexts when one is not comparing like with like. In fact, as well as the usually quoted RPI, the UK Central Statistical Office also publishes RPIs that omit respectively housing and seasonal foods as well as indices for the main heads and further subdivisions of these. An excellent detailed description of the RPI is given in an article in the *Employment Gazette*, Volume 95, August 1987, pp. 393–406, entitled 'A short guide to the retail prices index'. Table 15.5 gives the weights used in 1989 calculations for the five main groupings (total 1000) and the indices for each on 15 August 1989 referred to a base of 100 on 13 January 1987. At the later date, the *all items* RPI stood at 115.8, the index for all items except housing stood at 111.8, and that omitting seasonal foods stood at 116.2.

Some of the limitations of even complex and carefully compiled indices like the RPI may in part be ameliorated by having a series of indices measuring slightly different things. This is indeed the role of indices omitting housing, seasonal foods, etc. The fact that the RPI ignore tax payments stimulated the case for introducing an alternative index of prices that allows for tax changes, called the Taxation and Price Index (TPI). The difficulty now is that politicians tend to quote the RPI when it suits them better as the 'correct' index, and the TPI as the 'correct' index when that suits them better. Some politicians probably change their mind about which is correct as often as they change their underwear.

15.4 CHANGING THE BASE YEAR

We mentioned that the base year for the RPI was changed in 1987 from 1 January 1974 to 13 January 1987. There is no difficulty in changing the base year once the index is calculated. We often change the base when, as in the case of the RPI, the index gets so far removed from 100 that it becomes difficult to visualize changes in simple terms. For example, an increase from 100 to 115 is a 15% increase and we have a good conception of what such a percentage change means. An increase from 370 to 425.5 is also a 15% change, but it is less obvious that it is. We see this easily if we change the 370 to a new base value of 100. The index 425.5 to that base is then $100 \times 425.5/370 = 115$. The difficulty of interpretation with large departures from the common base of 100 becomes particularly marked for the Nikkei index of prices on the Japanese stock exchange. On 17 August 1990, it dropped 763 points, from 27 539 to 26 786.

Exercise   Verify that this fall of 763 points is a drop of less than 3%.

The general rule for changing the base of an index is to divide all indices in the series by the index for the new base year expressed relative to the old base, and to multiply the results by 100.

Example 15.6   A meat seller's wholesale cooperative works out the following indices for the prices of beef on the hoof relative to a 1980 base of 100. What is the effect of changing the base year to 1984?

Year	1980	1981	1982	1983	1984	1985	1986	1987	1988
Index	100	104	107	123	151	163	174	189	207

Solution   We divide each entry above by the 1984 value of 151 and multiply by 100, to get

Year	1980	1981	1982	1983	1984	1985	1986	1987	1988
Index	66.2	68.9	70.9	81.5	100	107.9	115.2	125.1	137.1

15.5   WHAT AND WHERE?

What skills have we mastered?

We have developed the basic methods of constructing indices from the idea of a simple price index evaluated as

$$100 \times \text{(current cost per unit)}/\text{(base year cost per unit)}.$$

Weighted aggregate or weighted relative indices may be calculated for prices, quantities, etc. Those using base year weights are called Laspeyres indices and those using current year weights are Paasche indices. In comparing indices, it is important to indicate the base year, weighting system and whether weighted aggregate or weighted relative indices, are being quoted.

Major indices such as the RPI or TPI are complex in structure, and to interpret such single figures as trend measures in a sensible way requires an understanding of their method of construction.

An easily made change of base for an index is desirable when its value deviates so markedly from 100 that changes become difficult to appreciate as proportions or percentages.

Where can I read more?

Many statistics textbooks (especially those with an emphasis on applications to business or the social sciences) have a chapter on indices. They are discussed in a management examinations context by Francis (1988: Chaps. 22–25), Bancroft and O'Sullivan (1988: Chap. 11), and Jones and McKay (1988: Chap. 17).

EXERCISES

*15.1   The price in pence of a standard can of soup in a London supermarket chain on 1 July of each of six years is:

1983	1984	1985	1986	1987	1988
62	65	69	68	74	79

Calculate a price index for the soup in that supermarket chain on 1 July in each of the above years taking 1 July 1983 as base.

15.2   If the index calculated in Exercise 15.1 stood at 129.03 on 1 July 1989, what would then be the price of a can of soup?

15.3   Recalculate the indices in Exercise 15.1 taking the base year as 1987.

*15.4   Given the following prices and quantities sold for each of three commodities for 1986 and 1988, calculate Laspeyres and

Paasche aggregate weighted price indices for 1988 with 1986 as base year. Explain the main reason for any differences between the index values.

Commodity	1986		1988	
	Quantity	Price	Quantity	Price
A	5	20	50	50
B	10	10	8	12
C	10	10	10	15

*15.5   For the data in Exercise 15.4, compute weighted relatives prices indices analogous to the Laspeyres and Paasche aggregate weighted price indices. Discuss the main reasons for any differences between each and also for any differences between these and the corresponding indices in Exercise 15.4.

15.6   A company manufacturing a product known as K257 uses 5 components in its assembly.

The quantities and prices of the components used to produce a unit of K257 in 1982, 1983 and 1984 are tabulated as follows:

Production of 1 unit of K257

Commodity	1982		1983		1984	
	Quantity	Price £	Quantity	Price £	Quantity	Price £
A	10	3.12	12	3.17	14	3.20
B	6	11.49	7	11.58	5	11.67
C	5	1.40	8	1.35	9	1.31
D	9	2.15	9	2.14	10	2.63
E	50	0.32	53	0.32	57	0.32

Required:

(a) Calculate Laspeyres type price-index numbers for the cost of 1 unit of K257 for 1983 and 1984 based on 1982.
(b) Calculate Paasche type price-index numbers for the cost of 1 unit of K257 for 1983 and 1984 based on 1982.
(c) Compare and contrast the Laspeyres and Paasche price-index numbers you have obtained in (a) and (b).

[ACCA, part question]

15.7 A cost accountant has derived the following information about basic weekly wage rates (W) and the number of people employed (E) in the factories of a large chemical company.

Basic weekly rates (£'s) and number of employees (100's)

Technical group of employees	July 1979		July 1980		July 1981	
	W	E	W	E	W	E
Q	60	5	70	4	80	4
R	60	2	65	3	70	3
S	70	2	85	2	90	1
T	90	1	110	1	120	2

(i) Calculate a Laspeyres (base weights) all-items index number for July 1980 basic weekly wage rates, with July 1979 = 100.
(ii) Calculate a Paasche (current weights) all-items index number for July 1981 basic weekly wage rates, with July 1979 = 100.
(iii) Briefly compare your index numbers for the company with the official government figures for the Chemical and Allied Industries which are given below.

Yearly annual averages	1979	1980	1981
Weekly wage rates	156.3	187.4	203.4

(July 1976 = 100) (Source: *Employment Gazette*, November 1981)

[CIMA, part question]

16 Dynamic Programming

16.1 A TOOL WITH MANY USES

In this final chapter, we use simple examples to demonstrate the basic idea behind a powerful technique called *dynamic programming*. It provides an alternative to some of the methods we have used in networks, decision analysis, inventory and stock control, and financial planning. Like linear programming, most real-life dynamic programming requires computer power for a solution.

Most examples in this chapter could be solved by other methods: in some cases (e.g. Example 16.3), that would be easier; in others, more difficult (e.g. if it required complete enumeration of all possible strategies). We take an 'intuitive' approach in our first example, and then indicate a little more formally the key concept behind dynamic programming. The name stems from the 'dynamic' nature of many of the problems where we apply the method. The problems are 'dynamic' in the sense that interrelated decisions have to be taken at various stages in a process and these have a knock-on effect that influences the optimal solution. Dynamic programming often starts by making what is virtually an obvious decision; usually the last decision in a chain. We then work back recursively to see what earlier decisions should be made when we know what all later decisions are going to be.

Example 16.1 A chemical company makes two highly corrosive chemicals, A and B. They may make batches of only one chemical at a time until they have produced three batches (these may be all A, all B, or some A others B). After three batches are produced the plant is stripped completely, many parts replaced to give virtually a 'new' plant and the cycle is repeated. If chemical A is produced at any batch then the profit from the next batch is reduced to 70% of what it would have been if the same chemical had been made at the previous batch, and if chemical B is produced at any batch then the profit from the next batch is only 30% of what it would have been if the same chemical had been made at the previous batch. The respective profits for batch 1 (the first batch of a cycle) are £1200 for A and £1800 for B. What strategy maximizes profits?

Solution   Clearly chemical B will give the largest batch-1 profit. However, making chemical B in batch 1 will seriously reduce the profit from whatever we make in batch 2 – to 30% of £1800 (i.e. £540) if we make B again and to 30% of £1200 (i.e. £240) if we make A in batch 2. On the other hand, had we made A in batch 1, then profits for A in batch 2 would be 70% of £1200 (i.e. £360) and those for B in batch 2, would be 70% of £1800 (i.e. £1260). Thus 'doing the (apparently) obvious' and maximizing batch-1 profit greatly reduces potential batch-2 profit. Indeed, if we made B in all three batches, the batch-3 profit would be £162 (i.e. 30% of £540), giving a three-batch total profit of £(1800 + 540 + 162) = £2502. In Exercise 16.1, we show that if chemical A were made in all three batches the total profit would be £2628.

Can we do even better by making some batches A and other batches B?

The one easy-to-make decision is what to do in the third batch, for whatever we do in the first two batches determines the 'profit capacity' c_1, i.e. the proportion of profitable output relative to the maximum possible. Past history (what we made at batches 1 and 2) has fixed c_1 when we start batch 3. Further, we do not care what capacity for profit is left after batch 3, for the plant is then completely overhauled and the process restarted. If we were to make A in batch 3 our profit would be $1200c_1$, and if we make B it would be $1800c_1$. Clearly, then, whatever we make in batches 1 and 2, we should make B in batch 3. We now work back one batch to see what we should do in batch 2 to maximize our profit over batches 2 and 3. We denote by c_2 the proportion of maximum profit we make from batch 2; this is determined by what we did in batch 1. We now know that we are making B in batch 3, so we must examine the total profit for batches 2 and 3 when we make A in batch 2 and when we make B in batch 2 and choose the greater. If we make A in batch 2, we make a profit of $1200c_2$ in that batch, and the capacity c_1 for the final batch is $c_1 = 0.7c_2$. Thus the total profit from batches 2 and 3 when we make A in batch 2 (and knowing we make B in batch 3) is $1200c_2 + 1800c_1 = 1200c_2 + 1800 \times 0.7c_2 = 2460c_2$. If we make B in batch 2, profit from that batch is $1800c_2$, but now $c_1 = 0.3c_2$, so that the total profit from batches 2 and 3 would now be $1800c_2 + 1800 \times 0.3c_2 = 2340c_2$. Thus the profit over batches 2 and 3 is optimized if we make A in batch 2 (and B in batch 3). We must now choose for batch 1 the chemical which will maximize overall profit knowing already that we make A in batch 2 and B in batch 3. For reasons that become apparent below, we may formally write c_3 for the profit proportion for batch 1, though, since it is the full possible profit, $c_3 = 1$. If we make A in batch 1, the profit is $1200c_3$, and $c_2 = 0.7c_3$. Since the maximum profit from batches 2 and 3 is $2460c_2$, this gives a total profit over all three batches of $1200c_3 + 2460 \times 0.7c_3 = 2922c_3$. Similarly, by making B in batch 1, we compute total profit as $1800c_3 + 2460 \times 0.3c_3 = 2538c_3$. Thus, since $c_3 = 1$, the maximum profit is £2922, obtained by making A in batch 1, A in batch 2, and B in batch 3, a result we verify directly in Exercise 16.2.

Since $c_3 = 1$, it may seem perverse to retain it in the above argument, but had we worked in say four- or five-batch cycles we could, by doing so, have extended the argument immediately to earlier batches.

Example 16.2 Had we made A at a batch preceding batch 1 with a profit proportion c_4 we easily see that our total profit would be $1200c_4 + 2922 \times 0.7c_4 = 3245.4c_4$, whereas had we made B in that preceding batch it would only have been $1800c_4 + 2922 \times 0.3c_4 = 2676.6c_4$.

We can now formally set out our recursive method.

1. First, we determine the optimum final batch decision. In the above example, this is (trivially obvious) make B.
2. We then move back to the penultimate batch and calculate the total profit for this plus the final batch under the conditions (i) make A and (ii) make B at the penultimate batch. We choose the condition that maximizes profit over the penultimate plus the final batch.
3. This process is continued, moving back one batch at a time, in each case selecting the maximum for that and the already optimized later strategy until all stages are covered.

Another way of looking at the process is that we first maximize one-stage profit (where that one stage is the last stage): the maximum we get is optimum whatever we have done earlier. We then maximize over two stages (the last and the last but one): the maximum is again optimum whatever we have done earlier. We then introduce one more stage (an earlier one) and maximize over the last three stages, and so on.

This stagewise build-up of optimality depends upon what is known as the Bellman optimality principle after its originator Richard Bellman (see Bellman, 1957), who expressed it in the following form:

> An optimal policy has the property that whatever the initial state and the initial decision are, the remaining decisions must constitute an optimal policy with regard to the state resulting from the first decision.

We shall not dwell upon the many and far reaching consequences of this simply expressed, but rather abstract, statement. It suffices to say that in Example 16.1 we applied it first to the final batch, where our policy 'make B' was optimal whatever we did at earlier stages. Then our two-stage decision 'make A in batch 2 and B in batch 3' became optimal whatever we did in batch 1. Finally we chose in batch 1 to make A, and the three-stage decision 'make A in batch 1, A in batch 2, and B in batch 3' became optimal. Further, as we indicated in Example 16.2, these decisions remain optimal if we add earlier batches.

16.2 DYNAMIC PROGRAMMING APPLIED TO A NETWORK PROBLEM

Here is an application of dynamic programming to a network problem that could also be solved by Dijkstra's algorithm described in Chapter 8 or even by a common-sense inspection of the network!

Example 16.3   The network illustrated in Fig. 16.1 represents a series of bus routes between towns P and Q. Each route passes through two intermediate towns. The fare in pence for the single fare stages between these intermediate towns is indicated beside each stage and fares are additive for two or more stages. Find the cheapest route from P to Q.

Solution   In a dynamic programming approach, our objective is, given all one-stage fares, to determine a minimal three-stage fare (from P to Q via two intermediate points). Knowing all the one-stage fares, it is easy to work out all the two-stage fares. For some 'two stages', there are two or more possible routes, e.g. from A to Q we may proceed via D or via E, and from B to Q we may

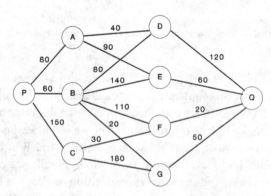

Figure 16.1 What is the minimum fare from P to Q?

proceed via D, E, F or G. Once we have worked out all two-stage fares, we seek a route giving a minimum fare between any pair of destinations. Then we next work out three-stage fares by adding relevant two- and one-stage fares.

More formally, and more generally, we denote by $f_i(X, Y)$ the fare for the optimal (here the lowest) i-stage fare between any two points X and Y. In this example, for instance, $f_2(A, Q)$ denotes the optimal two-stage fare between A and Q. It is associated with one of the routes (i) A to D to Q or (ii) A to E to Q, and it may be broken down to the sum of one-stage optima. This gives us a key to using dynamic programming in this problem, for since there is only a single one-stage route between any two points that route is optimal. This suggests working backward from our destination as we did in the previous example. We can immediately write down the optimal fares for the one-stage routes DQ, EQ, FQ, GQ. Further we may split fares for the two-stage routes from A, B or C to Q into the sum of two one-stage route fares and find which of these is optimal. Having determined these, we finally find an optimal three-stage route fare from P to Q as the sum of one-stage fares from P to A or B or C and optimal two-stage routes from each of these points to Q.

Formally we may set out the breakdown from three- to two- to one-stage optimal route fares relevant to the problem as

$$f_3(P, Q) = \text{minimum} \{[f_1(P, A) + f_2(A, Q)], [f_1(P, B) + f_2(B, Q)],$$
$$[f_1(P, C) + f_2(C, Q)]\}.$$

The two-stage optima involved in this breakdown may be written as the optimum sum of one-stage optima:

$$f_2(A, Q) = \text{minimum} \{[f_1(A, D) + f_1(D, Q)],$$
$$[f_1(A, E) + f_1(E, Q)]\},$$
$$f_2(B, Q) = \text{minimum} [\{f_1(B, D) + f_1(D, Q)],$$
$$[f_1(B, E) + f_1(E, Q)], [f_1(B, F) + f_1(F, Q)],$$
$$[f_1(B, G) + f_1(G, Q)]\},$$

$$f_2(C, Q) = \text{minimum}\{[f_1(C, F) + f_1(F, Q)],$$

$$[f_1(C, G) + f_1(G, Q)]\}.$$

Since all one-stage optimum fares can be read from the graph, we may immediately work out all these minima in reverse order. Thus,

$$f_2(C, Q) = \text{minimum}\{30 + 20, 180 + 50\} = 50,$$

$$f_2(B, Q) = \text{minimum}\{80 + 120, 140 + 60, 110 + 20, 20 + 50\}$$

$$= 70,$$

$$f_2(A, Q) = \text{minimum}\{40 + 120, 90 + 60\} = 150,$$

whence

$$f_3(P, Q) = \text{minimum}\{80 + 150, 60 + 70, 150 + 50\} = 130.$$

Thus the minimum fare is 130, and examination of the above steps starting now from the three-stage result shows the route is from P to B to G to Q.

As indicated, this problem could be solved more easily by a common-sense inspection of the diagram or using Dijkstra's algorithm; the strength of dynamic programming is its generality.

16.3 A FRIVOLOUS EXAMPLE OF AN IMPORTANT TYPE OF APPLICATION

As our final worked example in this short introduction to dynamic programming, we take ourselves to the mythical state of Sprentsylvania where the marriage customs are, to say the least, quaint.

Example 16.4 In the state of Sprentsylvania, each man on his 18th birthday, or on one of the three days thereafter, must take unto himself a bride from one of the maidens of the state whom the Elders decree. One girl will be presented to him on his birthday and he is told she will bring with her a dowry, the amount of which will be decided by an NBG computer (NBG are the leading computer

Table 16.1 Probability of various dowries on each of four days.

Dowry	Probability			
	Day 1	Day 2	Day 3	Day 4
$200	0.1	0.2	0.3	0.5
$150	0.2	0.2	0.3	0.3
$100	0.2	0.2	0.2	0.1
$50	0.5	0.4	0.2	0.1

manufacturers in Sprentsylvania). The dowry (in Sprentsylvanian dollars) will be either $200, $150, $100 or $50. In Sprentsylvania, $200 is virtually a king's ransom. The young man is also told that on each day the girl presented to him will be less pretty than any girl on preceding days, and that on the last day the girl will be a right ugly duckling. He is also told in advance the probabilities that the NBG computer will decree a dowry of each of the four amounts. To compensate for the decreasing beauty of the girls, the probabilities of the larger dowries are increased from day to day as set out in Table 16.1. The man must decide, after the NBG computer has indicated the dowry he will receive that day if he selects the girl on offer, whether to accept that girl (in which case his quest for a bride ends) or reject her (in which case the procedure is repeated the next day). On the final day, however, if he has not already selected his bride, he must take the girl that is then offered and will receive the dowry indicated by the computer for that day.

Being a normal Sprentsylvanian male, he is not averse to beauty, but even less averse to money. Clearly, if the NBG computer gives him the $200 dowry on the first day, when he gets the most beautiful girl as well, he will accept that girl as his bride. But if that day the dowry is only $50 he may well be tempted to try his luck next day for perhaps a slightly less beautiful bride but hopefully more lovely lolly. However, being not entirely averse to beauty, he feels that he

Table 16.2 Discounted cash value of dowries to compensate for increasing ugliness.

Day 1	Day 2	Day 3	Day 4
200	190	170	150
150	140	120	100
100	90	70	50
50	40	20	0

should discount the values of the dowry on later days and look upon the dowry on the second day as really being worth $10 less than its face value, and discounting those on each of the third and fourth days by a further $20 each day to give the discounted cash values in Table 16.2. Using these discounted cash values, he decides the best strategy is to maximize his discounted expected monetary value for the dowries (the discounting, he feels, compensates adequately for any regrets from perhaps marrying a bride lacking in beauty). Thus, on each day, he makes his decision to accept or reject the girl on offer so as to maximize his expected financial gain. Only if he gets to day 4 is the decision taken from his hands; he must accept the girl offered that day and the dowry that goes with her.

Solution It is easy to work out his expected gain if he does leave acceptance to day 4. It is (section 9.5.1), remembering to use his discounted cash value of the dowry,

$$150 \times 0.5 + 100 \times 0.3 + 50 \times 0.1 - 0 \times 0.1 = 110.$$

In the spirit of dynamic programming, we now look at what decisions he should make if he is faced with a choice on day 3. Clearly, if the choice on offer on day 3 is worth less than $110, he should reject it and move to day 4, because he has higher financial expectations. Thus, from Table 16.2, we see he should accept the girl on offer on day 3 only if the (discounted) dowry is $170 or $120. We are now in a position to work out his expected gain if he adopts this optimum strategy. A little care is needed here. His expectations are $170 with probability 0.3 (Tables 16.1 and 16.2), $120 with probability again 0.3, but, since he moves to day 4 if the dowry is $70 or $20 (with associated probabilities totalling 0.4), his expectation is then the day 4 expectation of $110. Thus the expected gain from optimum strategy at day 3 is

$$170 \times 0.3 + 120 \times 0.3 + 110 \times 0.4 = 131.$$

This knowledge now influences his decision on the previous day, day 2. He should accept on day 2 only if the dowry exceeds $131. Otherwise, he proceeds to day 3 with the higher expectation of $131. By similar arguments to those used above, his expected gain with optimum strategy at day 2 is

$$190 \times 0.2 + 140 \times 0.2 + 131 \times 0.6 = 144.6.$$

On day 1, therefore he should accept a girl that brings a dowry exceeding $144.6; that is, a dowry of $150 or $200. Thus his decisions on each day should be as follows.

First day. Accept for dowries of $200 or $150, otherwise reject.
Second day. Accept for dowries (after discounting) of $190 or $140, otherwise reject.
Third day. Accept for dowries (after discounting) of $170 or $120, otherwise reject.
Fourth day. No choice, and bad luck if the discounted dowry is zero!

We might regard this man's strategy, with a small risk of an ugly duckling bride coupled to what he regards as a worthless dowry, though in real money terms it is $50 before he discounts it (doing this perhaps because he'd spend the $50 on the services of a plastic surgeon to make the duckling less ugly) as a gambling man's approach. Had the suitor adopted a maximin strategy to maximize his minimum (discounted) dowry, his choice is obvious. Do you see what it is? See Exercise 16.5.

This is a frivolous example of an important type of problem. The more serious type is the problem facing a house seller who has to accept some offer. Over a period of days he may receive offers ranging from £50 000 to £70 000. None will be repeated. He may know that he must accept one offer not later than ten days after the present date. He may in his own mind associate personal probabilities with offers of varying amounts, perhaps even deciding that if the market is improving, better offers have a greater probability near the end of the period, or conversely if the market is dropping, that lower offers are more likely later. He wants to work out a strategy for accepting/rejecting offers to maximize the expected price he receives. To get a solution, certain restrictions must inevitably be built in, e.g. that only one offer can be accepted, that the buyer cannot change his mind, etc. This is not a trivial point, English rules on house purchase make it easier to change one's mind about accepting an offer than do Scottish laws. How good a solution is in practice depends on how reasonable are the assumptions we build in, not only in the form of rules about not changing one's mind, but also with respect to our assessment of future market trends, probability of various offers, etc.

16.4 OUTLINE OF A PRACTICAL DYNAMIC PROGRAMMING PROBLEM

From a rather frivolous numerical example in the last section, we turn to a widely occurring type of problem that is often solved by dynamic programming. We formulate our problem algebraically, so if you find algebra not very user-friendly just skim through this section to get the main ideas. Algebraic formulation demonstrates the generality of this problem. It is one in which there is a split allocation of resources; in an economics context this may involve optimum allocation between the proportion of income to be paid as dividends and the proportion to be reinvested over a period of years. It is also relevant to policy regarding other resources where returns may vary from year to year, often in some very complex way, and one wants to maximize income over a period of serveral years. Problems of this type are relevant in forestry, where timber cutting usually extends over a period of years and decisions must be made on how much to cut and how much to leave to maximize income over, say, a ten-year period. Here prices are often relatively low for young timber but better for more developed trees, but there may be some doubt whether long term prospects are for lower timber prices all round. Even if we leave out such stochastic elements in price, optimum policy still depends on timber volumes, which increase with age in standing timber, providing a certain amount of thinning is done in earlier years.

Farmers face similar problems about selling a portion of, say, a cereal crop and keeping some back for seed to provide the following year's crop. We use an example covering this latter situation which has been widely quoted but which was originally given in Houlden (1962) and in modified form involving forestry by Hollingdale (1978). We deal here simply with the formulation of the farm problem without delving into the solution.

Example 16.4 A farmer harvests z tons of wheat in a given year. His policy is to sell x and retain $y = z - x$ tons for seed, which will produce a larger crop the following year of ay tons where $a > 1$. He repeats the process for a further two years, when he sells the entire crop. (It is bad farming practice to keep using seed from the same source on the same ground for too long a period.) If any crop he sells produces an income of £$f(x)$, what is his optimum policy regarding the amounts to sell and the amounts to be replanted each year? We assume a and $f(x)$ remain unchanged from year to year. Here $f(x)$ simply means some (specified) function of x, e.g.

$$f(x) = 15x - 0.01x^2 \quad \text{or} \quad f(x) = \log x.$$

Comments on the solution The problem is trivial if $f(x)$ is an increasing function of x, for then the optimum policy is to resow the entire crop in every year but the last and then sell the entire crop in that last year, because, since $a > 1$, this will give him the maximum amount for sale. Apart from the fact that this might be impracticable, because he might run out of land on which to plant the ever-increasing amount of seed, it is often realistic to assume that income may not be an increasing function of x, since offering too much for sale might lower demand and reduce prices per tonne, or there may be subsidy payments involved, the subsidy being reduced or withdrawn if the crop sold exceeds certain target thresholds. We may summarize his yearly allocations as follows:

Year	Sells	Sows	Available following year
1	x_1	y_1	ay_1
2	x_2	y_2	ay_2
3	x_3	y_3	ay_3
4	x_4	0	0*

*The entire crop is sold at end of year 4.

Conventional approaches lead to a problem of maximizing his income $f(x_1) + f(x_2) + f(x_3) + f(x_4)$ subject to a constraint that may be written in terms of the known a, z, and the four variables x_i. We omit details, but suffice to say that such problems are extremely difficult to solve for all but the simplest forms of $f(x)$.

The dynamic programming approach replaces the problem of one maximization involving four variables to a series of four one-variable maximization problems. We go about this by introducing a new variable $g_n(q)$, which we define as the total income the farmer would receive if he started with q tons of seed and adopted an optimum policy of sales and resowing over n years. In our example, we are interested in $n = 4$, but, if the farmer were only interested in a one-year programme (and did not want to sow seed for a future crop), his optimum policy would be to sell all his seed that year. In that case, if he started the year with q tons of seed, he would sell it all for $£f(q)$, whence

$$g_1(q) = f(q).$$

What about $g_2(q)$? This is the optimum if he sells some seed in the first year, saves some to sow in the second year, and sells all the second-year crop. *If he knew* that the optimum tonnage to sell in the first year was x, bringing in an income $£f(x)$, then, if he started with q tons, with $q \geqslant x$, he would have $q - x$ tons for seed in the second year, giving a yield $a(q - x)$, all of which would be sold in the second year. Assuming then that x has been chosen to maximize total income, the second-year problem becomes one of maximizing the yield $a(q - x)$ over the remaining one year. The income from this is $f(a(q - x))$ or $g_1(a(q - x))$. All we know about x at this stage is that it must lie between 0 and q. We have to obtain it to maximize the sum of $f(x)$ and $g_1(a(q - x))$. This we write as

$$g_2(q) = \text{max over all } x \text{ in } (0, q) \text{ of } [f(x) + g_1(a(q - x))].$$

We know $g_1(a(q - x)) = f(a(q - x))$, and so, depending on the nature of $f(x)$, this maximum can be determined by use of the calculus or numerically – methods beyond the scope of this book. A little careful (but far from trivial) thought shows that

$$g_3(q) = \text{max over all } x \text{ in } (0, q) \text{ of } [f(x) + g_2(a(q - x))],$$

where we may again determine x after having determined $g_2(q)$ above.

Finally, for Example 16.4, we require

$$g_4(q) = \text{max over all } x \text{ in } (0, q) \text{ of } [f(x) + g_3(a(q - x))].$$

The recursive nature of the problem should now be clear. The formulation as above is not too difficult; obtaining a solution for most realistic $f(x)$ is very often a computer job, although a special simple form of $f(x)$ is used for demonstrating the solution to a slight modification of this problem by Hollingdale (1978).

We hope this chapter has given something of the flavour, if not of the subtlety, of this powerful technique.

16.5 WHAT AND WHERE?

What skills have we mastered?

We can cope with a few numerical problems involving discrete variables that have several 'dynamic' stages. The process usually involves a backward recursive method in which multiple stages are broken down to a sum of single stages, the solution for the last of these usually being self-evident.

Where can I read more?

A simple account is given by Hollingdale (1978: Chap. 3, §5), and mathematically more sophisticated treatments are given in Houlden (1962: Chap. 4) and by French *et al.* (1986: Chap. 12).

EXERCISES

16.1 Determine the total profit in Example 16.1 if chemical A were made in all three batches.

16.2 Verify, by direct calculation, that the total profit by making A in batch 1, A in batch 2, and B in batch 3 in Example 16.1 is £2922.

*16.3 In some network problems of the type considered in Example 16.2, the number of stages for different routes between P and Q may not all be the same. For example, there might be an additional two-stage route P to H to Q not shown on Fig. 16.1, with appropriate single-stage fares given. How might you modify the problem to apply dynamic programming in such a situation? If, in addition, a route from H to A were included to allow travel from P to H to A and onward by other routes from A, what modifications would be appropriate to allow a dynamic programming solution?

16.4 Solve Example 16.3 using Dijkstra's algorithm.

16.5 What is the strategy to maximize the minimum dowry in Example 16.4?

16.6 A boatbuilder has orders for boats of a certain type to be delivered at the end of the months shown below.

Boatbuilder's Orders

Month	Number of boats
February	1
March	2
April	5
May	3
June	2
July	1

Stock is zero at the beginning of February and is to be zero after the July delivery. If any boats are built in a particular month, there is an overhead cost of four units, independent of the number built. Stockholding costs one unit per boat per complete month. Every order must be met in the month in which it is due. No more than four boats can be built in one month and no more than three stored.

Use dynamic programming to determine in what months boats should be built, and in what quantities, in order to minimize cost. [Oxford GCE AS level]

*16.7 In Example 16.3 suppose that a new company provides the service from P to A and as an introductory offer on the first day instead of charging a fare pays 50p to each passenger using the route (effectively equivalent to a fare of − 50p). Use dynamic programming to determine the routing from P to Q at minimum fare on that day. Could Dijkstra's algorithm be used to solve the problem?

Appendix

A.1 SUM OF n TERMS IN GEOMETRIC PROGRESSION

Denote the terms of the geometric progression by a, ar, ar^2, ..., ar^{n-1}. To establish (3.1), we write

$$S = a + ar + ar^2 + \cdots + ar^{n-1}. \tag{A1.1}$$

Multiplication of both sides of (A1.1) by r gives

$$rS = ar + ar^2 + ar^3 + \cdots + ar^n. \tag{A1.2}$$

When we subtract (A1.1) from (A1.2), all terms on the right except a and ar^n cancel, and we are left with

$$(r - 1)S = ar^n - a,$$

whence $S = a(r^n - 1)/(r - 1)$, which is (3.1).

A.2 INTERPOLATION AND ITERATION

Linear interpolation is the simplest form of interpolation. If we know the value of some function $y = f(x)$ is y_1 when $x = x_1$ and is y_2 when $x = x_2$, then, if x' is a value of x between x_1 and x_2, the linear interpolation estimate of $y' = f(x')$ is

$$y' = y_1 + \frac{(x' - x_1)(y_2 - y_1)}{x_2 - x_1}. \tag{A2.1}$$

Only if $f(x)$ is a straight line is it certain that y' is the exact value of $f(x')$. For a great many functions, if x_1 and x_2 are not very different, linear interpolation gives a good approximation for intermediate values. For example, if $y = x^2 + 3$, then, if $x_1 = 5$, $x_2 = 6$ and $x' = 5.4$, (A2.1) gives

$$y' = 28 + 0.4 \times 11/1 = 32.4.$$

In this simple case, it is easily verified that the exact value is 32.16. The method is particularly valuable when we are dealing with complicated functions that may be extremely difficult to specify. In section 3.3, we suggested that interpolation might be appropriate for internal rate of return problems where the objective is to find a discounting rate that gives a zero net present value (NPV) for a cash flow. It is relatively easy to calculate the NPV for two different discount rates, one of which gives a positive NPV, and the other a negative NPV for cash flow. Linear interpolation may then be used to estimate a discount rate that will give zero cash flow.

For example, suppose discounting at 12% p.a. gives an NPV of £600 and discounting at 18% gives an NPV of $-£200$. We want to estimate a discount rate that will give zero NPV. We may use (A2.1), setting $x_1 = 600$, $x_2 = -200$, $y_1 = 12$, $y_2 = 18$ and $x' = 0$. Substituting in (A2.1) gives

$$y' = 12 + (-600) \times 6/(-800) = 16.5$$

In general, this will not give an exactly zero NPV. The estimate can be improved by what is called an iteration procedure. Basically this involves repeating the above procedure with new data values closer to our solution. For example, on calculating the NPV by the method given in section 3.3, for a discounting rate of 16.5% we might find that, instead of being exactly zero, it is $-£20$. Intuitively it is clear that a slightly lower discount rate, say 15.5% is likely to give a small positive NPV. Suppose we calculate it and find it is £30. Applying

(A2.1) to this new data gives a revised estimate of the discount y' for zero NPV of

$$y' = 15.5 + (-30) \times 1/(-50) = 16.1.$$

In practice, this is likely to be a good estimate, but, if desired, the exact NPV for discounting at 16.1% could be calculated and a further iteration performed.

There are more sophisticated methods of interpolation and iteration that can be used especially if we are given the values of the function $f(x)$ corresponding to the n values $x_1, x_2, \ldots, x_n$. In most cases, an appropriate formula using information from all these points will give a better estimate of $y' = f(x')$ for a given x' than that obtained by linear interpolation.

In our account of linear interpolation, we assumed x' was intermediate in value between x_1 and x_2. If x' lies outside this range, the procedure is called extrapolation. Extrapolation should be used with caution; in practice, it is likely to give less satisfactory approximations than those given by interpolation.

A.3 INEQUALITIES

The only point we emphasize about inequalities in this appendix is that one can do with them some of the things that are permissible with equalities, but not others. In particular, as for equalities, we may add or subtract the same constant from both sides of an inequality without changing its nature, i.e. a 'greater than' inequality remains a 'greater than' inequality, and a 'lesser than' inequality remains a 'lesser than' inequality. The same applies if we multiply both sides of an inequality by the same *positive* constant. However, if we multiply both sides of an inequality by the same *negative* constant, the inequality changes in sense, e.g. a 'greater than' inequality becomes a 'less than' inequality, and a 'less than or equals' inequality becomes a 'greater than or equals' inequality.

Examples   Since $17 < 21$, if we add 25 to both sides we find $42 < 46$, an obvious truism; if we now subtract 50, we get $-8 < -4$, which is also true. If we multiply each side of the original inequality $17 < 21$ by 2 we get $34 < 42$, but if we multiply it by -2 we get $-34 > -42$. Note that the sense of the inequality changes from $<$ to $>$.

These operations may be applied to the type of inequalities that arise in linear programming. The reader should verify that the following are all equivalent, and be clear about which of the operations suggested above are being performed in each case:

$$x + 3y \geqslant z + 17,$$

$$x + 3y - z \geqslant 17,$$

$$4x + 12y - 4z \geqslant 68,$$

$$z - x - 3y \leqslant -17,$$

$$x + 3y - z - 17 \geqslant 0,$$

$$z - x - 3y + 17 \leqslant 0.$$

Answers to Exercises

Chapter 1 (p. 15)

1.1 £4. **1.2** $\frac{9}{59}$. **1.3** £1493.85, £1532.82. **1.4** £1260.87. **1.5** £228.81.
1.6 £1461.86. **1.7** $\frac{7}{47}$.

Chapter 2 (p. 31)

2.1 £58.33, £6.25. **2.2** £25 000. **2.3** £21 000. **2.4** £500.73.
2.5 £21.14. **2.6** £521.87 (no difference: in each case total interest is
£$[1000 \times (1.07)^3 \times (1.075)^3 - 1000]$). **2.7** £513.45. **2.8** £510.78.
2.9 (c) **2.10** £2969.37.

Rate (mth)	1	1.5	1.75	2	3	4	5	6
2.11 APR	12.68	19.56	23.14	26.82	42.58	60.10	79.59	101.22

2.12 Corrections are weekly 1.0 = APR 67.77; weekly 1.5 = APR
116.89. APR of 1164.28 corresponding to weekly 5.0 may surprise as annual interest is more than 11 times capital: the moral
is always check APR even if a short term rate looks not unattrac-
tive.
2.13 APR in leap year or non-leap year is 8.32776% to five decimal
places; no practical difference for investors. **2.14** £1506.96. **2.15**
12.75 years (13 if interest only credited at year end). **2.16** 12.48
years (12.5 if interest only credited half yearly). **2.17** 9.25%. **2.18**
8.31 yr. **2.19** Bank pays me £24.33 net. **2.20** Bank B. £75.04
additional interest. **2.21** No. Bank A. £74.92 additional interest.
2.22 Bank B pays £6.29 net more than NS on £25 000. Bank A pays
£14.94 more net than bank B and £25 more than NS on £40 000.

2.23 9.02%. **2.24** £394 704.62. **2.25** (a) £243.20. (b) 6.74%, (c) £267.52, (d) 6.0%.

Chapter 3 (p. 50)

3.1 £47.07. **3.2** £100.12; repayments in Ex. 3.2 exceed those in Ex. 3.1 by £71.76. If inflation very high second method may be advantageous; exact balance may depend upon use made of the money in the intervening period. **3.3** £6810.86. **3.4** £1761.16 **3.5** £3586.51. **3.6** £5392.39 (Immediately after 10th payment fund is £54 489.59. At 10% p.a. after a further 11 years this accrues to £155 465.16; thus £94 534.84 required from a new fund with 10 payments first made one year later, giving above pyament.) **3.7** £250 000 grows to £332 750 in 3 years at 10% p.a. compounded, so ample funds available. **3.8** NPV 1st option £2700, second option £2224.02, so choose second. **3.9** NPVs (return on capital) in £ thousand are A = 283.58, B = 718.55, C = 64.41. B preferred. **3.10** £11 554.15. **3.11** Net outflows are (i) £150 073, (ii) £128 334 and (iii) £129 195, so (ii) preferred. **3.12** (a) assuming £100 paid off each month, monthly interest added is £0, £10, £7.75, £5.44, £3.08, £0.66. Final payment of £26.93 required. (b) Schedule is based on annual repayment of £1003.14. Annual interest component is £600, £519.37, £422.62, £306.51, £167.19.

Chapter 4 (p. 91)

4.1 15 Megacat, 12.5 Moggycat. **4.2** 3 gloss, 5 matt, £370. **4.3** No change. **4.4** Solution in Ex. 4.2 still optimal, but profit reduced to £360. This solution no longer unique. Any x, y in segment joining (3, 5) to (6, 2.5) also optimal. Solution (3, 5) may appeal as only integer optimum (see section 5.1). **4.5** 2 parts A, 1 part B, £11.67 per bag. **4.6** Equal parts A and F or 3 parts A to 1 part D; cost 10.5. First preferred if A in short supply. **4.7** No solution as no feasible region; constraints incompatible. **4.8** 16A, 2B. **4.9** No upper limit to amount of fertilizer is specified, so no finite optimum; i.e. feasible region extends to infinity so 'maximum' is infinite. **4.10** 20 sherry, no whisky. **4.11** 5 sherry, 6 whisky. **4.12** If x, y, z are tonnages of

A, B, C problem is maximize $U = 4x + 2.5y + 3z$ subject to

$$0.015x + 0.024y + 0.021z \leqslant 0.02(x + y + z),$$
$$0.0006x + 0.0007y + 0.0002z \leqslant 0.005 (x + y + z),$$
$$x, y, z \geqslant 0,$$
$$x + y + z = 1.$$

Final equality enables us to express z in terms of x, y, and eliminate z from U and inequality constraints. Solution $x = 75$, $y = 0$, $z = 25$; maximum profit £375. **4.16** (a) $U = x + y$, (b) $40x + 30y \leqslant 24\,000, 4x + 2y \geqslant 1800, y \geqslant x, x, y \geqslant 0$, (c) feasible region is triangle with vertices at (300, 300), (150, 600), (342.9, 342.9), (d) $U = 600$ (min) if 300 of each bought.

Chapter 5 (p. 114)

5.1 $3A$, $5B$. **5.2** Optimum is (A, 1), (B, 2), (C, 3), (D, 4), (E, 5). Total cost £63 000. **5.3** Optimum is (A, 1), (B, 3), (C, 2), (D, 4), (E, 6), (F, 5). Total score 497. **5.4** Optimum is (E, 1), (C, 2), (B, 3), (F, 4). A, D unallocated; total score 349. **5.5** Optimum is (A, 6), (B, 3), (C, 2), (D, 4), (F, 5). **5.6** Optima are CG, NP, DA, EI or CG, EP, DA, NI; 467 miles. Perhaps surprising that shortest route DP not used. This reflects fact that DA appreciably shorter than other routes to A. Fact that one optimum uses longest route NI also surprising; this is compensated for by relative shortness of other routings in this optimum; note also that NP + EI = EP + NI explains why there is not a unique optimum.

Chapter 6 (p. 138)

Note that some of the routings given in the solutions below are not unique, but any alternative routing will give the same total cost.

6.1 One optimal allocation is

	A	B	C	D
I	50			
II	10	50	20	
III	10			30

Total cost £5400

6.2 One optimal allocation is

	A	B	C	D
I	30	20		
II		30	20	30
III	40			

Total cost £6300, increase £900.

6.3 (1) Rearrange tableau, placing depot D in first column, then use NW corner rule. (2) Determine alternative feasible solution at start; any will do, the NW corner rule is just a convenient rule of thumb for obtaining one.

6.4 One optimal allocation is

	A	B	C	D
I	10	50		
II	60		20	
III				30

70 loads from I, 10 from III not required. Total cost £5300; saving £100.

6.5 One optimal allocation is

	A	B	C	D
I	20		20	
II	40	40		
III	10			30

Depot B does not get full requirement; total cost £4800.

6.6 Allocation in Ex. 6.5 is still optimal, but there is now an additional penalty of £200 for failure to supply full requirement.

6.7 An optimal allocation is

	A	B	C	D
Ia	50			
Ib		10		
II	20	40	20	
III				30

70 units from I(b) and 10 from III not allocated. Total cost £5400 (cf. Ex. 6.4). Are you surprised that total cost is the same as in Ex. 6.1? Verify that allocation in Ex. 6.1 is also optimal here. Does this surprise you?

6.8 In Ex. 6.4 there is spare capacity that can be moved at no additional cost; this may allow better use of cheaper routes. In Ex. 6.7 additional costs are incurred for 'use' of this spare capacity.

6.9 Make full quota each month in normal time, 4 overtime in January, 1 overtime in February. Hold 3 January overtime to February, and 4 February normal time + 1 February overtime to March.

6.10 All feasible allocations are optimum with loading + unloading costs totalling £475 (see Ex. 6.11).

6.11 These are identical to shadow costs. They reflect the *exact* costs on any route. This is why all feasible routes are optimal in Ex. 6.10.

6.12 If maximum bonus payable on any route is M, we might subtract all bonuses from M and minimize the resulting deficiencies. This would maximize the total bonus payments. A non-unique allocation giving maximum bonuses is

	I	II	III
A	13		7
B	2	8	

Total bonus £371.

6.13 An optimal allocation is

	A	B	C
I		10	40
II	20	50	
III	60		

Total profit £870.

6.14 An optimal allocation is

	A	B	C
I			60
II	10	70	
III	40		

Total profit £920.

He does not buy 20 from wholesaler III. Do you see why it is intuitively reasonable that profit should be greater than it was in Ex. 6.13?

6.15 $x_{21} + x_{22} + x_{23} \leqslant 130$, $x_{11} + x_{21} = 40$, $x_{13} + x_{23} = 70$, all $x_{ij} \geqslant 0$.

6.16 (a) 120, 100, 94 (solution not unique). £252.24 per day. (b) £9.60.

6.17 The cost matrix is formed as production + cleaning + transport costs. (a) Optimum allocation is

	1	2	3	4	5
A	70		40		140
B	50	150			
C			40	160	

30 from a dummy mine 6 goes to plant A at zero cost. (b) No changes since all production is allocated and the effect is to reduce relevant shadow costs for column 3 by same amount. (c) Extra production should go to plant A as this has spare capacity and (equal) lowest cost from mine 5.

Chapter 7   (p. 175)

7.1. 2.24, 1.96.   **7.2** 0.62.   **7.3** One job (first) moved to end of schedule.   **7.4** Max. tardiness 6 days; schedule in order of increasing due dates.   **7.5** Max. tardiness increased to 14 days. **7.6** J_2, J_1, J_3, J_4, J_6, J_5. Max penalty 12 on J_3.   **7.7** See Fig. S.1. Minimum time to publication now 186 days. Amended table easily deduced from Fig. S.1; main differences are that G, I now on critical path, H has total float and free float of 3, all floats on L increased by 3 and a number of consequential start and finish time alterations, often an increase of 3.

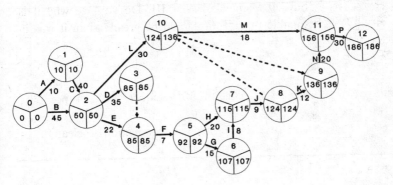

Figure S.1 CPA diagram for Exercise 7.7.

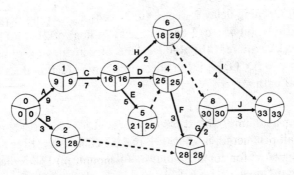

Figure S.2 CPA diagram for Exercise 7.8.

7.8 See Fig. S.2. Float table is as follows:

Activity	ET	LT	EH	LH	D	TF	FF	IF
A*	0	0	9	9	9	0	0	0
B	0	0	3	28	3	25	0	0
C*	9	9	16	16	7	0	0	0
D*	16	16	25	25	9	0	0	0
E	16	16	21	25	5	4	0	0

Activity	ET	LT	EH	LH	D	TF	FF	IF
F*	25	25	28	28	3	0	0	0
G*	28	28	30	30	2	0	0	0
H	16	16	18	29	2	11	0	0
I	18	29	33	33	4	11	11	0
J*	30	30	33	33	3	0	0	0

7.9 (i) Opening delay 2 weeks. (ii) No effect as within float.
7.10 (b) 47, (c) 45, (d) I has independent float of 21. **7.11** (a) No, 19 weeks required. (b) Reduce time of activities on critical path which is B, D, G, K, L but check that any reduction does not alter critical path.

Chapter 8   (p. 202)

8.1 See Fig. 8.7 **8.2** See Fig. 8.11(a). **8.3** See Fig. 8.11(b).
8.4 $S \to 5 \to 2 \to 6 \to F$; unique; total cost 27. **8.5** Same, but total cost now 29. **8.6** $S \to 1 \to 2 \to 3 \to F$ or any route avoiding $S \to 5$, $2 \to 4$, $4 \to 2$, $7 \to 6$, $2 \to 6$ or $6 \to 2$. 7 m. **8.7** 11 m; $F \to 6 \to 4 \to 7 \to 5$. **8.8** $S \to C \to E \to H \to J$ or $K \to M \to F$; minimum cost 30. **8.9** 8 000 gallons; S, C on one side of cut, all remaining nodes on other side.

Chapter 9   (p. 234)

9.1 $\frac{723}{2419} = 0.299$. **9.2** $\frac{103}{1000}$, (ii) $\frac{308}{3000}$, (iii) $\frac{259}{3000}$, (iv) $\frac{843}{2483}$. **9.3** (i) 0.3, (ii) 0.5, (iii) 0.8, (iv) 0.2 (opposite event to (iii)). **9.4** (i) 0.2, (ii) 0.08, (iii) 0.28, (iv) 0.72. **9.5** 0.45. **9.6** $\frac{1}{3}$, 3.33%. **9.7** 0.725. Probably not reasonable. Probabilities of not turning up may differ between businessmen and tourists. Probabilities may not be independent (e.g. family groups). **9.8** 11.2, 1.249. **9.9** See Example 9.8.

9.10

Digit	0	1	2	3	4	5	6	7	8	9
Frequency	19	18	17	17	17	19	21	23	22	27

Not unreasonable for sample of 200. A little surprising that for all digits below 6, numbers less than the expected 20, but an appropriate test shows this is not cause for alarm.

9.11 First interval 0.088, second 0.078, third 0.31, and so on.

9.12

Interval	0–0.4	0.4–0.8	0.8–1.2	1.2–1.6	1.6–2.0	2.0–2.4	2.4–2.8
Probability	0.330	0.221	0.148	0.099	0.067	0.045	0.030

Interval	2.8–3.2	3.2–3.6	3.6–4.0	4.0–4.4	4.4–4.8	4.8–5.2
Probability	0.020	0.013	0.009	0.006	0.004	0.003

Sum of above probabilities is 0.995; $\Pr(X > 5.2) = 1 - 0.995 = 0.005$. A more accurate estimate putting $t_1 = 0$, $t_2 = 5.2$ in (9.8) gives $\Pr(X \leqslant 5.2) = 0.99448$.

9.13 5.9, 1.375.   **9.14** 6.08, close to population mean of 5.9.

9.15 (a) (i) 0.941, (ii) 0.000392, (iii) 0.00192. (b) $\frac{28}{41}$.

9.16 (a) 0.0041. (b) 0.9959. (c) 0.3110. (d) 0.1866.

Chapter 10   (p. 259)

10.1 698, 26.2, 150 (in practice orders would probably be placed for 700 units each time).   **10.2** No. Inventory costs would increase by £157 p.a.   **10.3** (i) Increase to 854, (ii) decrease to 604, (iii) no change, (iv) increase to 854, (v) decrease to 493.   **10.4** Ex. 10.1 allocation optimal, total cost approx. £11871. Ex. 10.3 (v) least favourable; total cost approx. £12453.

10.5 1; expected stock-out cost £23.28.   **10.6** 8; expected stock-out cost £25.35; probabilities of stock-out for various buffer levels are:

Buffer	0	1	2	3	4	5	6	7	8	9
Probability	$\frac{3}{5}$	$\frac{8}{15}$	$\frac{1}{2}$	$\frac{13}{27}$	$\frac{23}{54}$	$\frac{17}{54}$	$\frac{5}{27}$	$\frac{2}{27}$	$\frac{1}{54}$	0

10.7 (a)

Orders	20	40	60	80	100
Cost (£)	51 880	51 440	51 960	52 720	53 576

(purchase cost of £48 000 included – this is often subtracted as it is not really an inventory cost). (b) £51 394 for orders of 1414 units. (c) Cost may be reduced to £49 200 assuming discount is on purchase cost only and *not* on cost of placing order.

Chapter 11   (p. 284)

11.3 20.   **11.4** (a) Order 20 or 30 pints, EMV 100; (b) 40 pints, EMV 146.   **11.9** A1 in first year and A2 in second year. Maximin 670 if sales steady in first year and drop in second.   **11.10** Car B, minimum expected net outlay of £2200. Car A minimizes maximum outlay of £2250.   **11.11** Loan to Bones and Shanks gives max. EMV £34 000; split loan ensures profit of at least £6000.   **11.2** (a) £9277.50. (b) £722.50 (since perfect information would give a profit of £10 000).

Chapter 12   (p. 309)

12.4 11 (98.1% certain).   **12.5** £303.03; yes, 4 months.   **12.6** 0.90; 0.02.   **12.7** 0.474.   **12.8** 0.929.   **12.9** Average monthly cost for replacement on failure is £1194.03. Average for replacement after 1, 2, 3, 4, 5 months respectively £1400, £1020, £1055, £1168.10, £1214.37. (c) Complete replacement every 2 months is optimum.

Chapter 13   (p. 333)

13.1 Inner warning lines 50.41, 51.59; outer action lines 50.07, 51.93. Stop after 5th, 9th, 14th samples.   **13.4** Poisson approximations are respectively 1, 0.910, 0.736, 0.558, 0.406, 0.199, 0.091, 0.040, 0.017. Comparison with Table 13.4 shows maximum discrepancy between binomial and Poisson probabilities is 0.004.

Chapter 14   (p. 351)

14.4 0.7, 23.33, 16.33, (i) 0.875, 56, 49; (ii) 0.75, 30, 22.5; (iii) 0.935, 120, 112.5. Waiting time in queue (especially in (iii)) perhaps rather longer than intuition might suggest.   **14.5** For example 14.1: 1770, 1740.5. For Example 14.2: 55.7, 36.2. Times less in practice since distribution of service times more 'compact' than exponential (some of which could be very long).

Chapter 15   (p. 374)

15.1

Year	1983	1984	1985	1986	1987	1988
Index	100	104.8	111.3	109.7	119.4	127.4

15.2 80p.   **15.3** 83.8, 87.8, 93.2, 91.9, 100, 106.7.   **15.4** Laspeyres 175.3; Paasche 232.7. Higher value of Paasche reflects large increase in weighting for commodity A, which is the item that also shows greatest price rise per unit.   **15.5** Laspeyres 158; Paasche 220. The indices are both lower than corresponding aggregate weighted indices because they are less influenced by a combination of increased prices and quantities sold.   **15.6** (a) 100.5, 104.0. (b) 100.4, 103.9. **15.7** (i) 116.9, (ii) 128.4. (iii) Government indices for 1980, 1981 with 1979 as base are 119.1, 130.1, suggesting company indices lagging official figures. This does not necessarily mean the company are paying lower than average rates in those years, for they may have been paying above average in base year.

Chapter 16   (p. 392)

16.1 £2628.   **16.3** Introduce a point H′ with fare stages P to H′, H′ to H and H to Q. Associate zero fare with the 'dummy' stage H′ to H to make all routes three stages. If, in addition, a route from H to A were included, this would give one four-stage route, so all other routes would require a zero fare dummy stage included to make all routes four stages.   **16.5** Accept any bride offered on the first day, ensuring at least $50.   **16.6** Feb 4, Mar 0, April 4, May 3, June 3, Jul 0.   **16.7** P to A to E to Q. Dijkstra's algorithm requires modification to deal with the negative fare (add 50p to all fares temporarily).

References

Bancroft, G. and O'Sullivan, G. (1988). *Maths and Statistics for Accounting and Business Studies*, 2nd edn. McGraw-Hill, London.

Bellman, R. (1957). *Dynamic Programming*. Princeton University Press.

Ehrenberg, A.C. (1983). *A Primer in Data Reduction*, Wiley, New York.

Francis, A. (1988). *Business Mathematics and Statistics*, 2nd edn. D.P. Publications, Eastleigh.

French, S., Hartley, R., Thomas, L.C. and White, D.J. (1986). *Operational Research Techniques*, Edward Arnold, London.

Gomory, R.E. (1958). Outline of an algorithm for integer solutions to linear programs. *Bulletin of the American Mathematical Society* **64**, 275–8.

Hollingdale, S.H. (1978). Methods of operational research. In: *Newer Uses of Mathematics* (ed. J. Lighthill). Penguin Books, London, pp. 176–277.

Houlden, B.T. (ed.) (1962). *Some Techniques of Operational Research*, English Universities Press, London.

Jones, R. and MacKay, J. (1988). *Business Mathematics and Information Technology*. Pitman, London.

Lawler, E.L. (1973). Optimum sequencing of a single machine subject to precedence constraints. *Management Science* **19**, 544–6.

Lucey, T. (1988). *Quantitative Techniques*, 3rd edn. D.P. Publications, London.

McLewin, W. (1980). *Linear Programming and Applications*. Input–Output Press, London.

Marquardt, D.W. (1984). New technical and educational directions for managing product quality. *The American Statistician* **38**, 8–14.

Moore, P.G. (1980). *Reason by Numbers*. Penguin Books, London.

Moore, P.G. (1986). *Basic Operational Research*, 3rd edn. Pitman, London.

Moore, P.G. and Thomas, H. (1988). *The Anatomy of Decisions*, 2nd edn. Penguin Books, London.

Potts, R.B. (1978). Networks. In: *Newer Uses of Mathematics* (ed. J. Lighthill). Penguin Books, London, pp. 281–325.

Rowntree, D. (1981). *Statistics Without Tears*. Penguin Books, London.

Sasieni, M., Yaspan, M. and Friedman, L. (1959). *Operational Research Methods and Problems*. Wiley, New York.

Sprent, P. (1977). *Statistics in Action*. Penguin Books, London.

Sprent, P. (1988a). *Understanding Data*. Penguin Books, London.

Sprent, P. (1988b). *Taking Risks, The Science of Uncertainty*. Penguin Books, London.

Tufte, E.R. (1983). *The Visual Display of Quantitative Information*. Graphics Press, Cheshire, Conn.

Wagner, H.M. (1975). *Principles of Operational Research*, 2nd edn. Prentice-Hall, London.

Waters, C.D.J. (1989). *A Practical Introduction to Management Science*. Addison-Wesley, Wokingham.

Wetherill, G.B. (1977). *Sampling Inspection and Quality Control*. Chapman and Hall, London.

Index

FOR THE BEST IN PAPERBACKS, LOOK FOR THE

In every corner of the world, on every subject under the sun, Penguin represents quality and variety – the very best in publishing today.

For complete information about books available from Penguin – including Puffins, Penguin Classics and Arkana – and how to order them, write to us at the appropriate address below. Please note that for copyright reasons the selection of books varies from country to country.

In the United Kingdom: Please write to *Dept E.P., Penguin Books Ltd, Harmondsworth, Middlesex, UB7 0DA.*

If you have any difficulty in obtaining a title, please send your order with the correct money, plus ten per cent for postage and packaging, to *PO Box No 11, West Drayton, Middlesex*

In the United States: Please write to *Dept BA, Penguin, 299 Murray Hill Parkway, East Rutherford, New Jersey 07073*

In Canada: Please write to *Penguin Books Canada Ltd, 2801 John Street, Markham, Ontario L3R 1B4*

In Australia: Please write to the *Marketing Department, Penguin Books Australia Ltd, P.O. Box 257, Ringwood, Victoria 3134*

In New Zealand: Please write to the *Marketing Department, Penguin Books (NZ) Ltd, Private Bag, Takapuna, Auckland 9*

In India: Please write to *Penguin Overseas Ltd, 706 Eros Apartments, 56 Nehru Place, New Delhi, 110019*

In the Netherlands: Please write to *Penguin Books Netherlands B.V., Postbus 195, NL–1380AD Weesp*

In West Germany: Please write to *Penguin Books Ltd, Friedrichstrasse 10–12, D–6000 Frankfurt/Main 1*

In Spain: Please write to *Alhambra Longman S.A., Fernandez de la Hoz 9, E–28010 Madrid*

In Italy: Please write to *Penguin Italia s.r.l., Via Como 4, I-20096 Pioltello (Milano)*

In France: Please write to *Penguin Books Ltd, 39 Rue de Montmorency, F-75003 Paris*

In Japan: Please write to *Longman Penguin Japan Co Ltd, Yamaguchi Building, 2-12-9 Kanda Jimbocho, Chiyoda-Ku, Tokyo 101*

FOR THE BEST IN PAPERBACKS, LOOK FOR THE 🐧

PENGUIN DICTIONARIES

Abbreviations
Archaeology
Architecture
Art and Artists
Biology
Botany
Building
Business
Chemistry
Civil Engineering
Computers
Curious and Interesting
  Words
Curious and Interesting
  Numbers
Design and Designers
Economics
Electronics
English and European
  History
English Idioms
French
Geography
German

Historical Slang
Human Geography
Literary Terms
Mathematics
Modern History 1789–1945
Modern Quotations
Music
Physical Geography
Physics
Politics
Proverbs
Psychology
Quotations
Religions
Rhyming Dictionary
Saints
Science
Sociology
Spanish
Surnames
Telecommunications
Troublesome Words
Twentieth-Century History

FOR THE BEST IN PAPERBACKS, LOOK FOR THE

PENGUIN REFERENCE BOOKS

The New Penguin English Dictionary

Over 1,000 pages long and with over 68,000 definitions, this cheap, compact and totally up-to-date book is ideal for today's needs. It includes many technical and colloquial terms, guides to pronunciation and common abbreviations.

The Penguin Spelling Dictionary

What are the plurals of *octopus* and *rhinoceros*? What is the difference between *stationary* and *stationery*? And how about *annex* and *annexe*, *agape* and *Agape*? This comprehensive new book, the fullest spelling dictionary now available, provides the answers.

Roget's Thesaurus of English Words and Phrases   Betty Kirkpatrick (ed.)

This new edition of Roget's classic work, now brought up to date for the nineties, will increase anyone's command of the English language. Fully cross-referenced, it includes synonyms of every kind (formal or colloquial, idiomatic and figurative) for almost 900 headings. It is a must for writers and utterly fascinating for any English speaker.

The Penguin Dictionary of Quotations

A treasure-trove of over 12,000 new gems and old favourites, from Aesop and Matthew Arnold to Xenophon and Zola.

The Penguin Wordmaster Dictionary
Martin H. Manser and Nigel D. Turton

This dictionary puts the pleasure back into word-seeking. Every time you look at a page you get a bonus – a panel telling you everything about a particular word or expression. It is, therefore, a dictionary to be read as well as used for its concise and up-to-date definitions.

FOR THE BEST IN PAPERBACKS, LOOK FOR THE

PENGUIN REFERENCE BOOKS

The Penguin Guide to the Law

This acclaimed reference book is designed for everyday use and forms the most comprehensive handbook ever published on the law as it affects the individual.

The Penguin Medical Encyclopedia

Covers the body and mind in sickness and in health, including drugs, surgery, medical history, medical vocabulary and many other aspects. 'Highly commendable' – *Journal of the Institute of Health Education*

The Slang Thesaurus

Do you make the public bar sound like a gentleman's club? Do you need help in understanding *Minder*? The miraculous *Slang Thesaurus* will liven up your language in no time. You won't Adam and Eve it! A mine of funny, witty, acid and vulgar synonyms for the words you use every day.

The Penguin Dictionary of Troublesome Words   Bill Bryson

Why should you avoid discussing the *weather conditions*? Can a married woman be *celibate*? Why is it eccentric to talk about the *aroma* of a cowshed? A straightforward guide to the pitfalls and hotly disputed issues in standard written English.

The Penguin Spanish Dictionary   James R. Jump

Detailed, comprehensive and, above all, modern, *The Penguin Spanish Dictionary* offers a complete picture of the language of ordinary Spaniards – the words used at home and at work, in bars and discos, at cafés and in the street, including full and unsqueamish coverage of common slang and colloquialisms.

The New Penguin Dictionary of Geography

From *aa* and *ablation* to *zinc* and *zonal soils*, this succinct dictionary is unique in covering in one volume the main terms now in use in the diverse areas – physical and human geography, geology and climatology, ecology and economics – that make up geography today.

Political Ideas   David Thomson (ed.)

From Machiavelli to Marx – a stimulating and informative introduction to the last 500 years of European political thinkers and political thought.

On Revolution   Hannah Arendt

Arendt's classic analysis of a relatively recent political phenomenon examines the underlying principles common to all revolutions, and the evolution of revolutionary theory and practice. 'Never dull, enormously erudite, always imaginative' – *Sunday Times*

Ill Fares the Land   Susan George

These twelve essays expand on one of the major themes of Susan George's work: the role of power in perpetuating world hunger. With characteristic commitment and conviction, the author of *A Fate Worse than Debt* and *How the Other Half Dies* demonstrates that just as poverty lies behind hunger, so injustice and inequality lie behind poverty.

The Social Construction of Reality   Peter Berger and Thomas Luckmann

Concerned with the sociology of 'everything that passes for knowledge in society' and particularly with that which passes for common sense, this is 'a serious, open-minded book, upon a serious subject' – *Listener*

The Care of the Self   Michel Foucault
The History of Sexuality Vol 3

Foucault examines the transformation of sexual discourse from the Hellenistic to the Roman world in an inquiry which 'bristles with provocative insights into the tangled liaison of sex and self' – *The Times Higher Education Supplement*

Silent Spring   Rachel Carson

'What we have to face is not an occasional dose of poison which has accidentally got into some article of food, but a persistent and continuous poisoning of the whole human environment.' First published in 1962, *Silent Spring* remains the classic environmental statement which founded an entire movement.

FOR THE BEST IN PAPERBACKS, LOOK FOR THE

PENGUIN HISTORY

Modern Ireland 1600–1972   R. F. Foster

'Takes its place with the finest historical writing of the twentieth century, whether about Ireland or anywhere else' – Conor Cruise O'Brien in the *Sunday Times*

Death in Hamburg   Society and Politics in the Cholera Years 1830–1910   Richard J. Evans

Why did the cholera epidemic of 1892 kill nearly 10,000 people in six weeks in Hamburg, while most of Europe was left almost unscathed? The answers put forward in this 'tremendous book' (Roy Porter in the *London Review of Books*) offer a wealth of insights into the inner life of a great – and uniquely anomalous – European city at the height of an industrial age.

British Society 1914–1945   John Stevenson

A major contribution to the *Penguin Social History of Britain*, which 'will undoubtedly be the standard work for students of modern Britain for many years to come' – *The Times Educational Supplement*

A History of Christianity   Paul Johnson

'Masterly … a cosmic soap opera involving kings and beggars, philosophers and crackpots, scholars and illiterate *exaltés*, popes and pilgrims and wild anchorites in the wilderness' – Malcolm Muggeridge

The Penguin History of Greece   A. R. Burn

Readable, erudite, enthusiastic and balanced, this one-volume history of Hellas sweeps the reader along from the days of Mycenae and the splendours of Athens to the conquests of Alexander and the final dark decades.

Battle Cry of Freedom   The American Civil War   James M. McPherson

'Compellingly readable … It is the best one-volume treatment of its subject I have come across. It may be the best ever published … This is magic' – Hugh Brogan in *The New York Times Book Review*

PENGUIN HISTORY

The Penguin History of the United States   Hugh Brogan

'An extraordinarily engaging book' – *The Times Literary Supplement*.
'Compelling reading ... Hugh Brogan's book will delight the general
reader as much as the student' – *The Times Educational Supplement*. 'He
will be welcomed by American readers no less than those in his own
country' – J. K. Galbraith

The Making of the English Working Class   E. P. Thompson

Probably the most imaginative – and the most famous – post-war work of
English social history.

The Waning of the Middle Ages   Johan Huizinga

A magnificent study of life, thought and art in 14th- and 15th-century
France and the Netherlands, long established as a classic.

The City in History   Lewis Mumford

Often prophetic in tone and containing a wealth of photographs, *The City
in History* is among the most deeply learned and warmly human studies of
man as a social creature.

The Habsburg Monarchy 1809–1918   A. J. P. Taylor

Dissolved in 1918, the Habsburg Empire 'had a unique character, out of
time and out of place'. Scholarly and vividly accessible, this 'very good
book indeed' (*Spectator*) elucidates the problems always inherent in the
attempt to give peace, stability and a common loyalty to a heterogeneous
population.

Inside Nazi Germany   Conformity, Opposition and Racism in Everyday Life
Detlev J. K. Peukert

An authoritative study – and a challenging and original analysis – of the
realities of daily existence under the Third Reich. 'A fascinating study ...
captures the whole range of popular attitudes and the complexity of their
relationship with the Nazi state' – Richard Geary

FOR THE BEST IN PAPERBACKS, LOOK FOR THE

PENGUIN SCIENCE AND MATHEMATICS

QED   Richard Feynman
The Strange Theory of Light and Matter

Quantum thermodynamics – or QED for short – is the 'strange theory'
– that explains how light and electrons interact. 'Physics Nobelist Feynman simply cannot help being original. In this quirky, fascinating book, he
explains to laymen the quantum theory of light – a theory to which he
made decisive contributions' – *New Yorker*

God and the New Physics   Paul Davies

Can science, now come of age, offer a surer path to God than religion?
This 'very interesting' (*New Scientist*) book suggests it can.

Does God Play Dice?   Ian Stewart
The New Mathematics of Chaos

To cope with the truth of a chaotic world, pioneering mathematicians have
developed chaos theory. *Does God Play Dice?* makes accessible the basic
principles and many practical applications of one of the most extraordi-
nary – and mindbending – breakthroughs in recent years. 'Engaging,
accurate and accessible to the uninitiated' – *Nature*

The Blind Watchmaker   Richard Dawkins

'An enchantingly witty and persuasive neo-Darwinist attack on the anti-
evolutionists, pleasurably intelligible to the scientifically illiterate'
– Hermione Lee in the *Observer* Books of the Year

The Making of the Atomic Bomb   Richard Rhodes

'Rhodes handles his rich trove of material with the skill of a master
novelist ... his portraits of the leading figures are three-dimensional and
penetrating ... the sheer momentum of the narrative is breathtaking ... a
book to read and to read again' – Walter C. Patterson in the *Guardian*

Asimov's New Guide to Science   Isaac Asimov

A classic work brought up to date – far and away the best one-volume
survey of all the physical and biological sciences.

FOR THE BEST IN PAPERBACKS, LOOK FOR THE 🐧

PENGUIN SCIENCE AND MATHEMATICS

The Panda's Thumb   Stephen Jay Gould

More reflections on natural history from the author of *Ever Since Darwin*. 'A quirky and provocative exploration of the nature of evolution ... wonderfully entertaining' – *Sunday Telegraph*

Gödel, Escher, Bach: An Eternal Golden Braid   Douglas F. Hofstadter

'Every few decades an unknown author brings out a book of such depth, clarity, range, wit, beauty and originality that it is recognized at once as a major literary event' – Martin Gardner. 'Leaves you feeling you have had a first-class workout in the best mental gymnasium in town' – *New Statesman*

The Double Helix   James D. Watson

Watson's vivid and outspoken account of how he and Crick discovered the structure of DNA (and won themselves a Nobel Prize) – one of the greatest scientific achievements of the century.

The Quantum World   J. C. Polkinghorne

Quantum mechanics has revolutionized our views about the structure of the physical world – yet after more than fifty years it remains controversial. This 'delightful book' (*The Times Educational Supplement*) succeeds superbly in rendering an important and complex debate both clear and fascinating.

Einstein's Universe   Nigel Calder

'A valuable contribution to the demystification of relativity' – *Nature*

Mathematical Circus   Martin Gardner

A mind-bending collection of puzzles and paradoxes, games and diversions from the undisputed master of recreational mathematics.

FOR THE BEST IN PAPERBACKS, LOOK FOR THE 🐧

PENGUIN BUSINESS AND ECONOMICS

Almost Everyone's Guide to Economics
J. K. Galbraith and Nicole Salinger

This instructive and entertaining dialogue provides a step-by-step explanation of 'the state of economics in general and the reasons for its present failure in particular in simple, accurate language that everyone could understand and that a perverse few might conceivably enjoy'.

The Rise and Fall of Monetarism   David Smith

Now that even Conservatives have consigned monetarism to the scrapheap of history, David Smith draws out the unhappy lessons of a fundamentally flawed economic experiment, driven by a doctrine that for years had been regarded as outmoded and irrelevant.

Atlas of Management Thinking   Edward de Bono

This fascinating book provides a vital repertoire of non-verbal images that will help activate the right side of any manager's brain.

The Economist Economics   Rupert Pennant-Rea and Clive Crook

Based on a series of 'briefs' published in *The Economist*, this is a clear and accessible guide to the key issues of today's economics for the general reader.

Understanding Organizations   Charles B. Handy

Of practical as well as theoretical interest, this book shows how general concepts can help solve specific organizational problems.

The Winning Streak   Walter Goldsmith and David Clutterbuck

A brilliant analysis of what Britain's best-run and most successful companies have in common – a must for all managers.